High Leverage Practices and Stu
with Extensive Support Needs

Building on the formative work of *High Leverage Practices for Inclusive Classrooms*, this critical companion explores how high leverage practices (HLP) can be applied to the education of students with extensive support needs (ESN). Each chapter walks readers through a different HLP, exploring implications for students with ESN and aligning with current practice, supports, and terminology. Edited by researchers and teacher educators with decades of experience in serving students with ESN and their teachers, this book is packed with rich examples of and detailed supports for implementing HLPs to ensure every student has access to all aspects of their school community.

Robert Pennington is the Lake & Edward J. Snyder, Jr. Distinguished Professor in Special Education at University of North Carolina-Charlotte, USA.

Melinda Jones Ault is a Professor at University of Kentucky, USA.

Ginevra Courtade is a Professor at University of Louisville, USA.

J. Matt Jameson is a Professor at University of Utah, USA.

Andrea Ruppar is an Associate Professor at University of Wisconsin-Madison, USA.

High Leverage Practices for Inclusive Classrooms, Second Edition
James McLeskey, Lawrence Maheady, Bonnie Billingsley, Mary T. Brownell, and
Timothy J. Lewis

Universal Design for Learning in the Early Childhood Classroom:
Teaching Children of all Languages, Cultures, and Abilities, Birth - 8 Years,
Second Edition
Pamela Brillante and Karen Nemeth

Social-Emotional Learning Through STEAM Projects, Grades 4-5
Season Mussey

Developing Teacher Leaders in Special Education: An Administrator's Guide to
Building Inclusive Schools
Daniel M. Maggin and Marie Tejero Hughes

The Brain-Based Classroom: Accessing Every Child's Potential Through
Educational Neuroscience
Kieran O'Mahony

Specially Designed Instruction: Increasing Success for Students with Disabilities
Anne M. Beninghof

Rigor for Students with Special Needs, Second Edition
Barbara R. Blackburn and Bradley S. Witzel

High Leverage Practices and Students with Extensive Support Needs

Edited by Robert Pennington,
Melinda Jones Ault,
Ginevra Courtade,
J. Matt Jameson, and
Andrea Ruppar

A Co-publication with the Council for Exceptional Children

Routledge
Taylor & Francis Group

NEW YORK AND LONDON

Cover image: ©Shutterstock

First published 2023
by Routledge
605 Third Avenue, New York, NY 10158

and by Routledge
4 Park Square, Milton Park, Abingdon, Oxon, OX14 4RN

Routledge is an imprint of the Taylor & Francis Group, an informa business

Library of Congress Cataloging-in-Publication Data
Names: Pennington, Robert C. (Robert Clyde), editor. | Ault, Melinda Jones, editor. | Courtade, Ginevra, editor. | Jameson, J. Matt, editor. | Ruppar, Andrea, editor.
Title: High leverage practices and students with extensive support needs / edited by Robert Pennington, Melinda Jones Ault, Ginevra Courtade, J. Matt Jameson & Andrea Ruppar.
Description: New York, NY : Routledge, 2023. | "A copublication with the Council for Exceptional Children." | Includes bibliographical references.
Identifiers: LCCN 2022021151 (print) | LCCN 2022021152 (ebook) | ISBN 9781032007908 (hardback) | ISBN 9780367772550 (paperback) | ISBN 9781003175735 (ebook)
Subjects: LCSH: Children with disabilities--Education--United States. | Students with disabilities--United States--Services for. | Inclusive education--United States.
Classification: LCC LC4015 .H54 2023 (print) | LCC LC4015 (ebook) | DDC 371.9/0460973--dc23/eng/20220916
LC record available at https://lccn.loc.gov/2022021151
LC ebook record available at https://lccn.loc.gov/2022021152

ISBN: 9781032007908 (hbk)
ISBN: 9780367772550 (pbk)
ISBN: 9781003175735 (ebk)

DOI: 10.4324/9781003175735

Typeset in Minion Pro
by KnowledgeWorks Global Ltd.

Council for Exceptional Children

Contents

List of Contributors

Melinda Jones Ault, University of Kentucky
Jessica Bowman, University of Minnesota
Sarah Bubash, University of Wisconsin-Madison
Rachel Cagliani, University of Georgia
Belva C. Collins, University of North Carolina-Charlotte
Jennifer Cook, East Tennessee State University
Ginevra Courtade, University of Louisville
Janet Sanchez Enriquez, University of North Carolina Charlotte
Anya S. Evmenova, George Mason University
Caroline Fitchett, University of Louisville
Grace Francis, George Mason University
J. B. Ganz, Texas A&M University
Shari L. Hopkins, Western Oregon University
Channon K. Horn, University of Kentucky
Maureen Howard, George Mason University
Roba Hrisseh, George Mason University
Sarah Ivy, University of Utah
J. Matt Jameson, University of Utah
Bree Jimenez, University of Texas-Arlington
Meagan Karvonen, Achievement and Assessment Institute, University of Kansas
Jacqui Kearns, Human Development Institute, University of Kentucky
Jennifer Kurth, University of Kansas
Sheldon Loman, Portland State University
Katherine Lynch, University of Kentucky
Addie McConomy, Florida State University
Pamela J. Mims, East Tennessee State University
Kai O'Neill, University of Kentucky
Jamie N. Pearson, North Carolina State University
Robert Pennington, University of North Carolina Charlotte

Shamby Polychronis, University of Utah
Timothy Riesen,Utah State University
Daira Rodriguez, Texas A&M University
Jenny Root, Florida State University
Andrea Ruppar, University of Wisconsin-Wisconsin-Madson
Joanna Ryan, University of North Dakota
Sally Shepley, University of Kentucky
Sara Snyder, James Madison University
Michael Stoehr, National Technical Assistance Center on Transition: The Collaborative, University of North Carolina Charlotte
Teresa Taber Doughty, University of Texas-Arlington
Melissa Tapp, University of North Carolina Charlotte
Shawnee Wakeman, University of North Carolina Charlotte
Virginia Walker, University of North Carolina Charlotte
Samantha Walte, University of Louisville
Margaret G. Werts, Appalachian State University
Amarachi Yoro, Texas A&M University
Alison Zagona, University of Kansas

Introduction

One of the essential functions of public education is to provide all students with the skills necessary to be agents of change within their own lives. To facilitate this agency or self-determination, educators must provide all students with the opportunity to access and make progress within a curriculum that is personally relevant, broadly applicable, and capitalizes on students' diverse background knowledge. They also must provide all students with learning experiences that reflect real-world contexts in that they are inclusive, interactive, collaborative, and designed such that students are afforded the dignity of learning from their mistakes. Finally, educators must prepare all students to communicate effectively to navigate ever-changing social landscapes and advocate for their interests.

Meeting this charge for students with disabilities often requires educators to use a broad range of strategies and supports to respond to the unique strengths, experiences, and needs of each of their students. This is especially true for many students with extensive support needs (ESN). These students often have developmental or intellectual disability and, in some cases, other support needs (e.g., physical disabilities, sensory impairments), and require comprehensive programmed (i.e., formal) and natural supports to access educational and social opportunities available to their peers without ESN. When carefully designed interventions and supports are provided, students with ESN have more opportunities in academic, social, and postsecondary learning contexts. Unfortunately, researchers have suggested that some students with ESN may not have access to high quality educational practices. As a result, they often are not actively engaged during the school day, have fewer opportunities to interact with peers without disabilities, and sometimes experience harm and isolation.

To facilitate the preparation of educators to implement high quality educational programs for students with disabilities, the Council for Exceptional Children appointed a team of experienced teacher educators to identify a set of high-leverage practices (HLPs) in special education. HLPs are educational practices considered to be the most critical for improving student outcomes and broad sets of HLPs have been established for all students (https://library.teachingworks.org/curriculum-resources/high-leverage-practices/). These HLPs are supported by research, can be applied across content and contexts, and are emitted by effective teachers with high frequency (McLeskey et al., 2019a). The team identified 22 HLPs to be emphasized in preparing teachers to serve students with disabilities. The HLPs are organized into four sets of practices under the headings (a) Collaboration, (b) Assessment, (c) Social/Emotional/Behavioral, and (d) Instruction. See Table 0.1 for a complete list of HLPs.

DOI: 10.4324/9781003175735-1

Table 0.1 The Council for Exceptional Children's 22 High Leverage Practices

HLP #	High Leverage Practice
1	Collaborating with Colleagues to Increase Student Success
2	Leading Effective Meetings with Professionals and Families
3	Collaborate with Families to Support Student Learning and Needed Services
4	Use Multiple Sources of Information to Develop a Comprehensive Understanding of a Student's Strengths and Needs
5	Interpret and Communicate Assessment Information with Stakeholders to Collaboratively Design and Implement Educational programs
6	Use Student Assessment Data, Analyzing Instructional Packages, and Making Necessary Adjustments that Improve Student Outcomes
7	Establish a Consistent, Organized, and Respectful Learning Environment
8	Use Feedback to Improve Student Outcomes
9	Teach Social Behaviors
10	Conduct Functional Behavior Assessment to Develop Individualized Behavior Support Plans
11	Identify and Prioritize Long- and Short-term Learning Goals
12	Systematically Design Instruction toward a Specific Learning Goal
13	Adapt Curriculum Tasks and Materials for Specific Learning Goals
14	Teach Cognitive and Meta Cognitive Strategies to Support Learning and Independence
15	Provide Scaffolded Supports
16	Use Explicit Instruction (We have combined HL 16 & 20 in a single chapter)
17	Use Flexible Grouping
18	Use Strategies to Promote Active Engagement
19	Use Assistive and Instructional Technologies
20	Provide Intensive Instruction
21	Teach Students to Maintain and Generalize New Learning Across Time and Settings
22	Provide Positive and Constructive Feedback to Guide Students' Learning and Behavior

Detailed information related to these HLPs are available in the HLP writing teams' published report *High Leverage Practices in Special Education* (Council for Exceptional Children, 2017), the book *High Leverage Practices for Inclusive Classrooms* (McLeskey et al., 2019b), and a High Leverages Practices website (https://highleveragepractices.org/). Further, several articles have been published describing their development and offering recommendations for implementation within teacher preparation programs (e.g., Brownell et al., 2019; Maheady et al., 2019; McLeskey et al., 2019a).

The identification of HLPs more specific to enhancing outcomes for students receiving special education services provides a unique opportunity for broad dissemination and ultimately, the scaling up of foundational practices to support learners with disabilities and their teachers. Though HLPs are broadly applicable to students with a range of learning differences, their application may look different for some learners with ESN. Though students with ESN are certainly more like their peers than different, they often require additional supports to maximize the effectiveness of any HLP. For example, many students with ESN have complex communication needs (CCN) that require teachers to provide communication supports to fully participate during the application of HLPs. Additionally, these students often require significant modifications and adaptations to the general education curriculum to acquire grade-level academic skills. Finally, students with ESN often receive supports from collaborative educational teams comprised of several members from different disciplines (e.g., speech language pathologist, board certified behavior analyst, vision teacher, nurse).

The purpose of this book is to help educators understand how the Council for Exceptional Children's (CEC) HLPs can assist in improving outcomes for their students with ESN. We selected authors with years of experience in working with students with ESN and their teachers, and asked them to frame each HLP in the context of their experiences. Specifically, we asked them to identify research-based strategies within each HLP demonstrated to be effective with students with ESN, to describe the HLP using terminology familiar to those working in the area of ESN, and to provide multiple examples representing the HLP applied to different students with ESN.

The 22 HLPs are described in the 21 chapters in this book. We have combined HLP 16 *Use Explicit Instruction* and HLP 20 *Provide Intensive Instruction* into a single chapter entitled *Systematic Instruction* to reflect common usage in the field of ESN. The chapters are organized by introducing the HLP in the context of ESN, offering strategies for implementing the HLP, summarizing the five main ideas in the chapter, providing guidance for educators on how to start using the HLP, and finally, offering a list of additional resources. We hope that educators use this book as a guide to improving their own teaching practice through the adoption of HLPs. We recommend that after reading this book, educators reflect on their own practice and identify HLPs for adoption or improvement in the next year. We encourage teachers to set realistic goals for adoption; enlist teaching colleagues, mentors, and administrators to support their efforts; and find ways to measure their incremental progress. Most importantly, we remind educators to be kind to themselves when they face hurdles in the adoption of these HLPs, and to look for new solutions toward supporting changes in their own teaching behavior and the behavior of others.

Finally, we appreciate the work of the Council for Exceptional Children and McLeskey and colleagues toward the identification of HLPs in Special Education and the opportunity to further disseminate this important work. All children, including those with ESN, deserve access to HLPs, and we hope this book will serve as a resource toward the realization of this promise.

References

Brownell, M. T., Benedict, A. E., Leko, M. M., Peyton, D., Pua, D., & Richards-Tutor, C. (2019). A continuum of pedagogies for preparing teachers to use high-leverage practices. *Remedial and Special Education*, 40(6), 338–355.

Maheady, L. J., Patti, A. L., Rafferty, L. A., & del Prado Hill, P. (2019). School–university partnerships: One institution's efforts to integrate and support teacher use of high-leverage practices. *Remedial and Special Education*, 40(6), 356–364.

McLeskey, J., Barringer, M.-D., Billingsley, B., Brownell, M., Jackson, D., Kennedy, M., Lewis, T., Maheady, L., Rodriguez, J., Scheeler, M. C., Winn, J., & Ziegler, D. (2017). *High-leverage practices in special education*. Council for Exceptional Children & CEEDAR Center.

McLeskey, J., Billingsley, B., Brownell, M. T., Maheady, L., & Lewis, T. J. (2019a). What are high-leverage practices for special education teachers and why are they important? *Remedial and Special Education*, 40(6), 331–337.

McLeskey, J., Maheady, L., Billingsley, B., Brownell, M., & Lewis, T. (Eds.). (2019b). *High leverage practices for inclusive classrooms*. Routledge.

1
Collaborate with Colleagues to Increase Student Success
Alison Zagona

Collaboration with general education teachers, paraprofessionals, and support staff is necessary to support students' learning toward measurable outcomes and to facilitate students' social and emotional well-being across all school environments and instructional settings (e.g., co-taught). Collaboration with individuals or teams requires the use of effective collaboration behaviors (e.g., sharing ideas, active listening, questioning, planning, problem-solving, and negotiating) to develop and adjust instructional or behavioral plans based on student data, and the coordination of expectations, responsibilities, and resources to maximize student learning.

Supporting Students with Extensive Support Needs

Collaboration among professionals who support students with extensive support needs (ESN) is a style of interaction that involves communication, co-planning, and consultation (Cook & Friend, 2010). Effective collaboration includes the consideration of team member roles and contributions made to support a student. Collaboration to support students with ESN is most successful when professionals engage in interdisciplinary teaming practices that focus on supporting the student to practice and meet all of their goals in natural settings.

Importance of Collaboration and Interdisciplinary Teaming to Ensure Student Success

Collaboration and interdisciplinary teaming between all professionals who support students with ESN are critically important to ensure student success (Giangreco et al., 2011). Students with ESN may have support needs in the following domains: academics, communication, social, behavior, sensory, gross motor, fine motor, and health. Students with ESN may benefit from support from the following professionals in schools: special education teacher, general education teacher, the student's family, speech–language pathologist, occupational therapist, physical therapist, school social worker, behavior analyst, nurse, teacher for students who are blind or have low vision, and teacher for students who are deaf or hard of hearing. It would be nearly impossible for one professional to possess all of the knowledge and skills necessary to support a student with ESN simply because of the value and expertise each professional brings to the team. Team members from across

DOI: 10.4324/9781003175735-2

disciplines must come together to share ideas and strategies to support students with ESN to be successful. As part of this process, professionals must consider their individual and collective roles within the team, and it is important for team members to use strategies for effective collaboration, communication, co- planning, and consultation. It is also critically important for team members to engage with each other in professional ways that respect individuals with ESN and their families. Students with ESN benefit from individualized supports to ensure they achieve positive outcomes in school and beyond, and it is important for students to receive supports from professionals who engage in interdisciplinary teaming efforts.

For example, a fourth-grade student with ESN (e.g., severe intellectual disability, deafblindness, and complex health care needs) would likely benefit from a range of supports in order to make progress in the English language arts curriculum. This fourth-grade student may benefit from the support of a general education teacher, special education teacher, speech–language pathologist, occupational therapist, physical therapist, and teacher for students with low vision. The team must work together, communicate, and focus on shared goals to ensure the student is supported to learn the content and express responses to demonstrate her learning. Professionals must collaborate with each other and engage in interdisciplinary teaming practices to ensure they are working toward common goals with the student and to ensure the recommended and implemented strategies complement each other. The student's goals must be identified based upon the student and family priorities, and the team should collaborate to ensure the student is supported to practice the skills in each goal area across settings. All members of the team should be focused on supporting the student to achieve their individualized goals across settings (Giangreco et al., 2011).

Chapter Objectives

Upon reading this chapter, you should be able to do the following:

1. Describe the roles of different professionals who may support students with ESN in school settings.
2. Describe and implement strategies for successfully communicating and co-planning with professionals to increase the success of students with ESN in inclusive classrooms.
3. Describe and implement strategies for consulting with all professionals to ensure implementation of supports for students with ESN in inclusive classrooms.
4. Describe strategies for ensuring team members work together toward common goals for the student in order to avoid providing fragmented services in isolation.
5. Describe features of professional interactions and communication that respects individuals with ESN and their families.

Roles of Different Professionals Supporting Students with ESN to Experience Success

All team members should collaborate to support the student to make progress in the general education curriculum (Giangreco et al., 2011). Professionals should avoid providing fragmented supports and recommendations, and they should avoid working in isolation on goals that are not connected to the general education curriculum. Professionals can achieve the necessary collaboration to support students with ESN by coming together to focus on supporting the student to practice and meet all of their goals in natural environments. Professionals who engage in this collaborative process to support students with ESN each fulfill a valuable role in the team.

The general education teacher is responsible for creating a culture of inclusion and belonging in the classroom, being knowledgeable about student skills and individualized learning goals, planning instruction, and implementing supports and assessments to ensure student progress in the curriculum. The special education teacher is responsible for working together with the general education teacher to plan for the inclusion of students with ESN through curriculum supports, cooperative learning groups, and/or physical room arrangement to ensure equitable access to all aspects of the classroom. The general and special education teachers are responsible for designing and implementing instruction for the student with ESN using evidence-based practices such as embedded instruction (Jimenez & Kamei, 2015). The special education teacher is typically responsible for supervising and training paraprofessionals who support the students with ESN in the classroom; however, the general education teacher should be empowered to engage in this supervision and collaboration as well. The special education teacher is typically responsible for coordinating the special education and related services for the student with ESN, and this involves communicating with all team members and the student's family. Paraprofessionals provide support for students with ESN, and they should be viewed as a second teacher who can provide support to all students in the classroom or lead small-group instruction; such practices prevent an overreliance on paraprofessionals and ensure the student with ESN is not socially isolated. Paraprofessionals may also assist with data collection and facilitate peer supports or coordinate other supports to support the student with ESN (Giangreco et al., 2011).

Students with ESN may also receive support from speech–language pathologists (SLPs) who may provide direct and/or consultative services as a support for the student with ESN to develop their skills in expressive and receptive communication as well as their language development. Services from an SLP intersect with skills the student needs to learn to make progress in the general education curriculum (e.g., reading, writing, comprehension, and communicating during class and group work), so it is important for the SLP to engage in interdisciplinary collaboration to ensure the student with ESN receives supports in a meaningful way in the natural classroom environment. Occupational therapists may also provide support for the student as a related service to support progress in daily living skills. Occupational therapists may address the student's fine motor skills including typing and writing as well as other skills such as feeding and communication or the use of physical access to their augmentative and alternative communication (AAC) device (if the student uses an AAC device; Causton & Tracy-Bronson, 2015). Physical therapists support a student's development of gross motor skills and the student's mobility support needs. These supports may involve equipment for positioning and use of a wheelchair or individualized equipment needed to physically access the classroom, playground, cafeteria, or other school locations. When physical therapists address student needs in the general education classroom or other natural environments, then the student with ESN receives the support needed to physically access the learning environment in meaningful and effective ways (Causton & Tracy-Bronson, 2015).

Students with ESN may also receive support from health care professionals, behavior analysts, teachers for students who are blind or have low vision, and/or teachers for students who are deaf or hard of hearing. Students with ESN may have complex health needs, and they may receive direct or consultative services from nurses or nursing assistants to address health needs related to feeding, respiration, severe allergies, diabetes, or other health needs. Behavior analysts may also provide support for students with ESN, and they may be board-certified behavior analysts, or they may have specialized training such that they are in the role of a behavior specialist. These professionals must work closely with all members of the team to ensure the student is supported to learn and demonstrate behaviors that are efficient for meeting their needs. Communication supports should be integrated with behavior supports for students with ESN when needed; thus, the behavior analyst must collaborate with all members of the team including the SLPs. Students with ESN may also have sensory impairments in vision or hearing and receive support from teachers for the visually impaired or teachers for the deaf or hard of hearing. These teachers must work closely with all members of the team, especially the classroom teacher and the special education teacher, because they are often responsible for providing services for students at multiple school sites and may not spend large portions of time at one school day-to-day. The direct or consultative services from these professionals address the student's access to instruction as well as supports to ensure their access such as training educators on the students' hearing aids, use of an FM system, or coordinating access to large-print or braille books.

Strategies for Collaborating with All Professionals to Ensure Student Success

Collaboration among the professionals who support students with ESN is essential to ensure student success, and it is critically important for professionals to use strategies for effective collaboration. Interdisciplinary teaming and maintaining a focus on shared goals is a process in which professionals engage to support the student to practice skills in a meaningful way across school settings and content areas. Additionally, communication and co-planning among the professionals who support students with ESN can ensure all team members are working with the knowledge of the student's current performance levels as well as knowledge of the current areas of focus in the curriculum.

Interdisciplinary Teaming

Interdisciplinary teaming refers to a process in which all team members address all of the student's goals in natural settings such as the general education classroom. This method for service delivery prevents the provision of fragmented services in isolated settings. For example, when an SLP addresses a student's expressive language goals in a separate office outside of the classroom, then the general education teacher and special education teacher may not have the opportunity to learn strategies for supporting the student to develop the skills, and the student may miss the opportunity to practice generalizing the skill to the activities and interactions in the classroom. Instead of providing fragmented services on goals practiced in isolation, it is important for professionals to engage in interdisciplinary teaming practices to ensure the student is supported to practice goals in the relevant settings, and to ensure that they have the support needed from the professionals who possess the necessary knowledge.

For example, a student with ESN may have an intellectual disability and complex communication needs such that they benefit from supports such as content area modifications in reading and supports to learn to use an AAC device. An elementary student with these support needs would benefit from interdisciplinary teaming to address goals involving expressive language across content areas and across settings in the school. For example, if the student has a goal to increase responses to wh-questions, this goal should be practiced across settings (e.g., classroom, cafeteria, and elective periods), and it could be practiced in both academic and social times. This would necessitate the support and interdisciplinary collaboration of the general education teacher, special education teacher, SLPs, and possibly peer supports who have learned how to support the student to use their AAC device to answer such questions. The SLPs could model ways for supporting the student to practice this skill during literacy activities or during recess with a peer. The general and special education teachers could watch this process that the SLP is implementing, and then they will be able to implement it themselves even if the SLP is not present. When the student has the opportunity to practice this skill across settings and is supported to do so by multiple members of the team, the student benefits by having many opportunities to practice and by having the expertise and support of multiple professionals. These opportunities for practicing skills will support skill acquisition and generalization.

Co-planning

A strategy for collaboration that is beneficial for school professionals and students with ESN is co-planning. Professionals may choose to schedule recurring meetings to ensure a constant flow of communication and to avoid the formation of silos in which general and special education teachers and related services providers work separately from each other. It is important for professionals to establish this common planning time to the greatest extent possible, and it is important to recognize that this can occur in person or virtually. Because some team members may visit multiple schools, keeping the option available for virtual co-planning sessions is important. During these co-planning meetings, it is important for one person to be designated as the facilitator, and this does not need to be the same person for each meeting. Additionally, it is important for the team to use an agenda to remain focused and efficient.

Example 1: Co-planning Meetings

Tyler, a preschool student with ESN (multiple disabilities including complex health care needs and physical support needs), benefits from the support of several professionals including teachers and related services providers. To organize a co-planning meeting, the special education teacher contacts the team members (general education preschool teacher, paraprofessional, physical therapist, occupational, therapist, speech–language pathologist, and school nurse) to schedule a time to get together at the beginning of the school year. After identifying a common time to meet, the team gathers to discuss the student and develop an initial plan to begin the school year. During the meeting, the special education teacher begins by asking each team member to share what they would like to accomplish during the meeting, and the special education teacher takes notes. The agenda is adjusted to reflect these priorities, and the team discusses plans for supports for the first two weeks of school, keeping a focus on routines taught during the first two weeks of school as well as curriculum modifications and supports needed for academics. At the end of the meeting, the team decides to meet every two weeks after school for 30 minutes. As the team continues to meet throughout the school year, they share accomplishments and celebrate the student's progress. Table 1.1 includes a list of questions to guide a team discussion during a co-planning meeting at the beginning of the school year.

Table 1.1 Questions to Guide a Co-planning Meeting at the Beginning of the Year

1. What would you like to accomplish during this meeting or a future meeting with this team?

2. What do you envision as your role in supporting the student this year?

3. What challenges do you anticipate while attempting to support the student this year? How can we, as members of the team, offer support to overcome those challenges?

4. What questions do you have for the team?

Communication

School professionals will benefit from developing an efficient system for communication that is accessible for all team members. Because each professional may be supporting many students at different schools, and recurring meetings with all team members might not always be possible, it is imperative to identify other ways to successfully communicate. The special education teacher can lead the effort to identify a communication system that is accessible for all members of the team. The special education teacher should ask team members for their preferred method of communication, try a discussion board in a shared electronic platform, and/or use email.

Example 2: Team Communication Strategies

Ana, a student with ESN in an inclusive postsecondary program, receives supports from a special education teacher, peer mentors, course instructors, and an employment coach. The special education teacher must find a way to communicate with team members to ensure the proper supports are designed and implemented for Ana. As one possibility, the team may choose to develop a shared folder in a platform such as Google Drive. In this folder, the team members can store plans for upcoming projects and special events, and they can also store a log for notes. This log could be a running log with dates, topics, and questions or comments. Keeping a log of this information and communicating in this way can support the team to remain focused on the student and avoid confusion that can arise when an email chain becomes lengthy. When the team members view the shared folder, they have the opportunity to be more focused on the student and their supports than if they were communicating through email alone.

Strategies for Consulting with All Professionals to Ensure Implementation of Supports for Students with ESN

Oftentimes, special education teachers who support students with ESN do so through a consultative service delivery model in which they provide support and services for several students who may all be in different classrooms (King-Sears et al., 2015). Collaborative consultation may be an indirect service for students with ESN because the professionals communicate about strategies to use as supports for the student. Collaborative consultation may also involve the provision of direct services in which the special education teacher provides services to the student with ESN in the general education classroom (King-Sears et al., 2015). When consulting with team members, special education teachers should plan to share information about the student, schedule time to visit the classroom, model strategies for the professionals in the classroom, and follow up on recommended strategies.

Share Information about the Student

The special education teacher should meet with team members, including the general education teacher, to share information about the student at the beginning of the year and throughout the school year. This helps to prevent the formation of silos in which the general and special education teachers are working completely separately on isolated goals. Additionally, sharing information with the general education teacher supports the student by empowering the general education teacher to learn and become proficient at providing individualized supports. In addition to sharing general information about the student, the special education teacher should ensure access to the student's individualized education plan (IEP) content after each new meeting. The special education teacher may want to consider using an "IEP at a Glance" form to ensure the most pertinent information about the student's IEP is readily accessible for all team members. A sample IEP at a Glance form is provided in Figure 1.1.

Example 3: IEP at a Glance as a Strategy for Sharing Information

Miguel, a tenth-grade student with ESN (autism and severe intellectual disability), receives support from many team members including several different general education teachers. An IEP at a Glance would be one way the special education teacher can ensure all team members have current information about Miguel's strengths, support needs, goals, services, and accommodations and modifications. Miguel attends grade-level classes with five teachers and receives support from a paraprofessional throughout the day. Miguel also receives services from an SLP and occupational therapist. Miguel has many IEP goals, all of which can and should be addressed throughout his classes and school routines. Because of the large number of professionals who support Miguel, it is critically important for the special education teachers to communicate IEP content with the team. Although all members of the team may have been present at the IEP meeting to discuss these items, having a document with this information readily available as a reminder will be important for continuity of services.

Schedule Time to Visit the Classroom and Model Instructional Strategies

In addition to sharing information about the student, special education teachers should schedule time to visit the classroom and spend dedicated time modeling for the general education teacher and paraprofessional (if the student receives support from a paraprofessional). The special education teacher should communicate with the general education teacher in advance of the visit to plan any needed supports and gather materials in order to prevent the need for the adults to have a conversation during instructional time. General education teachers have expressed an appreciation for learning strategies from the special education teacher, especially when these strategies are shared or modeled in the general education classroom (Zagona et al., 2021).

Student Initials: _____

Date of IEP: _____

Student Strengths (Specific, Observable skills):

Reading	Social Skills
Writing	Behavior
Math	Other
Communication	Other

Student IEP goals:

Reading	Social Skills
Writing	Behavior
Math	Other
Communication	Other

Accommodations and Modifications:

Services/ Anticipated Schedule (Days) for Receiving Services:

Figure 1.1 Sample IEP at a Glance

Example 4: Special Education Teacher as a Supportive Consultant

For example, Nicole, a kindergarten student with ESN (multiple disabilities including severe intellectual disability and low vision), would benefit from the support of a special education teacher who visits the classroom frequently. Nicole's kindergarten teacher is new at the school this year, and he had limited training and practice in inclusive education and students with ESN during his teacher training program. The special education teacher has arranged her schedule to visit the kindergarten classroom for 45 minutes three times per week. During this time, the special education teacher becomes another teacher in the classroom, working alongside the general education teacher so that he can learn how to best support the student. This 45-minute time block ensures the special education teacher is able to see and participate in a full instructional cycle including whole group and centers (Sterling-Turner et al., 2002). The special education teacher may choose to develop a daily schedule to organize her time and to ensure she is able to visit all of her student's classrooms to provide consultative services. A sample weekly schedule is included in Table 1.2. This weekly schedule could be shared with the general education teachers so they know when she is planning to visit the classroom. This schedule may be adapted for teachers who have students who are fully included in general education classrooms and students who spend part of their day in a classroom facilitated by the special education teacher. The purpose of the schedule is to ensure the special education teacher has a way of organizing and communicating time to visit the student's classroom to provide consultative support or to provide direct support to the student. The schedule also allows the special education teacher to plan times to visit classrooms to check in and follow up on recommended strategies.

Table 1.2 Sample Weekly Schedule for Special Education Teacher

	Monday	Tuesday	Wednesday	Thursday	Friday
7:45–8:00	Student drop-off/ recess	Student drop-off/ recess	Student drop-off/ recess	Student drop-off/ recess	Student drop-off/ recess
8:00–8:45	Tyler's classroom	Sam's classroom	Ana's classroom	Allen's classroom	Tyler's classroom
8:45–9:30	Miguel's classroom	Additional planning	Nicole's classroom	Check-in/ follow-up	Sam's classroom
9:30–10:15	Ana's classroom	Miguel's classroom	Data collection organization	Ana's classroom	Nicole's classroom
10:15–11:00	Planning	Planning	Planning	Planning	Planning
11:00–11:45	Lunch room support for students	Lunch room support for students	Lunch room support for students	Lunch room support for students	Lunch room support for students
11:45–12:30	Check-in/ follow-up	Check-in/ follow-up	Check-in/ follow-up	Check-in/ follow-up	Check-in/ follow-up
12:30–1:00	Lunch	Lunch	Lunch	Lunch	Lunch
1:00–2:00	Data collection organization	Allen's classroom	Sam's classroom	Additional planning	Data collection organization
2:00–2:45	Nicole's classroom	Check-in/ follow-up	Tyler's classroom	Miguel's classroom	Allen's classroom
2:45	Dismissal	Dismissal	Dismissal	Dismissal	Dismissal

Follow-up on Recommended Strategies

An important aspect of collaboration is trust, and it is important for professionals to convey a desire for supporting not only the student but also other team members as well. One way professionals can build trust with each other and support the team process is to follow up with each other after making recommendations. If the special education teacher makes a recommendation to try a certain type of modification, for example, then it will be important to follow up on that recommendation to be sure it is effective. Is the modification supporting the student to experience success and make progress? Does the teacher or paraprofessional know how to create and/or implement the modification? Following up with team members during the consultative process can provide the special education teacher with answers to these questions. Following up on recommendations can also support team members to trust the individual and their recommendations because they will feel supported throughout the implementation process.

Essential Features of Professional Interactions and Communication

As professionals interact during meetings and informal conversations as well as through online methods such as email and shared documents, it is important to maintain a high level of respect for the individuals with ESN and their families. Professionals must use preferred language, talk about the students and their families in respectful ways, recognize the student and family point of view, and maintain confidentiality. Unless individuals with ESN express an alternative preference, professionals should use "person first" language, meaning that they always put the individual first when talking about them. Additionally, professionals should focus on the student's "support needs" rather than any "deficits" (Thompson et al., 2018). For example, a student with ESN may have needs for support in mobility, health, and communication. Such focus on the student's support needs should be discussed only in ways that are relevant to the conversation.

When professionals discuss the student with ESN and their family, it is important to avoid making any assumptions, and it is important to maintain respect for their point of view. While the professionals may have known the student with ESN for several years, the student with ESN and their family know what they have experienced best, and that forms the foundation for their perspectives (Turnbull et al., 1999). These experiences and perspectives should be respected during direct interactions with families as well as when discussing the student with ESN and their family with other professionals.

Professionals should also always maintain a high level of confidentiality when sharing information about the student with ESN. Conversations between professionals should occur in a private setting, away from the student, other students, and professionals who are not involved in supporting the student. Information about the student should never be shared in a public place or where others could hear. Paperwork containing the student's name should be secured in ways that are compliant with the Family Educational Rights and Privacy Act, and IEP at a Glance forms that might be stored outside of a locked cabinet should contain minimal information such as the student's initials. All of these procedures should be in alignment with Family Educational Rights and Privacy Act and the school and district policies for confidentiality.

Next Steps toward Better Practice

1. Review the list of students who you support. Begin by identifying one student as an opportunity to improve and expand the collaboration with professionals who support that student. Consider selecting a student who has not made as much progress as was expected in the last month or two. Alternatively, consider selecting a student who will be having an IEP meeting in the next few months.
2. Contact one professional who supports the student you identified in number 1, and invite that professional to meet with you or to connect with you virtually, using a platform such as Google Drive. Consider identifying a specific lesson plan or assignment on which to focus the discussion during this initial meeting.
3. Contact one professional who supports one of your students and ask how you can support them. For example, contact a general education teacher or elective teacher who supports one of your students and ask how they are doing, how the student is doing, and what you might be able to do to support their classroom.
4. Review the list of IEP goals for one of your students. Consider ways that you can support the student to practice the skills in natural environments across the school. Have you considered any goals to be "speech goals"? Consider how you as a special education teacher can support the student to practice skills in *all* of their goals across various school settings. Alternatively, consider how you might be able to train or support others to address multiple skills across various school settings.

The Big Five

1. Students with ESN are often supported by many school professionals, including educators, related services providers, behavior support providers, and nurses, and interdisciplinary collaboration is imperative to ensure effective supports for students with ESN.

2. Because of the many professionals who support students with ESN, it is imperative that team members have opportunities to build relationships, communicate, and work together to address shared goals for the students with ESN.
3. The special education teacher can support professionals, including general education teachers and paraprofessionals by scheduling time to spend in the classroom and directly supporting the student alongside the general education teacher and paraprofessional.
4. Professionals should engage in interdisciplinary teaming, and they must focus their efforts toward supporting the student to meet goals within natural environments. Professionals should avoid providing fragmented services in isolated settings.
5. Professional interactions must respect and support the student's preferences, strengths, support needs, and confidentiality.

Resources

https://iris.peabody.vanderbilt.edu/module/v03-focusplay/cresource/q1/p03/#content
https://connectmodules.dec-sped.org/connect-modules/learners/module-3/
https://tiescenter.org/resource/dl24-the-5-15-45-tool-grab-a-partner-and-lets-collaborate
https://tiescenter.org/resource/dl23-pivoting-between-paraprofessional-support-in-inclusive-schools-and-distance-learning
https://tiescenter.org/resource/1q/pKnJgOQzqwfLf-87mpDg

References

Causton, J., & Tracy-Bronson, C. P. (2015). *The educator's handbook for inclusive school practices.* Paul H. Brookes Publishing Company.

Cook, L., & Friend, M. (2010). The state of the art of collaboration on behalf of students with disabilities. *Journal of Educational and Psychological Consultation, 20*(1), 1–8. https://doi.org/10.1080/10474410903535398

Giangreco, M. F., Cloninger, C. J., & Iverson, V. S. (2011). *COACH 3. Choosing outcomes and accommodations for children: A guide to educational planning for students with disabilities* (3rd ed.). Brookes Publishing.

Jimenez, B. A., & Kamei, A. (2015). Embedded instruction: An evaluation of evidence to inform inclusive practice. *Inclusion, 3*(3), 132–144. https://doi.org/10.1352/2326-6988-3.3.132

King-Sears, M. E., Janney, R., & Snell, M. E. (2015). *Collaborative teaming.* Paul H. Brookes Publishing Company.

Sterling-Turner, H. E., Watson, T. S., & Moore, J. W. (2002). The effects of direct training and treatment integrity on treatment outcomes in school consultation. *School Psychology Quarterly, 17*(1), 47–77. https://doi.org/10.1521/scpq.17.1.47.19906

Thompson, J. R., Walker, V. L., Shogren, K. A., & Wehmeyer, M. L. (2018). Expanding inclusive educational opportunities for students with the most significant cognitive disabilities through personalized supports. *Intellectual and Developmental Disabilities, 56*(6), 396–411. https://doi.org/10.1352/1934-9556-56.6.396

Turnbull, A. P., Blue-Banning, M., Turbiville, V., & Park, J. (1999). From parent education to partnership education: A call for a transformed focus. *Topics in Early Childhood Special Education, 19*(3), 164–172. https://doi.org/10.1177/027112149901900308

Zagona, A. L., Lansey, K. R., Kurth, J. A., & Kuhlemeier, A. (2021). Fostering participation during literacy instruction in inclusive classrooms for students with complex support needs: Educators' strategies and perspectives. *The Journal of Special Education, 55*(1), 34–44. https://doi.org/10.1177/0022466920936671

2

Lead Effective Meetings with Professionals and Families

Grace Francis and Maureen Howard

Teachers lead and participate in a range of meetings (e.g., meetings with families, individualized education program [IEP] teams, individualized family services plan [IFSP] teams, instructional planning) with the purpose of identifying clear, measurable student outcomes and developing instructional and behavioral plans that support these outcomes. They develop a meeting agenda, allocate time to meet the goals of the agenda, and lead in ways that encourage consensus building through positive verbal and nonverbal communication, encouraging the sharing of multiple perspectives, demonstrating active listening, and soliciting feedback.

Supporting Students with Extensive Support Needs

There are numerous stakeholders who serve critical roles in supporting students with disabilities who have extensive support needs (ESN) as they navigate the K-12 school system. Such stakeholders include families of students with ESN, special education professionals (e.g., educators, paraprofessionals, occupational and physical therapists), general education professionals (e.g., educators), and school administration and staff (e.g., principal, school nurse, secretary, custodian, counselor, librarian, social worker). Further, stakeholders may include members of the community (e.g., close family friend, advocate) or representatives from disability organizations/programs (e.g., job coach, case manager, advocate).

Effective meetings among these stakeholders are found to enhance relationships among professionals and families, ultimately leading to enhanced student outcomes (Haines et al., 2017). In fact, research indicates that multidisciplinary collaboration in schools can lead to increased satisfaction among professionals (Pufpaff et al., 2015), as well as more seamless implementation of home-school programming (e.g., healthcare plans, transition planning; Francis et al., 2018; Pufpaff et al., 2015). In K-12 settings, special education educators (hereafter referred to as "educators") often serve as the "point person" for organizing and facilitating meetings among multidisciplinary stakeholders with respect to students with ESN.

DOI: 10.4324/9781003175735-3

Chapter Objectives

Upon reading this chapter, you should be able to do the following:

1. Identify opportunities for key stakeholders (e.g., students, professionals, family members) to meet.
2. Describe facilitation strategies to increase accessibility and equity among participants before, during, and after meetings.
3. Describe strategies to support meaningful participation among students with ESN.

Opportunities for Stakeholders to Meet

There are numerous opportunities for stakeholders to engage in meaningful informal and formal meetings. Examples of informal meetings among professionals may include school-wide staff meetings, professional development, as well as grade level or subject team meetings during which school staff may discuss school, class, or individual student data or needs. These meetings may serve as opportunities for professionals to brainstorm ways in which to address trends in data, student concerns, as well as to innovate opportunities to strengthen school programs or initiatives (e.g., behavior systems, ways to build a positive school culture). Less formal but important opportunities for professionals and families to meet include person-centered planning meetings. Person-centered planning is a team process designed to help students with disabilities, including students with ESN, plan for the future, with the goal of students living fulfilling, self-directed lives (Wehman, 2011).

In addition to informal meetings, there are many formal opportunities for professional and family meetings. Parent–teacher conferences required under the Every Student Succeeds Act (ESSA, 2015) are one example. The Individuals with Disabilities Act (IDEA, 2004) also includes numerous meeting opportunities, including student eligibility and re-evaluation meetings, Individualized Family Service Plan (IFSP) meetings, and Individualized Education Program (IEP) meetings. Moreover, students may also have meetings to develop Individual Plans for Employment (IPE) meetings through vocational rehabilitation.

Strategies to Increase Accessibility and Equity among Meeting Participants

In this section, we describe strategies to engage professionals and families in meetings, including (a) pre-meeting, (b) during meeting, and (c) post-meeting strategies.

Pre-meeting Strategies

Positive communication and rapport-building are essential components of establishing equity among meeting participants (Ladson-Billings, 2017). As a result, educators may consider (re)introducing themselves to meeting participants before coming together. Educators who are the "point person" for a student's family at the school (e.g., special education case manager) may introduce themselves using several strategies, such as making a brief phone call, texting, or emailing to share a little about themselves (e.g., name, a photograph), the role they play in the student's team, and the role they will play in the upcoming meeting. An example of this might look like the following: "Hello! My name is Ms. Petrell and I am Gino's special education teacher. This means I am your main contact this year and will support you and Gino throughout the IEP and special education process. I am also one of Gino's teachers and teach him History and Science." Educators may also encourage other stakeholders (including families) to do the same (e.g., "Please take a minute to introduce yourself to the team prior to our meeting on March 8th.") to build a more equitable sense of belonging among meeting participants.

Further, examining how educator background, experiences, values, biases, and beliefs influence the ways in which one interacts with and perceives people, environments, cultures, and behaviors is a critical process prior to facilitating meetings (Rowe & Francis, 2020). Acknowledging and understanding the implications of individual's own biases and assumptions can help one better understand how and why they have positive and/or negative responses to people or contexts that differ from their experiences (Turnbull et al., 2021). Educators may complete an activity such as a "Social Identity Wheel" (https://sites.lsa.umich.edu/inclusive-teaching/social-identity-wheel/) to recognize their identities (e.g., gender identity, first/preferred language, race/ethnicity) that feel the most important to them and how those identities may influence their reactions to others. Although self-analysis is an important, ongoing process, educators may consider revisiting the potential influence of identities before meetings by journaling on questions such as (a) What assumptions do I have about people attending this meeting? (b) How do I feel about previous communication with attendees? (c) What about this meeting makes me excited? or (d) What about this meeting makes me nervous? This process will help educators be more self-aware going into meetings, and thus better equipped to facilitate equitable and effective meetings (Turnbull et al., 2021). Figure 2.1 provides a template educators may use and/or adapt to consider how their identities may influence their perceptions of teaching, disability, ability, students, and parents.

Pre-Meeting Reflection

Reflect on and write notes about your identities. Use the extra row of boxes to list and describe additional identities, as needed.

Race	Socio-economic Status	Gender	Disability
Ethnicity	Sexual Orientation	First Language	National Origin/Nations of Origin
	Age	Religious or Spiritual Affiliation	Body Size/Type

Reflect on the following questions.
1. Which identities do you feel the strongest when you think about your profession?
2. Which identities make you feel the most confident in your job?
3. Which identities do you believe result in positive biases related to students with extensive support needs?
   a. Which result in negative biases?
4. Which identities do you believe result in positive biases related to parents of students with extensive support needs?
   a. Which result in negative biases?
5. What actions can or should you take to tackle negative biases?

Figure 2.1 Identity Consideration Template

Prior to meetings, it is important to recognize when to collaborate with translators (e.g., professionals who translate written materials from one language into another), interpreters (e.g., professionals who interpret speech from one language into another), and/or cultural brokers (e.g., professionals with knowledge of two cultures who mediate differences between the two). This is particularly true when a student/parents' primary language or country of origin differs from the educator's (which may be determined by student documentation or by collaborating with other school professionals such as administration, social workers, or counselors). Not only are translators and interpreted materials required by IDEA (to the greatest degree possible), partnering with these professionals is likely to "level the playing field" by supporting equitable access and communication among attendees whose first/preferred language and culture differ from each other. While some school districts may have a list of translators, interpreters, and/or cultural brokers, in some cases, educators may need to collaborate with administrators or other school staff to locate and plan with personnel (Francis et al., 2017). Prior to meetings, educators should provide all materials to translators, interpreters, and cultural brokers so they have appropriate time to translate materials and ask clarifying questions, as needed.

Due to work schedules, childcare, and other competing demands, families are likely to have limited time for meetings. Therefore, educators should prioritize family availability and preferences when selecting the time and setting for meetings. Further, educators may consider providing families and professionals multiple options for meeting settings, including school, community organizations (e.g., parent training and information center), or the family home, as appropriate. Moreover, while in-person meetings can help develop positive relationships between professionals and families (Faber, 2015; Turnbull et al., 2021), recent research indicates that families and professionals find virtual meetings on platforms such as Zoom beneficial, and, in some cases, even preferred over in-person meetings due to increased flexibility in scheduling meetings, increased levels of family comfort, and the ability for families to invite additional people to contribute to the meeting (e.g., at-home therapists, family members to help translate; Francis et al., 2020).

Typical school-based computer software often generates a generic invitation document for formal meetings such as student IEP or re-evaluation meetings. These forms include jargon and language that is difficult for stakeholders to decipher. A simplified version of meeting invitations (in addition to the legal invitations that provide information regarding rights such as procedural safeguards) can increase access and generate excitement among all attendees. Further, prior to meetings, educators should consider sharing a draft agenda that includes meeting norms and expectations, as well as dedicated opportunities for attendees to share information. Sharing a draft agenda before meetings can better prepare and alleviate stress among attendees, as well as allow attendees to request needed changes (e.g., one attendee may need to share information at the beginning of the meeting instead of at the end; Howard et al., 2021). Figure 2.2 displays an example of a virtual meeting agenda that sets expectations for attendee participation, meeting norms, and prompting questions for attendees to consider prior to the meeting.

Similarly, stakeholders feel more prepared to communicate collaboratively with the knowledge of what will be discussed, by whom, and when and after they have had the opportunity to review draft materials (Howard et al., 2021). Educators can share drafts of materials that will be discussed at the meeting to ensure that attendees have an opportunity to provide feedback and reflect on the materials prior to meetings. To the greatest degree possible, educators should distribute all materials in plain language (e.g., writing that is easily and quickly understood by most readers) or include a plain language accompanying document for legal documents (e.g., Social Security documents) to help ensure that complex information or wording does not interfere with attendee understanding or participation. Finally, educators may ask about needed accommodations (e.g., accessible seating) when distributing the finalized agenda and meeting materials to be discussed during the meeting and finalize the number of attendees to ensure they plan accordingly (e.g., room size).

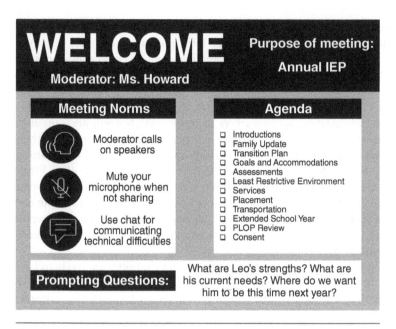

Figure 2.2 Virtual IEP Meeting Agenda

Note. An example of an agenda that sets expectations, meeting norms, and prompting questions for attendees. Reprinted with permission from Spoonful of Sped https://www.teacherspayteachers.com/Store/Spoonful-Of-Sped.

During-meeting Strategies

There are many approaches to build a sense of belonging at the onset of meetings, whether they be in-person or virtual. One approach is to greet attendees as they enter the meeting space. This act is especially important for families, as families often feel overwhelmed and isolated when entering a meeting outnumbered by professionals about their child (Mueller & Buckley, 2014). This is also an opportunity to make the most of the rapport built through pre-meeting communication by discussing common connections and other information learned about stakeholders during introductions. For example, something as simple as asking about weekend plans goes a long way in creating a safe and welcoming space and sparking dialogue that may lead to increased discussion during meetings. Further, educators may disrupt power hierarchies during meetings by encouraging families to speak first (and last) during meetings ("Why don't you start us off, Rich?"). In addition, it is also critical to seat interpreters and families next to each other and provide time for interpreters and families to converse with each other to learn communication styles, linguistic nuances, and build a level of comfort, as needed (Francis et al., 2017).

Once all attendees are present, educators may facilitate introductions (e.g., name, relation to the student, goal for the meeting) and distribute the agenda. During this time, educators can highlight the order of topics and opportunities for questions on the agenda. Educators should also clarify the approximate time allotted for the meeting and clearly state that part of the educator's role is to make sure that the meeting stays true to the norms included on the agenda (see Figure 2.2 for example norms), that everyone has an opportunity to share information, and that discussions remain centered on the student.

Educators should take their time as they move through the meeting agenda. This is especially important when interpreters are present. In addition to asking the interpreter to sit next to the family member(s), educators should be sure to speak directly to the family member in 2–3 sentences at a time to allow the interpreter to relay real-time information as accurately as possible (Zagelbaum

& Carlson, 2011). Further, as mentioned, documents such as IEPs often include dense language (Turnbull et al., 2021). Using plain language to the greatest degree possible, as well as visuals (e.g., use of an icon on the agenda for when a legal decision needs to be made or a signature is necessary) can support understanding among all attendees. Educators should prioritize student strengths throughout the meeting and find ways for all attendees to contribute their experiences and ideas. Educators can also encourage attendees to share items, stories, and videos to demonstrate student progress or areas of concern. For example, during the review of the student's transition plan, the educator and student could share pictures of the student engaging in vocational and life skills work at school. Next, parents could share anecdotes if the student does those same activities at home and what that looks like. Although meetings can run longer than expected, educators should provide a time check at approximately five minutes before the agreed upon meeting closure on the agenda before thanking attendees for joining and collaborating. If all aspects of the agenda have been discussed, this is an appropriate time for educators to request consent on documents, if necessary. If meeting topics remain unresolved, educators may use the last few minutes of the meeting to set up a time to reconvene and continue the conversation.

Post-meeting Strategies

As mentioned, self-awareness is an ongoing process. Engaging in self-reflection following meetings will further an understanding of the influence of their biases and perceptions. Educators may do this by journaling on their role in the meeting, the meeting process, meeting outcomes, the way educators feel about themselves and the others who attended the meeting, and by challenging themselves to consider *why* they feel certain ways (Rowe & Francis, 2020). In addition, emailing a brief summary of meeting notes (e.g., who attended, a summary of key points, and next steps) and a statement of appreciation (e.g., "Thank you for meeting yesterday- please let me know if you have any questions!) within 24–48 hours following the meeting can demonstrate commitment to attendees (Turnbull et al., 2021). This is also an opportunity to set up or confirm a follow-up meeting, as needed. In addition to an immediate follow-up email with all attendees, educators may elect to send individual emails to attendees who asked for extra information, who had individual questions, or whose comments or body language indicated that they may have felt uncomfortable during the meeting (e.g., shifting back and forth, avoiding eye contact). Figure 2.3 provides an example of an email educators may send to attendees whom they suspect felt uncomfortable during a meeting.

Facilitate Meaningful Participation among Students with ESN

Facilitating student participation in meetings is not only encouraged in IDEA (e.g., requirements to invite students to their IEP meetings starting no later than age 16; Sec. 300.322), but participating in meetings also provides students opportunities to develop critical communication, self-advocacy, and self-determination skills (Biegun et al., 2020; Newman et al., 2016). Person-centered planning involves several basic strategies including (1) students selecting stakeholders they would like to attend, (2) students leading a conversation about important personal information (e.g., relationships, needs, strengths, goals), (3) meeting attendees brainstorming strategies (e.g., resources, services) to address barriers and maximize student strengths and opportunities, and (4) students leading a closing conversation-delegating responsibilities related to their goals (Haines et al., 2017; Wehman, 2011). Many tenets of person-centered planning meetings can apply to all meetings, including centering conversations around students and helping students assume leadership roles. In this section, we use these tenets as a foundation to present strategies to support meaningful student participation (a) prior to, (b) during, and (c) after meetings in primary and secondary school settings.

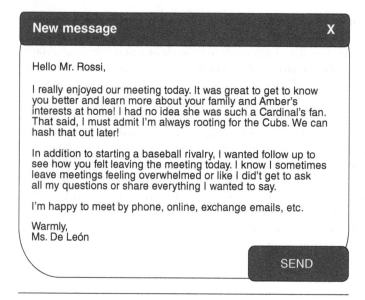

New message   X

Hello Mr. Rossi,

I really enjoyed our meeting today. It was great to get to know you better and learn more about your family and Amber's interests at home! I had no idea she was such a Cardinal's fan. That said, I must admit I'm always rooting for the Cubs. We can hash that out later!

In addition to starting a baseball rivalry, I wanted follow up to see how you felt leaving the meeting today. I know I sometimes leave meetings feeling overwhelmed or like I did't get to ask all my questions or share everything I wanted to say.

I'm happy to meet by phone, online, exchange emails, etc.

Warmly,
Ms. De León

SEND

Figure 2.3 Follow-up Email Example

Note. An example of an email educators may send to an attendee whom they suspect felt uncomfortable during a meeting.

Pre-meeting Strategies

Collaborating with students to create meeting invitations can develop a sense of ownership among students with ESN, as well as set expectations for student involvement among other attendees. One way to involve students in creating invitations is to include student preferences on the invitation such as a "dress code" consistent with their favorite color ("Please wear blue to my meeting.") or bring the student's favorite snack ("Waffles will be provided."). Educators may also include meeting expectations developed by the student. Examples include addressing sensory issues the student may have (e.g., "No gum chewing in my meeting, please" or "Please use level 2 voices in my meeting."), in addition to other expectations such as taking turns, professionals and family members asking questions to the student first, and following the agenda. Students can also help with the distribution of invitations to attendees digitally, in-person, or via mail (e.g., delivering in-person at school, creating a video to include with email distribution, signing or stamping printed invitations, adding photos or icons to the invitation).

As mentioned, meeting agendas provide structure and clarity for all attendees. Educators can support students to create agendas to ensure the meeting remains student-centered and establishes equity among team members. When creating an accessible agenda, educators should consider utilizing a combination of text, symbols, and/or images to signal when and how each attendee contributes to the meeting. For example, educators could place a picture of the student next to parts when they will share information. In addition, educators can include sentence stems as prompts to support student participation during each section of the agenda. Moreover, educators may use a stem that says, "I do my best work when I have _____" when discussing student accommodations or needed support. Students can read the sentence stems aloud or use a communication device to finish sentence stems. Figure 2.4 illustrates a sample agenda with student prompts.

In addition to creating an agenda, educators can also prepare students to participate in their meeting by co-creating a presentation for students to share. Educators should take care in considering students' preferred means of presenting information, such as using poster boards, virtual slide decks, pre-recorded videos, and/or using low-tech communication tools. After selecting the desired medium for presenting, educators should review the different sections of the meeting based on the

My IEP Agenda

✓	👋	Team member introductions "My name is .... This is ...."
✓		Transition plan "I am good at .... I like to .... I want to work at ...."
	📋	Goals "In the next year, I will ...."
		Accommodations "I do my best work when I have ...."
		Assessment (testing)
		Testing accommodations
		Least restrictive environment
		Services (hours)
		Placement, Transportation, and ESY
	✓	Agenda review
		Consent

Figure 2.4 Sample Agenda with Student Prompts

Note. The Picture Communication Symbols©1981–2016 by Tobii Dynavox. All Rights Reserved Worldwide. Used with permission. Boardmaker® is a trademark of Tobii Dynavox.

agenda. Next, educators can work with students to select what and when they would like to share information. For example, educators might suggest that students share their preferences and dislikes with regard to leisure activities or future employment when discussing goals. The use of icons on presentation materials or meeting agendas could also serve as a prompt for students and other attendees to indicate when the student will contribute information.

Once the agenda and presentation are created, educators can use multiple strategies to prepare students to participate and take on leadership roles during meetings such as direct instruction, modeling, prompt hierarchies (Orelove et al., 2017) and assistive technology (e.g., high and/or low-tech communication devices, projectors, pointers; Howard et al., 2021). For example, educators may use direct instruction to teach students how to use technology during meetings (e.g., advancing slides) or how to use meeting agendas as a tool to contribute during meetings (e.g., taking notes, letting attendees know when it is their turn to contribute, highlighting parts when they want to share, crossing out sections as the meeting progresses). Educators may also use direct instruction and modeling to teach students how to welcome individuals to the meeting (e.g., "Welcome, here is your seat); pre-programming communication devices, as needed. In addition, educators may model and role-play to teach students to indicate if they want meeting attendees to slow down, speak more loudly, indicate if they want to ask a question, or ask for a break during the meeting.

During-meeting Strategies

As the meeting begins, students can prepare attendees by distributing the agenda or setting out agendas at participant seats prior to the meeting. Students may also share the agenda on the projector, or in the case of an online meeting, on their screen/chat function for attendees to access. In addition to welcoming attendees, students can direct attendees to their seats, depending on where students would like each attendee to sit. After situating all attendees, students can present or co-present their presentation. During this time, educators may model providing ample wait time for students to provide information (e.g., "Let's give Adam a few moments to respond"). These actions demonstrate respect for the student, signal the value they contribute to the conversation, and may encourage other attendees to listen and respect the contributions of students. To help students share information, educators may pre-program communication devices with comments (e.g., "I don't like that," "Please say that again," "I agree," "Time to stop"). As mentioned, educators can also encourage students to control the presentation by advancing slide decks or using a pointer to gesture to the poster board or screen.

In addition to the presentation, students also can share artifacts with attendees. Artifacts may include videos of the student completing tasks, hanging out with friends, or working on a job site. Documents such as data sheets, awards, or their work schedule could be provided, as well. As mentioned, students can also keep time according to the agenda using a stopwatch or timer and announce when it is time to move on throughout the meeting. Educators can support student efforts to progress the meeting by asking attendees to write down remaining questions or comments on a particular section that can be addressed later during the meeting, time permitting, or after the meeting.

Post-meeting Strategies

Post-meetings provide a great opportunity to capture student feedback via an exit interview regarding ways to support their successful participation in future meetings. Educators may consider asking students what they liked about the meeting, what they did not like, and what they would like to happen next time. Educators can approach the exit interview process in multiple ways, such as creating a yes/no survey consisting of plain language statements (e.g., "I liked my meeting.") and including various response opportunities such as circling picture answer choices, gesturing yes or no, or using a student communication device. Finally, educators may consider collaborating with students to create a follow-up letter to send to attendees, thanking them for their attendance and participation. Educators can use the same process in which they developed the agenda to send the follow-up letter to provide students closure and keep all attendees engaged in meeting outcomes and next steps.

Next Steps toward Better Practice

1. It is imperative that educators are compliant with the "letter" of the law (e.g., inviting parents to annual IEP meetings). However, educators should also embody the "spirit" of the law by considering families and other professionals as partners in the education of students with ESN. Build-in time before, during, and after meetings to collaborate with students, families, and other key stakeholders.

2. Plain and accessible language is important to us all. Consider collaborating with school/district administration to create plain language documents to make legal documents (e.g., procedural safeguards) more accessible.

3. While the behavior of families and other professionals may not always be consistent with personal perceptions of what is "good" (e.g., attending all school-based meetings), educators may lessen the impact of negative biases by maintaining the position that all stakeholders share the common goal of student success. Specifically, educators may engage in reflexivity to consider and reflect on the identities that have the most influence on their profession.

4. In addition to formal meetings, teachers may also collaborate with families and other professionals to create more informal opportunities to interact that move away from school-centric activities (or when professional–family interactions center around the needs of the educator and school; Herrera et al., 2020). Some examples include person-centered planning meetings, conversations during school events, or brief check-in phone calls/notes/emails to families.

The Big Five

1. Many opportunities exist to meet outside mandated meetings (e.g., IEP meetings), including home visits and during school and community events.

2. Meetings between professionals and families are especially effective in supporting outcomes of students with ESN when educators consider strategies that occur before, during, and after meetings.

3. Educators must be reflexive regarding their own cultures and identities and aware of how their biases and perceptions may influence the ways in which they interact with meeting attendees.

4. Educators can facilitate meaningful collaboration during meetings by preparing attendees for meetings, including gathering attendee feedback to create the agenda and meeting more frequently in informal settings to build rapport.

5. Educators may engage in various methods to facilitate the participation of students with ESN during meetings, including the use of visual agendas and student-created presentations.

Resources

1. The Arc of the United States: https://thearc.org/about-us/
2. Parent Training and Information Centers: https://www.parentcenterhub.org/find-your-center/
3. Bridging Refugee Youth and Children's Services: https://brycs.org/
4. Global Family Research Project: https://globalfrp.org/Our-Work/Family-Engagement
5. SpoonfulofSpedIEPNotebook:https://www.teacherspayteachers.com/Store/Spoonful-Of-Sped
6. I'm Determined!: https://imdetermined.org/

References

Biegun, D., Peterson, Y., McNaught, J., & Sutterfield, C. (2020). Including student voice in IEP meetings through use of assistive technology. *Teaching Exceptional Children*, *52*(5), 348–350. https://doi.org/10.1177/0040059920920148

Every Student Succeeds Act (ESSA), 20 U.S.C.§ 1177 (2015).

Faber, N. (2015). The professional educator: Connect with students and families through home visits. *American Educator*, *39*(3), 24–27.

Francis, G. L., Gross, J. M. S., Magiera, L., Schmalzried, J., Monroe-Gulick, A., & Reed, S. (2018). Supporting students with disabilities, families, and professionals to collaborate during the transition to adulthood. *International Review of Research in Developmental Disabilities*, *54*, 71–104. https://doi.org/10.1016/bs.irrdd.2018.07.004

Francis, G. L., Haines, S. J., & Nagro, S. A. (2017). Developing relationships with immigrant families: Learning by asking the right questions. *TEACHING Exceptional Children, 50*(2), 95–105. https://doi.org/10.1177/0040059917720778

Francis, A., Raines, G. L., & Kinas-Jerome, A. M. (2020). *Accessing education in the time of coronavirus* [Conference session]. TASH Virtual Conference.

Haines, S. J., Francis, G. L., Mueller, T. G., Chiu, C., Burke, M. M., Kyzar, K., Shepherd, K. G., Holdren, N., Aldersey, H. M., & Turnbull, A. P. (2017). Reconceptualizing family-professional partnership for inclusive schools: A call to action. *Inclusion, 5*(4), 234–247. https://doi.org/10.1352/2326-6988-5.4.234

Herrera, S. G., Porter, L., & Barko-Alva, K. (2020). *Equity in school-family partnerships: Cultivating community and family trust in culturally diverse classrooms.* Teachers College Press.

Howard, M., Reed, A. S., & Francis, G. L. (2021). "It's my meeting!" Involving high school students with significant disabilities in the individualized education program process. *TEACHING Exceptional Children, 53*(4), 290–298. https://doi.org/10.1177/0040059920958739

Individuals with Disabilities Education Act (IDEA), 20 U.S.C. § 1400 (2004).

Ladson-Billings, G. (2017). The (r)evolution will not be standardized. In D. Paris, & S. Alim (Eds.), *Culturally sustaining pedagogies* (pp. 141–156). Teachers College Press.

Mueller, T. G., & Buckley, P. C. (2014). Fathers' experiences with the special education system: The overlooked voice. *Research and Practice for Persons with Severe Disabilities, 339*(2), 119–135. https://doi.org/10.1177/1540796914544548

Newman, L., Madaus, J., & Javitz, H. (2016). Effect of transition planning activities on postsecondary support receipt by students with disabilities. *Exceptional Children, 82*(4), 497–514. https://doi.org/10.1177/0014402915615884

Orelove, F. P., Sobsey, R., & Gilles, D. L. (Eds.). (2017). *Educating students with severe and multiple disabilities: A collaborative approach.* Brookes Publishing.

Pufpaff, L. A., Mcintosh, C. E., Thomas, C., Elam, M., & Irwin, M. K. (2015). Meeting the health care needs of students with severe disabilities in the school setting: Collaboration between school nurses and special education teachers. *Psychology in the Schools, 52*(7), 683–701. https://doi-org.mutex.gmu.edu/10.1002/pits.21849

Rowe, D. A., & Francis, G. L. (2020). Reflective thinking: Considering the intersection of microcultures in IEP planning and implementation. *Teaching Exceptional Children, 53*(1), 4–6. https://doi.org/10.1177/0040059920952007

Turnbull, A., Turnbull, R., Francis, G. L., Burke, M., Kyzar, K., Haines, S. J., Gershwin, T., Shepherd, K. G., Holdren, N., & Singer, G. (2021). *Families and professionals: Trusting partnerships in general and special education* (8th ed.). Pearson.

Wehman, P. H. (2011). Employment for persons with disabilities: Where are we now and where do we need to go? *Journal of Vocational Rehabilitation, 35*(3), 145–151.

Zagelbaum, A., & Carlson, J. (Eds.). (2011). *Working with immigrant families: A practical guide for counselors.* Taylor & Francis/Routledge.

3
Collaborate with Families to Support Student Learning and Secure Needed Services

Jamie N. Pearson, Jared H. Stewart-Ginsburg, and Shari L. Hopkins

Teachers collaborate with families about individual children's needs, goals, programs, and progress over time and ensure families are informed about their rights as well as about special education processes (e.g., IEPs, IFSPs). Teachers should respectively and effectively communication considering the background socioeconomic status, language, culture, and priorities of the family. Teachers advocate for resources to help students meet instructional, behavioral, social, and transition goals. In building positive relationships with students, teachers encourage students to self-advocate, with the goal of fostering self-determination over time. Teachers also work with families to self-advocate and support their children's learning.

Supporting Students with Extensive Support Needs

Before special education, professional services, and legal mandates, family members of students with extensive support needs (ESN) advocated for their loved ones to be treated with dignity and equity. Historians can trace a direct line between parent advocacy (particularly leadership from mothers) and modern federal policy requirements related to special education (Carlson et al., 2019; Harry, 2008). Families play an important role in shaping the lives of students with ESN. Consequently, including families of students with ESN in educational planning is a cornerstone of the Individuals with Disabilities Education Improvement Act (IDEA, 2004). Family engagement in special education services across the lifespan (i.e., during early intervention, transition to school, transition to adulthood) benefits students and their families (Burrell & Borrego, 2012; Mazzotti et al., 2021). However, many educators do not feel prepared or equipped to partner with families of students with ESN (Robertson et al., 2017). In this chapter, we will offer considerations and practices for partnering with family members of students with ESN in the education process. First, we describe legal and cultural aspects of family involvement for students with ESN. Then, we suggest how to build family–school partnerships with families of students with ESN. Family–school partnerships require educators to both fully understand families and take action toward partnership (Mortier et al., 2021). At the end of each section, we suggest tangible actions educators can take to collaborate with families.

DOI: 10.4324/9781003175735-4

Chapter Objectives

Upon reading this chapter, you should be able to do the following:

1. Describe the role of families in supporting students with ESN.
2. Depict the experiences of and challenges faced by families of students with ESN.
3. Convey the importance of family–school partnerships.
4. Identify effective partnership strategies to engage families and support students with ESN.

"Come Together:" What Are Family–School Partnerships?

Engaging students with ESN and their families as active partners in special education services leads to positive outcomes for children, caregivers, and families. Parents and caregivers of students with ESN who participated in special education service planning have reported increased perceived self-efficacy, confidence, competence, caregiver well-being, family well-being, and satisfaction with school services (Dunst et al., 2007; Zablotsky et al., 2012). Additionally, when parents and caregivers are knowledgeable and active participants in transition planning for students' future, their students are more likely to hold competitive employment after graduation (Mazzotti et al., 2021).

Unlike Beetlejuice, saying "family involvement" three times will not make it appear (Burton, 1988). Family engagement requires educators to intentionally invite, include, and partner with parents, caregivers, and family members from families of all cultural, linguistic, and socioeconomic backgrounds (Herman & Reinke, 2016; Pearson et al., 2021). Family–school partnerships are characterized by relationships where families and educators each contribute expertise and resources in ways that benefit students, their families, and the educators who support them (Mortier et al., 2021). In addition to the long-term benefits, family–school partnerships are critical for students with ESN because students with ESN often benefit from coordinated services and tools accessed across home, school, and community environments (e.g., behavior support plans, augmentative and alternative communication; Mortier et al., 2021). Family–school partnerships can lead to more effective service implementation and positive student outcomes such as IEP goal attainment and acquisition of skills for daily living (Azad & Mandell, 2016; Mapp & Kuttner, 2013; Topar et al., 2010). Despite the short- and long-term benefits for students with ESN, families, and teachers, collaborative partnerships between educators and family members of students ESN are often not fully developed (Azad & Mandell, 2016; Olmstead, 2013). Underdeveloped family–school partnerships can impact the quality of interactions with families, student achievement outcomes, and inclusive placement decisions (Zagona et al., 2019).

"We Are Family:" Defining Families

Supporting students with ESN requires educators to hold an expansive definition of *family* (Turnbull et al., 2016). The family unit is a complex system where interconnected individuals (e.g., spouses, siblings) interact in ways that influence each other's behavior (Kerr et al., 1988). In special education law, *family* is equally expansive. Under IDEA (2004), *family* describes children, parents, siblings, grandparents, extended family members, and non-related adults who act in the role of a family member (OSEP, 2020, p. 3). *Parent* includes natural parents, adoptive and foster parents, guardians, and any individual acting in the role of the parent (i.e., the primary decision maker for a student). In some cases, the term *caregivers* is used to describe guardians such as grandparents, siblings, aunts, and uncles who provide daily support to the student. Educators supporting students with disabilities have a responsibility to obtain parental consent prior to conducting evaluations for special education eligibility, instituting special education services, and making programmatic changes to special education service delivery. Educators must invite parents to attend and participate in individualized education program (IEP) meetings and regularly inform parents of their child's progress (IDEA, 2004).

STOP, COLLABORATE, LISTEN: Encourage parents and guardians to invite *any* family members who provide support to the student (e.g., siblings, grandparents) to attend or offer insight for the IEP meeting.

Historically Marginalized Families

Parent advocacy paved the way for special education services. However, not all families were initially included. Parental advocacy groups typically comprised mostly White membership with high social capital necessary for advocacy work (Harry, 2008; Trainor, 2010). As a whole, culturally and linguistically diverse students with ESN receive fewer disability-related services (e.g., Maenner et al., 2020). Because of this, we refer to culturally and linguistically diverse students and families (e.g., Black, Latinx, English Learners) as *historically marginalized* because they were often excluded from equitable services.

In addition to services, cultural backgrounds often shape practices, definitions, and compositions of families. Historically marginalized students with ESN are more likely to live in multi-generational homes with multiple adults who share care-giving responsibilities (Oberlander et al., 2007). The specific family members who participate in IEP meetings, educational planning, and supporting the needs of historically marginalized students with ESN may fluctuate over time. For example, if a grandparent comes to stay with a student and their parent(s), the students' parent(s) may direct you to include them in communication about the students' progress. A parent may share with teachers a cousin will be picking the student up from school and ensuring they complete their homework.

STOP, COLLABORATE, LISTEN: When meeting with parents (e.g., IEP meeting), ask what services have been provided for their student and what their experience was like receiving those services. Be mindful that families may not be aware of services available to them. Honor families' cultural and ethnic backgrounds by making a concerted effort to understand families' beliefs and practices, even if they differ from your own (Turnbull et al., 2016). Look for strengths family members bring to the IEP and educational process.

"Winds of Change:" How Students with ESN Shape Families

Raising a student with ESN affects the family system in unique ways. Families of students with ESN often experience a disruption in expectations, schedules, routines, and daily considerations after receiving a diagnosis (Carlson et al., 2019). This transition results in a forced adjustment to a new normal (Kerr et al., 1988). Parents may experience grief from altered expectations or increased stress from managing daily routines (Dababnah et al., 2018; Kinnear et al., 2016).

Stigma

Despite the potential for positive outcomes, one of the most notable challenges that families of students with ESN experience is stigma. Stigma is a process by which students with ESN are marginalized and undervalued by society based on their disability label (Goffman, 1963). Stigma often occurs in the form of stereotyping, prejudice, and discrimination (Ali et al., 2012). Students with ESN and their families experience stigmatization within schools and communities (Carter et al., 2016). For example, middle school students expressed negative stereotypes about their peers with ESN, which may have influenced their acceptance of students with ESN (Carter et al., 2016). Students with ESN are often socially excluded and experience violence and significant barriers that restrict their basic rights (Ali et al., 2012). Students with ESN may experience isolation from peers due to placement in segregated environments (i.e., self-contained classrooms), which restricts opportunities to form meaningful relationships outside of school (Ali et al., 2012; Carter et al., 2016).

Stigma is not just limited to students. Families of students with ESN can also experience being excluded or undervalued. Some parents feel shamed by others because they are raising a student with ESN (called *courtesy stigma*; Ali et al., 2012; Goffman, 1963). Stigma also can be internalized, where family members blame themselves for their student's disability or characteristics (called *affiliate stigma,* Ali et al., 2012; Goffman, 1963). Stigma can result in negative self-perceptions and emotions that cause family members to withdraw from others. In addition, people experiencing affiliate stigma might be reluctant to divulge family information due to fears and perceptions about parenting practices (Ali et al., 2012).

While all families can experience stigma, stigma is often most impactful in historically marginalized communities. Family members from historically marginalized communities sometimes do not seek services and support for their students with ESN due to historical oppression and cultural stigma associated with having ESN (Fripp & Carlson, 2017). For example, Black families supporting children with ESN shared stories of biases and community stigma of disability (e.g., Dababnah et al., 2018; Howard et al., 2021; Pearson et al., 2020). One example of practitioner biases is when educators suggest that behaviors and support needs in students of color are a result of the student's cultural background or parenting practices (i.e., as opposed to a disability; Pearson & Meadan, 2018; Pearson et al., 2020; Stanley, 2015). When families experience stigma (particularly, historically marginalized families), they often feel isolated or hesitant to seek support or services for their student with ESN or their family as a whole (Ali et al., 2012; Howard et al., 2021).

STOP, COLLABORATE, LISTEN: Recognize the role that stigma may play in families and parenting decisions (e.g., shame, withdrawal, isolation). Don't take it personally if family members are hesitant, reluctant, or distrustful! Look for signs that family members are experiencing isolation.

"I'll Be There:" Developing Family–School Partnerships

As educators begin to understand the roles, routines, and experiences of families, they can begin building positive family–school partnerships (see Table 3.1). In effective family–school partnerships, educators, family members, and the student share expertise (e.g., prioritizing student needs) and resources (e.g., community services, planning documents) with each other. As depicted in Table 3.1, effective partnerships are built on several important features. We provide an overview here, followed by a description of each in subsequent sections. Effective partnerships between educators and families of students with disabilities begin with four interpersonal characteristics: professional competence, communication, equality, and trust (Turnbull et al., 2016). On top of this foundation, partners (i.e., family members, the student, educators) determine support needs, make placement decisions, and promote self-determination (Mapp & Kuttner, 2013). Through this

Table 3.1 Establishing a System for Family-School Communication

Purpose	Characteristics	Mode	Examples
Relaying Information	1. One-directional 2. Episodic 3. No response	1. Hard copy 2. LMS 3. Text or phone call	1. After school events 2. Remind family to turn in signed permission slip 3. Need supplies
Planning and Problem Solving	1. Two-directional 2. Episodic or transient 3. Collaboration	1. In-person 2. Video conferencing 3. Phone call	1. Transition to another class 2. IFSP/IEP meetings 3. Conflict with another student
Ongoing Partnership	1. Two- or multi-directional 2. Sustained, long-term 3. Collaboration	1. Hard copy 2. Digital tools 3. Video/audio recordings	1. Inclusion/participation plan 2. Consistent expectations across environments 3. Increasing student self-determination

process, partners advocate and gain respect for each other. Engaging in advocacy and demonstrating respect helps connect the student and family members to community resources.

Communication

Communication between schools and family members can form a foundation for promoting positive outcomes for students with ESN. Families play an essential role in providing input during person-centered planning for all areas of their child's education, including student goals and educational placement (Shogren et al., 2017). Successful inclusion of students with ESN requires ongoing communication with families (York-Barr et al., 2005). With large educational teams involved in supporting students with ESN, parents (historically marginalized parents, in particular) can feel overwhelmed and unheard (Cooper-Duffy & Eaker, 2017). Positive family–school communication requires an established method of communication and an established schedule of communication.

Communication Methods

It is important to identify families' preferred method of communication (Pearson et al., 2018; Pearson et al., 2020). A variety of modalities exist which can serve a variety of functions (e.g., phone calls, email, text messages, notebook exchange; Turnbull et al., 2016). Considerations around internet availability and the communication needs of the family (i.e., limited English proficiency) may influence preferred modes of communication. Educators should determine the best and most consistent method of communication early on in supporting a student and use the method in the manner that best meets families' needs. Communication with families should also take place in the family's preferred language (Pearson et al., 2021; Turnbull et al., 2016).

   STOP, COLLABORATE, LISTEN: When a student is assigned to your caseload, ask family members what their preferred method, language, and frequency of communication is (e.g., text message, email, printed memos). Ask family members who should receive communication in addition to the student's parent(s)/ guardian(s) (e.g., aunt, adult sibling). Document these in the student's IEP and verify that this information is current at each IEP meeting.

Relaying: Brief Communication

One component of family–school communication is relaying information. Teachers and families of students with ESN often relay information, which is a one-direction communication where the sender (i.e., teacher, family member) shares relevant information with no response expected from the receiver other than an acknowledgement. Information relays typically communicate information about school or classroom related events (e.g., family literacy night, field trips). Teachers can consistently relay information to parents through structured modes such as class schedules, calendars, or newsletters. Information relays aid families in preparing ahead of time for important dates and events and allow teachers to engage in effective communication that takes less time than dialogic communication. For younger students, teachers may choose to send home hard copies of these items or post them on a class website. For older students, teachers may choose to utilize the school's learning management system (LMS) to post this type of information to a calendar for students and families to easily access (e.g., Blackboard, Canvas, Schoology). E-mails with or without attachments can be sent to families of all students through the LMS, which is often a family's preferred method because of ease of use and immediacy of delivery (Thompson et al., 2015). For students with ESN, teachers can relay consistent information about a student's progress toward academic, behavior, or transition-related goals. Teachers can also encourage families to relay information they believe will benefit the teacher, such as information about appointments, interfering behaviors, or forgotten items the student needs (e.g., medication, materials).

Some families may prefer to utilize digital tools for this purpose. In these instances, communication logs can also take the form of Google Docs, which are designed for collaboration between multiple parties. This has additional benefits in that they are using a secure, online resource. This is especially relevant for students with ESN who may have more personal, confidential information (e.g., medical, self-care) shared between parents and staff. Families or educators may also wish to use audio or video recordings. Additionally, educators can record informational videos to demonstrate instructional strategies so families are able to mirror school-based learning in both home and community settings (Pearson et al., 2019).

STOP, COLLABORATE, LISTEN: Establish an ongoing, two-way communication system through communication logs in accordance with family member preferences (e.g., home–school notes, daily updates, journals). Establish the purpose of daily communication logs with family members by discussing priorities (e.g., academics, services). Develop a form or template with the agreed-upon priorities listed. This will decrease the amount of information you send back and forth and ensure that family members feel the communication is responsive to their needs (Goldman et al., 2019). Make sure you include a section for achievements related to priority areas to act on a strength-based approach.

Problem Solving: Two-Way Communication

Educators and families expect to communicate with one another during the annual IEP team meetings. However, there are also times outside of these meetings when the educational team may need to discuss the student's needs and two-way communication is necessary. These meetings are generally episodic and issue specific (e.g., inclusion plan, updating health care plan). Families and related school personnel meet to address the issue at hand. Because these meetings require discussion and problem-solving, in-person interaction is helpful to ensure participants are able to contribute meaningfully. While teachers may prefer holding these discussions through virtual methods (e.g., video conferencing, phone call), family members may prefer communicating in person as nonverbal cues are often an important aspect in communication for family members from historically marginalized backgrounds (Pearson et al., 2018). When proposing in-person, face-to-face meetings, educators should understand that inviting families to meet before, during, or after school hours may be problematic for some families of students with ESN due to other support needs (e.g., scheduled respite care, health care appointments). In these instances, educators should partner with families to find a time and place to meet that is convenient for the family members and educator. If families prefer meeting in person but are unable to meet at the school or during school hours, educators may consider holding meetings off school property or at the family home. Meeting locations must be agreed upon by family members and the educator (IDEA, 2004).

STOP, COLLABORATE, LISTEN: As your schedule allows, offer multiple options for meeting times. Consider offering multiple meeting locations. When face-to-face is not an option, use video or audio call platforms where multiple participants can join in (e.g., Zoom, AppleFaceTime, GoogleMeet). This allows multiple family members to join or invite others who may contribute expertise to the discussion. Ensure platforms do not require a subscription or paywall for family members.

Professional Competence, Equality, and Respect

As educators communicate with families, they must take a strength-based approach (Steiner, 2011). The presumption of competence is a guiding philosophy in the education of students with ESN. Presumption of competence asserts that every student should be provided with opportunities to learn alongside their peers without having to first prove that they benefit from and learn in inclusive, academic settings (e.g., Biklen & Burke, 2006). Educators' approach to family partnerships should maintain this same philosophy. Communication with families should highlight student and family abilities and assets even when addressing challenges and needs (Pearson et al., 2018; Ruppar et al., 2018). Educators should take extra effort to convey and document student and family strengths when planning student services (e.g., IEP meeting, person-centered planning).

STOP, COLLABORATE, LISTEN: When you first begin working with a family, state explicitly that family members are equal members of the educational team and experts on their student's strengths and preferences. Approach conversations with families with a positive, collaborative spirit by asking questions that elicit the family's knowledge and expertise of their student. Defer to parents' priorities when appropriate or find compromises when you believe deference is not in the best interest of the student.

Advocacy

Educators supporting families of students with ESN should help develop families' advocacy capacity (e.g., knowledge of disability services, proactive communication) so family members can advocate for their student(s) in and beyond special education services. Teachers can partner with families to help parents and caregivers develop the knowledge and expertise they need to advocate for their children. Parent advocacy is the active engagement of parents and caregivers to ensure that the educational rights of students with disabilities are being met (Trainor, 2010). Parent advocacy can result in students receiving more services (Burke et al., 2018) and students being placed in inclusive educational settings (Trainor, 2010). One of the greatest barriers to family advocacy is with the design of the special education system itself (Pearson et al., 2021). Families often feel unheard and left out of decision-making processes. Given that students with ESN may have a large number of related and outside services, meetings with school personnel (e.g., IEP, person-centered planning, transition planning meetings) can feel like an "us" vs. "them" prospect from the start where family members are outnumbered by professional service providers (Mortier et al., 2021). This is especially true for historically marginalized families, as family members often convey they do not feel informed or capable of advocating for their student(s) (Burke et al., 2018; Pearson et al., 2020).

In addition to working directly with family members to build their advocacy capacity, educators can also develop parent-led discussions. Parent-led discussions increase knowledge and empowerment in family members, thereby increasing social and cultural capital where family members develop the knowledge, confidence, and experience to successfully advocate complex systems (Carter et al., 2012). During parent-led discussions, parents/caregivers develop an agenda (sometimes with the support of a teacher) and lead a discussion concerning their student's progress. In these agendas, caregivers typically include: (a) their student's academic, behavior, or transition aims; (b) discussion of the student's progress relative to their aims; and (c) area(s) of needs. By facilitating the discussion, family members can center their voices (i.e., instead of the teacher's voice) and demonstrate increased agency over decision-making processes for their child. Parents can lead discussions for formal meetings (e.g., IEP meetings) or informal meetings (e.g., episodic discussions about the student's progress).

STOP, COLLABORATE, LISTEN: As you lead meetings with family members, take time to explain the rationale, steps, and legal requirements involved in processes. Seek or create opportunities for family members (particularly from historically marginalized backgrounds) to participate in special education family advocacy training (e.g., Volunteer Advocacy Project; Burke et al., 2016; FACES; Pearson et al., 2021). Provide opportunities and support for parents to create agendas and lead discussions.

Trust

Trust is an important part of family–school partnerships (Turnbull et al., 2016). Family members and educators must each believe that each has the student's best interest in mind and will act with integrity to support the student. Similarly, family members and educators must agree to offer each other the benefit of the doubt when they describe differing experiences. Similar to presuming competence, educators should assume that families are sharing authentic experiences and parenting to the best of their ability.

Trust, however, is typically earned rather than given. One way to increase trust is through cultural brokering (Mortier et al., 2021). Historically marginalized families may especially benefit from this process. Cultural brokers are defined as liaisons who purposefully connect people of different cultural backgrounds, to improve their collaboration (Mortier et al., 2021). Educators can work with families to identify cultural brokers within the school community. For example, educators can reach out to community-based agencies such as parent training and information centers (PTI) found in every state, to identify cultural brokers who are trusted in their students' communities. Cultural brokers can provide additional insight into family systems and facilitate ongoing family–school communication by informing and assisting families.

STOP, COLLABORATE, LISTEN: Work to earn family's trust by keeping your commitments regarding service delivery, interventions, and communication. Be "impeccable with your word": do what you say you will do when you say you will do it (Ruiz, 1997, p. 24). Give families the benefit of the doubt by believing them when they describe experiences of the student that contrast your own, such as when describing the frequency or pervasiveness of interfering behaviors. When helpful, consider cultural brokers to help build trust with a family.

Support Needs and Placement Decisions

As the label suggests, students with ESN often demonstrate they will benefit from services addressing several needs (e.g., communication, numeracy). Prioritizing or minimizing areas of need should be a team effort whereby educators and family members are contributing knowledge of the student's strengths, preferences, interests, and needs in deciding which services, interventions, and opportunities to pursue (Trainor, 2007). Similarly, educational placement decisions (e.g., inclusive setting, self-contained setting) require consensus on what is most appropriate for the student. Second, educators must have an understanding of the family's priorities for these complex and nuanced decisions (Kurth, 2019).

When educators and family members do share consensus on what is most appropriate, discrepancies over placement or services may create barriers to building relationships with educators (Azad & Mandell, 2016). When discrepancies occur, educators may consider deferring to parents as a way of acknowledging their expertise and priorities. Other times may require a compromise between family members and educators where they agree to address one need first and then another or opt for a placement that is agreeable to both entities even if one expert (i.e., teacher, family member) believes it is less preferable than another.

STOP, COLLABORATE, LISTEN: Structure discussions regarding student needs and placement as a dialog where all relevant family members can share their opinion. When helpful, intentionally with hold your opinion until family members have weighed in. Seek to find compromise when possible.

Self-determination

A key tenant of promoting self-determination for students with ESN is to place the student at the center of all decision-making (Trainor, 2007). Person-centered planning (PCP) brings together all individuals (e.g., student, family members, friends, community members, service providers) who are or will be involved in the student's life to cultivate a plan for their future, empowering them to direct their own lives (Meadan et al., 2010; Trainor, 2007). While PCP is often used to develop a system for supporting students as they transition from adolescence to adulthood, it is also effective for school age students with ESN who require a larger network of supports and services, such as skills for daily living and individualized supports such as sensory regulation. One specific model of PCP frequently used in education is the McGill Action Planning Systems (MAPS; Vandercook et al., 1989). MAPS is used to prioritize personally relevant, meaningful goals for students and identify the environmental supports and services needed to achieve those goals. All stakeholders, including students, families, and schools, provide input.

Given the collaborative nature of MAPS, teachers should connect with family members to obtain information about student preferences, interests, needs, and strengths, either through interviews or a written questionnaire. Questions should be designed to obtain information relevant to the students' educational plan to identify student and family priorities. For example, the MAPS facilitator might ask students and family members to identify and describe their priorities. It is important to collect this information in ways that are most accessible to the student and their family. In some cases, families may prefer to participate in an oral interview. One benefit of oral interviews is that the facilitator can probe responses from participants to get more details about the student's history, needs, and goals, for example. Other students and families may prefer to answer written questions where they are able to think through their responses and respond at their own pace. Written questionnaires, however, may require follow-up to ensure that the team accurately interprets the responses. In the next section, we describe ways that educators can support parent empowerment and advocacy during PCP.

Connecting to Community Resources

Students with ESN benefit when they have access to community experiences (e.g., Mazzotti et al., 2021). Students with disabilities who participated in community experiences were more likely to be employed after graduation (Mazzotti et al., 2021).Community resources, such as disability services, nonprofit organizations, or activity groups, are an often-overlooked building block of family–school partnerships. Community resources can be both formal (e.g., vocational rehabilitation, parent advocacy classes, speech-language therapy) or informal (e.g., religious congregations, parent support groups, play groups; Kyzar et al., 2012) and provide support to students and families that are specific to students with ESN or for students with and without ESN. While community resources often exist outside the official jurisdiction of educators, educators may consider how community resources benefit a particular student or all students with ESN (Stewart-Ginsburg & Kwiatek, 2020).

Community resources are especially important for historically marginalized families. Historically marginalized families often rely on informal supports (e.g., support groups, religious congregations) more than formal support (e.g., mental health counseling), due to historic oppression (Avent et al., 2015; Avent Harris, 2019; Dempsey et al., 2016; Gourdine et al., 2011; Ward & Besson, 2012). Considering how community resources support families, helps educators become more culturally competent (Pearson et al., 2021). Families also may already receive support from community resources. Considering the community resources a student or family utilizes, helps educators and families build and maintain connections that will outlast the educator's tenure with the family.

Community Resource Mapping

To connect families with community resources, educators must be aware of community resources. Educators can assist families by identifying and connecting them with community services and resources through community-resource mapping (CRM). CRM is a systematic method for identifying a variety of community agencies and organizations which may be able to provide support for students with ESN at the national, state, and local levels (Morningstar & Clavenna-Deane, 2018). Educators identify formal and informal or natural supports to enable meaningful participation of students within the community setting and discover strengths in the community. Through the CRM process, educators become empowered and knowledgeable about opportunities available to students and their families and share the information with students and family members. By engaging in CRM, educators are better prepared to connect students with ESN with community resources in ways that support their visions and goals (Crane & Skinner, 2003; Morningstar & Clavenna-Deane, 2018). Connection with community resources may serve different purposes across school environments. As educators navigate these conversations, they should keep in mind the presumption of competence and maintain high expectations for the student.

STOP, COLLABORATE, LISTEN: Ask families what resources they find valuable and important in the community. Consider formal resources (e.g., autism-related services) and informal resources (e.g., peer relationships). Go through the CRM process (e.g., transitiontn.org/virtual-community-resource-maps-tools-tips-and-tricks/) and discover important resources in your community. Create (or find) a document outlining resources available to family members of students with ESN.

The Big Five

Family collaboration is a crucial part of education, especially for students with ESN. Collaboration with families may feel like a careful dance: partners (i.e., educators, family members, students with ESN) move in response to each other and support each other within the context of a trusting relationship. Educators are presented with several opportunities for partnership with family members throughout the year through the IEP and PCP processes. By establishing competence, communication, equality, and trust, educators build a strong foundation for partnership. Strong family–school partnerships benefit students, family members, and educators (Pearson et al., 2021). Most importantly, by collaborating with families, educators and family members gain valuable allies as they empower students with ESN to realize the lives they desire (Pearson et al., 2020). We leave you with the Big Five ideas for collaborating with families of students with ESN:

1. Establish a partnership foundation based on professional competence, communication, equality between partners, and trust.
2. Identify and utilize accessible communication systems that address family–school priorities.
3. Acknowledge and embrace the diversity of family structures and support needs, the various roles of family members who support students with ESN, and the values students and families hold.
4. Let families lead the dance! Share information with family members to help them build advocacy skills. Encourage family members to lead meetings. Support and promote students' self-determination.
5. Identify and connect students and families to community resources that support family quality of life and adjustment.

Resources

1. Beach Center on Disability: https://beachcenter.lsi.ku.edu/beach-families
2. Center for Parent Information and Resources: https://www.parentcenterhub.org
3. Child Mind Institute: https://childmind.org
4. Illinois Early Learning Project: https://illinoisearlylearning.org
5. National Technical Assistance Center on Transition – the Collaborative: https://transitionta.org

References

Ali, A., Hassiotis, A., Strydom, A., & King, M. (2012). Self stigma in people with intellectual disabilities and courtesy stigma in family carers: A systematic review. *Research in Developmental Disabilities, 33*(6), 2122–2140. https://doi.org/10.1016/j.ridd.2012.06.013

Avent Harris, J. R. (2019). The blacksuperwoman in spiritual bypass: black women's use of religious coping and implications for mental health professionals. *Journal of Spirituality in Mental Health*, 1–17. https://doi.org/10.1080/19349637.2019.1685925

Avent, J. R., Cashwell, C. S., & Brown-Jeffy, S. (2015). African American Pastors on mental health, coping, and help seeking. *Counseling and Values*, 60(1), 32–47. https://doi.org/10.1002/j.2161-007X.2015.00059.x

Azad, G., & Mandell, D. S. (2016). Concerns of parents and teachers of children with autism in elementary school. *Autism*, 20(4), 435–441. https://doi.org/10.1177/1362361315588199

Biklen, D., & Burke, J. (2006). Presuming competence. *Equity & Excellence in Education*, 39(2), 166–175. https://doi.org/10.1080/10665680500540376

Burke, M. M., Goldman, S. E., Hart, M. S., & Hodapp, R. M. (2016). Evaluating the efficacy of a special education advocacy training program. *Journal of Policy and Practice in Intellectual Disabilities*, 13(4), 269–276. https://doi.org/10.1111/jppi.12183

Burke, M. M., Meadan-Kaplansky, H., Patton, K. A., Pearson, J. N., Cummings, K. P., & Lee, C. E. (2018). Advocacy for children with social-communication needs: Perspectives from parents and school professionals. *The Journal of Special Education*, 51(4), 191–200. https://doi.org/10.1177/0022466917716898

Burrell, T. L., & Borrego, J. Jr (2012). Parents' involvement in ASD treatment: What is their role? *Cognitive and Behavioral Practice*, 19(3), 423–432. https://doi.org/b9tf94

Burton, T. W. (Director). (1988). *Beetlejuice* [Film]. Warner Bros. Pictures.

Carlson, S. R., Manundar, V. D., Wehmeyer, M. L., & Thompson, J. R. (2019). Special education transition services for students with Extensive Support Needs. In *Special education transition services for students with disabilities* (Vol. 35, pp. 117–136). Emerald Publishing Limited. https://doi.org/10.1108/S0270-401320190000035015

Carter, E. W., Biggs, E. E., & Blustein, C. L. (2016). Relationships matter: Addressing stigma among children and youth with intellectual disabilities and their peers. In: K. Scior & S. Werner (Eds.), *Intellectual Disability and stigma: Stepping out from the margins* (pp. 149–164). Palgrave Macmillan UK. https://doi.org/10.1057/978-1-137-52499-7_10

Carter, E., Swedeen, B., Cooney, M., Walter, M., & Moss, C. K. (2012). "I don't have to do this by myself?" Parent-led community conversations to promote inclusion. *Research and Practice for Persons With Severe Disabilities*, 37(1), 9–23. https://doi.org/hcrr

Cooper-Duffy, K., & Eaker, K. (2017). Effective team practices: Interprofessional contributions to communication issues with a parent's perspective. *American Journal of Speech-Language Pathology*, 26(2), 181–192. https://doi.org/gk6n26

Crane, K., & Skinner, B. (2003). Community resource mapping: A strategy for promoting successful transition for youth with disabilities. *Information Brief: Addressing Trends and Developments in Secondary Education and Transition*, 2(1), 1–7.

Dababnah, S., Shaia, W. E., Campion, K., & Nichols, H. M. (2018). "We had to keep pushing": Caregivers' perspectives on autism screening and referral practices of black children in primary care. *Intellectual and Developmental Disabilities*, 56(5), 321–336. https://doi.org/10.1352/1934-9556-56.5.321

Dempsey, K., Butler, S. K., & Gaither, L. (2016). Black churches and mental health professionals: Can this collaboration work? *Journal of Black Studies*, 47(1), 73–87. https://doi.org/10.1177/0021934715613588

Dunst, C. J., Trivette, C. M., & Hamby, D. W. (2007). Meta-analysis of family-centered help giving practices research. *Mental Retardation and Developmental Disabilities Research Reviews*, 13, 370–378. https://doi.org/10.1002/mrdd.20176

Fripp, J. A., & Carlson, R. G. (2017). Exploring the influence of attitude and stigma on participation of African American and latino populations in mental health services. *Journal of Multicultural Counseling and Development*, 45(2), 80–94. https://doi.org/10.1002/jmcd.12066

Goffman, E. (1963). Embarrassment and social organization. In N. J. Smelser & W. T. Smelser (Eds.), *Personality and social systems* (pp. 541–548). John Wiley & Sons Inc. https://doi.org/10.1037/11302-050

Goldman, S. E., Sanderson, K. A., Lloyd, B. P., & Barton, E. E. (2019). Effects of school-home communication with parent-implemented reinforcement on off-task behavior for students with ASD. *Intellectual and Developmental Disabilities, 57*(2), 95–111. https://doi.org/10.1352/1934-9556-57.2.95

Gourdine, R. M., Baffour, T. D., & Teasley, M. (2011). Autism and the African American community. *Social Work in Public Health, 26*(4), 454–470. http://doi.org/fd52h7

Harry, B. (2008). Collaboration with culturally and linguistically diverse families: Ideal versus reality. *Exceptional Children, 74*(3), 372–388. https://doi.org/gnfhfq

Herman, K., & Reinke, W. (2016). Improving teacher perceptions of parent involvement patterns: Findings from a group randomized trial. *School Psychology Quarterly, 32*. https://doi.org/10.1037/spq0000169

Howard, J., Copeland, J. N., Gifford, E. J., Lawson, J., Bai, Y., Heilbron, N., & Maslow, G. (2021). Brief report: Classifying rates of students with autism and intellectual disability in North Carolina: Roles of race and economic disadvantage. *Journal of Autism and Developmental Disorders, 51*(1), 307–314. https://doi.org/10.1007/s10803-020-04527-y

Individuals with Disabilities Education Improvement Act (IDEA), 20 U.S.C. § 1400 (2004).

Kerr, M. E., Bowen, M., & Kerr, M. E. (1988). *Family evaluation.* WW Norton & Company.

Kinnear, S. H., Link, B. G., Ballan, M. S., & Fischbach, R. L. (2016). The impact of parenting stress: A meta-analysis of studies comparing the experience of parenting stress in parents of children with and without autism spectrum disorder. *Journal of Autism and Developmental Disorders, 46*(3), 942–953. https://doi.org/10.1007/s10803-015-2637-9

Kurth et al. (2019). A description of parent input in IEP development through analysis IEP documents. *Intellectual and Developmental Disabilities, 57*(6), 485–498. https://doi.org/10.1352/1934-9556-57.6.485

Kyzar, K. B., Turnbull, A. P., Summers, J. A., & Gómez, V. A. (2012). The relationship of family support to family outcomes: A synthesis of key findings from research on severe disability. *Research and Practice for Persons With Severe Disabilities, 37*(1), 31–44. https://doi.org/10.2511%2F027494812800903247

Maenner, M., Shaw, K., Baio, J., Washington, A., Patrick, M., DiRienzo, M., Christensen, D., Wiggins, L., Pettygrove, S., Andrews, J., Lopez, M., Hudson, A., Baroud, T., Schwenk, Y., White, T., Rosenberg, C., Lee, L.-C., Harrington, R., Huston, M., & Dietz, P. (2020). Prevalence of autism spectrum disorder among children aged 8 years: Autism and developmental disabilities monitoring network, 11 sites, United States, 2016. *MMWR. Surveillance Summaries, 69*, 1–12. https://doi.org/10.15585/mmwr.ss6904a1

Mapp, K. L., & Kuttner, P. J. (2013). *Partners in education: A dual capacity building framework for family-school partnerships.* Southwest Educational Development Laboratory. https://www2.ed.gov/documents/family-community/partners-education.pdf

Mazzotti, V. L., Rowe, D. A., Kwiatek, S., Voggt, A., Chang, W., Fowler, C. H., Poppen, M., Sinclair, J., & Test, D. W. (2021). Secondary transition predictors of post-school success: An update to the research base. *Career Development and Transition for Exceptional Individuals, 44*(1), 47–64. https://doi.org/10.1177/2165143420959793

Meadan, H., Shelden, D. L., Appel, K., & DeGrazia, R. L. (2010). Developing a long-term vision: A road map for students' futures. *Teaching Exceptional Children, 43*(2), 8–14. https://doi.org/10.1177/004005991004300201

Morningstar, M. E., & Clavenna-Deane, B. (2018). *Your complete guide to transition planning and services.* Paul H. Brookes Publishing.

Mortier, K., Brown, I. C., & Aramburo, C. M. (2021). Cultural brokers in special education. *Research and Practice for Persons With Severe Disabilities*, *46*(1), 3–17. https://doi.org/10.1177%2F1540796920975386

Oberlander, S. E., Black, M. M., & Starr, R. H. (2007). African American Adolescent mothers and grandmothers: A multigenerational approach to parenting. *American Journal of Community Psychology*, *39*(1), 37–46. https://doi.org/10.1007/s10464-007-9087-2

Office of Special Education Programs (2020). *OSEP expectations for engaging families in discretionary grants*. https://bit.ly/3qkXxUd

Olmstead, C. (2013). Using technology to increase parent involvement in schools. *TechTrends*, *57*(6), 28–37. https://doi.org/10.1007/s11528-013-0699-0

Pearson, J. N., Akamoglu, Y., Chung, M., & Meadan, H. (2019). Building family-professional partnerships with culturally, linguistically, and economically diverse families of youngchildren. *Multicultural Perspectives*, *21(4),* 208–216. https://doi.org/hcrs

Pearson, J. N., Hamilton, M. B., & Meadan, H. (2018). We saw our son blossom": A guide for fostering culturally responsive partnerships to support African American autistic children and their families. *Perspectives of the ASHA Special Interest Groups*, *3*, 84–97.

Pearson, J. N., Meadan, H., Malone, K. M., & Martin, B. M. (2020). Parent and professional experiences supporting African-American children with autism. *Journal of Racial and Ethnic Health Disparities*, *7*(2), 305–315. https://doi.org/10.1007/s40615-019-00659-9

Pearson, J. N., Hamilton, M. B., Stansberry Brusnahan, L. L., & Hussein, D. (2021). Empowering families by utilizing culturally responsive strategies in the education of children with multi-layered identities. In E. A. Harkins Monaco, M. C. Fuller, & L. L. Stansberry Brusnahan (Eds.), *Diversity, Autism, and developmental disabilities: Guidance for the culturally sustaining educator.* (Vol. 13, pp. 131–156). Council for Exceptional Children and Division on Autism and Developmental Disabilities.

Robertson, P. M., McCaleb, K. N., & Smith, N. J. (2017). Future education leaders' needs in serving students with severe disabilities: A call for intentional preparation. *Inclusion*, *5*(1), 60–76. https://doi.org/10.1352/2326-6988-5.1.60

Ruppar, A. L., Roberts, C. A., & Olson, A. J. (2018). Developing expertise in teaching students with extensive support needs. *Intellectual and Developmental Disabilities*, *56*(6), 412–426. https://doi.org/10.1352/1934-9556-56.6.412

Shogren, K. A., Wehmeyer, M. L., Schalock, R. L., & Thompson, J. R. (2017). Reframing educational supports for students with intellectual disability through strength-based approaches. In M. L. Wehmeyer & K. A. Shogren (Eds.), *Handbook of research-based practices for educating students with intellectual disability* (pp. 17–30). Routledge.

Stanley, S. L. G. (2015). The advocacy efforts of African American mothers of children with disabilities in rural special education: Considerations for school professionals. *Rural Special Education Quarterly*, *34*(4), 3–17. https://doi.org/10.1177%2F875687051503400402

Steiner, A. M. (2011). A strength-based approach to parent education for children with autism. *Journal of Positive Behavior Interventions*, *13*(3), 178–190. https://doi.org/10.1177%2F1098300710384134

Stewart-Ginsburg, J. H., & Kwiatek, S. M. (2020). Partnerships from the pews: Promoting interagency collaboration with religious organizations. *Career Development and Transition for Exceptional Individuals*, *43*(3), 187–192. https://doi.org/d7dz

Thompson, B. C., Mazer, J. P., & Flood Grady, E. (2015). The changing nature of parent– teacher communication: Mode selection in the smartphone era. *Communication Education*, *64*(2), 187–207. https://doi.org/10.1080/03634523.2015.1014382

Topar, D. R., Keane, S. P., Shelton, T. L., & Calkins, S. D. (2010). Parent involvement and student performance: A multiple meditational analysis. *Journal of Prevention & Intervention in the Community*, *38*(3), 183–197. https://doi.org/10.1080/10852352.2010.486297

Trainor, A. A. (2007). Person-centered planning in two culturally distinct communities: Responding to divergent needs and preferences. *Career Development for Exceptional Individuals, 30*(2), 92–103. https://doi.org/10.1177/08857288070300020601

Trainor, A. A. (2010). Diverse approaches to parent advocacy during special education home-school interactions: Identification and use of cultural and social capital. *Remedial and Special Education*, 31(1), 34–47. https://doi.org/10.1177/0741932508324401

Turnbull, A. P., Turnbull, H. R., Erwin, E., Soodak, L., & Shogren, K. A. (2016). *Families, professionals, and exceptionality: Positive outcomes through partnerships and trust* (7th ed.). Pearson.

Vandercook, T., York, J., & Forest, M. (1989). McGill action planning system (MAPS). *Journal of the Association for Persons With Severe Handicaps, 23*(2), 119–133. https://doi.org/10.1177/154079698901400306

Ward, E. C., & Besson, D. D. (2012). African American men's beliefs about mental illness, perceptions of stigma, and help-seeking barriers. *The Counseling Psychologist, 41*(3), 359–391. https://doi.org/10.1177/0011000012447824

York-Barr, J., Sommerness, J., Duke, K., & Ghere, G. (2005). Special educators in inclusive education programmes: Reframing their work as teacher leadership. *International Journal of Inclusive Education, 9*(2), 193–215. https://doi.org/10.1080/1360311042000339374

Zablotsky, B., Boswell, K., & Smith, C. (2012). An evaluation of school involvement and satisfaction of parents of children with autism spectrum disorders. *American Journal on Intellectual and Developmental Disabilities, 117*(4), 316–330. https://doi.org/10.1352/1944-7558-117.4.316

Zagona, A. L., Miller, A. L., Kurth, J. A., & Love, H. R. (2019). Parent perspectives on special education services: How do schools implement team decisions? *School Community Journal, 29*(2). https://www.adi.org/journal/2019fw/ZagonaEtAlFW2019.pdf

4

Use Multiple Sources of Information to Develop a Comprehensive Understanding of a Student's Strengths and Needs

Shawnee Wakeman, Meagan Karvonen, Jacqui Kearns, and Michael Stoehr

To develop a deep understanding of a student's learning needs, special educators compile a comprehensive learner profile through the use of a variety of assessment measures and other sources (e.g., information from parents, general educators, other stakeholders) that are sensitive to language and culture, to (a) analyze and describe students' strengths and needs and (b) analyze the school-based learning environments to determine potential supports and barriers to students' academic progress. Teachers should collect, aggregate, and interpret data from multiple sources (e.g., informal and formal observations, work samples, curriculum-based measures, functional behavior assessment [FBA], school files, analysis of curriculum, information from families, other data sources). This information profile of the student's strengths and needs.

Supporting Students with Extensive Support Needs

Assessment data are the sources of planning in every area of education for every student. The use and the types of assessments, however, can vary greatly. For students with extensive support needs (ESN) who potentially produce variable performances and need multiple experiences to master content and skills, best practice is the collection of multiple sources of data from the student over time rather than a single point in time assessment. Comprehensive assessment is necessary to ensure developing appropriate individualized education program (IEP) goals and designing the most effective instruction and interventions to support students in any content or context.

High leverage practice (HLP) 4 specifically addresses the use of multiple types of assessments and the utilization of multiple opportunities for the student to provide data to create a thorough picture of the student's strengths and needs for educational programming. HLP 4 is **Use multiple sources of information to develop a comprehensive understanding of a student's strengths and needs.** The description provided by McLeskey et al. (2017) includes

> …compile a comprehensive learner profile through the use of a *variety of assessment measures and other sources* (e.g., information from parents, general educators, other stakeholders) that are sensitive to language and culture, to (a) analyze and describe students' strengths and needs and (b) analyze the school-based learning environments to determine potential

DOI: 10.4324/9781003175735-5

supports and barriers to students' academic progress. *Teachers should collect, aggregate, and interpret data from multiple sources (e.g., informal and formal observations, work samples, curriculum-based measures, functional behavior assessment [FBA], school files, analysis of curriculum, information from families, other data sources)*

(p. 21)

Accessible, authentic assessments are essential if the data collected accurately represent what students with ESN know and can do. The collection of data from these assessments over time is also essential if the purpose of the assessment is to not only gauge student performance but to also inform the use of supports and strategies most appropriate for the student within instruction.

In this chapter, we will emphasize the importance of comprehensive assessment for the purposes of identifying students' strengths and areas where supports should be provided. We will describe a range of assessments including those especially relevant for many students with ESN (e.g., academics, communication, assistive technology, transition, ecological) and will describe ways to ensure that preferences of students with ESN are included within assessment data. We also will provide guidance in practically collecting assessment data from the transdisciplinary team.

Chapter Objectives

Upon reading this chapter, you should be able to do the following:

1. Identify the sources of assessment data available across multiple domains for the purpose of education planning.
2. Determine flexible ways to collect data that is an accurate representation of student strengths and needs.
3. Identify how to actively engage students (understanding of and preference for) within the assessment process.
4. Consider ways to make sense of data to create comprehensive student profiles in collaborative teams.

Considerations for Assessment

The first step when considering the use of any assessment is to determine the purpose of the assessment and how the results will be used. Not all assessments are created equal, nor are they designed to meet all purposes. For example, states administer alternate assessments based on alternate academic achievement standards to many students with ESN. These assessments have at least one designated purpose, most likely determining student achievement of grade-level academic expectations as defined by the state. Alternate assessment results can be used for different purposes. For example, parents use the results to learn how their student performed academically that year. States include those assessment results in accountability reporting. IEP teams may mention the results when describing the student's present levels of performance because they could inform goals or priorities for next year. When assessments are used for purposes for which they are not designed, the results can be distorted or misinterpreted. For example, some benchmark assessments provide information about how a student did compared to peers. Comparing scores for a student with ESN to the whole population of students in the same grade could be misleading and is not likely to be useful when planning how to adjust instruction. It is essential to determine the purpose of any assessment data prior to administering any assessment.

The use of appropriate assessments and best assessment practices is essential if data collected are to be considered an accurate representation of the student's performance. This speaks directly to the **reliability** of scores, **validity** of interpretations made about the scores, and **fairness** of the assessment for all students (American Educational Research Association et al., 2014). Reliability refers to the precision of results and consistency with which an assessment would produce similar results over different administrations, assuming consistent administration conditions and consistent student knowledge. It is especially important for assessments for students with ESN to be precise and consistent over time. It is best practice to use multiple data points to understand a student's performance, since students with ESN do not necessarily demonstrate what they know and can do consistently. A *reliable* assessment administered repeatedly reduces the imprecision of results and provides a clearer picture of the student. *Valid* score interpretations require evidence that the assessment has certain characteristics and that it was administered as intended. For example, an academic assessment covering a large instructional unit would need to include items that cover the breadth of the content at the depth of expected learning. An inventory designed to predict success in a transition program would need evidence that its scores are actually linked to transition outcomes. A communication assessment that involves multiple people rating the student needs to have evidence that its descriptors are clear and can be consistently interpreted by a range of people (including those from different cultural and linguistic backgrounds) so the combination of ratings produce results that can guide good decisions about the student's educational program.

An assessment is considered *fair* when it is designed for a wide range of students and options for flexible administration, accessibility supports, or accommodations may be used to ensure all students have access to the assessment and can show what they know and can do. Assessments can be designed and administered using universal design for learning (UDL) principles to support the goal of fair assessment. When assessments are developed using principles of UDL, learner variability is considered by design so teachers do not have to make as many accommodations for each student's unique circumstances. For example, an assessment that allows the student to respond using any preferred response mode means the teacher does not have to choose accommodations for students who do not use speech to communicate. Students must also be familiar with the assessment process for the assessment to be fair. For assessments of knowledge and skills, students must receive equal opportunities to learn the content that is assessed. Scores must not be biased for any subgroup (e.g., based on disability, language, or cultural background), and results should be interpreted in the context of other information available about the student.

The concepts of reliability, validity, and fairness apply to each assessment. Collectively, the data sources should be appropriate for the student to reduce potential bias based on disability or other characteristics (e.g., cultural or linguistic background), promote valid interpretations of assessment results, and support teams in synthesizing the information to develop a profile that can guide educational decisions.

A final caution when assessing students is the use of a single assessment at a single point in time to make descriptions, decisions, or determinations. The value of using multiple sources or multiple points of data to create a comprehensive profile of a student is the inclusion of data that is verified by more than one measure or verified by multiple data points over time. For example, a student with ESN may be assessed on their ability to identify phonemes. If the student is only assessed once and is only asked to produce the phonemes, the data could be misleading for multiple reasons—if the student has communication needs and cannot produce some of the sounds but could identify the sound; if the student is distracted on the day; if the student is assessed after lunch when the student may be more fatigued; or if the student is presented the written letter versus presented the letter orally.

Common Data Collection Methods

There are several commonly used formats for measures—observations, interviews, scales, assessments—for data collection when working with students with ESN and their families.

Observations

Observations of the performance of students with ESN are one of the most common types of measures used for data collection. Data collection using data sheets (described in detail in Chapter 6) are most frequently associated with observations. The key for observations is reliability between observers. Collins (2012) noted that behaviors must be observable and measurable for data collection. There must be clear definitions or descriptions of what the observer records as being an example of the behavior or an instance of the correct response. Interrater reliability—agreement between multiple observers when recording data—increases credibility of the data. Examples of observations include FBAs, ecological inventories (observation of typical routines and skills by individuals without a disability and compared to a specific student, Browder et al., 2020) and data sheets that capture student demonstrations of a targeted skill or behavior. Common types of data sheets are task analytic, repeated or distributed trial, frequency, duration, and repeated opportunity. See the MAST module resource for more information about designing or selecting the correct data sheet for a skill (Resource section of this chapter).

Interviews and Questionnaires

Interviews and questionnaires are often used with students with ESN and their families to determine priorities and preferences. Protocols for interviewing stakeholders are often included within ecological inventories and adaptive behavior assessments to identify routines or processes that take precedence or are identified by the student or family as problematic. Preference assessments also typically take an interview or questionnaire format. These types of measures are critical when creating a comprehensive student profile to help identify the areas of interest within the domains of instruction (e.g., academic, social, leisure, vocational).

Rating Scales

Similar to surveys or questionnaires, rating scales ask a respondent to rate successful performance of a concept or behavior on some type of scale (such as a Likert scale). A typical rating scale for students with ESN is an adaptive behavior scale. While behavior rating scales typically examine behavior, emotional regulation, and social skills (Hosp et al., 2003), adaptive behavior scales are described by Pearson and Lachar (1994) as "...the practical skills used for negotiating one's physical and social environment, including communication skills, daily living skills, and social skills" (p. 33). Rating scales are often completed by multiple respondents to establish reliability (i.e., the student, parents, teachers).

Assessments

Perhaps the most recognizable source of information about student knowledge and skills is an assessment. Assessment results can be used for formative or summative purposes. The purpose of the assessment, the point in time, and the goal for its use (e.g., planning, evaluation) significantly influence the choice of assessment. When results of assessments are used within a process to adjust instruction and learning, the assessments are formative in nature (Brookhart & Lazarus, 2017). Formative assessments may be more formal, such as published curriculum-based measures used to monitor progress within an multi-tiered system of supports (MTSS) framework; or they may be more informal or teacher-created, like descriptive feedback on a draft of a student work product (Wylie, 2008). Summative assessments are typically more evaluative in nature to determine proficiency or summarize what has been learned after instruction (Brookhart & Lazarus, 2017). A final grade for a unit and a score on a statewide academic assessment are both examples of summative assessment results. Some assessments can fulfill both summative and formative purposes. An end-of-unit assessment score provides summative information on what a student knew and could do relative to the learning objectives for that unit. But if the teacher also used results to identify gaps in the student's understanding, they might use the information formatively by planning for how to remediate while working on the next unit. Regardless of the use, it is essential that students with ESN are given appropriate accessibility supports or accommodations so that they may participate in the assessment and produce data that are an accurate representation of their learning. Both formative and summative assessment results can and should be used to create profiles for students with ESN.

Another area to measure performance of students with ESN is within the domain of community-based learning. While a comprehensive assessment system for community-based instruction includes each type of measure listed in this section, informal vocational assessments also exist to measure student learning and mastery of knowledge and skills specific to a work environment.

Areas for Assessment

As we have discussed the uses and types of measures, it is also beneficial to discuss these in context of the content to be assessed. Depending upon what you are assessing, you may be more likely to find a measure of a specific type. For example, behavior is typically observed or reported on a rating scale. In the following sections, we discuss ways to collect and use data within different content areas to create a comprehensive profile. While this chapter introduces assessment of several broad areas, other chapters (e.g., Chapter 10 regarding behavior and functional behavior assessments [FBA]) go into more detail regarding specific content assessments.

Communication

Assessing students with ESN necessarily includes communication as an essential component. All areas of development—social, academic, and behavioral—depend on the ability of a student to communicate. Yet, historically, approximately 10% of students with ESN who participate in alternate assessments are assessed as pre-symbolic (i.e., no regular use of gestures, signs, words, or other indications of communication; Kearns et al., 2011). Furthermore, a similar percentage of high-school-age students continue to be assessed as pre-symbolic in communication. Of the students who are emerging in their use of symbols, fewer than 50% have no form of augmentative alternative communication (AAC; Kearns et al., 2011). Communication assessments represent the foundation for students with ESN. Without a robust communication system, assessment that rely on responses to prompts such as those that typically measure academic achievement (versus assessments that measure observable student behaviors) will yield inconclusive results.

Because of the complexity of the support needed for this population, the determination of communicative intent relies largely on observation of behavior (Downing et al., 2015). For this reason, convening a multi-disciplinary team to determine the types of assessment protocols is an important first step. Team members are selected based on the identified needs of the learner - including family members, the student/child, speech-language/audiology, occupational and physical therapy, vision, AAC, and English language expertise. The team can best match the assessment protocols with the unique characteristics of the learner. Indeed, team assessment and intervention result in higher levels of AAC use among students with ESN (Kleinert et al., 2019).

The purpose of the assessment guides the team's decision-making about the assessment types and tools. The primary communication assessment purpose, in most cases, is to determine goals and objectives, intervention strategies, and the selection of AAC tools that are likely to improve communication for the individual learner. It is important to note that there are no prerequisites for communication intervention or the use of AAC (Brady et al., 2016). Given the complexity of communication, a valid representation of the student's communication should occur during typical routine activities. The team may use a variety of assessment types and tools to gather the information necessary for team decision-making.

Ecological models are generally preferred for most assessment purposes because of the importance of the communication context (Downing et al., 2015). Ecological models include observations of the student's communication in familiar settings/routines, or activities, and with familiar partners. The expressive and receptive communication including the communicative form/behavior used by the student, the intent or function of the form, and content of the message are documented. Ecological protocols also can include the opportunities to observe initiations, responses, repairs, and/or turn taking during typical daily routines.

Family and peer interview protocols also can be important tools for assessing communication. Family members can identify communicative forms and intents that occur regularly and assist with documenting the communicative forms, intents, and messages in a communication diary. These observations can be recorded in writing or with video clips. Similarly, peers can assist by providing their interpretations of a student's communication forms and intents.

Communication partner skills are critically important to emerging communicators as observation and interpretation are critical to identifying and shaping clear messages, socially appropriate forms, and AAC use (Blackstone & Hunt-Berg, 2003; see resources for additional information). The communication partner shares an important responsibility as the use of AAC and other forms require supportive engagement, wait time, and interaction skills. Informally, video clips can be used to assess communication partner skills. The *Social Network Inventory* (Blackstone & Hunt-Berg, 2003) assesses AAC users and their communication partners across the age span.

Dynamic assessment (Snell, 2002) is another type of communication assessment strategy. This assessment strategy involves the assessor, the student, and environment. The assessor engages the student with highly preferred items and activities by responding to any student action, commenting and expanding on the student's communication, modeling, or waiting expectantly for student responses. The assessor may also manage the environment with the highly preferred items to elicit communication from the student by "forgetting" or providing the "wrong" selection. For example, Amy chose the color red—her favorite color to paint her poster—but the teacher, in order to elicit additional communication, gave her the green paint. Amy then had to get the teacher's attention, show her the green paint, and use her device to ask for her favorite color of red paint.

The Communication Matrix tool (Rowland, 2021; see resources for additional information) can be used to assist the team in identifying the student's level of communication ranging from preintentional to symbolic for a range of purposes. The communication matrix is a useful tool for determining a student's skills at a particular point in time, for determining next steps, and for monitoring on-going progress.

The Student Environment Task Tool or SETT Framework (Zabala, 2005), originally designed for any type of assistive technology, can provide teams with a framework for determining appropriate AAC tools, strategies, or devices. A SETT Framework adapted to include communication information can be used by the team initially to identify specific areas in which assessment is needed. It can also be used as a framework to integrate the information gathered from the family surveys, ecological and dynamic observations to identify AAC tools and strategies. The *Student* section of the adapted SETT Framework includes determining how the student communicates currently, identifying preferred and non-preferred items/actions/activities and facilitating the identification of AAC access pathways including hearing, vision, motor/positioning, motor/tactual, and English learner status. Once the *Student* portion of the framework is completed, the *Environment*, *Task*, and *Tool* sections are completed. The *Environment* section identifies the types of environments and routines that the student may access (e.g., the classroom—putting away materials; the playground—taking turns; the library—checking out a book). The *Task* section identifies specific communication tasks that are required in that environment (e.g., for recess or snack—telling a story, telling a joke, asking/answering a question, offering a comment/compliment; for class activities—asking/answering questions, suggesting ideas, commenting). Finally, the *Tool* section assists the team in determining the communication tool or device most appropriate for that environment. For example, a student traveling down the hall to class may wave or smile to communicate "hello," but to tell a story or joke, they would need their AAC system.

Academic

Collecting and using student performance data is essential for designing academic instruction to effectively meet the needs of all students so they can make progress in the general curriculum. This is true regardless of whether the student has a disability, what context the instruction occurs in, or what academic standards are being taught.

There are several best practices when designing and utilizing assessments of academic content. One important consideration is determining how much and what type of assessment data is enough to create a comprehensive profile. Statewide assessments like alternate academic assessments provide information about how much a student achieved in a subject overall, but a comprehensive profile should also include some information about strengths and areas for growth within each subject. A teacher will likely want to use several different types of academic assessment. For example, an IEP team might use the past year's alternate assessment scores and current year's alternate assessment performance level descriptors to set instructional goals in English language arts. The teacher might then administer a curriculum-based measure of several literacy skills or complete a district literacy checklist every six weeks to monitor progress each marking period and communicate with parents about that progress. The teacher also might collect observational data twice per week to monitor student learning on a cluster of English language arts content standards, adjust instruction, and make suggestions for how the family can help the student make progress on those standards at home. At the end of the year, the IEP team could then review a profile that includes all previous data plus a portfolio of student artifacts and the latest alternate assessment results to develop an overall evaluation of the student's academic progress and plan for the next year. In this example, the teacher follows HLP 4 by gathering different types of data, using each type of assessment consistent with its intended purpose, and collecting data over time to develop the student's academic profile.

Second, academic assessments need to meet standards for reliability, validity, and fairness that are consistent with the stakes involved in decisions that will be made using the results. Large-scale alternate assessments used to determine if a student is proficient in grade-level academics need more rigorous evidence than a teacher-made assessment designed to guide instruction. All assessments, including teacher-made assessments, can benefit from UDL principles to promote fairness. Educators can utilize the UDL guidelines and checkpoints (CAST, 2018) to design and administer an assessment that minimizes barriers and promotes engagement for a wide range of students with ESN. For example, the teacher could give students the option to show their understanding of an event in a book by composing sentences using a preferred writing tool, making a picture, or giving a presentation to their classmates using a preferred expressive communication mode and AAC as needed. This approach addresses UDL guidelines related to engagement and expression. Again, a key goal of applying UDL principles to assessment design and administration is to minimize potential barriers for students to demonstrate what they know and can do. For example, a paper and pencil assessment could represent a barrier for a student with ESN who does not have the motor skills to write, but the student could select response options in a variety of ways or type their responses on a computer or tablet. The link to the UDL guidelines is included in the resources for this chapter and is described in depth in Chapters 13 and 19.

A third consideration for academic assessment is the measurement of student performance during instruction. Designing effective, efficient, reliable ways to collect formative academic performance of learning and achievement can be a challenge, especially when multiple instructors are collecting data over time. Attention to the method of data collection within instruction is essential so there are opportunities for assessment that fit within evidence-based instruction. For example, in inclusive classrooms, students with ESN often participate in the evidence-based practice of embedded instruction (instruction typically designed for students with ESN that occurs throughout the day in activities or routines in a general education classroom; Jimenez & Kamei, 2015). An example of embedded instruction is when a student with ESN identifies vocabulary definitions using response options as each vocabulary word is read within a text. Assessment of content taught or reinforced through embedded instruction requires an efficient method for gathering performance data at each assessment opportunity regardless of who is teaching the lesson. All instructors must first be trained on collecting data for the correct response to increase accuracy of data collection and then must find a system for collecting that data that is stored in one location (such as on an app or using a data sheet on a clipboard kept in one location in the classroom).

Transition

Assessment for transition age students is the ongoing process of collecting and synthesizing information about students' interests, preferences and needs as they relate to the current and future demands of working, education, living, personal, and social environments (Neubert & Leconte, 2013). This information provides a common thread across the transition process and forms the basis for goal setting and identification of service needs that can support the individual in achieving their desired post-school outcomes (i.e., post-secondary education, competitive integrated employment, and independent living). Figure 4.1 is a process by which assessment related to transition occurs.

Because a student's transition happens across multiple environments including school, home, work, and community, collaboration across agencies to collect and use assessment information is critical to the development of common transition plans and delivery of services needed to support the student in achieving his or her goals. Collaboration among professionals and service systems has long been understood as an important component of effective initiatives and programs that support the transition of students with disabilities from school to work and adult life (Haber et al., 2016; Kellems et al., 2016). Collaboration among professionals assists students and their families in navigating the transition process, and is a predictor of successful employment outcomes for students with disabilities (Haber et al., 2016; Oertle & Seader, 2015). The Individuals with Disabilities Education Act (IDEA, 2004) and the Rehabilitation Act, as amended by Workforce Innovation and Opportunity Act (WIOA, 2014), both place a strong emphasis on collaboration and coordination in planning and providing transition services (Office of Special Education and Rehabilitation Services, 2017).

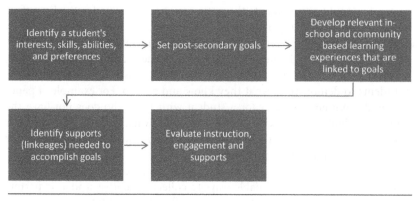

Figure 4.1 A Common Process for Secondary Transition Assessment

Table 4.1 Types of Transition Assessments

Formal Assessment Examples	Informal Assessment Examples
• Achievement tests	• Situational assessments
• Aptitude tests	• Work-based learning experiences
• Adaptive behavior scales	• Interviews
• Intellectual functioning assessment	• Direct observation
• Temperament inventories	• Curriculum-based assessment
• Self-determination scales	• Social history
• Pre-vocational-employability scales	• Surveys
• Interest inventories	• Rating scales for specific areas

There are numerous types of assessments used to inform the transition process for a student. Examples of the types of transition assessments typically included are listed in Table 4.1.

Results from the age-appropriate transition assessments serve as the common thread in the transition process and form the basis for a student's present levels of academic achievement and adaptive performance. The student's comprehensive profile mirrors the present levels and should be the foundation to define transition goals and services to be included in the IEP.

Collaboration to Create Profile

Creating a student profile should be a collaborative effort. As the teacher, it is critical to engage others in the assessment process to not only collect information from diverse perspectives but to also build trust within the instructional team that everyone's perspectives are valued. Assessment data should be collected from and by general and special education teachers, parents, students, related service providers, and other support personnel such as behavior specialists and vocational support specialists. It is important for educators of secondary students to engage with outside agencies and professionals in vocational rehabilitation services. The team, with the student at the center, will want to develop a profile that describes important information about the student to assist others in getting to know them. The profile allows the team to connect with the student's strengths and preferences and avoid using strategies and practices that have evidence of not being effective for the student. The necessity to engage others to create a profile that accurately represents a student is apparent, particularly when data may be conflicting from different situations and environments. It is necessary that a team provide data and context to help make sense of any data from one source that may conflict with data from another. For example, students with ESN may be able to complete a skill or task such as make a request or navigate in one environment and not in another environment. Conversely, students with ESN may produce unwanted behavior in one setting and not in another for various reasons. Discussions among the team can help identify issues and subsequently brainstorm solutions.

Student Engagement in the Process

One of the most important reasons for completing assessments is to empower a student to learn about themselves so they can take an active role in their educational and career development process. A student should be directly involved in all phases of the assessment process and should understand why they are being assessed and how to interpret and utilize the assessment information to reach their educational and life goals. One way to actively engage students in the assessment process is through the use of person-centered planning (PCP). PCP is an ongoing engaging process that is used to assist students with disabilities to plan for their future. In PCP the student and those individuals who know the student the best, assist in developing a vision regarding how that person wants to live their life and what is required to make that vision a reality. Another way to effectively support this goal is by engaging students in the assessment process itself. UDL principles, such as providing options for self-regulation, can be helpful here. For example, the teacher could design a formative assessment approach that includes a clear learning goal of what the student knows. The teacher can reinforce that goal during instruction, give relevant and timely feedback, and have the student record how they did with the goal during instruction. All of those strategies support learner engagement.

Next Steps toward Better Practice

For students with ESN, creating a comprehensive profile is more complex than administering only academic assessments. The entire student must be represented to create a complete picture of the student's strengths and needs across domains. So how do educators begin the process? We recommend the following steps.

1. Identify a student-centered, multidisciplinary team who currently works or will work with the student.
2. Identify the purpose (why do we need these data) and use (what will we use these data for) for any planned data. If necessary, re-read the Considerations for Assessment section to understand the differences between purpose and use.
3. Identify a method of data collection that matches the intended purpose and use AND produces accurate, unbiased information about the student.
4. Collect data across any and all areas that inform the student profile:
   a. Communication and, if appropriate, assistive technology
   b. Social skills
   c. Academic knowledge/skills aligned to grade-level standards
   d. Behavior- adaptive, engagement
   e. Transition
5. Discuss data and craft the student profile as a collective team. The student and team should be active in the data analysis and decision process regarding next steps for the student which are reflected in the student profile.

The Big Five

In this chapter, we describe HLP 4 in depth by explaining several types of measures and best practice for collecting data to create a comprehensive profile for students with ESN. *The profile must be comprehensive reflecting strengths and needs to accurately represent the student.* The process to collect and evaluate data within the team is the foundation for the development of the IEP. *It is essential that a multidisciplinary team be assembled to create a comprehensive profile-* the teacher should not be the only person collecting data from the student. HLP 4 is clear that data must come from multiple sources to build a comprehensive profile to best identify barriers and supports for the student. As outlined in this chapter, each team member plays a vital role in providing information and perspective so that a clear understanding of the student's strengths and needs is articulated. Instructional planning (strategies, supports, adaptations) should only be designed using ample student data that is thorough in nature.

The most effective and useful assessment systems are those in which students with ESN and their families are partners with school personnel. *When students and families are engaged meaningfully in the assessment process, the data on which identified learning targets are the lynchpin for communication and collaboration.* The potential for student progress is boundless when school and home are working in tandem to collect and use assessment data to develop IEPs and design strategies, supports, and adaptations that can be used universally.

As students with ESN can produce variable performance in a number of areas, *data collection should occur using a number of different methods.* Observations of student performance, interviews of and rating scales completed by stakeholders, and assessments of what students know and can do all play a role in the development of a student profile. It is important to remember that one assessment may not be appropriate for all students and that adaptations and accommodations will likely be necessary. Some measures may be more appropriate than others depending upon the content, context, and student characteristics. Assessments must be free from any culture or language bias if the data collected are to represent the student accurately. It is essential to determine the purpose of collecting assessment data and the use of the data before the measure is identified. For example, if data are to be used for an evaluative purpose, the better measures are likely observations of student performance and assessments.

One content area that can easily influence data collected within every other area is communication. *Communication is the foundation for all other assessments*- academic, social, transition across the age span. Yet approximately 10% of students with ESN leave school without a reliable system of symbolic communication. Furthermore, students who leave high school without a reliable system of symbolic communication are at significantly higher risk of poor post school outcomes. Assessment of communication is essential when creating a comprehensive student profile as a student must be able to make a reliable response if data are to be trustworthy.

Resources

Best Practice

The *MAST module on data collection* includes designing and selecting data sheets (observation, assessment) to match a task or skill. https://mast.ecu.edu/Data%20Collection/Data%20Collection/index.html

The *Universal Design for Learning Guidelines* "offer a set of concrete suggestions that can be applied to any discipline or domain to ensure that all learners can access and participate in meaningful, challenging learning opportunities." https://udlguidelines.cast.org/

Communication

AssistiveWare has a webpage with explanation and demonstration videos that support understanding how to set up communication partner skill opportunities with students with ESN. https://www.assistiveware.com/learn-aac/build-communication-partner-skills This supports the work by Blackstone and Hunt-Berg (2003).

Home Talk is a parent interview inventory designed to provide communication information about children who are Deafblind or have unique communication forms. Harris, J., Hartstorne, N., Jess, T., Mar, H., Rowland, C., Sall, N., Schmoll, S., Schweigert, P., Unruh, L., Vernon, N., & Wolf, T. (2003). *Home Talk.* https://www.designtolearn.com/uploaded/pdf/HomeTalk.pdf

The *Communication Matrix* (Rowland, 2021) is a communication assessment resource available for minimal charge to help anyone understand the communication status and needs of an individual who is in the early stages of communicating. https://communicationmatrix.org/

Transition

A Transition Guide to Postsecondary Education and Employment for Students and Youth with Disabilities, August 2020 includes information about the need for collaborative teams using data to make informed decisions regarding transition planning for students with disabilities. https://www2.ed.gov/about/offices/list/osers/transition/products/postsecondary-transition-guide-08-2020.pdf

Quickbook of Transition Assessments is a resource with multiple transition assessments that can help districts and agencies provide the necessary services based upon student needs, preferences, and abilities. https://www.ocali.org/up_doc/Quickbook_of_Transition_Assessment.pdf

References

American Educational Research Association [AERA], American Psychological Association, & National Council on Measurement in Education (2014). *Standards for educational and psychological testing.* AERA.

Blackstone, S., & Hunt-Berg, M. (2003). *The social network inventory.* Attainment Company.

Brady, N. C., Bruce, S., Goldman, A., Erickson, K., Mineo, B., Ogletree, B. T., Paul, D., Romski, M., Sevcik, R., Siegel, E., Schoonover, J., Snell, M., Sylvester, L., & Wilkinson, K. (2016). Communication services and supports for individuals with severe disabilities: Guidance for assessment and intervention. *American Journal on Intellectual and Developmental Disabilities, 121*(2), 121–138. https://doi.org/10.1352/1944-7558-121.2.121

Brookhart, S., & Lazarus, S. (2017). *Formative assessment for students with disabilities.* Commissioned by the Council of Chief State School Officers State Collaboratives on Assessing Special Education Students and Formative Assessment. https://ccsso.org/sites/default/files/2017-12/Formative_Assessment_for_Students_with_Disabilities.pdf

Browder, D., Spooner, F., Courtade, G., Brosh, C. R., & Knight, V. (2020). Promoting social skills and positive behavior support. In D. Browder, F. Spooner, & G. Courtade (Eds.), *Teaching students with moderate and severe disabilities* (2nd ed., pp. 301–320). Guilford Press.

CAST (2018). *Universal design for learning guidelines version 2.2 [graphic organizer].* Wakefield, MA: Author. https://udlguidelines.cast.org/more/downloads

Collins, B. (2012). *Systematic instruction for students with moderate and severe disabilities.* Brookes.

Downing, J. E., Peckham-Hardin, K., & Hanreddy, A. (2015). Assessing communication. In J. E. Downing, A. Hanreddy, & K. Peckham-Hardin (Eds.), *Teaching communication skills to students with severe disabilities* (pp. 51–83). Paul Brookes.

Haber, M. G., Mazzotti, V. L., Mustian, A. L., Rowe, D. A., Bartholomew, A. L., Test, D. W., & Fowler, C. H. (2016). What works, when, for whom, and with whom: A meta-analytic review of predictors of postsecondary success for students with disabilities. *Review of Educational Research, 86*, 123–162. https://doi.org/10.3102/0034654315583135

Hosp, J. L., Howell, K. W., & Hosp, M. K. (2003). Characteristics of behavior rating scales: Implications for practice in assessment and behavioral support. *Journal of Positive Behavior Interventions, 5*(4), 203–208. https://doi.org/10.1177/10983007030050040301

Individuals with Disabilities Education Act, 20 U.S.C. § 1400 (2004).

Jimenez, B., & Kamei, A. (2015). Embedded instruction: An evaluation of evidence to inform inclusive practice. *Inclusion, 3*(3), 132–144. https://doi.org/10.1352/2326-6988-3.3.132

Kearns, J., Towles-Reeves, E., Kleinert, H., Kleinert, J., & Thomas, M. (2011). Characteristics of and implications for students participating in alternate assessments based on alternate academic achievement standards. *Journal of Special Education, 45*(1), 3–14. https://doi.org/10.1177/0022466909344223

Kellems, R. O., Springer, B., Wilkins, M. K., & Anderson, C. (2016). Collaboration in transition assessment: School psychologists and special educators working together to improve outcomes for students with disabilities. *Preventing School Failure, 60*(3), 215–221. https://doi.org/10.1080/1045988Z.2015.1075465

Kleinert, J., Kearns, J., Liu, K. K., Thurlow, M. L., & Lazarus, S. S. (2019). *Communication competence in the inclusive setting: A review of the literature* (TIES Center Report 103). Minneapolis, MN: University of Minnesota, The TIES Center. https://files.tiescenter.org/files/g93yqc4Knm/ties-center-report-103

McLeskey, J., Barringer, M.-D., Billingsly, B., Brownell, M., Jackson, D., Kennedy, M., & Ziegler, D. et al. (2017). *High-leverage practices in special education*. Council for Exceptional Children & CEEDAR Center. https://ceedar.education.ufl.edu/wp-content/uploads/2017/07/CEC-HLP-Web.pdf

Neubert, D. A., & Leconte, P. J. (2013). Age-appropriate transition assessment: The position of the division on career development and transition. *Career Development and Transition for Exceptional Individuals, 36*, 72–83. https://doi.org/10.1177/2165143413487768

Oertle, K., & Seader, K. (2015). Research and practical considerations for rehabilitation transition collaboration. *The Journal of Rehabilitation, 81*(2), 3–18. Retrieved from https://www.proquest.com/scholarly-journals/research-practical-considerations-rehabilitation/docview/1695783728/se-2?accountid=14605

Office of Special Education and Rehabilitation Services. (2017). *Transition activities in the Office of Special Education and Rehabilitative Services*. Retrieved from https://www2.ed.gov/about/offices/list/osers/transition/products/osers-transition-activities-2017.pdf

Pearson, D. A., & Lachar, D. (1994). Using behavioral questionnaires to identify adaptive deficits in elementary school children. *Journal of School Psychology, 32*(1), 33–52. https://doi.org/10.1016/0022-4405(94)90027-2

Rowland, C. (2021) *Communication matrix*. https://communicationmatrix.org

Snell (2002). Using dynamic assessment with learners who communicate nonsymbolically. *Augmentative and Alternative Communication, 18*(3), 163–176. https://doi.org/10.1080/07434610212331281251

Workforce Innovation and Opportunity Act (WIOA) of 2014, PL 113–128.

Wylie, C. (2008). *Formative assessment: Examples of practice*. Council of Chief State School Officers. https://ccsso.org/resource-library/formative-assessment-examples-practice

Zabala, J. (2005). Ready, SETT, GO! Getting started with the SETT framework. *Closing the Gap, 23*(6), 1–3. https://manage42.rockyview.ab.ca/Plone/assets/archive/learning/teaching/assistive-technology/atl-assets/Ready-SETT.pdf

5

Interpret and Communicate Assessment Information with Stakeholders to Collaboratively Design and Implement Educational Programs

Bree Jimenez and Teresa Taber Doughty

Teachers interpret assessment information for stakeholders (i.e., other professionals, families, students) and involve them in the assessment, goal development, and goal implementation process. Special educators must understand each assessment's purpose, help key stakeholders understand how culture and language influence interpretation of data generated, and use data to collaboratively develop and implement individualized education and transition plans that include goals that are standards-based, appropriate accommodations and modifications, and fair grading practices, and transition goals that are aligned with student needs.

Supporting Students with Extensive Support Needs

Understanding and interpreting assessment results and subsequently communicating that information to stakeholders is vital to ensure success in meeting the learning needs of all students, including those with extensive support needs (ESN). In this chapter, we will describe the purpose of various assessments and those factors to consider when interpreting assessment data to make educational programming decisions (e.g., culture and language influence, stakeholder voice, targeting skills with broad impact). We will offer guidance for avoiding bias in the interpretation of results, and strategies for clearly communicating results to families, students, the transdisciplinary team, and other stakeholders.

HLP 5 focuses on understanding student data and effectively communicating the meaning of those data to stakeholders. It underscores the special educator's need to understand assessment and recognize the influence of culture and language when interpreting and communicating assessment results for students with ESN. Ultimately, communicating with stakeholders about assessment, including parents and families, includes describing the purpose of the various assessments used, explaining in clear terms the meaning of the test scores achieved, and connecting assessment results to the everyday life of the student with ESN (Pierangelo, 2003).

While teachers are quite skilled in recording students' grades, progress, and levels of independence over time, making meaning of those data and subsequently acting based on results often can be challenging. Also somewhat complex is a teacher's skillfulness in subsequently communicating data results to parents, students, and other professionals so that understanding occurs, and evidence-based instructional planning and student learning follows. Because effective interpretation

DOI: 10.4324/9781003175735-6

and communication of assessment information is critical to student success, this chapter will focus on several objectives.

Chapter Objectives

Upon reading this chapter, you should be able to do the following:

1. Identify the purposes of assessment for students with ESN.
2. Describe how presumed competence promotes high expectations for students with ESN.
3. Identify how contextual considerations influence data interpretation and collaboration.
4. Implement specific steps for communicating data to stakeholders including parents/caregivers, students, and education professionals.

Purposes of Assessment

Assessment occurs in multiple forms and formats (see Chapter 4). Its purpose is to gather student performance data so that teachers, parents/caregivers, and educational teams can make informed decisions about students' educational services and learning outcomes. Assessment is a major component in meeting the legal requirements for serving students with ESN. Results aid in determining student eligibility for special education services and each student's ongoing instructional needs based on present levels of performance (Kamman & McCray, 2019). The Individuals with Disabilities Education Act (IDEA, 2004) guarantees several rights related to assessment as part of individual's procedural safeguards. Parents/caregivers have the right to request an evaluation, they must receive written notice of assessment results, they retain the right of consent/refusal, and the ability to request prompt and thorough evaluations for their student using multiple measures. All assessments conducted must be free from bias/discrimination. Concurrently, the Elementary and Secondary Schools Act (ESSA, 2015) requires annual monitoring of student progress in mathematics, reading or language arts, and science as aligned to the state's academic and achievement standards. This law requires that all students participate in the same annual academic assessments with a limited exception for students with ESN. For these students, guidelines for administering alternative assessments are offered.

Present Levels of Performance

Assessments offer frequent information about where a student is currently performing and allows for the adjustment of instruction to accommodate changing needs. Formative and summative assessments given throughout the academic year (e.g., daily exit tickets, teacher checklists, homework, portfolio projects, video demonstration of student performing skill) illustrate and provide regular evidence of how a student is progressing in his or her academic work. Special educators use these results, in addition to other assessment information, to determine an individual's present level of performance. As IDEA requires a statement of each child's current level of academic and behavioral performance (IDEA, 34 C.F.R. § 300.347[a][1]), these statements must be based on current and accurate assessment data.

Because assessment plays a pivotal role for students with ESN from determining eligibility for initial special education services to measuring instructional effectiveness and learning, ongoing and meaningful communication with parents/caregivers and other relevant stakeholders is essential. Special education teachers must effectively describe the purpose of various assessments, accurately interpret assessment results, and subsequently link assessment findings to meaningful skills and outcomes for students with ESN. These actions are central to meeting HLP 5.

Presumed Competence

The assumption that all students can and will learn with high-quality instruction is essential during the educational assessment and planning process. Data are used to determine a student's strengths and needs followed by learning goals for progression through the stages of learning in a skill or concept (Jimenez et al., 2021). Donnelan (1984) introduced the concept of "the Least Dangerous Assumption" suggesting that in the absence of data, danger lies in assuming that someone cannot and therefore will not—learn, think, or do. HLP 5 specifically addresses the alignment between assessment, lesson planning, accommodations/modifications, and culture (e.g., beliefs) and communication. For students with ESN, the impact of low expectations has amplified bias towards this population for generations (Thurlow & Quenemoen, 2019). For example, in the 1990s, students with disabilities were excluded from educational assessments, as they were not expected to acquire the same knowledge and skills as their peers without disabilities. When appropriate access to high-quality curriculum and instruction is provided, students can meet or exceed established proficiency levels. Subscribing to high accountability standards for student progress ultimately leads to improved instruction and learning for all students. While expectations increased over the last several decades (e.g., alternate assessments), it is important for educational teams to assess their own presumptions related to academic success for students with ESN. Decision-maker (i.e., IEP team) self-reflection may uncover long held beliefs and biases regarding ability and performance outcomes of the students they serve (Thurlow & Quenemoen, 2019).

Context Matters

Context is defined as the "circumstances that form the setting for an event, statement, or idea, and in terms of which it can be fully understood and assessed" (Oxford University Press, n.d.). An essential element of HLP 5 is the use of assessment information and the consideration of how to develop curriculum and align instruction within the various contexts for target individuals. For students with ESN, assessment drives all aspects of their educational experience from initial eligibility assessment to ongoing assessment measuring instructional effectiveness and learning. Assessment data inform whether a student is eligible for special education services and subsequently play a pivotal role in prioritizing instruction. A holistic and contextual or ecological view is needed and should be included within the student's present levels of performance. To "fully understand" and therefore respond to the student's learning needs, the IEP team should use an ecological lens to communicate and plan.

Ecological Framework

The ecology framework was conceptualized in education to identify and teach the routines, activities, and skills that students need to learn to support their full participation in home, school, work, and community settings. When using an ecological lens to develop curriculum, student expectations are individualized based upon his or her strengths and needs. The framework articulates a process of working with students and their families to identify needed supports, adaptations, and modifications that personalize the curriculum, thus providing specially designed instruction that assigns accountability to educational teams for appropriate and ambitious student goals and outcomes.

Research examining the post-school outcomes of young adults with ESN repeatedly affirms the benefits of the ecological approach to assessment and curriculum development. For example, studies indicate that educational programs developed and aligned with individually prioritized activities and skills needed to participate in the community promote social connectedness and result in improved student adjustment to employment (White & Weiner, 2004), independent living

(Stancliffe & Lakin, 2007), and the development of social relationships with peers without disabilities (Chadsey, 2007; Giangreco & Putnam, 1991). Given these empirically demonstrated outcomes, it is not surprising that an ecological approach to collaboratively design and implement educational programs has strong support from the field today (Hunt et al., 2012).

Hunt et al. (2012) suggest the use of an ecological framework to guide stakeholders to maintain a clear focus on individual student needs as they provide access to general curriculum for students with ESN. Trela and Jimenez (2012) suggest use of the terminology "personally relevant," to interpret and talk about curricular adaptations made within the ecological framework providing access to both curriculum and individualized support. Educational teams should take time to self-reflect on how educational plans, goals, and assessment data reflect a personally relevant ecological lens, promoting high expectations across all domains: academic, social, and life skills.

Cultural and Linguistic Diversity

The influence of culture and language on assessment and communicating assessment results is considerable for effective instructional planning and implementation. Cultural perspectives directly affect understanding of assessment results and decision-making around instruction (Palawat & May, 2012). Unilateral communication about assessment results and resulting instructional goals and strategies may be limited to a teacher's understanding of cultural and linguistic diversity (CLD; Gonzales & Gabel, 2017). Yet, the needs of CLD students with ESN are unique and complex. While these students may face many of the same issues as their CLD peers without disabilities, the nature of their disability may preclude access to the general curriculum, appropriate services, and materials; and meaningful collaboration between families and educators (Rivera et al., 2016). *Funds of Knowledge* (Vélez-Ibáñez & Greenberg, 1992) is a concept describing the cultural practices that are part of a family unit's culture and daily routines based upon each family member's roles within their own family and community. This theory focuses on students' competences and identity (Esteban-Guitart & Moll, 2014) as it builds individual skills and knowledge that students acquire and may not be recognized by teachers. Effectively communicating assessment results with culturally and linguistically diverse stakeholders requires educational professionals ensure full language access to information. Parents, family members, and other stakeholders with limited English proficiency must have access to information in their first language. This may include involving an interpreter during meetings while concurrently ensuring written information is available in the primary language. Asking CLD stakeholders their preferences for communication also will aid in effective communication (Rossetti et al., 2017).

CLD families should be given the chance to openly discuss the options that are available and how these options can benefit the family and child, thus leading to more positive outcomes (Rivera et al., 2016). Kim and Morningstar (2005) identified four concerns that CLD families have during IEP and transition planning meetings: (a) professional attitudes, (b) diversity concerns, (c) contextual barriers, and (d) bureaucratic barriers. This lack of communication could lead to mistrust and feelings of isolation. A lack of services, such as translators, can negatively influence communication of assessment data, hindering implementation of HLP 5. Family-centered approaches set the needs, desires, and customs of the child and family as a key element for improving educational outcomes (Kim & Turnbull, 2004). It is imperative to respect the cultural values of all families, allow them to lead meetings, and provide equality in decision-making (Rivera et al., 2020).

For example, family members may prefer to review assessment information in writing prior to meeting to allow for processing information, family discussion, and the generation of clarifying questions. Rossetti and colleagues (2017) also identified commitment, equity, professional competence, and mutual trust and respect as aspects of strong collaborative partnerships when addressing effective communication involving CLD stakeholders.

Cultural Information Seeking

Taking time to understand a student's cultural heritage/socio-cultural background can help educators determine what skills should be linked to class assignments that aid in understanding new materials. Open communication systems that acknowledge a family and student's "funds of knowledge" and the cultural household knowledge needed for functional well-being, can be used to access a rich source of cognitive wealth (Rivera et al., 2016). Educators and collaborative teams should use their student's experiences (i.e., prior knowledge; possibly communicated through the family) to develop culturally responsive assessment and curriculum, making learning less demanding (Krashen, 1982).

CLD families often develop knowledge based on their own experiences and those of extended family members; therefore, these diverse families are often willing to assist in planning for their child's education; behavioral, medical, and social support needs; and post-secondary transitions but are often undermined by others' perceptions based on their ethnicity or socioeconomic status. Educators can use this collection of knowledge and perspectives to better assist families in selecting and accessing educational opportunities that are the best fit for their child and family.

Systems that Support Communication

Ensuring that all stakeholders have access to assessment data and subsequent interpretations is imperative for cohesive and evidence-based planning and appropriate support services to occur. As the coordinator of services for students with ESN, the special education teacher should take the lead in communicating and interpreting information to all stakeholders: students, family members, and professional education service providers (e.g., OT, PT, BCBA, SLP, administrators). This information should be shared, at minimum, on an annual basis at the IEP meeting. However, data sharing frequency should be determined based on the immediate need of information. For example, if a student with ESN is being assessed on challenging and/or dangerous behaviors, assessment information may need to be shared more frequently whereas data related to longitudinal academic goals may be shared on an annual or twice annual basis. Using technology tools (see next section) may assist special educators in sharing information and its frequency with all stakeholders.

Kamman and McCray (2019) recommend using a summary sheet for communicating formative (e.g., data sheets, weekly assessments) and summative assessment and re-evaluation results, when appropriate. Table 5.1 is one such summary document that communicates assessment results (formative, summative, criterion/norm-referenced), a real-world interpretation, and IEP/instructional implications. Individuals reviewing this table would receive information about the assessment instrument used, the specific scores obtained and a brief discussion on how these assessment results might be used when planning for instruction. This document may be reviewed by the IEP team and other stakeholders in advance of the IEP or other assessment meeting for planning instructional goals.

Use of Technology to Collaborate

As technology advanced over the past decade, increasingly free and easy to use tech resources were made available to educational teams to ease the time constraints of meaningful collaboration. Assessment data (formative and summative) can be used to both collaboratively design and implement educational programs and may be enhanced by the various digital systems available to effectively share knowledge (e.g., Slack.com, Google features, Loom or Screencastify screen recording). For example, Google Docs allows real-time access to student data to all members of an educational team. By uploading a student's data sheet for a current goal, the student's entire team (e.g., general education math teacher, paraprofessional, special education, parents/caregivers) can see daily progress, record data on the same data sheet, and even track progress across settings. This ongoing data

Table 5.1 Summary Sheet of Data Results

Data	Results	Clinical Interpretation	Real World Interpretation	IEP Implications
Wechsler (WISC-V)	FSIQ = 41	Below average functioning in non-verbal index measures, visual spatial index, fluid reasoning, working memory, and processing skills. Reading, writing, and math skills fall in the low average range, social-emotional functioning in the below average range.	Sally's results indicate that her visual and auditory working memory are strengths, meaning that when provided with clear visual and auditory directions, she can follow them through conclusion. She struggles with reading, writing, and math skills with difficulty in sight-word recognition, decoding, reading comprehension, spelling, composing sentences, and using appropriate grammar and sentence structure. She demonstrates strong behavioral skills.	Further assess current level of academic skills according to grade-level standards and to determine a baseline. Develop age/grade appropriate goals and objectives for reading, writing, and mathematics. Support positive social and emotional skills with peers and adults.
Math—increasing accuracy in addition and subtraction using decimals.	25% accuracy over a 6-week period.	The fourth-grade standards emphasize that mathematically proficient students are able to recognize and solve problems that contain place values. Following six weeks of direct instruction in solving addition and subtraction problems including place values (decimals) using paper and pencil, Sally is demonstrating considerable below average performance when compared to her fourth-grade peers.	Sally successfully identifies coins and bills but struggles with representing them accurately in writing.	Continue direct instruction in counting real money. Continue instruction in solving addition and subtraction problems that include a decimal (place value) in writing. Introduce using a hand-held calculator (or calculator app on phone), or virtual manipulatives (place value number line) for solving problems.

(Continued)

Table 5.1 Summary Sheet of Data Results (*Continued*)

Data	Results	Clinical Interpretation	Real World Interpretation	IEP Implications
Reading	Word recognition = 30% mastery of 4th-grade vocabulary list for Weeks 3, 4, and 5.	Fourth-grade curriculum standards in vocabulary development and word recognition allow students to connect essential ideas, arguments, and perspectives using text. Sally demonstrates below average mastery of printed words when read verbally over a 3-week period.	Sally is learning 3 of every 10 new vocabulary words presented each week in class. She is able to read these words when they are part of a sentence or represented in context (e.g., on the school lunch menu).	Present vocabulary words with pictures to illustrate the words during practice. Continue to teach the words in the context in which they will typically be seen. For example, in the school building, in worksheet directions, and in her other daily reading materials for different academic subjects.
KeyMath3	Composite score = 68 Standard scores Basic concepts -68 Basic operations = 71 Applications = 65	Sally's scores fall in the 1-2 percentile and 2 to 3 standard deviations below the mean for all math functions. Her overall performance is considered well-below average for her age and grade level.	Sally can complete basic addition problems using a calculator but struggles with subtraction, counting money, multiplication, and basic division.	Instruction should continue to focus on basic math skills (addition and subtraction) using a calculator and money). In January, begin introducing single-digit multiplication when applied to everyday activities such as preparing a shopping list (e.g., There are four people, and each will need two snacks for their lunch… 4x2=8).

(*Continued*)

Table 5.1 Summary Sheet of Data Results (*Continued*)

Data	Results	Clinical Interpretation	Real World Interpretation	IEP Implications
ABC Analysis	60% antecedent 40% consequence Conclusion: Escape from Demand.	Behavior appears to be under antecedent control and reinforced by consequence.	"Escape behavior" occurs most frequently (60% of the time) when the teacher asks Sally to complete independent seatwork. Sally will argue with the teacher, talk to her friends, ask to go to the restroom, and draw doodles on her work instead of completing the academic work (requiring reading and/or numerical calculations). The teacher often responds to this behavior by engaging with Sally and inadvertently allowing her to delay or avoid having to complete independent and academic tasks. Need to determine if instructions are confusing, if the requested academic task is above Sally's ability to complete, and if additional instruction is required.	Determine if Sally can complete academic tasks independently. Provide additional focused instruction in academic areas that Sally seeks to escape/avoid. Identify and implement the use of reinforcers for Sally's completion of requested independent academic work. Shorten assignments. Add a timer and provide her a choice of other activities once assigned tasks are completed.

analysis allows a student's team to quickly respond to the data and make data-based instructional decisions (see Chapter 6).

Self-determination

Students with ESN can gain independence through self-determined learning (Wehmeyer et al., 2012). Student-directed learning strategies should be embedded within the learning environment and throughout ongoing communication regarding learning (with students and IEP teams) to allow them to guide their own learning and communicate with stakeholders. The Self-Determined Learning Model of Instruction (SDLMI; Wehmeyer et al., 2000) was developed to teach students how to set goals, take action, and adjust their plans. Aligned with HLP 5 (identify student's strengths and needs), this model teaches students to identify problems, solutions, barriers, and consequences for these solutions. Studies confirm that students with ESN can use such skills to communicate with educational teams to increase their performance on academic, transition, and self-determination goals (Agran et al., 2012). Additionally, despite cultural differences within the value of self-determination, educators can support students who are CLD to be causal agents in a way that is reflective of their needs (Rivera et al., 2016; Rivera et al., 2020). By preparing students, even young students with ESN, to practice skills such as choice-making, goal-setting, and self-monitoring, educators are providing them the tools needed to become active members of a collaborative educational team.

Self-determined people have self-caused, rather than other-caused occurrences in their lives (Wehmeyer et al., 2012). Recently, research on formative assessments has included both summative and interim assessments in the development of "balanced assessment systems" (e.g., Darling-Hammond & Pecheone, 2010). Effective formative assessment involves teachers adjusting teaching and learning in response to data, as well as students receiving feedback about their learning with advice on what they can do to improve (Black & Wiliam, 1998). As highlighted in HLP 5, stakeholders (including the student) need to communicate on their own data, to determine and self-advocate for clear learning goals/targets and criteria for success. Results of a study led by Jimenez and Warren (in press) indicate that teachers of students with ESN were able to initiate and lead meaningful formative assessment conferences to increase communication of their own assessment data across academic goals and skills.

Another way in which a student can become more involved as a key stakeholder in the communication of educational programming and assessment is through student-led IEP meetings. Students need to have the opportunity to indicate preferences and choices and make decisions in order to have control (self-caused); and these decisions may be informed by educational assessments and ongoing formative data analysis. Kellems and Morningstar (2010) suggest that one way to build student self-determination skills is through student-led IEP meetings. Inviting students to participate in their IEP meetings is not only important, but also mandated for transition-aged students by IDEA; however, inviting students is not enough. Teachers will need to teach students with ESN the importance of attending and participating in their IEP meetings and help students develop the skills needed to actively participate as the key stakeholder.

Next Steps toward Better Practice

Actions that special education providers might take to successfully facilitate the implementation of HLP 5 activities include:

1. Establish monthly meetings with school-based colleagues and service providers to share and reflect upon gathered data. These meetings might take place at a regularly occurring and convenient time that that allows for professionals to review data for students with ESN and collaboratively reflect upon those data to determine best next steps.

2. Build standardized reporting forms to use to share data with professionals, family members/caregivers, and students. These forms could include information about the instructional/behavioral goal for the student with ESN, information about data being gathered (e.g., frequency, observations), environmental factors (e.g., A-B-C analysis), and a space for interpreting results. These templates can provide a snapshot or executive summary of the data gathered on students.

3. Use progress reports for parents/caregivers and students. These progress reports can include digital/video examples of student learning/behaviors, examples for follow-up instruction, and other information to demonstrate how a student with ESN is progressing in meeting target goals or when being assessed for services.

4. Schedule regular meetings with family members that are flexible and meet the various needs of participants. These meetings can be in-person or virtual but regardless of how meetings occur, they must be flexible to ensure active participation. Meetings might take place at a local library, a fast-food restaurant, or virtually using appropriate technology.

5. Always ensure that information is available to culturally and linguistically diverse stakeholders in their primary language, if requested; provide this information in advance of any meeting to allow for them to review information, seek translation of any information, and generate any questions.

The Big Five

In this chapter, we describe HLP 5 in depth by explaining factors to consider when interpreting assessment data to make educational programming decisions. We would like to leave you with a summary presented as five take-aways.

1. Conduct different forms of assessment to gather student performance data. Use those data with stakeholders to make informed decisions about students' educational services and learning outcomes.

2. Don't forget to stop and check your own expectations of student learning. The least dangerous assumption we can make as educators is to assume that with quality instruction a student will learn! If a student is not responding to an intervention, stakeholders need to determine what needs to change to support that student's success.

3. Provide all team members equity in decision-making. An ecological framework can allow us to "see" all contexts that matter to the learner.

4. Assessment data can include large amounts of information and be complex. Summarize assessment data to allow real-time collaboration of data collection and analysis.

5. Students should be a part of their own assessment and learning! Teach students how to meaningfully participate and involve them in their day-to-day analysis of assessment data and in annual IEP meetings.

Resources

- Harkins Monaco, L., Fuller, M., & Stansberry Brushnahan, L. (2021). Diversity, Autism and Developmental Disabilities: Guidance for the Culturally Sustaining Educator. Prism Series Volume 13, Council for Exceptional Children. https://exceptionalchildren.org/store/books/diversity-autism-and-developmental-disabilities-guidance-culturally-responsive-educator
- What Works Clearinghouse
  - Using Student Achievement Data to Support Instructional Decision Making https://ies.ed.gov/ncee/wwc/PracticeGuide/12
- IRIS Center
  - Family Engagement: Collaborating with Families of students with Disabilities https://iris.peabody.vanderbilt.edu/module/fam/

- CONNECT Modules
  - Communication for Collaboration https://connectmodules.dec-sped.org/connect-modules/learners/module-3/
- Equity in Special Education Placement: A school self-assessment guide for culturally responsive practice https://fndusa.org/wp-content/uploads/2015/05/Equity-in-Special-Education-Placement-A-School-Self-Assessment-Guide-for-Culturally-Responsive-Practice.pdf
- CADRE (The Center for Appropriate Dispute Resolution in Special Education)
  - Student Led IEPs https://www.cadreworks.org/cadre-continuum/stage-i-prevention/participant-stakeholder-training/student-led-ieps-district

References

Agran, M., Cavin, M., Wehmeyer, M., & Palmer, S. (2006). Participation of students with moderate to severe disabilities in the general curriculum: The effects of the self-determined learning model of instruction. *Research and Practice for Persons With Severe Disabilities, 31*(3), 230–241. https://doi.org/10.1177/154079690603100303.

Agran, M., Krupp, M., Spooner, F., & Zakas, T. L. (2012). Asking students about the importance of safety skills instruction: A preliminary analysis of what they think is important. *Research and Practice for Persons with Severe Disabilities, 37*(1), 45–52. https://doi.org/10.2511/027494812800903265

Black, P. J., & Wiliam, D. (1998). Assessment and classroom learning. *Assessment in Education: Principles, Policy and Practice, 5*(1), 7–73. https://doi.org/10.1080/0969595980050102.

Chadsey, J. (2007). Adult social relationships. In S. Odom, R. H. Horner, M. E. Snell, & J. Blacher (Eds.), *Handbook of developmental disabilities* (pp. 449–466). Guilford Press.

Darling-Hammond, L., & Pecheone, R. (2010). *Developing an Internationally Comparable Balanced Assessment System That Supports High-Quality Learning*. Educational Testing Services.

Donnellan, A. M. (1984). The criterion of least dangerous assumption. *Behavioral Disorders, 9*(2), 141–150. https://doi.org/10.1177/019874298400900201.

Esteban-Guitart, M., & Moll, L. C. (2014). Funds of identity: A new concept based on the funds of knowledge approach. *Culture & Psychology, 20*(1), 31–48. doi: https://doi.org/10.1177/1354067X13515934.

Every Student Succeeds Act of 2015, Pub. L. No. 114-95 § 114 Stat. 1177 (2015).

Giangreco, M. F., & Putnam, J. W. (1991). Supporting the education of students with severe disabilities in regular education environments. In L. H. Meyer, C. A. Peck, & L. Brown (Eds.), *Critical issues in the lives of people with severe disabilities* (pp. 245–270). Paul H. Brookes.

Gonzales, S. M., & Gabel, S. L. (2017). Exploring involvement expectations for culturally and linguistically diverse parents: What we need to know in teacher education. *International Journal of Multicultural Education, 19*(2), 61–81. doi: https://doi.org/10.18251/ijme.v19i2.1376.

Hunt, P., McDonnell, J., & Crockett, M. A. (2012). Reconciling an ecological curricular framework focusing on quality of life outcomes with the development and instruction of standards-based academic goals. *Research and Practice for Persons With Severe Disabilities, 37*(3), 139–152. https://doi.org/10.2511/027494812804153471.

Individuals with Disabilities Education Act, 20 U.S.C. § 1400 (2004).

Jimenez, B., Root, J., Shurr, J., & Bouck, E. C. (2021). Using the four stages of learning to assess, set goals, and instruct. *TEACHING Exceptional Children.* https://doi.org/10.1177/00400599211054873.

Jimenez, B., & Warren, S. (in press). Building self-determination via student engaged formative assessments for students with intellectual disability. *Education and Training in Autism and Developmental Disabilities.*

Kamman, M., & McCray, E. D. (2019). Interpreting and communicating assessment information with stakeholders to collaboratively design and implement education programs. In J. McLeskey, L. Maheady, B. Billingsley, M. T. Brownell, & T. J. Lewis' (Eds.), *High leverage practices for inclusive classrooms* (pp. 67–79). Routledge.

Kellems, R. O., & Morningstar, M. E. (2010). Tips for transition. *TEACHING Exceptional Children*, 43(2), 60–68. doi: https://doi.org/10.1177/004005991004300206.

Kim, K. H., & Morningstar, M. E. (2005). Transition planning involving culturally and linguistically diverse families. *Career Development for Exceptional Individuals*, 28(2), 92–103. doi: https://doi.org/10.1177/08857288050280020601.

Kim, K. H., & Turnbull, A. (2004). Transition to adulthood for students with severe intellectual disabilities: Shifting toward person-family interdependent planning. *Research & Practice for Persons With Severe Disabilities*, 29(1), 53–57. http://hdl.handle.net/1808/6250

Krashen, S. D. (1982). *Child-adult differences in second language acquisition. Series on issues in second language research*. Newbury House Publishers.

Oxford University Press. (n.d.). *Oxford English dictionary*. Retrieved September 6, 2021, from https://www.lexico.com/en/definition/context

Palawat, M., & May, M. E. (2012). The impact of cultural diversity on special education provision in the United States. *Journal of the International Association of Special Education*, 13(1), 58–63.

Pierangelo, R. (2003). *The special Educator's book of lists* (2nd ed.). Jossey Bass.

Rivera, C., Haughney, K., Clark, K., & Werunga, R. (2020). Culturally responsive planning, instruction, and reflection for young students with significant disabilities. *Young Exceptional Children*. doi: https://doi.org/10.1177/1096250620951767.

Rivera, C. J., Jimenez, B. A., Baker, J. N., Spies, T., Mims, P. J., & Courtade, G. (2016). A culturally and linguistically responsive framework for improving academic and postsecondary outcomes of students with moderate or severe intellectual disability. *Physical Disabilities: Education and Related Services*, 35(2), 23–80. https://doi.org/10.14434/pders.v35i2.22171

Rossetti, Z., Sauer, J. S., Bui, O., & Ou, S. (2017). Developing collaborative partnerships with culturally and linguistically diverse families during the IEP process. *TEACHING Exceptional Children*, 49(5), 328–338. doi: https://doi.org/10.1177/0040059916680103.

Stancliffe, R. J., & Lakin, K. C. (2007). Independent living. In S. Odom, R. H. Horner, M. E. Snell, & J. Blacher (Eds.), *Handbook of developmental disabilities* (pp. 429–448). Guildford Press.

Thurlow, M. L., & Quenemoen, R. F. (2019). *Revisiting expectations for students with disabilities (NCEO brief #17)*. Minneapolis, MN: University of Minnesota, National Center on Educational Outcomes.

Trela, K., & Jimenez, B. (2013). From different to differentiated: Using "ecological framework" to support personally relevant access to general curriculum for students with significant intellectual disabilities. *Research and Practice for Persons With Severe Disabilities*, 38(2), 117–119. doi: https://doi.org/10.2511/027494813807714537.

Vélez-Ibáñez, C. G., & Greenberg, J. B. (1992). Formation and transformation of funds of knowledge among u.S. Mexican Households. *Anthropology & Education Quarterly*, 23(4), 313–335. doi: https://doi.org/10.1525/aeq.1992.23.4.05x1582v.

Wehmeyer, M. L., Palmer, S. B., Agran, M., Mithaug, D. E., & Martin, J. E. (2000). Promoting causal agency: The self-determined learning model of instruction. *Exceptional Children*, 66(4), 439–453. doi: https://doi.org/10.1177/001440290006600401.

Wehmeyer, M. L., Shogren, K. A., Palmer, S. B., Williams-Diehm, K. L., Little, T. D., & Boulton, A. (2012). The impact of the self-determined learning model of instruction on student self-determination. *Exceptional Children*, 78(2), 135–153. doi: https://doi.org/10.1177/001440291207800201.

White, J., & Weiner, J. S. (2004). Influence of least restrictive environment and community based training on integrated employment outcomes for transitioning students with severe disabilities. *Journal of Vocational Rehabilitation*, 21(3), 149–156.

6

Use Student Assessment Data, Analyze Instructional Practices, and Make Necessary Adjustments that Improve Student Outcomes

Samantha Walte, Caroline Fitchett, and Ginevra Courtade

After special education teachers develop instructional goals, they evaluate and make ongoing adjustments to students' instructional programs. Once instruction and other supports are designed and implemented, special education teachers have the skill to manage and engage in ongoing data collection using curriculum-based measures, informal classroom assessments, observations of student academic performance and behavior, self-assessment of classroom instruction, and discussions with key stakeholders (i.e., students, families, other professionals). Teachers study their practice to improve student learning, validate reasoned hypotheses about salient instructional features, and enhance instructional decision-making. Effective teachers retain, reuse, and extend practices that improve student learning and adjust or discard those that do not.

Supporting Students with Extensive Support Needs

Special educators take pride in delivering instruction that explicitly addresses students' needs. Evidence-based practices, research-based curricula, and a variety of complex interventions have been expertly designed to help students with disabilities successfully access and excel in the general education curriculum (Cook & Odom, 2013; Spooner et al., 2012). Underlying that instruction, however, needs to be a well-developed and accurately interpreted assessment. In this chapter, we will dive deeper into assessment from the lens of educating students with extensive support needs (ESN). We focus on HLP 6: Using student assessment data, analyzing instructional practices, and making necessary adjustments that improve student outcomes (McLeskey et al., 2017).

At its core, assessment results inform educators about how they can best support their students (Browder et al., 2020a). In special education, professionals use assessment results to build tailored programming for students with disabilities, and to determine the continued appropriateness of that programming. The Individuals with Disabilities Education Act (IDEA, 2004) calls for a process of determining specific educational needs through relevant, unbiased, ongoing assessment. This process requires the use of valid and robust tools, but also necessitates that anyone who interprets the results of assessments be knowledgeable enough to determine what

DOI: 10.4324/9781003175735-7

services and programming a student will receive. IDEA highlights the importance of assessment and professionals' accurate interpretation throughout students' educational careers. Part C of the law describes early intervention services that are specifically developed based on a team's interpretation of a battery of tests and observations, and students 16 and older are required by the federal law to have measurable goals based on age-appropriate transition assessments. To meet these requirements and provide powerful educational services to students, teachers, and all members of the individualized education program (IEP) team must be experts not only in choosing and administering assessments but, perhaps most importantly, in interpreting the results.

The skill of making instructional decisions informed by data, or data-based decision-making (DBDM), provides a specific framework for educational teams to determine what is working, what is not, and what to do in either case (Farlow & Snell, 1989). The simple but effective process involves collecting baseline data with valid measures, developing a goal for growth based on the student's baseline performance, implementing high quality intervention or instruction, collecting data to systematically monitor the student's progress, using clear rules to determine next steps based on the data collected, making an informed instructional change, continuing to monitor the student's progress, and repeating this cycle to consistently support the student (McLeskey et al., 2019). DBDM is both uniquely crucial and uniquely complicated for some students with ESN. Students with ESN may have a constellation of needs that can change the way their teams collect and interpret data, including academic, communication, social, behavioral, medical, sensory, mental health, and others (Browder et al., 2020b,c). Students with ESN often have some level of intellectual disability, which makes assessment methods that are sensitive to incremental change vital. When implemented with fidelity, DBDM supports teachers in identifying patterns of students' responding and pinpointing small changes, making it the perfect tool for teachers of students with ESN (Browder et al., 2010).

Teachers of students with ESN acknowledge the importance of DBDM and feel confident in their ability to collect data but are often not adequately prepared to interpret the data they collect and make decisions to improve their instruction (Demchak & Sutter, 2019). Teaching is a rewarding but incredibly difficult job, fraught with daily interruptions that distract even the best educators from their plans and practices. Additionally, the nature of supporting students with ESN involves the understanding that each student's needs will be different. This can lead teachers to struggle when applying general structures like DBDM to a variety of situations. In fact, teachers of students with ESN often master the principles of DBDM but have difficulty executing the steps with fidelity in their classrooms (Jimenez et al., 2016). Thus, teachers and teams need systematic guidelines to follow, rather than just knowledge of the principles of DBDM (Browder et al., 2010). To support their own practice, teachers also need strategies to help monitor their fidelity to the DBDM process, in the face of the chaos of a typical school day (Belfiore & Browder, 1992).

Chapter Objectives

Upon reading this chapter, you should be able to do the following:

1. Explain the steps in the DBDM process.
2. Identify patterns in graphed student data and make informed instructional decisions based on that data.
3. Adjust various dimensions of instruction and support.
4. Implement self-management strategies to ensure you are engaging in the DBDM process with fidelity.

Using Data to Make Decisions

In this section, we describe a DBDM system that has been implemented with students with ESN and evaluated through research for more than two decades (Belfiore & Browder, 1992; Browder et al., 1986; Jimenez et al., 2016). There are three steps in using this system: (a) analyzing the data, (b) making an instructional decision based on this analysis, and (c) deciding how to implement this decision. These steps require the prior collection of baseline data, development of a goal for growth based on the student's baseline performance, implementation of high-quality instruction, and the systematic collection of data to monitor student progress. For more information on data collection methods, please see **Resources** at the end of this chapter.

Step 1. Analyze the Data.

Any decision a teacher makes throughout this DBDM process must be based on student data. In this progress monitoring system, the teacher reviews each student's progress data once every two weeks to guide their next steps in instruction. Different goals will require different types and methods of data collection, but all data should be transferred to line graphs to make patterns clear. Many teachers will have multiple graphs of data for different skills their students are learning; however, the decision rules are applied to each graph separately. The more frequently teachers use the system, the easier it will become to review the graphs and make decisions. Each graph must have at least six data points to be reviewed, as six is the minimum number needed to draw a trend line using intersections. Teachers who have used this DBDM system find that collecting data six days out of the 10 days (i.e., two school weeks) is feasible (Browder et al., 2020c). Using guidance from the DBDM process, teachers will then identify the pattern represented on each graph.

Step 2. Use Decision Rules.

After the teacher has reviewed a graph with at least six data points and identified a pattern of responding, they will apply the decision rules to determine how to proceed with instruction. The decision rules shown in Figure 6.1 were originally developed by Haring et al. (1980) and Browder et al. (1986). The rules were further refined by Browder et al. (1991), Browder (2001), and Browder et al. (2011). These simple guidelines were designed to be easy for teachers to follow. Generally, they suggest that (a) students who make no progress need instruction of skills to be made simpler or more accessible; (b) students who make inadequate progress require instructional adjustments (e.g., changes in prompting, stimulus presentation); and (c) students who show inconsistent or decelerating data trends require adjustments in reinforcement contingencies unless there are extenuating circumstances (e.g., illness). Until teachers can use these patterns fluently, they can use Figure 6.1 to find the data pattern and note the decision rule.

Step 3. Implement the Decision to Change Instruction.

When a teacher identifies a student's pattern of response to instruction indicates a need for change, and determines the type of change needed, the teacher should quickly implement that instructional change (i.e., simplify the response, improve antecedent, improve motivation) to ensure student progress. Table 6.1 gives suggestions of instructional changes based on data patterns.

In Table 6.2, we give examples of two teachers that have used the DBDM rules to plan for an instructional change for their students as well as targeted IEP goals for each student.

In the next section, we outline steps to consider after the decision to change instruction has been made and continue with the examples of Mr. Gomez and Kaelin and Ms. Proctor and Carlos.

Data Pattern	Conclusion	Decision
1. The student reached the set criterion during the two weeks of instruction. 	Mastery	Develop a new instructional plan to maintain and extend performance (e.g., fluency, generalization).
2. All data points are at 0. Or the student has not made new independent responses since instruction began. 	No Progress	If this is the first 2 weeks of instruction, make no changes yet-continue with the current instructional plan. After the first 2 weeks, *simplify the skill*.
3. The data points above the baseline and improving (accelerating trend), but not yet at the mastery level. 	Adequate Progress	*Make no changes*. Continue instruction.
4. Only a few independent correct responses are being made after several weeks of instruction. 	Inadequate Progress	*Improve antecedents* (e.g., prompting strategies) so the student makes more independent, correct responses.
5. Student performance data are variable; the student responds independently some days but not others and there are no known extenuating circumstances. 	Inconsistent Progress	*Improve motivation* of student to perform responses correctly without assistance.

Figure 6.1 Data-based Decision-Making Rules
Note. Adapted from Browder et al. (2020c).

Table 6.1 Implementing Decisions to Change Instruction

To Simplify the Response	*To Improve Antecedents*	*To Improve Motivation*
Goal: Make it feasible for student to perform without assistance.	Goal: Increase the number of independent correct responses the student makes each day.	Goal: To help the student regain past performance after a regression and then, make continuous improvement.
Strategies	Strategies	Strategies
• Use forward or backward chaining: Teach only one step or one portion of the task analysis. • Use a more specific task analysis: Break the current task analysis down into smaller steps. • Use a simpler motor response: A motor response that requires less physical control or skill (e.g., touch a switch instead of pointing). • Make the discrimination simpler: Modify the materials so that it is easier to select the correct answer (e.g., choosing a letter from a field of a letter and number, instead of a field of two letters). • Use assistive technology • Select an alternative way to achieve the same outcome: Use an entirely different response or set of materials (e.g., have the student use a voice output device instead of handing a communicative partner a picture).	• Only use the least intrusive prompting needed (e.g., do not move immediately to a physical prompt if a student does not respond to the task direction). • Give more wait time before giving a prompt. • Revise the prompt to focus the learner's attention more on the natural cues (e.g., Prompting, "Your friend just walked in!" instead of "Say hi!"). • Use nonspecific verbal cues like "What's next?". • Use graduated guidance or that is, fade the amount of physical assistance given (e.g., using hand-over-hand when first teaching a skill like writing a name, and then fading to just lightly guiding the student's hand). • Have a peer model the response or give the prompts. • Use self-prompting with pictures or audio (e.g., video prompting on an iPad of the student performing the steps of the task correctly).	• Only praise independent correct responses. • Ignore errors and prompt the next step. • Emphasize the natural consequence for performing the response. • Embed choice in instruction (e.g., give the student a choice of manipulatives to use during instruction on 1:1 correspondence). • Involve student in self-monitoring and graphing daily performance. • Use tangible reinforcers for performance that is better than the prior day (e.g., picking a prize or getting a sticker or certificate). • Vary praise statements or increase enthusiasm of praise • Only give feedback for correct responses. • Have a peer lead or be a part of instruction.

Note. Modified from Browder et al. (2020c, p. 108).

Six Steps for Change to Instruction

The steps for making decisions based on data are clear and simple, and supported by years of research and practice. Within the complex environment of a school, however, teachers need to take additional steps to successfully implement changes to a student's instructional plan. In practice, there are multiple stakeholders who need to know and be able to effectively communicate changes, additional materials required (e.g., instructional materials, reinforcers), and training needs for the team to execute the change consistently. HLP 6 specifically highlights the need for teachers to "study their practice to improve student learning" (McLeskey et al., 2017, p. 20). The entire DMDB process falls apart if it is not being implemented with fidelity. To that end, this section also includes

Table 6.2 Student and Teacher Information Based on DBDM

	Kaelin	**Carlos**
IEP Goal	*Given a field of 3 picture cards and a "Wh" question (asked verbally) from an adapted book, Kaelin will make a choice by touching one picture card with her hand with 80% accuracy over 3 consecutive sessions.*	*Given 20 fractions written on index cards, Carlos will sort the fraction cards into "proper" and "improper" categories with 90% accuracy over 4 consecutive sessions.*
Description	*Mr. Gomez has decided to make an instructional change for his student. Kaelin is a first-grade student who communicates through eye gaze, facial expressions, and gestures. Mr. Gomez has reviewed Kaelin's data for her adaptive goal and noticed the data path is inconsistent. In response, Mr. Gomez has decided to modify his use of reinforcement. The change will be to only reinforce correct responses (in this case, touching either picture card is correct) and use only high value tangible reinforcers (sensory putty is Kaelin's favorite!).*	*Ms. Proctor is deciding if she should make an instructional change for her student. Carlos is a tenth-grade student with autism spectrum disorder that spends 70% of his time in the general education classroom with his peers. Carlos is a verbal communicator and enjoys talking about baseball with his peers. Ms. Proctor has noticed that Carlos is making great progress on his math goal, and faster than she anticipated. In response, Ms. Proctor has created a new goal that involves slightly more advanced mathematical reasoning.*

a structure for teachers and teams to evaluate their own performance regarding adhering to the DBDM process (see Figure 6.2).

Identify Who Needs to Know About the Change

Consistency is vital to skill acquisition for students with ESN (Collins, 2022). Special educators are responsible for the consistency of instructional procedures within their own classroom and to an extent, supporting programming outside of their classroom. Collaboration with stakeholders is among the most important aspects of a consistent school day for students. Further, collaboration among stakeholders in planning and implementing instructional programs is attributed to greater student outcomes (McLeskey et al., 2017). As stated in Chapter 4, students with ESN often receive supplementary services (e.g., speech-language therapy, occupational therapy, physical therapy, vision, audiology) in addition to everyday instruction. Many skills (e.g., choice making, attending behaviors) are used across contexts and communicative partners. Ensuring each person that works with the student is doing so in an intentional and consistent manner may not only result in increased skill acquisition but could also contribute to increased predictability of the student's day. Creating a working collaborative partnership with stakeholders also supports a sense of shared responsibility of the student and their success. This mindset could ultimately result in increased academic performance by students (Berry, 2021; Huberman et al., 2012). Identifying who needs to know the instructional changes can be determined by considering first, individuals on the IEP team, and second, the students' weekly schedule.

Teachers should remember that it is also important to communicate changes to the students themselves. While the student may not need to know the details of every small change made to their instructional experience, they are a crucial member of their own educational team and should be kept in the loop about what is being changed. When students with ESN are supported and

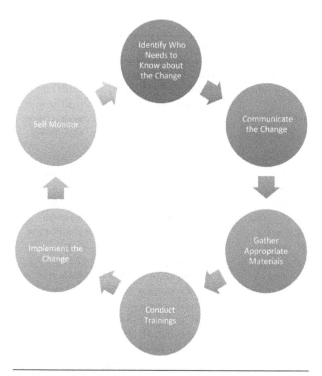

Figure 6.2 Six Steps for Change to Instruction

empowered, they can meaningfully participate in their own planning (Biegun et al., 2020; Johnson et al., 2020). Emphasizing this component of self-determination also may increase student's buy-in to instructional changes (Sebag, 2010).

When deciding who needs to know about the change in instruction, teachers must ask: *Which therapists support this student? Which paraprofessionals work with this student? Will the student be working on this skill at home? Are there other people within the school that work with this student (i.e., other teachers, mentors, student teachers, peer tutors)?*

Communicate the Change

Efficient use of time is critical for special educators to perform all teaching responsibilities. "Time" has been cited as a main barrier to collaboration among parties to serve students with disabilities (Da Fonte & Barton-Arwood, 2017; Lawrence-Brown & Muschaweck, 2004). Therefore, it is ideal to communicate the change in instruction to all stakeholders before it is rolled out. Aligning schedules of a group can be challenging, considering the change could be immediately relevant to only some members of the group. However, an attempt should be made to meet with stakeholders in small groups or individually to convey how the change might affect the student, their performance in other contexts, and future expectations of stakeholders. Aside from the student, the parent/caregiver is the most important member of the IEP team and should always be consulted and involved in any decisions made about their child's education. Active parent involvement in educational decision making can be a predictor of increased academic achievement of students with disabilities (Sheldon & Epstein, 2005).

Before communicating the change, teachers must ask: *How does my team usually communicate? Would video conferencing be more feasible than an in-person meeting for the group? How can I communicate this instructional change to the student?*

Gather Appropriate Materials

Sometimes an instructional change requires a change in materials, whether the team needs to add, create, or take materials away. Materials needed during a change in instruction should be identified and acquired prior to implementing the change so they can be used during training (see Step 3). Students with ESN often require multiple supports to access academic content, such as manipulatives (i.e., objects that can be manipulated by students to aid in their learning; Bouck & Flanagan, 2010), visuals (i.e., teaching aids that give concrete cues for skill development; Cohen & Demchak, 2018), and reinforcers (i.e., stimuli used to motivate and reward students; Da Fonte et al., 2016).

Examples of manipulatives include blocks to represent numbers, a stuffed pig to associate with the *Three Little Pig* story, counting bears, sand or rocks to supplement a science lesson, or a miniature American flag for an American history lesson. When selecting manipulatives for goals, teachers should consider the unique ways that some students with ESN receive sensory input and be mindful of textures, scents, and visual stimuli that might be aversive. Conversely, they might consider using sensory input that students enjoy during instruction. For example, if a student enjoys feeling rough textures, a teacher might include manipulatives with bumpy or abrasive surfaces (e.g., lava rock, sandpaper shapes). In addition, teachers might need to plan for the introduction and use of assistive technology (e.g., picture-based communication systems, exchange switches, pencil grips), and be prepared with materials required to record performance data (e.g., stopwatch for timing, pen, data sheet).

Before changing the materials, teachers must ask: *What new materials will we need to make this change? Do we still need all materials we were using before? How will the student feel about adding, changing, or removing these materials? Do we need to create anything new, or can we repurpose something we already have? Where can the materials be stored so they are easily accessible for anyone who needs to use them?*

Train

Training staff and other stakeholders to implement the instructional change is a crucial component in successfully advancing that change to action. Being "on the same page" contributes to the team's instructional consistency and ultimately, the predictability of instruction for students (Collins, 2022). Training stakeholders can take many forms; however, one easy and effective method of training is behavior skills training (BST). Sarokoff and Sturmey (2004) identified four essential components in teaching skills to others. BST involves four training phases: (1) instruction, (2) modeling, (3) rehearsal, and (4) feedback. BST has been used to teach a variety of skills (e.g., communication interventions, video modeling, interactive play, functional behavior assessments) to a variety of learners (paraeducators, university students, children, parents), and is commonly used across disciplines (Andzik et al., 2021; Covey et al., 2021; Shayne & Miltenberger, 2013).

During the instruction phase of BST, the trainer introduces the skill and describes the process of how to perform that skill. Instruction is typically performed in person and can be supplemented with visuals, such as a slide deck presentation or graphics. Modeling involves the trainer going through the physical motions of performing the skill while the trainees observe. Modeling is a time for the trainer to not only physically perform the skill, but also verbally describe the steps being taken at the same time. Rehearsal is conducted by pairing the trainees together and practicing what was just modeled. Rehearsal of the skill allows for the trainer to observe and offer corrective feedback in real time. Receiving feedback in real time supports the learning process of the trainee and allows for quick adjustments to be made while practicing.

Before training, teachers must ask: *Who needs to be trained? Can we train together as a group, or will we need individual sessions? Where can we do training? When can we do training? Who will train? How will feedback be provided? How can the student be involved?*

Implement the Change

Implementing the change in instruction should involve careful planning and frequent monitoring of student progress. To systematically determine if an instructional change impacts a student's performance, that change must be implemented consistently and accurately no matter who works with the student or where they work with them. To ensure consistency of the change, the team should take data on their implementation of the new intervention or strategy. Procedural fidelity is "the degree to which the provider uses procedures required to execute the treatment as intended" (Odom et al., 2010). Put differently, procedural fidelity can be viewed as how closely the instructor is following the procedures of implementation. Monitoring fidelity is especially important after a change of instruction. Proper implementation of instruction is not only a mediator of improved student outcomes (Durlak & DuPre, 2008; Stahmer et al., 2015), but also allows the instructor to detect student learning more confidently or troubleshoot lack of progress because the integrity of instruction isn't compromised.

Fidelity is typically monitored with a checklist, which also makes training (Step 4) easier. To create a fidelity checklist, first create a task analysis of your instructional procedures, or a step-by-step list of instructions for how to do them. For example, Collins (2022) provided a general structure of key elements that should be considered when delivering systematic instruction: (1) have appropriate materials ready for use, (2) gain the learner's attention, (3) give a clear task direction, (4) wait a specific interval of time for the learner to respond, (5) prompt correct performance according to the procedure being used, and (6) provide feedback (i.e., praise or error correction). Ideally, an observer should be present to record the fidelity data. However, a video recording of the instructional session could be used for the instructor to collect data. To calculate fidelity of implementation, first count the number of steps completed correctly by the instructor. Next, divide that number by the total number of steps in the procedure. Finally, multiply that number by 100 to produce a percentage of accuracy.

Often checking the data pattern after changing instruction can be especially informative. Refer to the Figure 6.1 to determine appropriate next steps for instruction. Checking the data path should be done about every 3 data points so adjustment can be made without time being compromised.

When implementing the change, teachers must ask: *What are the steps required to correctly perform this instructional change? Have I made a fidelity checklist? Have I shared the fidelity checklist with each stakeholder who is involved in this change? Will someone on the team observe implementation of the change, or will we record ourselves? When and how will I review the fidelity data to ensure the team is consistently performing the instructional change? What will I do if there is inconsistency?*

Self-Monitor

Making informed instructional decisions and implementing changes in programming is essential to student success. However, the process of decision-making also should be monitored. Teachers should monitor their consistency and accuracy in delivering instruction and its impact on student performance. In acknowledging their duty to remain agile and flexible in response to student performance, teachers can ultimately increase student achievement on both IEP goals and in the general education curriculum (Belfiore & Browder, 1992; Browder et al., 1989; Browder et al., 2005).

As discussed earlier, DBDM involves inspecting data for trends or patterns and making instructional decisions based on the decision-making "rules." Step 6 of Change in Instruction concerns adherence to those rules. The Data-based Decision-Making Self-Monitoring Checklist (Figure 6.3) was designed to support teachers in following the decision-making rules but can also be used as a running record of instructional decisions and the changes they might include.

Student Name:

Goal/Objective:

Mastery	Adequate Progress	Inadequate Progress	Inconsistent Progress	No Progress

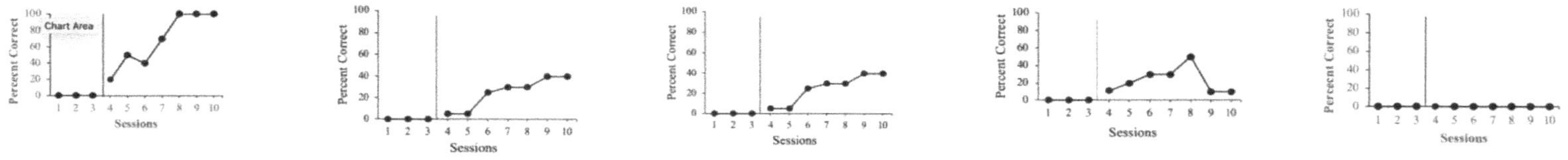

Date	Data Path	Decision
	☐ Mastery	Introduce new skill
	☐ Adequate Progress	Make no changes
	☐ Inadequate Progress	Improve antecedents
	☐ Inconsistent Progress	Improve motivation
	☐ No Progress	Simplify task or modify response mode

Change Made

Figure 6.3 Data-based Decision-Making Self-Monitoring Checklist

To use the DBDM self-monitoring checklist, teachers first write the goal of interest under the student's name at the top of the checklist. Second, they compare their student's data path to the samples presented in the tool and identify which graph most closely matches. Third, they record the date and indicate the progress level by placing a checkmark in the corresponding box. Finally, they note the rule associated with the progress level and document the change that was made in the right-hand column. The next time an instructional decision is made, it should be recorded in the same fashion in each subsequent table.

Table 6.3 shows the process of two teachers implementing instructional changes with their student using the Six Steps to Change Instruction outlined above.

Next Steps toward Better Practice

Because students with ESN may require support in numerous areas (e.g., communication, academic, social, behavior, sensory, health) and make progress at different rates, it is essential that their teachers are experts at assessing whether their instruction is working. Diligent use of DBDM empowers teachers to confidently tailor instruction for each student and facilitate measurable progress for all their students. Teachers should consider the following tips when starting the DBDM process.

1. *Learn the DBDM decision rules through practice* as to become fluent and confident in applying them to student data. Teachers might consider posting Figure 6.1 in the classroom.
2. *Organize the materials* consistently used during instruction, so everything is easily accessible to everyone who will work with the student.
3. *Gather contact information* for the team members communicated with most frequently, so any changes or calls for training meetings can be conveyed quickly.
4. Print or save the *DBDM Self-Monitoring Checklist* to ensure teachers and other team members follow procedures with fidelity.
5. Advanced Move: *Teach students* to collect data, interpret their graphs, and make decisions about their own instruction.

The Big Five

In this chapter, we describe HLP 6 in depth by explaining how to analyze student assessment and make necessary adjustments to improve student outcomes, and implement self-monitoring strategies to ensure implementation fidelity of the DBDM. We leave you with a summary presented as five take-aways.

1. Students with ESN need educators who can design and modify high quality systematic instruction and collect data that are sensitive to incremental change.
2. Using appropriate assessments and a DBDM process are not just good ideas, but legally required practices.
3. DBDM is a continuous process that entails taking baseline data, implementing high quality instruction with fidelity, monitoring student progress, using decision rules to evaluate progress, making instructional changes based on evaluation, and repeating these steps consistently.
4. Educational teams need to work together to support each student with ESN's related skills and needs that may impact learning, such as communication, motor skills, nutrition, vision, and hearing.
5. In addition to taking data on student progress, educators should monitor their own implementation of the DBDM process to ensure they are using it with fidelity.

Table 6.3 Examples of Using the Six Steps to Change Instruction

Action	Kaelin	Carlos
Identify who needs to know	*Mr. Gomez knows that choice making is embedded in his instruction, speech therapy, and vision. He informs each party of the coming change in instruction. Mr. Gomez also discusses this change with the parent.*	*Ms. Proctor informs the IEP team (including Carlos' caregiver) of the needed change, as well as the student teacher and peer tutors that often work with Carlos on his goals.*
Communicate the change	*Mr. Gomez has decided to communicate the change in instruction to his two instructional assistants, the speech therapist, and the vision teacher. A meeting was set to communicate this change. Vision teacher was unable to attend the meeting, so Mr. Gomez scheduled a zoom meeting to inform her of the change.*	*Since Carlos' change in instruction required a new goal, the IEP team met over Zoom to discuss and make the change. All stakeholders (including the student teacher) were present during the IEP meeting except the peer tutors. Ms. Proctor communicated the change in instruction to the peer tutors when they arrived at the classroom the next day before they began working with students.*
Gather materials	*Items needed for the change in Kaelin's instruction include an updated data sheet (see Kaelin's Adaptive Goal Data Sheet), "Good Morning!" adapted book with picture choices inside, a pencil or pen, tangible reinforcer (e.g., sensory putty, squish ball, fidget toy).*	*The new goal involves sorting index cards (with 2 fractions on each) into "equivalent" and "nonequivalent" categories. The items for the new goal include 20 index cards with 2 fractions written on each, "Equivalent" and "Nonequivalent" written on a laminated strip of paper, fraction circle manipulatives, and his updated data sheet to record the data.*
Train	*Mr. Gomez scheduled two separate meetings (to accommodate schedules) to train his two instructional assistants, the speech therapist, and the vision teacher. He used BST to train them on the change in instruction.*	*Ms. Proctor used BST to train the student teacher and the peer tutors on the instructional and data collection procedures of Carlos' new math goal.*
Implement the change/Check data path	*Mr. Gomez implemented the instructional change with Kaelin and checks the data path every two weeks.*	*Ms. Proctor implemented the new goal with Carlos and evaluated the data pattern once every 2 weeks.*
Self-monitor	*Mr. Gomez checks Kaelin's data path on her goal every two weeks and makes an instructional decision each time. He uses the Data-based Decision-Making Self-Monitoring Checklist to record his decisions and monitor adherence to the DBDM rules.*	*Ms. Proctor makes an instructional decision every two weeks after reviewing Carlos' data path on his new goal. She uses the Data-based Decision-Making Self-Monitoring Checklist to record her decisions and monitor adherence to the DBDM rules.*

Resources

Collins, B. (2022). Chapter 4: Developing data sheets and collecting baseline data. In B. Collins (Ed.), *Systematic instruction for students with moderate and severe disabilities* (pp. 43–62). Brookes Publishing.

Center on Multi-Tiered Systems of Support at the American Institutes for Research (MTSS Center) https://www.air.org/centers/center-multi-tiered-system-supports-mtss-center
- Data-based Decision-making

Missouri Educational Systems and Instruction for Learning (MoEdu-SAIL) https://www.moedu-sail.org/
- Common Formative Assessments

Modules Addressing Special Education and Teacher Education (MAST) https://mast.ecu.edu/
- Data Collection
- Data-based Decisions

References

Andzik, N. R., Schaefer, J. M., & Christensen, V. L. (2021). The effects of teacher-delivered behavior skills training on paraeducators' use of a communication intervention for a student with autism who uses AAC. *AAC: Augmentative & Alternative Communication*, *37*(1), 1–13. https://doi.org/10.1080/07434618.2021.1881823

Belfiore, P. J., & Browder, D. M. (1992). The effects of self-monitoring on teacher's data-based decisions and on the progress of adults with severe mental retardation. *Education and Training in Mental Retardation*, *27*(1), 60–67.

Berry, A. B. (2021). Understanding shared responsibility between special and general education teachers in the rural classroom. *Rural Special Education Quarterly*, *40*(2), 95–105. https://doi.org/10.1177/87568705211015681

Biegun, D., Peterson, Y., McNaught, J., & Sutterfield, C. (2020). Including student voice in IEP meetings through use of assistive technology. *TEACHING Exceptional Children*, *52*(5), 348–350. https://doi.org/10.1177/0040059920920148

Bouck, E. C., & Flanagan, S. M. (2010). Virtual manipulatives: What they are and how teachers can use them. *Intervention in School and Clinic*, *45*(3), 186–191. https://doi.org/10.1177/1053451209349530

Browder, D. M. (2001). *Curriculum and assessment for students with moderate and severe disabilities*. Guilford.

Browder, D. M., Demchak, M., Keller, M., & King, D. (1989). An in vivo evaluation of the use of data-based rules to guide instructional decisions. *The Journal of the Association for Persons With Severe Handicaps*, *14*(3), 234–240.

Browder, D. M., Karvonen, M., Davis, S., Fallin, K., & Courtade-Little, G. (2005). The impact of teacher training on state alternate assessment scores. *Exceptional Children*, *71*(3), 267–282. https://doi.org/10.1177/001440290507100304

Browder, D. M., Liberty, K., Heller, M., & D'Huyvetters, K. K. (1986). Self-management by teachers: Improving instructional decision making. *Professional School Psychology*, *1*(3), 165–175.

Browder, D. M., Spooner, F., & Courtade, G. (2020a). *Teaching students with moderate and severe disabilities*. Guilford Press.

Browder, D. M., Spooner, F., Courtade, G., & Jimenez, B. (2020b). Using assessment for planning standards-based individualized education programs. In D. M. Browder, F. Spooner, and G. Courtade (Eds.), *Teaching students with moderate and severe disabilities* (2nd ed.) (pp. 62–112). Guilford Press.

Browder, D. M., Spooner, F., Courtade, G., & Pennington, R. C. (2020c). Monitoring and enhancing student progress: Getting the most out of data. In D. M. Browder, F. Spooner, and G. Courtade

(Eds.), *Teaching students with moderate and severe disabilities* (2nd ed.) (pp. 93–113). Guilford Press.

Browder, D. M., Spooner, F., & Jimenez, B. (2011). Standards-based individualized education plans and progress monitoring. In D. M. Browder, & F. Spooner (Eds.), *Teaching students with moderate and severe disabilities* (pp. 42–91). Guilford Press.

Browder, D. M., Wakeman, S. Y., Ahlgrim-Delzell, L., & Hudson, M. (2010). Utilization of formative assessments within educational programs for students with significant cognitive disabilities: current practice, current research, and next steps. *Chief State School Officers: ASES-SCASS on Alternate Assessment.*

Cohen, A., & Demchak, M. (2018). Use of visual supports to increase task independence in students with severe disabilities in inclusive educational settings. *Education and Training in Autism and Developmental Disabilities, 53*(1), 84–99.

Collins, B. C. (2022). Systematic instruction for students with moderate and severe disabilities (2nd ed.). Brookes Publishing.

Cook, B. G., & Odom, S. L. (2013). Evidence-based practices and implementation science in special education. *Exceptional Children, 79*(2), 135–144. https://doi.org/10.1177/001440291307900201

Covey, A., Li, T., & Alber-Morgan, S. R. (2021). Using behavioral skills training to teach peer models: Effects on interactive play for students with moderate to severe disabilities. *Education & Treatment of Children, 44*(1), 19–30. https://doi.org/10.1007/s43494-020-00034-y

Da Fonte, M. A., & Barton-Arwood, S. M. (2017). Collaboration of general and special education teachers: Perspectives and strategies. *Intervention in School & Clinic, 53*(2), 99–106. https://doi.org/10.1177/1053451217693370

Da Fonte, M. A., Boesch, M. C., Edwards-Bowyer, M. E., Restrepo, M. W., Bennett, B. P., & Diamond, G. P. (2016). A three-step reinforcer identification framework: A step-by-step process. *Education and Treatment of Children, 39*(3), 389–409. https://doi.org/10.1353/etc.2016.0017

Demchak, M., & Sutter, C. (2019). Teachers' perception of use and actual use of a data-based decision-making process. *Education and Training in Autism and Developmental Disabilities, 54*(2), 175–185.

Durlak, J. A., DuPre, E. P. (2008). Implementation matters: A review of research on the influence of implementation on program outcomes and the factors affecting implementation. *American Journal of Community Psychology, 41*, 327–350. https://doi.org/10.1007/s10464-008-9165-0

Farlow, L. J., & Snell, M. E. (1989). Teacher use of student performance data to make instructional decisions: Practices in programs for students with moderate to profound disabilities. *Journal of the Association for Persons With Severe Handicaps, 14*(1), 13–22.

Haring, N. G., Liberty, K. A. and White, O. R. (1980). Rules for data-based strategy decisions in instructional programs: Current research and instructional implications. In W. Sailor, B. Wilcox, & L. Brown (Eds.), *Methods of instruction for severely handicapped students*. Paul H. Brookes.

Huberman, M., Navo, M., & Parrish, T. (2012). Effective practices in high performing districts serving students in special education. *Journal of Special Education Leadership, 25*(2), 59–72.

Individuals with Disabilities Education Act, 20 U.S.C. § 1400 (2004).

Jimenez, B. A., Mims, P. J., & Baker, J. (2016). The effects of an online data-based decisions professional development for in-service teachers of students with significant disability. *Rural Special Education Quarterly, 35*(3), 30–40. https://doi.org/10.1177/875687051603500305

Johnson, D. R., Thurlow, M. L., Wu, Y. C., LaVelle, J. M., & Davenport, E. C. (2020). IEP/transition planning participation among students with the most significant cognitive disabilities: Findings from NLTS 2012. *Career Development and Transition for Exceptional Individuals, 43*(4), 226–239. https://doi.org/10.1177/2165143420952050

Lawrence-Brown, D., & Muschaweck, K. S. (2004). Getting started with collaborative teamwork for inclusion. *Catholic Education: A Journal of Inquiry and Practice, 8*(2), 146–161. https://doi.org/10.15365/joce.0802022013

McLeskey, J., Barringer, M.-D., Billingsley, B., Brownell, M., Jackson, D., Kennedy, M., Lewis, T., Maheady, L., Rodriguez, J., Scheeler, M. C., Winn, J., & Ziegler, D. (2017). *High-leverage practices in special education*. Council for Exceptional Children & CEEDAR Center. https://ceedar. education.ufl.edu/wp-content/uploads/2017/07/CEC-HLP-Web.pdf

McLeskey, J., Maheady, L., Billingsley, B., Brownell, M., & Lewis, T. (Eds.). (2019). *High leverage practices for inclusive classrooms*. Routledge.

Odom, S. L., Boyd, B. A., Hall, L. J., & Hume, K. (2010). Evaluation of comprehensive treatment models for individuals with autism spectrum disorders. *Journal of Autism and Developmental Disorders, 40*(4), 425–436. https://doi.org/10.1007/s10803-009-0825-1

Sarokoff, R. A., & Sturmey, P. (2004). The effects of behavioral skills training on staff implementation of discrete-trial teaching. *Journal of Applied Behavior Analysis, 37*(4), 535–538. https://doi. org/10.1901/jaba.2004.37-535

Sebag, R. (2010). Behavior management through self-advocacy: A strategy for secondary students with learning disabilities. *TEACHING Exceptional Children, 42*(6), 22–29. https://doi. org/10.1177/004005991004200603

Shayne, R., & Miltenberger, R. G. (2013). Evaluation of behavioral skills training for teaching functional assessment and treatment selection skills to parents. *Behavioral Interventions, 28*(1), 4–21. https://doi.org/10.1002/bin.1350

Sheldon, S. B., & Epstein, J. L. (2005). Involvement counts: Family and community partnerships and mathematics achievement. *Journal of Educational Research, 98*(4), 196–206. https://doi. org/10.3200/JOER.98.4.196-207

Spooner, F., Knight, V. F., Browder, D. M., & Smith, B. R. (2012). Evidence-based practice for teaching academics to students with severe developmental disabilities. *Remedial and Special Education, 33*(6), 374–387. https://doi.org/10.1177/0741932511421634

Stahmer, A. C., Rieth, S., Lee, E., Reisinger, E. M., Mandell, D. S., & Connell, J. E. (2015). Training teachers to use evidence-based practices for autism: Examining procedural implementation fidelity. *Psychology in the Schools, 52*(2), 181–195. https://doi.org/10.1002/pits.21815

7

Establish a Consistent, Organized, and Respectful Learning Environment

Virginia Walker and Sheldon Loman

To build and foster positive relationships, teachers should establish age-appropriate and culturally responsive expectations, routines, and procedures within their classrooms that are positively stated and explicitly taught and practiced across the school year. When students demonstrate mastery and follow established rules and routines, teachers should provide age-appropriate specific performance feedback in meaningful and caring ways. By establishing, following, and reinforcing expectations of all students within the classroom, teachers will reduce the potential for challenging behavior and increase student engagement. When establishing learning environments, teachers should build mutually respectful relationships with students and engage them in setting the classroom climate (e.g., rules and routines); be respectful; and value ethnic, cultural, contextual, and linguistic diversity to foster student engagement across learning environments.

Supporting Students with Extensive Support Needs

HLP #7 focuses on establishing a consistent, organized, and respectful learning environment. To build positive learning environments that address the unique needs of students with ESN, special education teachers and other school members will need to gather information to understand student strengths and support needs and environmental demands specific to the settings in which students receive instruction and interact with their peers. The physical layout of the classroom and instructional arrangements should be designed in such a way that promotes accessibility, safety, peer relationships, and independence. Special education teachers will need to collaborate with other school members to establish and teach expectations, routines, and procedures using supports and instructional approaches that are effective and tailored to address the unique needs of students with ESN. Importantly, special education teachers will need to establish rapport and build respectful relationships with students by delivering feedback and reinforcement to encourage social/emotional/behavioral growth, using respectful language, encouraging and acknowledging communication, and relying on ethical and safe practices to address challenging behavior.

DOI: 10.4324/9781003175735-8

Chapter Objectives

Upon reading this chapter, you should be able to do the following:

1. Describe the importance of gathering critical information to plan and establish supportive and positive learning environments for students with ESN.
2. Identify strategies for arranging the physical learning environment to meet the needs of students with ESN.
3. Identify strategies for establishing expectations, routines, and procedures within different learning environments to meet the needs of students with ESN.
4. Identify strategies for establishing positive relationships with students with ESN.

Understanding Student Needs to Plan and Establish a Supportive and Positive Learning Environment

Special education teachers must consider the cultural, linguistic, and individual assets students bring to school in order to foster positive environments. Utilizing person-centered planning approaches (Holburn et al., 2007) with students and their families is an effective way to understand the cultural values and long-term vision for student outcomes. A person-centered plan involves a meeting (or multiple meetings) with the student, family, and other stakeholders (e.g., friends, community agencies, teachers, related services providers, paraprofessionals). These meetings can serve as a foundation for building a respectful relationship and establishing rapport with students with ESN and their families. During a meeting, the student and their team may identify important information pertaining to the student's values, educational history (what did and did not work in previous classrooms), relationships, instructional preferences, and support needs. This information can be used to develop a classroom environment where expectations and routines are meaningful to students.

In seeking to build a positive learning environment, HLP #4 recommends that teachers develop a comprehensive understanding of each student's individualized learning needs through a review of multiple sources of information. Specific sources of information that will be helpful in establishing a positive learning environment for students with ESN are provided in Table 7.1.

Understanding the culture, language, educational history, strengths, preferences, interests, and needs of students can be critical to designing classroom learning environments that promote positive relationships and outcomes for students with ESN. To ensure that a positive learning environment is maintained, HLP #6 suggests that teachers continuously monitor student engagement to make necessary adjustments. Ensuring that a classroom is a welcoming, positive, and respectful learning environment and consistent with the values of each student involves the use of person-centered approaches, assessment of each student's engagement within the classroom activities, and ongoing consideration of student and family perspectives.

Setting up the Physical Learning Environment

Teachers must carefully determine how to arrange the physical learning environment, including classrooms and other spaces in the school where instruction is delivered (e.g., gymnasium for a physical education class), to promote accessibility, safety, peer relationships, and independence. Initially, teachers will need to take inventory of the various settings their students will access, including any relevant sub environments within these settings. For example, there may be multiple learning zones within the same classroom that need to be considered. As a next step, educators will need to evaluate their students' strengths and support needs and the expectations and demands across all learning environments as described in the previous section. With this information, educators will have greater capacity to set up learning spaces that encourage student success.

Table 7.1 Essential Tools for Understanding Student Needs in the Classroom

Purpose	Description	Examples/References
Student/Person-Centered Planning	Process with students, their families, and stakeholders in identifying a plan for their future including: strengths and goals, and barriers to their goals, while recruiting possible supports.	Making Action Plans (MAPS; Forest et al., 2007) Planning Alternative Tomorrows with Hope (PATH; Forest et al., 1993)
Student Preferences	Rating scales or systematic preference assessments involving direct observations to identify student learning preferences and reinforcing activities or items.	Systematic Preference Assessments (Chazin & Ledford, 2016) Child Preference Indicators (Moss, 2006a.) Personal Preference Indicators (Moss, 2006b.)
Promoting Self-Determination	Practical tools available online where students can learn to share their strengths, interests, needs, goals, and preferences.	Good Day Plan, One-Pager, Goal Plan www.imdetermined.org
Assessing Environmental Barriers and Supports	Ecological Inventories or Assessments involve observations of students to identify tasks that need to be performed across instructional environments.	Ecological Assessments (Westling et al., 2015)
Understanding Communication and Function of Student Behavior	Functional Behavioral Assessment (FBA) identifies the communicative function of student behavior by identifying antecedents and consequences of behavior through the use of interviews and observations.	Functional Behavioral Assessment (Crone et al., 2015)
Comprehensive Planning for Accommodations for Students with Extensive Support Needs	Procedures for identifying values of students and their families aligned with school outcomes identified by school-based personnel.	Choosing Outcomes and Accommodations for Children (Giangreco et al., 2011)
Student Support Needs	The Supports Intensity Scale-C assesses specific supports needed by children ages 5-16 with ESN in typical, age-appropriate environments.	Supports Intensity Scale- Children's Version (SIS-C; Thompson et al., 2016)

Physical Arrangement

Once information has been gathered about the various settings in which students will receive instruction, teachers can begin to design the classroom's physical layout. A number of arrangements appropriate for different learning contexts can be used in classroom spaces. For example, desks can be placed side-by-side in rows, which takes up less classroom space and allows students to face the same direction. When desks are arranged in a U-shape (or horseshoe) around the perimeter of the room, educators can quickly access students who require support. Placing desks in groups or seating small groups of students at tables so that students are facing one another allows for better movement in the classroom and is conducive to learning activities involving group learning and peer interaction. Finally, desks can be pushed together to form pairs or individual desks can be placed in rows facing the front of the classroom, which takes up the most classroom space but can be helpful in establishing classroom expectations, routines, and procedures, especially at the start of a new school year. The arrangement should always allow for easy movement and ensure the safety of all classroom members, especially in the case of an emergency like a fire or intruder drill (Clarke et al., 2014). As teachers consider how to design their classrooms, they may find the design websites under Resources helpful (e.g., Classroom Architect).

Because each strategy has its own advantages and disadvantages, teachers will need to determine which strategy (or multiple strategies) best aligns to the learning context by considering the following: the number of students in the class, the content/subject matter, the learning activity types used during instruction (see, for example, https://activitytypes.wm.edu/), and, importantly, individual student characteristics and support needs. Based on guidelines from Rohrer and Samson (2014), the following planning questions can be useful to teachers in designing classroom environments that are accessible and appropriate for all students, including those with ESN:

1. Are different sizes of chairs, desks, and other furniture needed to ensure students are positioned properly?
2. Do students have behavioral needs that need to be considered (e.g., climbing on furniture, property damage)?
3. Do students have sensory impairments that need to be considered (e.g., student with hearing loss seated close to teacher)?
4. Do students have medical, physical, sensory, and/or communication needs that require special equipment (e.g., wheelchair, stander, augmentative and alternative communication device)? Where will special equipment be stored?
5. Do students require support for feeding (e.g., G-tube feeding), toileting, or other personal care activities (e.g., administering medication)? Where will these activities occur to ensure privacy?
6. Who should be consulted to support classroom arrangement (e.g., speech language pathologist, behavior analyst, physical therapist, school nurse)?

As teachers answer these questions, it will be equally important to consider the *accessibility of the learning environment* and whether Universal Design principles might be applied to improve accessibility. "Universal Design is the design and composition of an environment so that it can be accessed, understood and used to the greatest extent possible by all people regardless of their age, size, ability or disability" (The Centre for Excellence in Universal Design, n.p.). The Centre for Excellence in Universal Design offers thoughtful guidelines for universally designing environments that can be applied to school settings, including *equitable use* (e.g., avoid segregating or stigmatizing students, provide same means of use for all students), *low physical effort* (e.g., minimize physical effort, allow students to maintain neutral body position), and *size and space for approach and use* (e.g., make reach comfortable for all seated or standing students, provide adequate space for use of assistive devices or personal assistance). See Resources for the Centre's seven Universal Design guidelines.

Instructional Arrangement

The ways in which students are arranged during instruction (one-to-one, small group, whole group) is yet another consideration for developing a positive learning environment. Similar to physical classroom arrangements, decisions concerning instructional arrangements should be made based on the content being taught, the types of learning activities used during instruction, and individual student needs, while also weighing the advantages and disadvantages of each type of instructional arrangement. The most common arrangement for students with ESN, one-to-one instruction, allows teachers, paraprofessionals, and other school members to provide individualized support to students in an efficient and direct manner. However, because one-to-one instruction may present challenges (e.g., increased probability of students not generalizing acquired skills to different instructional contexts, separation from peers, increased use of teacher time), it has been suggested that it be utilized only when students require intensive instruction (e.g., learning a replacement behavior to address persistent challenging behavior), privacy is needed (e.g., learning toileting skills), and a peer or older student provides mentoring or tutoring (McDonnell et al., 2020).

Small group instruction and whole group instruction, both of which are common in general education classrooms, allow for more efficient delivery of instruction to a larger number of students and offer social opportunities for students with ESN and their peers. For example, friendships may develop when students have opportunities to socially interact with one another and students with ESN will have increased opportunities to work on social and communication skills goals (e.g., cooperating to work towards a shared goal, respecting personal space, turn taking during conversations; Winstead et al., 2019). Many individual learning goals of students with ESN can be addressed in small and whole group arrangements through strategies like embedded instruction.

Peer Support Arrangements

Even when students are placed in small and whole group instructional arrangements or have other opportunities to socialize with peers, meaningful interactions and relationship development are not guaranteed. Intentional efforts must be made to develop and arrange supports to encourage interaction and capitalize on relationship-building opportunities. A number of strategies have been effective in addressing the social needs of students with ESN, including delivering systematic instruction to teach critical social skills, encouraging students with ESN to develop age-appropriate interests and participate in activities with peers who share similar interests, providing students with ESN and peers opportunities to participate in shared activities, and arranging peer supports (Brock et al., 2020). As an effective practice for improving social skills among students with ESN, particularly in general education middle and high school settings (Brock & Huber, 2017), peer support arrangements involve one or more peer partners who are trained to provide academic, behavioral, and social support to students with ESN while receiving support from educators. Aside from enhancing social interactions, peer support arrangements can serve as a feasible and practical alternative to reliance on paraprofessionals. As discussed in greater detail in the section that follows, the overreliance and misuse of paraprofessionals, especially within general education classrooms, can have negative consequences for students (Giangreco, 2021).

Other Considerations

Considerations of when, where, and how adults in the classroom will be utilized is another important aspect of designing positive learning environments.

Paraprofessionals.

Paraprofessionals assist special education teachers and other professionals in delivering special education and related services to students with disabilities. Paraprofessionals can play an important role in educating students with ESN, and research suggests they can effectively support students with ESN across various skill domains and settings, particularly when they are provided with adequate training and supervision (Brock & Anderson, 2021; Walker et al., 2021). However, the overreliance and misuse of paraprofessionals, especially one-to-one paraprofessionals in general education classrooms, can be problematic and may serve as a barrier to promoting a positive learning environment. As Giangreco (2021) points out, paraprofessionals typically have limited preparation and training, yet they are often assigned to support students who have the most significant needs and often assume instructional responsibilities.

Because paraprofessionals are not certified teachers, teachers and others responsible for paraprofessional oversight must ensure that paraprofessionals are practicing within the scope of their responsibilities (see CEC standards under Resources). Overreliance on paraprofessionals also may negatively affect opportunities for students with ESN to develop relationships and interact with their peers and teachers. Finally, when paraprofessionals take on the role of primary instructor or support provider, the quality of instruction may be poor, students with ESN may become more dependent on adults, and students with ESN may experience separation from peers within the general education classroom (Giangreco, 2021). To ensure that paraprofessionals are practicing within the scope of their responsibilities, educators can develop and share paraprofessional lesson plans to clearly establish expectations and roles during learning activities (Yates et al., 2020).

General Education Teachers and Related Services Providers.

General education teacher involvement will be critical in establishing positive learning environments in general education settings, where students with ESN learn alongside peers without disabilities for part or all of the school day. Special education teachers may not be present in these settings, and therefore the general education teacher will take the lead in arranging the learning environment, delivering instruction to students with ESN, and supervising paraprofessionals. This will require ongoing collaboration and creative problem solving between the special and general education teachers (Thompson et al., 2018). Likewise, special education and general education teachers, regardless of learning environment, will need to collaborate with related services providers to determine where, when, and how related services will be delivered across learning environments.

Establishing and Teaching Expectations, Routines, and Procedures

Establishing clear, consistent expectations in the classroom sets the foundation for a safe, positive, and predictable environment that promotes social and academic success. State et al. (2019 recommend the following guidelines: expectations should be (a) positively stated, (b) brief and limited in number (no more than five), (c) easily remembered, and (d) broad enough to encompass multiple behaviors across different settings and activities. It is important to consider incorporating the school-wide behavioral expectations (when applicable) within classrooms to promote generalization of classroom learning to other school environments. For example, some schools may implement School-wide Positive Behavioral Interventions and Supports (SWPBIS) where there are usually three to five positively stated expectations (e.g., Be safe, Be respectful, Be responsible) that are publicly posted, taught, and acknowledged across all school environments (OSEP Technical Assistance Center on Positive Behavioral Interventions and Supports, 2015). If a school does not implement SWPBIS, teachers can still frame their specific classroom expectations around school-wide expectations to ensure common language and consistency across environments that will result in positive social outcomes and create opportunities for students to be included with their peers.

Involving students with ESN in establishing the classroom expectations can promote a classroom that is culturally sustaining and meaningful to all students. Some ways to engage students with ESN in defining classroom expectations may include (a) using visual supports or video models to represent the proposed expectations, (b) incorporating choice-making by presenting proposed expectations and having students identify preferred expectations, and (c) supporting students with complex communication needs in using their augmentative and alternative communication systems to express their ideas for expectations in the classroom. Figure 7.1 provides an example of how classroom expectations can align with school-wide

School-wide Expectations	Classroom Expectations Aligned with School-wide Expectations	What Does it Look Like? (examples from the student's perspective) 	What Does it Sound Like? (examples from the student's perspective) 
Be Safe	Walk at all times in the classroom 	"Regular or slow-motion walking like in a video" 	"Calm taps of footsteps on the ground" 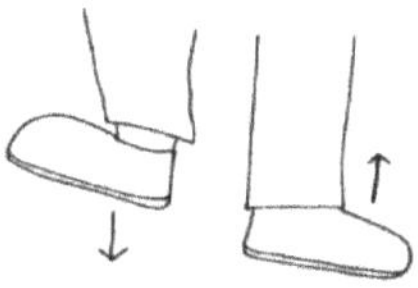
Be Responsible	Be in your seat when the bell rings 	"Your bottom on your chair" 	"Quiet voices" 
Be Respectful	Take turns- make sure everyone has an opportunity 	"I get a chance to do the activity and I wait for friends to try." 	"Quiet voice saying 'My turn' or 'Your turn'" 

Figure 7.1 Classroom Expectations Aligned with School-wide Expectations

Note. Images from LessonPix: www.lessonpix.com

expectations and includes visual supports for what the expectations might look and sound like from the student perspective.

Teaching Expectations

Once the classroom expectations are agreed upon and defined, they should be systematically taught to all students. Universal Design for Learning (UDL; Hitchcock et al., 2005) is a framework that can help teachers plan to effectively teach expectations to students with ESN in their classrooms. Teachers can use UDL to consider multiple ways to represent the expectations, multiple means to engage students, while also providing various ways for students to express their understanding of the expectations. Examples of the UDL principles include using visuals paired with text to explain behavioral expectations (*multiple means of representation*), involving peers to support teaching expectations (*multiple means of engagement*), and encouraging students to use a variety of communication modes to express understanding of expectations (e.g., speech generating device; *multiple means of expression*). The use of UDL is an important first step to ensuring students with ESN learn the expectations within classrooms and across school environments. See information about UDL under Resources.

Teachers should use evidence-based practices for students with ESN (see Browder et al., 2014 and Wong et al., 2015) in conjunction with UDL to teach expectations. In a recent study, teachers improved outcomes for students with ESN through adapting the school-wide expectations using UDL and several evidence-based practices for students with ESN (e.g., visual supports, social narratives, systematic instruction) to teach behavioral expectations (Loman et al., 2018). Other evidence-based practices that may be effective in teaching students with ESN classroom expectations include peer-mediated supports, video modeling, response prompting, and differential reinforcement strategies. Additional information about evidence-based practices can be found under Resources.

The UDL Classroom Expectations Lesson Design Worksheet (see Figure 7.2) can be used collaboratively by teachers and other school members to outline the instructional procedures for teaching expectations to students with ESN.

This tool can be used by the educational team for each specific classroom activity or environment (e.g., Classroom Group Instruction). The educational team will fill out the worksheet to identify the expectations or social skill outcomes (first column), how students will demonstrate learning of those outcomes (second column), and what is currently done to teach those outcomes (third column). After these columns are completed, the classroom teacher and the team can use their expertise (e.g., speech/language therapists in the use of language and communication strategies) to complete the remaining columns to determine how to (a) present the expectations in multiple ways (e.g., use of picture symbols, social narratives, video models), (b) encourage students to use multiple ways to express understanding of the expectations (e.g., use of speech generating device, pointing or gestures), and (c) engage and motivate students in multiple ways when teaching the expectations (e.g., peer-mediated supports, use of materials that are of interest). Once the use of UDL and evidence-based practices are outlined, the following steps can be used to systematically teach expectations to students with ESN: (a) define the expectation clearly, (b) teach relevant examples and non-examples, (c) provide feedback and guided practice, and (d) consistently monitor and review.

Teaching Classroom Routines and Procedures

Teaching classroom routines and procedures help set up a classroom that runs efficiently and effectively. As noted earlier, there may be sub environments within a particular learning environment. For example, teachers may create different learning spaces or "zones" in their classrooms that serve different purposes (e.g., library/quiet reading, technology center). These zones

UDL Classroom Expectations Lesson Design Worksheet Example

UDL Classroom Expectations Lesson Design Worksheet

Routine/Environment: <u>Classroom-Group Instruction</u>   Instructor(s): <u>Ms. Bell and Mr. Chavez</u>

Key Social Skill Goals/Outcomes Note: From the 3-5 SWPBIS expectations (e.g., "Be Safe, Be Respectful, Be Responsible")	What We Want Students to Do to Demonstrate Learning	What We Do Now	Applying UDL: Representation of Content	Applying UDL: Student Actions/ Expression	Applying UDL: Student Engagement/ Motivation
Students will **be safe** in the classroom	Keep hands, feet, and materials to themselves Walk at all times Ask permission to leave the room	Show students the expectations poster on the board Remind them of the rules	Provide pictures as prompts of the expectations. Use video examples of the expectations Role play and practice examples and non-examples Develop and use social narratives to explain the expectations	Students can use different ways to communicate their understanding of expectations (e.g., create posters or videos, use voice output devices) Students can illustrate what the expectations should look like and sound like	Meaningful reinforcement (finding incentives that students prefer). Peer-mediated Interventions where students can partner with other students in supporting safety at the playground Self-management and reinforcement strategies where each student can give themselves a "thumbs up, thumbs sideways, or thumbs down" for how they were safe in the classroom

Figure 7.2 UDL Classroom Expectations Lesson Design Worksheet Example

should be designed with accessibility and safety in mind, and it will be important to explicitly teach students with ESN the expectations and rules for each learning area. Once teachers and students are on the same page with everyday classroom routines, there is more time for teachers to focus on essential academic and social skills instruction.

In developing classroom routines and procedures, teachers should take inventory of all activities students are expected to perform within their classroom on a daily basis (e.g., entering/exiting the classroom, independent work time, getting supplies, emergency drills). A task analysis can be conducted to identify the steps students need to perform within each classroom routine by breaking down the routine into simple, observable steps that students have the prerequisite skills to perform (Westling et al., 2015). Prerequisite skills can be determined by informal observations of students within the classroom. See AFIRM modules under Resources about task analysis. As an example, the dismissal routine (Figure 7.3) is broken down into eight steps that

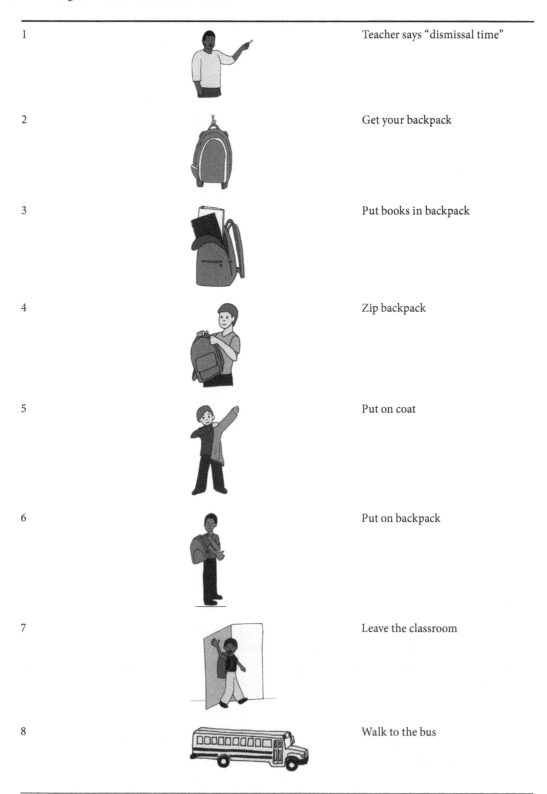

1		Teacher says "dismissal time"
2		Get your backpack
3		Put books in backpack
4		Zip backpack
5		Put on coat
6		Put on backpack
7		Leave the classroom
8		Walk to the bus

Figure 7.3 Dismissal Routine Example

were determined by observing students and identifying the appropriate skills that needed to be taught within that routine.

In this example, visual supports are provided to prompt students through each step along with text that can be used as cues to teach the dismissal routine. As discussed earlier, UDL principles and other evidence-based practices also can be used to teach classroom routines. In addition to incorporating visual supports, the use of systematic instructional strategies such as backward chaining, forward chaining, and total task presentation (Mims, 2020) along with video modeling (McCoy & Hermansen, 2007) have been well-established practices for teaching multi-step (or chained) routines.

The use of the "First-Then" strategy (Premack Principle) is another approach that can be useful to incorporate in teaching classroom routines that may be considered difficult by students with ESN. In using the "First-Then" strategy, a visual representation of a routine (e.g., dismissal) can be presented with a visual representation of a reinforcing activity (e.g., video game) that signals to the student that once they complete the "first" activity (usually a difficult or non-preferred activity), they will be able to receive the "then" activity (always a preferred activity).

Developing Positive Relationships with Students

One of the most important actions educators can take to create a positive learning environment is to develop positive relationships with students. This involves providing students with meaningful feedback and reinforcement, supporting student communication, and utilizing practices that are ethical and respectful.

Feedback and Reinforcement

HLP #8 calls for educators to provide positive and constructive feedback to guide students' learning and behavior. Specific strategies and considerations for delivering feedback to encourage positive student outcomes across skill domains are covered in detail in Chapter 8. However, it is important to note here that the assessments described earlier in this chapter, particularly those that focus on student support needs and preferences, can provide teachers with valuable information to guide the ways in which they deliver feedback and reinforcement (Cannella-Malone et al., 2013).

Another important aspect of developing positive relationships with students, especially while delivering feedback, is communicating in respectful ways. A teacher's body language, words, and tone convey a message to the student and will undoubtedly influence rapport with the student. Likewise, the way in which educators refer to students with ESN may have significant implications. For decades, disability advocates, researchers, and other stakeholders have promoted the use of person-first language, which puts the person before their disability (e.g., instead of referring to a student as a "wheelchair user," an educator might say, "the student uses a wheelchair."). The idea behind person-first language is that it emphasizes the value of the person with a disability by recognizing them as a person rather than by their disability. However, in recent years, concerns have been raised about person-first language, particularly that it separates people from their disability, which can be a central part of a person's identity and life experience. Identity-first language, on the other hand, acknowledges that a person's disability is a significant part of their identity and puts the disability first (e.g., autistic student vs. student with autism). Ultimately, decisions about whether to use person-first or identity-first language should be made based on the person with a disability's choice of language, and teachers should make every effort to ensure that students are comfortable with the language they are using.

Communication Supports

Many students with ESN have complex communication needs and, as a result, may use augmentative or alternative communication to replace or supplement speech (Andzik et al., 2018). Students also may communicate in unconventional ways, including unintelligible vocalizations and challenging behavior (Snell et al., 2010). In developing positive relationships with students who have complex communication needs, teachers are encouraged to collaborate with related services providers who have expertise in communication interventions and supports (e.g., speech language pathologist, assistive technology specialist, behavior analyst). Not only will teachers need to learn about a student's existing communication system and strategies to teach communication skills, they will also need to identify opportunities throughout the school day and across learning environments to promote and respond to communication. As educators consider ways to promote and respond to student communication across environments, they may find it helpful to consider the Communication Bill of Rights (Brady et al., 2016). See Communication Bill of Rights under Resources.

It is important to point out that choice-making is emphasized in the Communication Bill of Rights, which points to the critical role it plays in promoting communication, independence, and self-determination among students with ESN (Tullis et al., 2011; Wehmeyer & Shogren, 2016). Choice-making can even be used as a strategy to address challenging behavior (e.g., Shogren et al., 2004). Teachers and others who support students with ESN should provide students with opportunities to make meaningful decisions throughout the school day, while honoring these choices when appropriate and feasible.

One final point that bears repeating is that, for students who use aided augmentative and alternative communication, those communication systems should always be accessible and in working condition. Communication systems should never be removed on the basis of challenging behavior or learning activity, and backup systems should be available in the event that a student's primary system is damaged or otherwise unavailable. Brady et al. (2016) remind us that all students have the basic right to "affect, through communication, the conditions of their existence." Without access to a communication system, students with ESN face significant barriers to meaningfully participating and making progress toward their learning goals.

Utilizing Practices that Are Ethical and Respectful

One final consideration for establishing positive learning environments relates to the practices used by teachers and how these practices keep students with ESN safe and promote dignity and respect. Of course, teachers will need to abide by school and district policies and procedures, and when developing routines, procedures, and supports within the classroom, they should take special care to ensure that alternatives to practices that may be aversive to students are prioritized. For example, when addressing challenging behavior, some students may require intense, individualized interventions to encourage prosocial behavior, and as emphasized in the IDEA (2004). Positive behavioral interventions and supports (PBIS) should be considered over practices that may be aversive. Restraint and seclusion, in particular, are two practices that have been overused, misused, and can be dangerous when implemented in school settings. As Trader et al. (2017) point out, these practices should be limited to emergency situations only, and evidence-based practices that focus on the *prevention* of challenging behavior should be prioritized. In Chapter 8, strategies that can be used in lieu of aversive practices (e.g., differential reinforcement) are provided. Finally, educators must design physical learning spaces such that students and other school members can safely navigate the environment, and emergency plans will need to be developed (or adapted if following a school-wide plan) to ensure that all students, including those with ESN who may require individualized support, can follow the plan and remain safe during emergency drills and evacuations (e.g., tornado drill, intruder drill, fire evaluation).

Next Steps toward Better Practice

1. To organize a positive learning environment for students with ESN, engage the student and family in student-centered planning. Ecological assessments, preference assessments, and other assessments (e.g., SIS-C, FBA) can help educators understand student strengths and needs and the demands of the environments in which they will be educated.
2. The physical layout and design of a classroom is an important element of providing a positive learning environment for all students, including those with ESN. Conduct an ecological inventory to fully explore the learning environments and sub environments students will access as a first step in designing the classroom space. Work closely with general education teachers, paraprofessionals, and other school members (e.g., related services providers) to design a space that is accessible, safe, and that promotes student independence and peer interaction.
3. Students with ESN may require additional support to learn classroom expectations and routines. When planning how to teach classroom expectations and routines, problem solve using the UDL Worksheet. By applying the UDL principles to frame the use of evidence-based practices in teaching behavioral expectations and routines, educators ensure that students with ESN are meaningfully accessing the expectations.
4. Developing positive relationships with students is critical in establishing positive learning environments. Because many students with ESN have complex communication needs, identifying ways to promote communication will be important. Closely examine the Communication Bill of Rights and determine when and how you will honor these rights among students with complex communication needs and who rely on augmentative and alternative communication systems.

The Big Five

1. To establish a positive and supportive learning environment, it will be important to understand students' strengths and needs and the demands across school settings by gathering information from multiple sources.
2. To ensure students are effectively supported across environments, engage in collaborative teaming to utilize expertise across a range of professionals (e.g., general education teachers, special education teachers, speech/language pathologists, occupational and physical therapists, behavior analysts).
3. Design the physical environment of the classroom in such a way to promote engagement, peer interactions, safety, and accessibility.
4. Use UDL and evidence-based practices to teach three to five social/emotional/behavioral expectations embedded in classroom routines.
5. Create a climate that is safe, positive, and respectful by developing rapport and relationships with students and promoting independence.

Resources

1. Classroom Architect: http://classroom.4teachers.org/
2. Floor Planner: https://floorplanner.com/

3. Scholastic's Class Set-up Tool: http://teacher.scholastic.com/tools/class_setup/index.html
4. Learning Activity Types: https://activitytypes.wm.edu/
5. Centre for Excellence in Universal Design Principles: http://universaldesign.ie/what-is-universal-design/the-7-principles/the-7-principles.html
6. CEC Paraeducator Preparation Guidelines: https://exceptionalchildren.org/standards/paraeducator-preparation-guidelines
7. CAST Universal Design for Learning Guidelines: https://udlguidelines.cast.org
8. CEEDAR Center Evidence-based Practices for Students with Severe Disabilities: https://ceedar.education.ufl.edu/portfolio/evidence-based-practices-for-students-with-severe-disabilities/
9. Autism Focused Intervention Resources and Modules: https://afirm.fpg.unc.edu/afirm-modules
10. Communication Bill of Rights: https://www.asha.org/siteassets/uploadedFiles/NJC-Communication-Bill-Rights.pdf

References

Andzik, N., Schaefer, J. M., Nichols, R. T., & Chung, Y. M. (2018). National survey describing and quantifying students with communication needs. *Developmental Neuro Rehabilitation*, *21*(1), 40–47. https://doi.org/10.1080/17518423.2017.1339133

Brady, N. C., Bruce, S., Goldman, A., Erickson, K., Mineo, B., Ogletree, B. T., Paul, D., Romski, M., Sevcik, R., Siegel, E., Schoonover, J., Snell, M., Sylvester, L., & Wilkinson, K. (2016). Communication services and supports for individuals with severe disabilities: Guidance for assessment and intervention. *American Journal on Intellectual and Developmental Disabilities*, *121*(2), 121–138.

Brock, M. A., & Anderson, E. J. (2021). Training paraprofessionals who work with students with intellectual and developmental disabilities: What does the research say? *Psychology in the Schools*, *58*(2), 702–722. https://doi.org/10.1002/pits.22386

Brock, M. E., Carter, E. W., & Biggs, E. E. (2020). Supporting peer interactions, relationships, and belonging. In F. Brown, J. McDonnell, & M. E. Snell (Eds). *Instruction of students with severe disabilities* (9th ed., pp. 384–417). Pearson.

Brock, M. E., & Huber, H. B. (2017). Are peer support arrangements an evidence-based practice? A systematic review. *The Journal of Special Education*, *51*(3), 150–163. https://doi.org/10.1177/0022466917708184

Browder, D. M., Wood, L., Thompson, J., & Ribuffo, C. (2014). Evidence-based practices for students with severe disabilities (Document No. IC-3). Retrieved from University of Florida, Collaboration for Effective Educator, Development, Accountability, and Reform Center website: http://ceedar.education.ufl.edu/tools/innovation-configurations/

Cannella-Malone, H. I., Sabielny, L. M., Jimenez, E. D., & Miller, M. M. (2013). Pick one!: Conducting preference assessments with students with significant disabilities. *Teaching Exceptional Children*, *45*(6), 16–23. https://doi.org/10.1177/004005991304500602

Chazin, K. T., & Ledford, J. R. (2016). *Preference assessments*. Evidence-Based Instructional Practices for Young Children with Autsim and Other Disabilities. http://ebip.vkcsites.org/preference-assessments

Clarke, L. S., Embury, D. C., Jones, R. E., & Yssel, N. (2014). Supporting students with disabilities during school crises: A teacher's guide. *Teaching Exceptional Children*, *46*(6), 169–178. https://doi.org/10.1177/0040059914534616

Crone, D. A., Hawken, L. S., & Horner, R. H. (2015). *Building positive behavior support systems in schools*. Guilford.

Forest, M., O'Brien, J., & Pearpoint, J. (1993). *PATH: A workbook for planning positive possible futures*. Inclusion Press International.

Forest, M., Pearpoint, J., & O'Brien, J. (2007). 'MAPS': Educators, parents, young people, and their friends planning together. *Educational Psychology in Practice, 11*(4), 35–40. https://doi.org/10.1080/0266736960110407

Giangreco, M. F. (2021). Maslow's hammer: Teacher assistant research and inclusive practices at a crossroads. *European Journal of Special Needs Education, 36*(2), 278–293. https://doi.org/10.1080/08856257.2021.1901377

Giangreco, M., Cloninger, Chigee, J., & Iverson, V. S. (2011). *Choosing outcomes & accommodations for children: A guide to educational planning for students with disabilities* (3rd ed.). Brookes.

Hitchcock, C. G., Meyer, A., Rose, D., & Jackson, R. (2005). Equal access, participation, and progress in the general education curriculum. In D. Rose, A. Meyer, & C. Hitchcock (Eds.), *The universally designed classroom: Accessible curriculum and digital technologies* (pp. 37–68). Cambridge, MA: Harvard Education Press.

Holburn, S., Gordon, A., & Vietze, P. M. (2007). *Person centered planning made easy: The PICTURE method.* Brookes.

Individuals With Disabilities Education Act (IDEA), 20 U.S.C. § 1400 (2004).

Loman, S. L., Strickland-Cohen, M. K., & Walker, V. L. (2018). Promoting the accessibility of SWPBIS for students with severe disabilities. *Journal of Positive Behavior Interventions, 20*(2), 113–123. https://doi.org/10.1177/1098300717733976

McCoy, K., & Hermansen, E. (2007). Video-modeling for individuals with autism: A review of model types and effects. *Education and Treatment of Children, 30*, 183–213. https://www.jstor.org/stable/42899952

McDonnell, J., Snell, M. E., Brown, F., Bowman, J., & Conradi, L. (2020). Arranging the teaching environment. In F. Brown, J. McDonnel, & M. E. Snell (Eds). *Instruction of students with severe disabilities* (9th ed., pp. 137–155). Pearson.

Mims, P. J. (2020). Using instruction that works: Evidence-based practices. In D. M. Browder, F. Spooner, & G. R. Courtade (Eds.), *Teaching students with moderate and severe disabilities* (2nd ed., pp. 114–140). Guilford.

Moss, J. (2006a). Child Preference Indicators. Center for Learning and Leadership UCEDD University of Oklahoma Health Sciences Center. Retrieved from: https://ouhsc.edu/Portals/1154/EasyDNNnews/Uploads/4222/2_ChildPreferenceIndicators2.pdf

Moss, J. (2006b). Personal Preference Indicators. Center for Learning and Leadership UCEDD University of Oklahoma Health Sciences Center. Retrieved from: https://ouhsc.edu/Portals/1154/EasyDNNnews/Uploads/4233/12_PersonalPreferenceIndicators2.pdf

OSEP Technical Assistance Center on Positive Behavioral Interventions and Supports (2015). Positive Behavioral Interventions and Supports (PBIS) Implementation Blueprint: Part 1 – Foundations and Supporting Information. Retrieved from: www.pbis.org.

Rohrer, M., & Samson, N. (2014). *10 critical components for success in the special education classroom.* A SAGE Company.

Shogren, K. A., Faggella-Luby, M. N., Bae, S. J., & Wehmeyer, M. L. (2004). The effect of choice-making as an intervention for problem behavior: A meta-analysis. *Journal of Positive Behavior Interventions, 6*(4), 228–237. https://doi.org/10.1177/10983007040060040401

Snell, M. E., Brady, N., McLean, L., Ogletree, B. T., Siegel, E., Sylvester, L., Mollica, B. M., Paul, D., Romski, M., & Sevcik, R. (2010). Twenty years of communication intervention research with individuals who have severe intellectual and developmental disabilities. *American Journal on Intellectual and Developmental Disabilities, 115*(5), 364–380. https://doi.org/10.1352/1944-7558-115-5.364

State, T. M., Mitchell, B. S., & Wehby, J. (2019). Consistent, organized, respectful learning environment. In J. McLeskey, L. Maheady, B. Billingsley, M.T. Brownell, & T. J. Lewis (Eds.), *High leverage practices for inclusive classrooms* (1st ed., pp. 97–106). Routledge.

The Center for Excellence in Universal Design (n.d.). *What is Universal Design?* https://www. universaldesign.ie/what-is-universal-design/

Thompson, J. R., Walker, V. L., Shogren, K., & Wehmeyer, M. L. (2018). Expanding inclusive educational opportunities for students with significant cognitive disabilities through personalized supports. *Intellectual and Developmental Disabilities, 56*(6), 396–411. https://doi. org/10.1352/1934-9556-56.6.396

Thompson, J. R., Wehmeyer, M. L., Hughes, C., Shogren, K. A., Little, T. D., Hyojeong, S., Schalock, R. L., & Realon, R. E. (2016). *Supports intensity scale—Children's version: User's manual.* American Association on Intellectual and Developmental Disabilities.

Trader, B., Stonemeier, J., Berg, T., Knowles, C., Massar, M., Monzalve, M., Pinkelman, S., Nese, R., Ruppert, T., & Horner, R. (2017). Promoting inclusion through evidence-based alternatives to restraint and seclusion. *Research and Practice for Persons With Severe Disabilities, 42*(2), 75–88. https://doi.org/10.1177/1540796917698830

Tullis, C. A., Cannella-Malone, H. I., Basbigill, A. Y., Fleming, C. V., Payne, D., & Wu, P. (2011). Review of the choice and preference assessment literature for individuals with severe to profound disabilities. *Education and Training in Autism and Developmental Disabilities, 46*(4), 576–595.

Walker, V. L., Kurth, J., Carpenter, M. E., Tapp, M. C., Clausen, A., & Lockman Turner, E. (2021). Paraeducator-delivered interventions for students with extensive support needs in inclusive school settings: A systematic review. *Research and Practice for Persons With Severe Disabilities, 46*(4), 278–295. https://doi.org/10.1177/15407969211055127

Wehmeyer, M. L., & Shogren, K. A. (2016) Self-determination and choice. In N. Singh (Ed.), *Handbook of evidence-based practices in intellectual and developmental disabilities* (pp. 551–584). Springer. https://doi.org/10.1007/978-3-319-26583-4_21

Westling, D., Fox, L., & Carter, E. (2015). *Teaching students with severe disabilities* (5th ed.). Pearson.

Winstead, O., Lane, J. D., Spriggs, A. D., & Allday, R. A. (2019). Providing small group instruction to children with disabilities and same-age peers. *Journal of Early Intervention, 41*(3), 202–219. https://doi.org/10.1177/1053815119832985

Wong, C., Odom, S. L., Hume, K., Cox, A. W., Fettig, A., Kucharcyk, S., Brock, M. E., Plavnick, J. B., Fleury, V. P., & Schultz, T. R. (2015). *Evidence-based practices for children, youth, and young adults with autism spectrum disorder: A comprehensive review.* Frank Porter Graham Child Development Institute, Autism Evidence-Based Practice Review Group, The University of North Carolina.

Yates, P., Chopra, R., Sobeck, E., Douglas, S., Morano, S., Walker, V. L., & Schulze, R. (2020). Working with paraeducators: Tools and strategies for planning, performance feedback, and evaluation. *Intervention in School and Clinic, 56*(1), 43–50. https://doi.org/10.1177/1053451220910740

8

Provide Positive and Constructive Feedback to Guide Students' Learning and Behavior

Robert Pennington, Melissa Tapp, and Janet Sanchez Enriquez

The purpose of feedback is to guide student learning and behavior and increase student motivation, engagement, and independence, leading to improved student learning and behavior. Effective feedback must be strategically delivered and goal directed; feedback is most effective when the learner has a goal and the feedback informs the learner regarding areas needing improvement and ways to improve performance. Feedback may be verbal, nonverbal, or written, and should be timely, contingent, genuine, meaningful, age appropriate, and at rates commensurate with task and phase of learning (i.e., acquisition, fluency, maintenance). Teachers should provide ongoing feedback until learners reach their established learning goals.

Supporting Students with ESN

One of the most essential elements of any educational program is the provision of positive and constructive feedback in response to student behavior. Feedback has been defined broadly as information regarding one's performance (Hattie & Timperley, 2007) and is often discussed in the literature as behavior specific praise or error correction. This descriptive feedback has two interrelated functions: (a) to provide information confirming the accuracy of a response, or directions as to how to perform an accurate response, and (b) differential reinforcement of correct responding. Though seemingly subtle, educators' understanding of the distinctions between these two functions is important. One involves the use of carefully selected words, or other symbols to communicate a message related to performance, whereas the other involves the delivery of some desirable consequence that improves students' future performance (reinforcement). For some students, descriptive verbal praise may be informative but not reinforcing. Consider the teenager who raises his hand in class and is met with effusive teacher praise (e.g., Enrique, I really love that you raised your hand). Embarrassed, he lowers his head and the teacher notices less hand raising in the coming days. Other students, especially those with extensive support needs (ESN) and complex communication needs (CCN), may not have the listener (i.e., receptive) skills to understand and ultimately, benefit from the content of descriptive verbal feedback.

Though the research literature is replete with demonstrations of the effectiveness of descriptive feedback for students with a range of support needs, many students will require additional support to benefit from feedback on their performance. This is especially true for students with ESN, who

DOI: 10.4324/9781003175735-9

often have CCN, who require carefully designed instructional opportunities, and may have a limited and in some cases, highly idiosyncratic sets of reinforcers that may not be readily available in naturalistic instructional settings. These students will require educators to implement systematic procedures for identifying reinforcers, delivering reinforcers, and thinning reinforcer delivery to levels commensurate with natural environments.

Chapter Objectives

Upon reading this chapter, you should be able to do the following:

1. Discuss the relationships between feedback, reinforcement, and student behavior.
2. Describe strategies for identifying potential reinforcers for use during instruction and the provision of behavior supports.
3. Describe important features of positive feedback.
4. Describe systematic strategies for the delivery of feedback.

Behavior and Consequences

Educators often spend a great deal of time planning for instruction. They seek out or develop engaging materials, plan thoughtfully sequenced lessons, and carefully construct questions or activities to assess their students' understanding. The most effective educators also carefully attend to their use of feedback and other consequences while delivering their lessons. Consequences play an essential role in learning. When a response produces a desirable consequence, that response is more likely to occur in the future. We call this relationship between a consequence and an increase in behavior *reinforcement* and refer to the desirable consequence as a *reinforcer*. Materials and conditions that immediately and consistently precede a reinforced response often come to evoke that response. For example, a teacher prompts Katherine, who has ESN, CCN, and limited mobility, to press a switch that emits a recorded message "Hey, let's hang out" each time a peer approaches her. The teacher instructs several peers to come over and talk to Katherine when they hear the message. After several days, Katherine begins to hit the switch independently when a peer comes within close proximity to her.

Consequences also contribute to student problem behavior. Contextually inappropriate and sometimes harmful behaviors occur because of a learner's history of consequences. In other words, individuals emit problem behaviors because these behaviors have worked for them (or have been reinforced) in the past and under similar conditions. They have produced access to preferred conditions (e.g., attention, items, activities) or escape from challenging and aversive ones (e.g., difficult tasks, unpleasant social interactions). For some students without effective functional communication skills, problem behavior may be the only means by which they can control their access or exposure to preferred and aversive conditions.

Effective educators arrange their classrooms and instruction so that students frequently receive feedback and other reinforcing consequences for engaging in contextually appropriate academic, social, and adaptive skills. They also try to limit the reinforcement of errors, and other behaviors that might become persistent and prevent access to high quality educational, social, and employment opportunities. This strategy of rewarding some behaviors rather than others is referred to as differential reinforcement and stands as one of the most foundational principles in the science of learning.

Strategies for Identifying Potential Reinforcers

As previously mentioned, some students may require the use of other reinforcers in addition to vocal feedback. These reinforcers are often unique to the individual learner. For example, some students might find stickers and high fives as reinforcing and others, snacks or vibrating toys.

Table 8.1 Preference Assessments

Assessment	When to Use
Caregiver Interview	When student's preferred items are unknown.
Pre-task choice	Student can choose among items and can wait to earn the item.
Free Operant	Student's preferred items are unknown.
Single Stimulus	Student does not consistently choose between two items.
Paired Stimulus	Student can choose between two items (but not when given three or more).
Multiple Stimulus with Replacement	Given three or more choices, student consistently selects a single item AND the student engages in challenging behavior when favorite items are removed. Use for assessing toy preference.
Multiple Stimulus without Replacement	Given three or more choices, student consistently selects a single item AND the student does not engage in challenging behavior when favorite items are removed. Use for edibles preference.

Though some reinforcers may appear highly idiosyncratic or unnatural, it is important that educators overcome inclinations to using a one-size-fits-all approach to reinforcer delivery. Reinforcers are not defined by their form (e.g., praise vs. edibles) but by their actual effect on behavior. Educators must be careful to not blame students for their own failure to identify powerful reinforcers. It is the educator's responsibility to identify powerful reinforcers for each of their students, even when it may be challenging to do so—even when it may take some effort to do so—even when conventional reinforcers are not effective. Fortunately, researchers have established several strategies for helping educators identify potential reinforcers for use during instruction and intervention.

These strategies, collectively referred to as preference assessments, involve gathering information from students and in some cases, caregivers, to identify objects, activities, and other stimuli that may serve as reinforcers for a particular behavior. Preference assessments are especially useful when working with populations of students who may not vocally describe their preferences or may engage with a limited number of activities and items throughout the day.

There are several preference assessment procedures (see Table 8.1). Indirect preference assessments involve asking a caregiver or other person familiar to a student to identify highly preferred stimuli. Educators can conduct informal indirect assessment by asking caregivers about a child's interests or preferences. They also can use *structured interviews or checklists* (Fisher et al., 1996; Matson et al., 1999). For example, the Reinforcement Assessment for Individuals with Severe Disabilities (RAISD; Fisher et al., 1996) poses questions about a range of potential preferences and the conditions under which they may serve as reinforcers.

Direct preference assessments involve gathering information related to preferences directly from a learner. For some students, it may be appropriate to ask them to identify their preferences by responding to open-ended questions (e.g., What is your favorite candy?) or a presentation of choices (e.g., Which do you like most, video games or listening to hip hop?). Educators also might offer a pre-task choice prior to beginning an activity (e.g., What would you like to earn for working today, a snack or time reading your comic?). Some educators may conduct *free operant* preference assessments. This involves observing the student within a natural or contrived environment for a predetermined amount of time. In the assessment environment, the educator makes available a range of potential reinforcing items or activities. The educator or paraprofessional then observes the student and records the time they spend engaging with any item. At the end of the assessment, the educator identifies potentially reinforcing items by the total duration of time spent with each item.

Finally, educators can use *trial-based* stimulus preference assessments which involve systematically presenting potentially reinforcing stimuli and observing students' interaction with them. These trial-based preference assessments are especially advantageous for students with CCN, as they provide an opportunity for students to "show" their preferences instead of vocally reporting them. Further, they can be used to present new potential reinforcers to which students may not be familiar and evaluate their value against familiar stimuli. Researchers have established the efficacy of several trial-based preference assessments for use with students with ESN including single stimulus and multiple stimulus methods. The *single stimulus* preference assessment (Pace et al., 1985) has been used to assess the preferences of students who have difficulty making selections between two or more items. During the assessment, the educator presents multiple items, one at a time, and records approach, contact, or engagement with the item. Those items with the most approaches or longest duration of contact are considered most preferred. For those students able to choose between two stimuli presented simultaneously, educators may use a *paired-stimulus* preference assessment (Fisher et al., 1992). Prior to conducting this assessment, an educator identifies five to six potential reinforcers. During the assessment trials, they present two items, ask students to make a selection, and record their response. Throughout the assessment, pairs are varied so that each item is presented with every other item multiple times. At the end of the assessment, the teacher ranks items from most to least preferred based on the number of times each item was selected. Finally, educators can use *multiple stimulus* preference assessments (DeLeon & Iwata, 1996). These preference assessments often require less time than other assessments and can be easily conducted prior to an instructional session. The educator gathers five to six potential reinforcers, places them in an array and asks the student to "choose one." After the student makes a selection, the teacher records the response and either replaces the item (i.e., *multiple stimulus with replacement*) or does not replace the item and continues until all reinforcers have been selected (i.e., *multiple stimulus without replacement*). Again, preferences are identified based on the number of times items are selected.

It is important to note that preference assessments only identify potential reinforcers. Students may prefer one item over another, but that item may still be insufficient to serve as a reinforcer during difficult instructional tasks. Ultimately, only increases in student behavior can demonstrate that an item or type of feedback is a reinforcer under particular instructional conditions.

Functions of Feedback

Thus far, we have discussed feedback in relation to its use in reinforcing student behavior, but performance feedback also can be described in term of its three basic functions; (a) confirming and potentially reinforcing a correct response (i.e., positive feedback), (b) presenting additional instructional content (i.e., instructive feedback), and (c) providing information on accurate responding in response to an error (i.e., error correction). Positive feedback involves communicating to a student that a response is accurate or contextually appropriate. It can potentially reinforce a particular behavior and can be used to draw a student's attention to a particular response or feature of a response. For example, an occupational therapist might provide feedback to a student for improvement in writing a particular letter after writing their name.

Instructive feedback (see HLP 22) is provided to extend learning by providing additional non-targeted information following a student's response. For example, in response to the question, "Can you name something red?," a student touches the word "apple" on their speech generating device. The teacher responds by saying, "Yes, you touched a red apple" but then immediately follows with the instructive feedback, "Apple is a fruit!". Instructive feedback also can be used to provide information related to social performance. For example, after a student shares the control of a video game with a peer, a teacher might say, "Thank you for sharing. You also can tell your friend you like playing with them." When using instructive feedback, educators do not expect students to respond to the additional information.

Finally, educators can provide corrective feedback to assist students in identifying and correcting their errors. When using corrective feedback, the teacher identifies an error (e.g., "Duncan, I notice you just took Ryan's pencil without asking.") and provides information on how to perform the response correctly (e.g., "Ask Ryan if you can borrow his pencil."). For some students with ESN and CCN, corrective feedback may include minimal verbal feedback but instead might involve interrupting an error and providing a prompt (e.g., modeling the correct response) to support the student's accurate performance of the skill. It is important to note that corrective feedback should not be confused with verbal reprimands. It should be delivered in a neutral tone, stated positively (e.g., "Keep your feet on the floor" instead of "Don't kick your friend's chair," and when appropriate, should be paired with positive feedback following student performance of the corrected student response.

Forms of Feedback

There are countless ways that teachers can provide feedback to their students. For some, as described above, feedback involves providing access to a reinforcing item or activity. For others, it involves affirming or describing a student's response using vocal or written feedback. Table 8.2 provides several examples of feedback. When possible, educators should use multiple forms of feedback since students are likely to contact various types of feedback in the real world.

Educators also can combine forms of feedback to strengthen the effectiveness of a single form. For example, when working with students for which spoken positive feedback may be ineffective, a teacher might begin delivering spoken feedback as she delivers edible reinforcers. This process called "pairing" might increase the reinforcing effectiveness of the teacher's spoken feedback.

Teachers also should consider carefully how to deliver effective and noninvasive feedback to students with sensory impairments. For example, some teachers might use manual signs or written feedback for their students with hearing impairments. For deafblind students, educators might use appropriate "touch cues" or Pro-tactile American Sign Language (see Quartz, 2016) to provide positive feedback. For example, when it is time to line up and make a transition between classes, and teacher might consistently signal the transition is coming by gently tapping three times on the back of a student's arm.

Table 8.2 Examples of Feedback

Forms of Feedback	Examples
Access to reinforcing objects	Presenting edibles, tokens, or access to preferred activities.
Gestural	Thumbs up/down, smiles, pointing, "touch down sign," manual signs.
Written	Texted feedback, written comments, check marks.
Spoken	Whispered comments, enthusiastic praise, spoken model of correct responses.
Physical	Fist bump, high-five, pat on the back.

Table 8.3 Remote Instruction Resources

Online Tool	Link
Google Slides	https://www.google.com/drive/ Also see Mattson et al. (2020).
Boom Cards	https://wow.boomlearning.com/
Pear Deck	https://www.peardeck.com/
Brain Pop	https://www.brainpop.com/
Class Dojo	https://www.classdojo.com/
Seesaw	https://web.seesaw.me/
Edmodo	https://new.edmodo.com/

Virtual Feedback

With the shift from in person to virtual instruction (emergency remote, asynchronous, synchronous, hybrid) in 2020, teachers were required to consider how they might deliver feedback during remote instruction. Fortunately, an assortment of web-based platforms for educators is available to track student progress and provide immediate feedback. These technology-based tools can be used to provide audio, video, and written feedback in real time or post performance. For example, a teacher might use her cursor to provide error correction when a student points to the wrong vocabulary word during a lesson or may leave a video message on a student's learning management system in relation to their performance on a particular assignment. Teachers also might use digital classroom management systems where they award students for particular behaviors using digital tokens that can be exchanged for rewards (see Table 8.3).

It is also important to note that during remote instruction, some students may not respond to feedback provided virtually. As a result, teachers may need to recruit family members to provide direct feedback to their child. This will require that teachers provide training to parents to ensure feedback is delivered effectively (Stenhoff et al., 2020).

Providing Feedback and Other Potentially Reinforcing Stimuli

Feedback Should Be Immediate and Contingent

When providing feedback for student behavior, educators must make sure that it is both immediate and contingent. When feedback and reinforcers are delivered immediately (i.e., within a few seconds) following a target behavior, they are more likely to be effective (Cooper et al., 2020). Telling a student that they did a nice job on a task earlier in the day may evoke pleasant feelings but may have little effect on whether the performance is repeated in the future. Reinforcer delivery also should be contingent, meaning that feedback is delivered when and only when a student emits a particular response. Educators must be careful to only provide feedback contingent on target responses. Consider a student who is just learning to use eye gaze to make selections between two pictures. The student's teacher is so excited that the student is attempting to move her head and eyes towards a picture that she repeatedly offers praise for "trying" even when the student makes errors. Quickly, the student learns that moving her head produces positive teacher attention, instead of a particular response and persists in making errors during instructional sessions. Educators must heed that in the case of providing student feedback, timing *is* everything.

Schedules of Feedback Delivery

Closely related to timing is the consistency with which feedback is delivered. When teaching a new skill or trying to facilitate a student's use of one behavior (e.g., communication) over another (e.g., problem behavior) educators should provide feedback following every occurrence of the behavior. This continuous schedule of feedback/reinforcement helps students respond consistently to relevant instructional materials (e.g., saying "2" when presented the problem "1 +1") and environment conditions (e.g., asking for assistance when presented a difficult task). Once students respond consistently and accurately to instructional and environmental materials and conditions (e.g., three to five consecutive days with 100% accuracy), educators must start adjusting or thinning their schedules of feedback in order to promote the maintenance of performance in environments where feedback is in limited supply.

Thinning a schedule of feedback/reinforcement often involves shifting from a continuous to an intermittent schedule of delivery. For example, instead of providing positive feedback following every occurrence of a student's successful transition to a new activity, a teacher might provide praise or a token after every other transition. Gradually, the teacher shifts feedback delivery to every third, fourth, and fifth transition. Educators also might find it helpful to use a variable schedule of feedback and gradually increase the average ratio of feedback to student responses. For example, a teacher might provide feedback after every 2nd, 5th, or 3rd transition (i.e., average of 3). This variable schedule can make the delivery of feedback less predictable and reduce students' lapses in responding after receiving reinforcing feedback. When thinning schedules of feedback, it is important that educators make gradual changes to avoid what is referred to as ratio strain. Ratio strain occurs when the response requirement to access a reinforcer becomes too high and students stop responding.

When thinning feedback/reinforcement for target replacement behaviors, educators may note a resurgence or increase in the problem behavior. This is likely to occur because in the past a problem behavior has produced consistent and immediate reinforcement, so when the replacement behavior becomes less effective, the learner "shifts" back to using the more effective problem behavior. Consider that a young adult with ID has been taught to use appropriate conversation starters with a co-worker instead of invading their "personal space" to gain attention. Since the co-worker cannot respond to every bid for attention, they decide to only respond to their peer's bids for attention every now and again. After a day of thinning the delivery of attention, the young adult starts reinvading the coworker's personal space. One strategy that has been effective in reducing this resurgence, is providing noncontingent access to reinforcers during thinning. For example, when teaching a student to emit requests instead of problem behavior to access adult attention, a teacher might increase the frequency at which she interacts with the student during the school day. By providing access to reinforcers "for free" teachers can decrease students' motivation to engage in the problem behavior, decreasing the likelihood of resurgence. Other strategies involve teaching students when a replacement behavior will and will not produce reinforcement (multiple schedules), gradually increasing the length of time (i.e., delay interval) or a number of tasks demands (i.e., demand fading), or teaching student responses to a denial of a reinforcer (i.e., tolerance training). For more information on schedule thinning strategies see Muharib and Pennington (2019) and Hanley et al. (2014).

Considering the Content of Feedback

Educators also must consider the content of their feedback. In general, feedback should provide specific information to the learner about their behavior to avoid assigning attributes to students ("You are a good boy.") and help the learner clearly understand which response produced positive feedback. For example, during role plays of social interactions between peers, a speech language pathologist might tell a student with autism spectrum disorder, "Nice job, asking your friend how he felt about the movie." Educators also should consider students' receptive communication repertoire when providing feedback. For example, a student just learning to select objects in response to a teacher's directive (e.g., "Show me crayon") may not benefit from word-dense feedback. Instead of saying "Nice job, I like the way you touch the crayon," the teacher might offer a "Yes, crayon" while simultaneously pointing to the object.

Consider Culturally Responsive Feedback

Culturally and linguistically diverse (CLD) students with ESN experience similar challenges as their CLD peers without disabilities (i.e., gaining access to the general curriculum, services, materials, and purposeful collaboration between schools and families; Rivera et al., 2016). Supporting CLD learners with ESN begins with a classroom environment designed to be safe, inviting, and inclusive. Students' opinions are respected, and all are valued members of an extended classroom family (Cartledge & Kourea, 2008). Teachers can embed CLD practices into the delivery of effective feedback by considering students' culture when identifying reinforcers and using effective corrective and performance feedback. Teachers must acknowledge and accept that for CLD learners, what constitutes reinforcement may be at odds with cultural expectations (Sugai et al., 2012). Next, corrective feedback must be immediate, authentic, positive, and offered with sensitivity and respect (i.e., clear, free of innuendos, idioms, sarcasm, and plainly stated expectations). For example, if a student is being disruptive in the classroom, commenting, "Is that how you behave while you are in school?" may be too vague for some learners. Instead, a teacher might say, "You should lower your voice because we are in the classroom and do not want to disturb other students" and provide a model of using a lowered voice. Finally, performance feedback should address students' individual and cultural preferences by incorporating students' ideas, languages, and personal experiences (Gersten & Geva, 2003). Begin with establishing student connections and affirm student strengths to guide conversations and build positive relationships. Deliver feedback quickly, consistently, and provide specific actionable next steps for students. For example, by stating, "I was able to go over your test from earlier this morning, and we can talk about it more this afternoon" and "When you have finished your math assignment, you need to write the next problem, look over the notes we wrote in our folder for that." Last, remember to keep feedback focused and succinct. Point out explicitly where the learner was successful and where further support is needed. Culturally responsive practices promote the delivery of meaningful and timely feedback, thereby strengthening teacher rapport with students and facilitating successful self-directed learning opportunities (Hammond, 2014; McIntyre & Hulan, 2013).

Systematic Delivery of Feedback as a Behavior Support

Students with ESN are at risk for developing problem behavior. As mentioned above, this is often because they have not been taught more effective ways to change their circumstances. Educators can support their students in developing contextually appropriate skills while reducing problem behavior through the systematic application of differential reinforcement strategies. These strategies generally involve providing positive feedback (i.e., reinforcement) for desirable behavior while withholding or reducing the quality of feedback for problem behavior. Though there are multiple differential reinforcement strategies and several variations of each (see Cooper et al., 2020), three basic applications are functional communication training (FCT), differential reinforcement of alternative (DRA) behavior, and differential reinforcement of other (DRO) behavior.

Functional Communication Training

FCT is one of the most researched interventions for learners with ESN and involves teaching students to request reinforcers (Carr & Durand, 1985; Chezan et al., 2018). Prior to implementing FCT, the educational team conducts a functional behavior assessment (see Chapter 10) to determine the purpose a behavior serves for a learner (e.g., escaping a task to access the computer). Next, the team identifies a functional communication response (FCR) to replace the problem behavior (e.g., Saying, "Can I take a break," touching a break card). It is important to choose a response that is already in the student's repertoire and is easier to emit than the challenging behavior. Then, the teacher must prompt the student to use the FCR during a specified routine or activity (e.g., vocal model of "Take a Break"). This may require a high level of prompting at first which is ultimately faded (e.g., inserting time delay) as the student begins to emit the response independently. During the beginning stages of training, it is critical that all occasions of the FCR are reinforced while also withholding reinforcement as much as possible for problem behavior. Gradually, the team thins the schedule of reinforcement as described above.

Differential Reinforcement of Alternative Behavior

DRA behavior procedures are similar to those of FCT with the exception that the educational team can identify any alternative behavior (not just communicative) to serve as a replacement for the problem behavior. After conducting an FBA, the educational team identifies a behavior or set of behaviors that will produce the same reinforcers as problem behavior. The team then provides reinforcers for as many occurrences of the replacement behavior as possible while withholding reinforcers when the problem behavior occurs. Consider, a young man with Down Syndrome that frequently blows kisses towards his female classmates. His teacher decides to intervene by teaching him an alternative way to access his classmates' attention. She first selects a few target replacement behaviors (e.g., waves, asking about the weather) and tells the student that he can use them to get his peers' attention. She then coaches his classmates to acknowledge only his appropriate bids for attention and when possible, ignore his airborne kisses. In some cases, the educational team might target behaviors to reinforce that are physically incompatible with performing the problem behavior (i.e., differential reinforcement of incompatible behavior [DRI]). For example, a teacher might reinforce a student's in-seat behavior instead of wandering around the classroom.

Differential Reinforcement of Other Behavior

DRO behavior involves the delivery of a reinforcer for the nonoccurrence of problem behavior during or at the end of a predetermined interval of time. When planning for a DRO, a teacher first determines the DRO interval by dividing an observation period by the number of times a behavior occurs (e.g., 60 min/5 occurrences = 12-min interval). The teacher then reduces the length of the interval by half (e.g., 6 min) to increase the likelihood the student will earn a reinforcer. The teacher then informs the student that they will earn a reinforcer for not emitting the target problem during the interval. If the target behavior occurs during an interval, the teacher resets the timer and restates the rule. Some students may become frustrated if they do not meet the criterion for accessing reinforcers. To reduce this frustration and possible escalations in problem behavior, teachers can combine the DRO with DRA. For example, a teacher might use a DRO procedure to reinforce the absence of a student picking the skin on their fingers, while simultaneously using DRA to reinforce academic activities that involve her using her hands.

Withholding Reinforcement

One of the active ingredients in most differential reinforcement strategies is withholding reinforcers following the occurrence of problem behavior. For example, if a student engages in a tantrum to access their favorite game on an iPad, a teacher does not provide access to the iPad immediately following the tantrum. This "no reinforcement" or extinction schedule for problem behavior can be difficult to maintain in school settings. Consider the preschooler who stands on his desk or the adolescent who engages in self-injurious behavior to access teacher attention. In both cases, students are at risk for harm and thus, the adult must intervene. In these cases, a teacher should intervene but provide less of the reinforcer than available if the student engages in the replacement behavior. For example, the preschool teacher might walk over to the student, calmly say, "Get down" in a neutral voice and gently guide the student down from the desk or the high school teacher might use blocking procedures described in the behavior intervention plan but not provide verbal feedback of any kind related to the SIB. It is also important to note that it is not recommended to withhold reinforcement without providing an alternative way for students to access reinforcers. This withholding of reinforcers may result in an escalation of problem behavior and in some cases, the emergence of new ones.

Next Steps toward Better Practice

1. Since identifying powerful reinforcers is essential to effective programming for students with ESN, teacher should learn to conduct at least one preference assessment and use it frequently (e.g., at least weekly).
2. When planning for increasing a team's use of feedback, it will be helpful to determine currents levels of feedback delivery. Team members should spend some time observing each team member as they provide instruction to determine their current level of using feedback, and to set incremental goals for improving their feedback.
3. Educators should remember that feedback involves the behavior change of teachers, paraprofessionals, and sometimes, related service providers. It may be necessary to program supports to facilitate this behavior change including the use of self-management strategies, recruitment of peer feedback, and auxiliary cues (e.g., visual aids, timers).

The Big Five

1. Feedback is an essential component of instructional programming and behavior supports for all students, including those with ESN.
2. For some students, verbal or written feedback may not be sufficiently reinforcing to improve outcomes. For these students, educators should conduct preference assessments to identify potentially effective reinforcers.
3. Educators should align feedback to student's sensory and communication support needs to ensure feedback is both meaningful and dignifying.
4. When teaching new skills and establishing the effectiveness of new behaviors, feedback and other reinforcers should be delivered continuously but then ultimately thinned to reflect contingencies in natural environments.
5. When addressing problem behaviors, educators should use feedback and other reinforcers to guide students to engage in contextually appropriate behaviors instead of problem behaviors.

Resources

- Western Michigan University's Center of Excellence Autism Training Videos
  - https://wmuace.com/videos
- Autism Focused Intervention Resources & Modules
  - https://afirm.fpg.unc.edu/afirm-modules
- OCALI Autism Internet Modules
  - https://autisminternetmodules.org/

- Texas Statewide Leadership for Autism Training
  - https://www.txautism.net/

References

Carr, E. G., & Durand, V. M. (1985). Reducing behavior problems through functional communication training. *Journal of Applied Behavior Analysis*, *18*(2), 111–126. https://doi.org/10.1901/jaba.1985.18-111

Cartledge, G., & Kourea, L. (2008). Culturally responsive classrooms for culturally diverse students with and at risk for disabilities. *Exceptional Children*, *74*(3), 351–371. https://doi.org/10.1177/001440290807400305

Chezan, L., Wolfe, K., & Drasgow, E. (2018). A meta-analysis of functional communication training effects on problem behavior and alternative communicative responses. *Focus on Autism and Other Developmental Disabilities*, *33*(4), 195–205. https://doi.org/10.1177/1088357617741294

Cooper, J. O., Heron, T. E., & Heward, W. L. (2020). *Applied behavior analysis*. Pearson.

DeLeon, I. G., & Iwata, B. A. (1996). Evaluation of a multiple-stimulus presentation format for assessing reinforcer preferences. *Journal of Applied Behavior Analysis*, *29*(4), 519–533. https://doi.org/10.1901/jaba.1996.29-519

Fisher, W. W., Piazza, C. C., Bowman, L. G., & Amari, A. (1996). Integrating caregiver report with a systematic choice assessment to enhance reinforcer identification. *American Journal on Mental Retardation*, *101*(1), 15–25.

Fisher, W., Piazza, C. C., Bowman, L. G., Hagopian, L. P., Owens, J. C., & Slevin, I. (1992). A comparison of two approaches for identifying reinforcers for persons with severe and profound disabilities. *Journal of Applied Behavior Analysis*, *25*(2), 491–498. https://doi.org/10.1901/jaba.1992.25-491

Gersten, R., & Geva, E. (2003). Teaching reading to early language learners. *Educational Leadership*, *60*(7), 44–49.

Hammond, Z. (2014). *Culturally responsive teaching and the brain: Promoting authentic engagement and rigor among culturally and linguistically diverse students*. Corwin Press.

Hanley, G. P., Jin, C. S., Vanselow, N. R., & Hanratty, L. A. (2014). Producing meaningful improvements in problem behavior of children with autism via synthesized analyses and treatments. *Journal of Applied Behavior Analysis*, *47*(1), 16–36. https://doi.org/10.1002/jaba.10

Hattie, J., & Timperley, H. (2007). The power of feedback. *Review of Educational Research*, *77*(1), 81–112. https://doi.org/10.3102/003465430298487

Matson, J. L., Bamburg, J. W., Cherry, K. E., & Paclawskyj, T. R. (1999). A validity study on the questions about behavioral function (QABF) scale: Predicting treatment success for self-injury, aggression, and stereotypies. *Research in Developmental Disabilities*, *20*(2), 163–175. https://doi.org/10.1016/S0891-4222(98)00039-0

Mattson, S. L., Higbee, T. S., Aguilar, J., Nichols, B., Campbell, V. E., Nix, L. D., Reinert, K. S., Peck, S., & Lewis, K. (2020). Creating and sharing digital ABA instructional activities: A practical tutorial. *Behavior Analysis in Practice*, *13*(4), 772–798. https://doi.org/10.1007/s40617-020-00440-z

McIntyre, E., & Hulan, N. (2013). Research-based, culturally responsive reading practice in elementary classrooms: A yearlong study. *Literacy Research and Instruction*, *52*(1), 28–51. https://doi.org/10.1080/19388071.2012.737409

Muharib, R., & Pennington, R. C. (2019). My student cannot wait! Teaching tolerance following functional communication training. *Beyond Behavior*, *28*(2), 99–107. https://doi.org/10.1177/1074295619852106

Pace, G. M., Ivancic, M. T., Edwards, G. L., Iwata, B. A., & Page, T. J. (1985). Assessment of stimulus preference and reinforcer value with profoundly retarded individuals. *Journal of Applied Behavior Analysis*, *18*(3), 249–255. https://doi.org/10.1901/jaba.1985.18-249

Quartz. (2016, October 31). *Pro-tactile ASL: A new language for the deafblind* [video]. YouTube. https://www.youtube.com/watch?v=9GrK3P15TYU

Rivera, C. J., Jimenez, B. A., Baker, J. N., Spies, T., Mims, P. J., & Courtade, G. (2016). A culturally and linguistically responsive framework for improving academic and postsecondary outcomes of students with moderate or severe intellectual disability. *Physical Disabilities: Education and Related Services, 35*(2), 23–80. https://DOI:10.14434/pders.v35i2.22171

Stenhoff, D. M., Pennington, R. C., & Tapp, M. C. (2020). Distance education support for students with autism spectrum disorder and complex needs during covid-19 and school closures. *Rural Special Education Quarterly, 39*(4), 211–219. https://doi.org/10.1177/8756870520959658

Sugai, G., O'Keeffe, B. V., & Fallon, L. M. (2012). A contextual consideration of culture and school-wide positive behavior support. *Journal of Positive Behavior Interventions, 14*(4), 197–208. https://doi.org/10.1177/1098300711426334

9

Teach Social Communication Behaviors

J. B. Ganz, Daira Rodriguez, and Amarachi Yoro

Teachers should explicitly teach appropriate interpersonal skills, including communication, and self-management, aligning lessons with classroom, and school-wide expectations for student behavior. Prior to teaching, teachers should determine the nature of the social skill challenge. If students do not know how to perform a targeted social skill, direct social skill instruction should be provided until mastery is achieved. If students display performance problems, the appropriate social skill should initially be taught; then, emphasis should shift to prompting the student to use the skill and ensuring the "appropriate" behavior accesses the same or a similar outcome (i.e., reinforcing to the student) as the problem behavior.

Supporting Students with Extensive Support Needs

Emergent social communication and impacts on individuals with ESN. Social communication is central to quality of life, throughout the life span (Clarke et al., 2011; McNaughton & Light, 2015). It may be considered a basic human right that individuals, including those with disabilities, have the ability to impact their personal conditions, via communication (Brady et al., 2016). Communication is ubiquitous, observable in almost all contexts, and includes spoken, nonverbal, and written communication forms. Learners with ESN often display emergent social communication skills. That is, these learners may communicate through idiosyncratic behaviors or gestures, or via challenging behavior (American Psychiatric Association, 2013; Centers for Disease Control and Prevention, 2016) rather than age-expected language and nonverbal communication. They may not appear to be as socially engaged as their peers or display age-appropriate emotional learning and regulation. These social communication challenges can have negative impacts on academic learning and daily functioning.

Parents of children with ESN, especially those with emergent social communication, may express concern over the impact of their children's disabilities on short- and long-term outcomes for the child and for the family. These parents express challenges with chronic stress and fatigue (Krakovich et al., 2016), building warm and connected relationships with their children, and with caring for their children and managing challenging behaviors that result from communication challenges (Hirschler et al., 2015). Relatedly, these parents often face difficulties accessing resources and services.

DOI: 10.4324/9781003175735-10

Students with risk factors, such as poverty, or who are members of minoritized populations are particularly at risk for poor outcomes (Sacks & Murphey, 2018; Starr et al., 2016). These families typically face delays in referral for and access to timely diagnostic assessment (Mandell et al., 2009) and are more likely to experience misdiagnosis (Grindal et al., 2019), which also delays access to effective intervention (Amant et al., 2018). They face more challenges and inequities in accessing special education and other high-quality services than members of the dominant populations (Richards, 2020), particularly culturally responsive approaches (Becerra et al., 2015). English learners with disabilities are particularly vulnerable (Liu et al., 2015).

Learners with ESN often require direct teaching and attention to instruction across contexts for social communication skills. Without direct instructional consideration, this population is at risk for social isolation and limited participation in community settings (Clarke et al., 2011; McNaughton & Light, 2015). This chapter will focus on five key strategies to teach social communication to individuals with ESN including (a) naturalistic developmental behavioral interventions (NDBIs), (b) culturally responsive practices, (c) parent- and peer-mediated interventions, (d) focusing on generalization, and (e) integrating technology with instruction.

Chapter Objectives

Upon reading this chapter, you should be able to do the following:

1. Identify social communication challenges common in students with ESN.
2. Describe high-leverage strategies for teaching social communication to individuals with ESN.
3. Explain strategies to support diverse students with ESN and their families.

Naturalistic Developmental Behavioral Interventions

The use of NDBI is a key approach to teaching social communication behavior. Given the ubiquity of communication, instruction in social communication must be implemented across all contexts and with all individuals with whom the student with ESN interacts. Thus, unlike much academic instruction, social communication instruction must consider areas outside of classrooms that are affected by the student's needs. There is evidence that instruction in natural environments, with natural and distributed instruction, is effective in teaching new skills to students with some ESN (Gevarter & Zamora, 2018; Logan et al., 2017). Features of naturalistic interventions include implementing interventions within natural contexts, incorporating natural communicative partners, following the student's lead and responding to their initiations, and incorporating the student's preferred activities (Logan et al., 2017; Prizant et al., 2000). Naturalistic instruction involves preparing the environment and materials to elicit opportunities for instruction within natural contexts. Such approaches also frequently incorporate behavioral techniques, such as prompts and prompt fading, modeling, and programmed reinforcement, to provide direct instruction in emerging social communication skills (Logan et al., 2017).

NDBI refer to approaches that involve providing instruction within the natural contexts, with natural communicative partners, during naturally occurring routines, with natural reinforcement for targeted behaviors, and with natural materials in which the newly taught behaviors are needed (Ganz et al., 2019). These strategies typically involve child-directed activities and using materials that are reinforcing or motivating for the child. Further, they include strategies derived from behavioral principles and developmental science (Schreibman et al., 2015). This combination of empirically based approaches is particularly critical for teaching social communication behaviors, considering that much learning is based on the interactions between the instructor and learner or the learner and other communicative partners (Schreibman et al., 2015). Combining empirically supported behavioral strategies within naturalistic instruction increases opportunities for acquisition, fluency, maintenance, and generalization (Parker-McGowan et al., 2014). NBDIs have been found to improve outcomes, particularly in children with autism spectrum disorder (ASD), in social engagement, cognitive development, expressive language, and play skills (Tiede & Walton, 2019).

Researchers have identified several NBDIs with empirical support. In a recent comprehensive review of evidence-based practices for individuals with ASD, Hume et al. (2021) identified three manualized naturalistic interventions meeting their quality criteria: milieu teaching (Kaiser & Roberts, 2013), pivotal response trainings (PRT; Koegel & Koegel, 2006), and the Joint Attention Structured Play Engagement and Regulation (JASPER) approach (Kasari, 2014). Other NDBIs include incidental teaching (Hart & Risley, 1978), natural language paradigm, and the behavior chain interruption strategy (BCIS; Carnett et al., 2017). As described above, these approaches share several common features including environmental arrangement, prompting, and responding to learner interactions. For example, when using the BCIS, a communicative partner interrupts a routine (e.g., hides a straw needed to access a juice box), prompts a learner to respond (e.g., points to the picture of a straw on a speech-generating device [SGD]), and following the communicative response, provides the learner with the item or action needed to complete the routine (e.g., provides the straw).

Incentivizing Social Communication

Social communication may be challenging for individuals with ESN; thus, it is critical to incentivize communication and participation in communication instruction. This includes strategies such as interviewing stakeholders who are close to the child, asking educators or parents to complete checklists of potential reinforcers, and conducting preference assessments to determine the activities, items, and foods that are naturally motivating for that child (Ganz et al., 2019). Further, educators should provide high rates of praise and positive reinforcement and access to preferred materials throughout instruction to facilitate student motivation to practice new skills (Ganz et al., 2019). Identifying preferred routines and communicative responses that are immediately useful and naturally rewarding to that individual may also increase learners' willingness to participate in intervention. Communication temptations, such as enticing the child by showing them items they like without offering them, and BCIS techniques may be built into instruction to provide opportunities for the child to initiate learning opportunities (Carnett et al., 2017; Wetherby & Prutting, 1984). Finally, ending instruction when the child is enjoying the activity is preferable to drawing out instruction when the child is frustrated or bored, to maintain the reinforcing value of the activity and willingness of the child to participate (Ganz et al., 2019).

Behavioral Strategies for Social Communication

Modeling of social communication, including modeling of verbalizations, use of augmentative and alternative communication (AAC), and nonverbal communication, is a strategy frequently used with people with ESN and other disabilities (Drager et al., 2006; Ganz et al., 2019). If using communication devices, it is important to prepare pages in the system with adequate vocabulary prior to instruction; current technologies also offer just-in-time programming, allowing instructors to take photos of items and quickly record audio. Electronic AAC systems may offer a verbal model; when implementing lower-tech systems, such as picture point or picture exchange systems, it is important that the instructor also pairs the use of visual symbols with modeling the associated speech (Drager et al., 2006). Modeling of gestures, speech, and nonverbal communication is also critical, to provide the learner with numerous opportunities to associate those communication forms with their meaning. Prompting and prompt fading strategies (e.g., time delay and system of least prompts) are also critical for learners who require more direct instructional approaches, such as those with ESN (Ganz et al., 2019).

Culturally Responsive Practices

Culturally responsive teaching is defined as "using the cultural characteristics, experiences, and perspectives of ethnically diverse students as conduits for teaching them more effectively" (Gay, 2002, p. 106). Culturally responsive practices for educators have been part of the leading practices to reduce inappropriate referrals to special education and the disproportionate representation of students of color within special education (Cartledge & Kourea, 2008; National Center for Culturally Responsive Educational Systems, 2005). This is particularly critical when educators serve students with ESN, who may be less likely to code switch, or modify behavior based on the social norms across different settings, and who may not be able to communicate differences between home and school expectations. Culturally responsive practitioners understand how students' behavior reflect their cultural experiences and respond in ways that appropriately and proactively accept or redirect students' behaviors when necessary (Counts et al., 2018). A culturally responsive teacher exhibits an affirming attitude toward students who differ from the dominant culture, acknowledges the existence, and accommodates the diversity of thinking, talking, behaving, and learning in the classroom.

Parental beliefs and culture may impact parent behavior and parent–child relationships, and the responsiveness of parents and their children to educational strategies implemented by educators from the mainstream culture. Therefore, in order to effectively serve these parents, it is important for teachers or service providers to carefully consider cultural differences when providing services to parents. (Boyd & Correa, 2005). Being conscious of a parent's cultural heritage when providing services or directly working with them is another way of being culturally responsive.

During a training or coaching session, parents and service providers usually come together having different backgrounds as well as diverse experience and perceptions about their children with autism, services, and education (Boyd & Correa, 2005). The professional may often have a different opinion and belief which could be due to personal or educational experience. For example, a special education teacher could see disabilities differently because of the nature of their training and experience with this population of students.

Teachers who work on socio-communication for students with ESN need to be culturally responsive in order to respond appropriately to the diverse needs of their students. Classrooms contain students from different cultural backgrounds; thus, a one-size-fits-all approach may not support an inclusive classroom climate. Teachers must continually and deeply reflect on their practice to ensure its responsivity to the unique experiences of their students.

Cultural Self-examination

If a person's cultural background and/or life experiences are vastly different from those of people with whom he or she is interacting, there is a risk for culture clash or misunderstanding that can lead to conflict or misattribution (Gudykunst, 2003). This is particularly critical to consider in the case of students with ESN, who are less likely to communicate when they experience cultural clashes with educators or adjust to the differences between expectations within their home and communities, and their school. Therefore, teachers within diverse communities should become highly aware of their personal cultural background and lens for understanding behavior, as well as cultural norms of others, so that they can reduce attributions that may lead to prejudice. To conduct a cultural self-examination, teachers need to examine their beliefs and biases toward the students in their classes (e.g., Fiedler et al., 2008; Wisneski & Dray, 2009). Kendall (1996) suggests that teachers take the "emotional risk" to check their personal beliefs and consider how these beliefs impact their teaching. The essence of this inward reflection is for teachers to identify areas of change in how they respond to students who may be different from their peers.

Parent- and Peer-mediated Intervention

In addition to school professionals (e.g., teachers, speech–language pathologists, paraeducators, and behavior analysts), peers and parents are critical natural communication partners who are positioned to provide support in social communication learning to individuals with ESN. One approach to increase social interactions in individuals with ESN is through the use of peer-mediated interventions (PMIs). PMIs involve the use of typically developing peers to help model and prompt social skills to promote social interactions between individuals with ESN and peers (Sperry et al., 2010). These interventions allow individuals with ESN to practice social skills with different peers, thus increasing the likelihood that the newly learned skills will generalize across settings and individuals (Bambara et al., 2016). Typically, PMIs are implemented in naturalistic settings that involve daily activities. PMIs are particularly important as individuals with ASD often lack the ability to observe the behavior of their typical peers, therefore limiting their ability to acquire social skills (Brain & Mirenda, 2019). The aim of PMIs is to teach peers to interact more successfully with children with ESN, increase the frequency in which children and youth interact with typically developing peers, and promote positive and natural interactions between youth with ESN and typically developing students (Sperry et al., 2010).

To implement a PMI, it is important to consider the needs of the peer and the learner, by taking into account what goals may work best for the individual with ASD but also what will be feasible for the peer interventionist to implement (Simpson & Bui, 2016). Peer interventionists chosen to participate should exhibit good social skills, language, and age-appropriate play skills. Before peer interventionists can begin to implement the intervention, they must be trained on explicit support strategies. Successful implementation of PMIs require the peer interventionist to be confident in addressing challenges that arise while participating in the intervention.

Peer network interventions are a potential element of PMI. The focus of peer networks is to provide students with ESN with broader systems of supports in inclusive settings and to encourage increased social interaction between students with ESN and their peers (Carter et al., 2014). This systematic approach involves planning where, when, and how peers will be involved; recruiting appropriate peers; providing instruction to peers regarding their roles; facilitating interactions between peers; collecting data and making adjustments based on the impact; and generalizing implementation to new contexts (Carter et al., 2014). Expanding and supporting the peer support networks of students with ESN has been demonstrated to improve social interaction and engagement (Biggs et al., 2018; Herbert et al., 2020) and increase new social contacts (Asmus et al., 2017).

Through parent-mediated interventions, the parent takes the role of the interventionist to implement the intervention with their children (Oono et al., 2013). Parent-mediated intervention generally involves identifying potentially effective interventions, training parents how to implement the intervention, maintaining a collaboration relationship between parents and practitioners, and providing ongoing feedback to parents (Althoff et al., 2019). Initial parent training procedures may vary but typically involve behavioral skills training (BST). BST includes the provision of directions or written materials, modeling of the practice, and providing parents the opportunity to rehearse and receive feedback. Once parents are able to implement strategies with their children, practitioners provide ongoing support to facilitate maintenance of the practice and to help parents make adjustment as needed. Parents of children with ESN often face barriers to treatment and services; however, by engaging in parent-mediated interventions, educators can increase the accessibility and affordability to treatment (Trembath et al., 2019). Further, parent-mediated interventions may increase generalization of learning across environments and are associated with improved skill maintenance over time (Shalev et al., 2020).

Focus on Generalization

When teaching new skills to students with ESN, educators must consider whether those skills will be used or generalized outside of the instructional context to new people, materials, and settings (Johnston et al., 2012). Some students with ESN may have difficulty generalizing new skills without explicit programming (Brown & Bebko, 2012; Neely et al., 2016), especially those who use AAC. These students may be taught to use these AAC systems under conditions that may not reflect their daily experiences and as a result may abandon them (Moorcroft et al., 2019).

To facilitate generalization, educators should plan for and teach students to use social communication skills within naturalistic settings to the extent possible. This involves teaching students to initiate and respond to interactions about different stimuli, from different communicative partners, and in different settings. Further, educators should consider teaching students how to respond under different conditions. For example, students with ESN should learn how to recruit a communicative partner's attention, determine when potential reinforcers are and are not available, and how to use alternative forms of communication when necessary (e.g., SGD is not working). Finally, educators should evaluate whether their efforts at promoting generalization are effective by intermittently conducting generalization probes. These involve presenting new contexts to students and observing whether or not they can use the targeted skills under these new conditions.

Integrating Technology Tools

Some learners with ESN may not learn to use vocal speech to navigate the many complex interactions in the daily lives. For these students, the educational team may need to identify other forms of communication. These forms generally fall into one of two categories: unaided and aided communication. Unaided communication involves the use of speech or gestures (e.g., signs) and no periphery equipment (e.g., devices and picture boards). This form of communication is considered practical as learners, teachers, and parents are not required to maintain and make additional communication equipment available, but can be difficult to learn, especially for students without strong imitation skills. Aided communication involves selecting available words, pictures, or objects to communicate a message. This may involve exchanging a picture, pressing a word or picture on SGD, or hitting a switch with a part of the body to move a cursor through a menu of choices (i.e., scanning). Many students with ESN, much like students without disabilities, will use multiple forms of communication (Ganz et al., 2021).

Aided communication and gesture-based communication, commonly referred to as AAC, has garnered extensive research supports for its effectiveness in supporting social communication outcomes for students with ESN (Ganz et al., 2012; Ganz et al., 2021). Given the increased availability and rapid advancement of mobile technology, educators now have new opportunities to support the social communication development of students that use AAC (Edyburn, 2007; Zemla, 2012). For example, students for whom SGDs may be effective can now take their communication systems downloaded on a phone or tablet into a range of environments providing more opportunities to practice skills under natural conditions. These devices are equipped with increasingly natural digital speech and more fluid accessibility features. Further, technological advancements have made it easier for students with physical disabilities to express themselves using scanning software and a range of electronic methods of input (e.g., eye gaze and switches).

Next Steps toward Better Practice

This chapter presents five strategies that are effective in addressing social communication in individuals with ESN. To implement these strategies in-depth, readers are encouraged to seek further training in these areas and investigate relevant resources listed below. That said, there are some steps educators can take that may be manageable without extensive preparation and training.

Educators should implement social communication skill instruction within natural contexts, with natural communication partners, with natural contingencies, and with a wide range of materials and outcomes. Given the heterogeneity of effects of communication interventions across learners with ESN, it is critical that educators use professional judgment, knowledge of the individual with ESN, culturally sensitive and informative interviews and questionnaires with the individual or family members, and data on that particular individual when making instructional decisions. When implementing communication instruction for individuals with ESN, educators, in cooperation with family members and other service providers (e.g., speech–language professionals, behavior analysts, paraeducators, and general educators), should make decisions about what skills to teach, via what communication modes, in what contexts, with what communicative partners, and via what intervention strategies by considering data from numerous sources, including normed and other structured assessments, direct observation of current skills and deficits in authentic environments and contexts, family member input, and input from the individual, as possible. Given the ubiquitousness of communication, there should be ample opportunities to address skills deficits across settings, including any settings for which communication deficits are apparent and needed. Further, teaching skills across contexts and teaching a variety of skills from the outset is necessary to ensure skill generalization, particularly for learners with ASD and those who require a larger number of opportunities to practice skills.

Recruiting peers and parents as instructional or support agents will multiply the impact of instruction and is necessary, given that communication is used across settings. Some considerations include providing instruction to peers, parents, and other community members, to provide them with basic strategies (e.g., reinforcement and modeling) to support communication; we recommend teaching only a few strategies that may be most easily implemented and with high efficacy. By including family members in selection of goals and implementation, educators may better learn and use culturally responsive practices, such as including the parents' ideas regarding important social skills and necessary vocabulary and other social communication needs. Further, instruction should include rapidly expanding the individual's vocabulary, such as by continually adding icons to an individual's AAC system to allow them to communicate more broadly.

The Big Five

1. Naturalistic approaches that incorporate aspects of developmentally appropriate practices and empirical behavioral strategies are useful to increase opportunities for learning social communication, generalization of learned skills, and improvement in outcomes related to social engagement and communication. They involve strategies such as teaching within natural contexts, child-directed activities, using materials that the child enjoys, and incorporating behavioral strategies such as prompting, prompt fading, and reinforcement.
2. Culturally responsive practices should be considered where needed and involve engaging family members, understanding their backgrounds and experiences, and applying this knowledge to gain stakeholder buy-in and involving family members and their input into the education of their children with ESN. Key strategies include cultural self-examination, practicing mindfulness, having a plan for inclusion, and effective and culturally sensitive instruction.
3. Peers and parents may be the critical change agents in improving social communication in learners with ESN within natural environments and with natural communication partners. Teaching natural communication partners to encourage social communication skills may increase rates of acquisition and generalization of new learning across contexts.
4. Generalization must be planned for when teaching individuals with ESN new social communication skills, particularly those with ASD who may not generalize new learning without planned instruction. This is particularly critical given that communication is necessary across almost all contexts.
5. A range of technologies are available to increase the ability to communicate (e.g., AAC) and access services (e.g., telepractice for parents and educators in rural areas).

Resources

- What Works Clearinghouse (WWC). The WWC is a project of the U.S. Department of Education's Institute of Education Sciences. It provides reports of high-quality research to illustrate what works in education and includes intervention reports, practice guides, and resources for educators. https://ies.ed.gov/ncee/wwc/
- National Center on Intensive Intervention at American Institutes for Research. This national center is funded by the U.S. Department of Education's Office of Special Education Programs and provides support to educational institutions to implement intensive interventions for those with ESN, including resources on teaching social learning. https://intensiveintervention.org/
- National Clearinghouse on Autism Evidence and Practice (NCAEP). The NCAEP provides information on evidence-based practices for individuals with ASD and related abilities, a systematic review and report of these practices, and an evidence-based practice database. https://ncaep.fpg.unc.edu/
- Autism Focused Intervention Resources and Modules (AFIRM). AFIRM is a project affiliated with the NCAEP and provides instructional modules on planning, implementation, and monitoring of use of practices to improve outcomes for individuals with ASD and related abilities. https://afirm.fpg.unc.edu/node/137
- National Autism Center. The National Autism Center conducts systematic reviews of evidence-based practices for individuals with ASD and related abilities and provides related resources. https://www.nationalautismcenter.org/

References

Althoff, C. E., Dammann, C. P., Hope, S. J., & Ausderau, K. K. (2019). Parent-mediated interventions for children with autism spectrum disorder: A systematic review. *American Journal of Occupational Therapy, 73*(3). https://doi.org/10.5014/ajot.2019.030015

Amant, H. G. S., Schrager, S. M., Peña-Ricardo, C., Williams, M. E., & Vanderbilt, D. L. (2018). Language barriers impact access to services for children with autism spectrum disorders. *Journal of Autism and Developmental Disorders, 48*(2), 333–340. https://doi.org/10.1007/s10803-017-3330-y

American Psychiatric Association. (2013). *Diagnostic and statistical manual of mental disorders* (5th ed.). https://doi.org/10.1176/appi.books.9780890425596

Asmus, J. M., Carter, E. W., Moss, C. K., Biggs, E. E., Bolt, D. M., Born, T. L., Bottema-Beutel, K., Brock, M. E., Cattey, G. N., Cooney, M., Fesperman, E. S., Hochman, J. M., Huber, H. B., Lequia, J. L., Lyons, G. L., Vincent, L. B., & Weir, K. (2017). Efficacy and social validity of peer network interventions for high school students with severe disabilities. *American Journal on Intellectual and Developmental Disabilities, 122*(2), 118–137. https://doi.org/10.1352/1944-7558-122.2.118

Bambara, L. M., Cole, C. L., Kunsch, C., Tsai, S.-C., & Ayad, E. (2016). A peer-mediated intervention to improve the conversational skills of high school students with autism spectrum disorder. *Research in Autism Spectrum Disorders, 27*(1), 29–43. https://doi.org/10.1016/j.rasd.2016.03.003

Becerra, D., Androff, D., Messing, J. T., Castillo, J., & Cimino, A. (2015). Linguistic acculturation and perceptions of quality, access, and discrimination in health care among latinos in the United States. *Social Work in Health Care, 54*(2), 134–157. https://doi.org/10.1080/00981389.2014.982267

Biggs, E. E., Carter, E. W., Bumble, J. L., Barnes, K., & Mazur, E. L. (2018). Enhancing peer network interventions with students with complex communication needs. *Exceptional Children, 85*(1), 66–85. https://doi.org/10.1177/0014402918792899

Boyd, B. A., & Correa, V. I. (2005). Developing a framework for reducing the cultural clash between African American parents and the special education system. *Multicultural Perspectives, 7*(2), 3–11. https://doi.org/10.1207/s15327892mcp0702_2

Brady, N. C., Bruce, S., Goldman, A., Erickson, K., Mineo, B., Ogletree, B. T., Paul, D., Romski, M., Sevcik, R., Siegel, E., Schoonover, J., Snell, M., Sylvester, L., & Wilkinson, K. (2016). Communication services and supports for individuals with severe disabilities: Guidance for assessment and intervention. *American Journal on Intellectual and Developmental Disabilities*, *121*(2), 121–138. https://doi.org/10.1352/1944-7558-121.2.121

Brain, T., & Mirenda, P. (2019). Effectiveness of a low-intensity peer-mediated intervention for middle school students with autism spectrum disorder. *Research in Autism Spectrum Disorders*, *62*(1), 26–38. https://doi.org/10.1016/j.rasd.2019.02.003

Brown, S. M., & Bebko, J. M. (2012). Generalization, overselectivity, and discrimination in the autism phenotype: A review. *Research in Autism Spectrum Disorders*, *6*(2), 733–740. https://doi.org/10.1016/j.rasd.2011.10.012

Carnett, A., Waddinton, H., Hansen, S., Bravo, A., Sigafoos, J., & Lang, R. (2017). Teaching mands to children with autism spectrum disorder using behavior chain interruption strategies: A systematic review. *Advance in Neurodevelopmental Disorders*, *1*(4), 203–220. https://doi.org/10.1007/s41252-017-0038-0

Carter, E. W., Huber, H. B., & Brock, M. E. (2014). Developing effective peer networks. In J. E. H. Barnett & K. J. Whalon (Eds.), *Friendship 101: Helping students build social competence*. Council for Exceptional Children.

Cartledge, G., & Kourea, L. (2008). Culturally responsive classrooms for culturally diverse students with and at risk for disabilities. *Exceptional Children*, *74*(3), 351–371. https://doi.org/10.1177/001440290807400305

Clarke, M. T., Newton, C., Griffiths, T., Price, K., Lysley, A., & Petrides, K. V. (2011). Factors associated with the participation of children with complex communication needs. *Research in Developmental Disabilities*, *32*(2), 774–780. https://doi.org/10.1016/j.ridd.2010.11.002

Counts, J., Katsiyannis, A., & Whitford, D. K. (2018). Culturally and linguistically diverse learners in special education: English Learners. *NASSP Bulletin*, *102*(1), 5–21. https://doi.org/10.1177/0192636518755945

Drager, K. D. R., Postal, V. J., Carrolus, L., Castellano, M., Gagliano, C., & Glynn, J. (2006). The effect of aided language modeling on symbol comprehension and production in 2 preschoolers with autism. *American Journal of Speech-Language Pathology*, *15*(2), 112–125. https://doi.org/10.1044/1058-0360(2006/012)

Edyburn, D. L. (2007). Technology-enhanced reading performance: Defining a research agenda. *Reading Research Quarterly*, *42*(1), 146–152. https://doi.org/10.1598/RRQ.42.1.7

Fiedler, C. R., Chiang, B., Van Haren, B., Jorgensen, J., Halberg, S., & Boreson, L. (2008). Culturally responsive practices in schools: A checklist to address disproportionality in special education. *Teaching Exceptional Children*, *40*(5), 52–59. https://doi.org/10.1177/004005990804000507

Ganz, J. B., Earles-Vollrath, T. L., Heath, A. K., Parker, R. I., Rispoli, M. J., & Duran, J. B. (2012). A meta-analysis of single case research studies on aided augmentative and alternative communication systems with individuals with autism spectrum disorders. *Journal of Autism and Developmental Disorders*, *42*(1), 60–74. https://doi.org/10.1007/s10803-011-1212-2

Ganz, J. B., Hong, E. R., Leuthold, E., & Yllades, V. (2019). Naturalistic augmentative and alternative communication instruction for practitioners and individuals with autism. *Intervention in School and Clinic*, *55*(1), 58–64. https://doi.org/10.1177/1053451219833012

Ganz, J. B., Pustejovsky, J., Reichle, J., Vannest, K., Foster, M., Fuller, M. C., Pierson, L. M., Wattanawongwan, S., Bernal, A., Chen, M., Haas, A., Skov, R., Smith, S. D., & Yllades, V. (2021). Selecting communicative interventions targets for school-aged participants with ASD and ID: A Single-case experimental design meta-analysis. EdArXiv. https://doi.org/10.35542/osf.io/yx5au

Ganz, J. B., Pustejovsky, J., Reichle, J., Vannest, K., Foster, M., Pierson, L. M., Wattanawongwan, S., Bernal, A., Chen, M., Haas, A., Sallese, M. R., Skov, R., & Smith, S. D. (2021). Participant characteristics predicting communication outcomes in AAC implementation for individuals with ASD and IDD: A systematic review and meta-analysis. EdArXiv. https://doi.org/10.35542/osf.io/6sgba

Gay, G. (2002). Preparing for culturally responsive teaching. *Journal of Teacher Education*, 53(2), 106–116. https://doi.org/10.1177/0022487102053002003

Gevarter, C., & Zamora, C. (2018). Naturalistic speech-generating device interventions for children with complex communication needs: A systematic review of single-subject studies. *American Journal of Speech-Language Pathology*, 27(3), 1073–1090. https://doi.org/10.1044/2018_AJSLP-17-0128

Grindal, T., Schifter, L. A., Schwartz, G., & Hehir, T. (2019). Racial differences in special education identification and placement: Evidence across three states. *Harvard Educational Review*, 89(4), 525–553. https://doi.org/10.17763/1943-5045-89.4.525

Gudykunst, W. B. (2003). *Cross-cultural and intercultural communication*. Sage.

Hart, B., & Risley, T. R. (1978). Promoting productive language through incidental teaching. *Education and Urban Society*, 10(4), 407–429. https://doi.org/10.1177/001312457801000402

Herbert, M. E., Brock, M. E., Barczak, M. A., & Anderson, E. J. (2020). Efficacy of peer-network interventions for high school students with severe disabilities and complex communication needs. *Research and Practice for Persons With Severe Disabilities*, 45(2), 98–114. https://doi.org/10.1177/1540796920904179

Hirschler, Guttenberg, Y., Golan, O., Ostfeld, Etzion, S., & Feldman, R. (2015). Mothering, fathering, and the regulation of negative and positive emotions in high-functioning preschoolers with autism spectrum disorder. *Journal of Child Psychology and Psychiatry*, 56(5), 530–539. https://doi.org/10.1111/jcpp.12311

Hume, K., Steinbrenner, J. R., Odom, S. L., Morin, K. L., Nowell, S. W., Tomaszewski, B., Szendrwy, S., McIntyre, N. S., Yücesoy-Özkan, S., & Savage, M. N. (2021). Evidence-based practices for children, youth, and young adults with autism: Third generation review. *Journal of Autism and Developmental Disorders*, 51, 4013–4032. https://doi.org/10.1007/s10803-020-04844-2

Johnston, S. S., Reichle, J., Feeley, K. M., & Jones, E. A. (2012). *AAC strategies for individuals with moderate to severe disabilities*. Brookes Publishing Company.

Kaiser, A. P., & Roberts, M. Y. (2013). Parent-implemented enhanced milieu teaching with preschool children who have intellectual disabilities. *Journal of Speech, Language, and Hearing Research*, 56(1), 295–309. https://doi.org/10.1044/1092-4388(2012/11-0231)

Kasari, C. (2014). Are we there yet? The state of early prediction and intervention in autism spectrum disorder. *Journal of the American Academy of Child and Adolescent Psychiatry*, 53(2), 133–134. https://doi.org/10.1016/j.jaac.2013.11.007

Kendall, F. E. (1996). *Diversity in the classroom: New approaches to the education of young children*. Teachers College Press, Columbia University.

Koegel, R. L., & Koegel, L. K. (2006). *Pivotal response treatments for autism: Communication, social, & academic development*. Paul H Brookes Publishing.

Krakovich, T. M., McGrew, J. H., Yu, Y., & Ruble, L. A. (2016). Stress in parents of children with autism spectrum disorder: An exploration of demands and resources. *Journal of Autism and Developmental Disorders*, 46(6), 2042–2053. https://doi.org/10.1007/s10803-016-2728-2

Liu, K. K., Thurlow, M. L., & Quenemoen, R. F. (2015). *Instructing and assessing English learners with significant cognitive disabilities*. National Center on Educational Outcomes. https://nceo.umn.edu/docs/OnlinePubs/2015ELswSCDreport.pdf

Logan, K., Iacono, T., & Trembath, D. (2017). A systematic review of research into aided AAC to increase social-communication functions in children with autism spectrum disorder. *Augmentative and Alternative Communication*, 33(1), 51–64. https://doi.org/10.1080/07434618.2016.1267795

Mandell, D. S., Wiggins, L. D., Carpenter, L. A., Daniels, J., DiGuiseppi, C., Durkin, M. S., Giarelli, E., Morrier, M. J., Nicholas, J. S., Pinto-Martin, J. A., Shattuck, P. R., Thomas, K. C., Yeargin-Allsopp, M., & Kirby, R. S. (2009). Racial/ethnic disparities in the identification of children with autism spectrum disorders. *American Journal of Public Health, 99*(3), 493–498. https://doi.org/10.2105/AJPH.2007.131243

McNaughton, D., & Light, J. (2015). What we write about when we write about AAC: The past 30 years of research and future directions. *Augmentative and Alternative Communication, 31*(4), 261–270. https://doi.org/10.3109/07434618.2015.1099736

Moorcroft, A., Scarinci, N., & Meyer, C. (2019). Speech pathologist perspectives on the acceptance versus rejection or abandonment of AAC systems for children with complex communication needs. *Augmentative and Alternative Communication, 35*(3), 193–204. https://doi.org/10.1080/07434618.2019.1609577

National Center for Culturally Responsive Educational Systems. (NCCREST). (2005). Cultural considerations and challenges to response to intervention models: An NCCREST position statement. Retrieved from http://www.nccrest.org/publications/position_statements.html

Neely, L. C., Ganz, J. B., Davis, J. L., Boles, M. B., Hong, E. R., Ninci, J., & Gilliland, W. D. (2016). Generalization and maintenance of functional living skills for individuals with autism spectrum disorder: A review and meta-analysis. *Review Journal of Autism and Developmental Disorders, 3*(1), 37–47. https://doi.org/10.1007/s40489-015-0064-7

Oono, I. P., Honey, E. J., & McConachie, H. (2013). Parent-mediated early intervention for young children with autism spectrum disorders (ASD). *Evidence-Based Child Health: A Cochrane Review Journal, 8*(6), 2380–2479. https://doi.org/10.1002/ebch.1952

Parker-McGowan, Q., Chen, M., Reichle, J., Pandit, S., Johnson, L., & Kreibich, S. (2014). Describing treatment intensity in milieu teaching interventions for children with developmental disabilities: A review. *Language, Speech, and Hearing in School, 45*(4), 351–364. https://doi.org/10.1044/2014_LSHSS-13-0087

Prizant, B., Wetherby, A., & Rydell, P. (2000). Issues in enhancing communication and related abilities for young children with autism spectrum disorders: A developmental transactional perspective. In A. Wetherby, & B. Prizant (Eds.), *Autism spectrum disorders: A transactional developmental perspective* (pp. 193–214). Paul H. Brookes Publishing.

Richards, E. (2020, April 18). 'Historic academic regression': Why homeschooling is so hard amid school closures. *USA Today.* https://www.usatoday.com/story/news/education/2020/04/13/coronavirus-online-school-homeschool-betsy-devos/5122539002

Sacks, V., & Murphey, D. (2018, February 12). The prevalence of adverse childhood experiences, nationally, by state, and by race or ethnicity. Child Trends. https://www.childtrends.org/publications/prevalence-adverse-childhood-experiences-nationally-state-race-ethnicity

Schreibman, L., Dawson, G., Stahmer, A. C., Landa, R., Rogers, S. J., McGee, G. G., Kasari, C., Ingersoll, B., Kaiser, A. P., Bruinsma, Y., McNerney, E., Wetherby, A., & Halladay, A. (2015). Naturalistic developmental behavioral interventions: Empirically validated treatments for autism spectrum disorder. *Journal of Autism and Developmental Disorders, 45*(8), 2411–2428. https://doi.org/10.1007/s10803-015-2407-8

Shalev, R. A., Lavine, C., & Di Martino, A. (2020). A systematic review of the role of parent characteristics in parent-mediated interventions for children with autism spectrum disorder. *Journal of Developmental and Physical Disabilities, 32*(1), 1–21. https://doi.org/10.1007/s10882-018-9641-x

Simpson, L. A., & Bui, Y. (2016). Effects of a peer-mediated intervention on social interactions of students with low-functioning autism and perceptions of typical peers. *Education and Training in Autism and Developmental Disabilities, 51*(2), 162–178. https://www.jstor.org/stable/24827545

Sperry, L., Neitzel, J., & Engelhardt-Wells, K. (2010). Peer-Mediated instruction and intervention strategies for students with autism spectrum disorders. *Preventing School Failure: Alternative Education for Children and Youth, 54*(4), 256–264. https://doi.org/10.1080/10459881003800529

Starr, E. M., Martini, T. S., & Kuo, B. C. (2016). Transition to kindergarten for children with autism spectrum disorder: A focus group study with ethnically diverse parents, teachers, and early intervention service providers. *Focus on Autism and Other Developmental Disabilities*, *31*(2), 115–128. https://doi.org/10.1177/1088357614532497

Tiede, G., & Walton, K. M. (2019). Meta-analysis of naturalistic developmental behavioral interventions for young children with autism spectrum disorder. *Autism*, *23*(8), 2080–2095. https://doi.org/10.1177/1362361319836371

Trembath, D., Gurm, M., Scheerer, N. E., Trevisan, D. A., Paynter, J., Bohadana, G., Roberts, J., & Iarocci, G. (2019). Systematic review of factors that may influence the outcomes and generalizability of parent-mediated interventions for young children with autism spectrum disorder. *Autism Research*, *12*(9), 1304–1321. https://doi.org/10.1002/aur.2168

Wetherby, A., & Prutting, C. (1984). Profiles of communicative and cognitive-social abilities in autistic children. *Journal of Speech and Hearing Research*, *27*(3), 364–377. https://doi.org/10.1044/jshr.2703.364

Wisneski, D. B., & Dray, B. J. (2009). Examining diversity through mindful reflection and communication. *Focus on Teacher Education*, *9*(3), 2–4.

Zemla, J. (2012). *5 Great iPad apps for children with autism*. Yahoo voices. Retrieved from http://voices.yahoo.com/5-great-ipad-appschildren-8893899.html.

10

Conduct Functional Behavioral Assessments to Develop Individual Behavioral Support Plans

Sally Shepley, Kai O'Neill, and Katherine Lynch

Creating individual behavior plans is a central role of all special educators. The key to successful plans is to conduct a functional behavioral assessment (FBA) any time behavior is chronic, intense, or impedes learning. A comprehensive FBA results in a hypothesis about the function of the student's problem behavior. Once the function is determined, a behavior intervention plan is developed that (a) teaches the student a pro-social replacement behavior that will serve the same or similar function, (b) alters the environment to make the replacement behavior more efficient and effective than the problem behavior, (c) alters the environment to no longer allow the problem behavior to access the previous outcome, and (d) includes ongoing data collection to monitor progress.

Supporting Students with Extensive Support Needs

People behave in countless ways to improve their circumstances. They work, play, and engage in social interactions to access pleasant circumstances (e.g., increased attention and access to a preferred item or activity) and, in some cases, to avoid unpleasant ones (e.g., task demands and aversive conditions). Some individuals engage in contextually inappropriate or harmful behaviors to change their circumstances. These behaviors are problematic as they may impede learning, preclude access to typical or less restrictive educational environments, and result in harm. Students with extensive support needs (ESN) may be at more risk for engaging in these behaviors as they often have complex communication needs and, as a result, may not be able to use communication skills to control their access to preferred and nonpreferred circumstances. When students develop patterns of behavior that negatively impact learning and may be harmful, the educational team must engage in a process called FBA to determine the purpose (i.e., function) a behavior serves for a student. The FBA process serves as the foundation for building the behavior support plan (BSP) as the student's educational team uses data related to behavioral function, preferences, and strengths to develop an individualized BSP to teach the student alternative and safer ways to change their circumstances.

DOI: 10.4324/9781003175735-11

Chapter Objectives

Upon reading this chapter, you should be able to do the following:

1. Recognize the need for an FBA when students with ESN engage in challenging behaviors in school settings.
2. Describe steps for conducting an FBA, including both indirect and direct assessments, and how the results of these assessments lead to a hypothesis of behavioral function(s).
3. Describe how to use knowledge of behavioral function(s) to develop a BSP, using both antecedent interventions to prevent challenging behaviors and consequent interventions to improve appropriate alternative behaviors.
4. Recognize the importance of monitoring behavioral progress throughout FBA and BSP implementation.

Meet Lily and Manny

Lily is an energetic seven-year-old girl, who can often be observed smiling, laughing, and playing at the water table in her school's sensory room. Lily has a medical diagnosis of Angelman syndrome and a seizure disorder, and she is served under the IDEA eligibility of intellectual disability. Lily does not communicate vocally, instead she points to people (e.g., her dads and her special education teacher, Ms. Morelli), places (e.g., the playground and sensory room), or items she wants (e.g., water table and sink). In the last 6 months, Ms. Morelli has noticed some frustrating behaviors from Lily, which is unusual for her happy-go-lucky self. Some days, she will throw her work materials on the ground or push and hit the teachers working with her. Lily's dads indicate there have been no changes in the home or with her medical needs, but also that they do not observe these same behaviors at home. Ms. Morelli checked with the physical therapist to make sure Lily's ankle and foot orthodontics necessary for her gait and balance were not causing any pain, to which the physical therapist indicated everything properly fit. Ms. Morelli is very confused about these new behaviors, but also eager to figure out what function(s) this new behavior is serving for Lily.

Manny, or Manny the meteorologist, as he is proudly known around his high school, is a 14-year-old who desires social interactions with his peers and identifies as autistic. Manny has a medical diagnosis of level 2 autism spectrum disorder, moderate intellectual disability, and hypertonia. Manny requires reminders from his teachers and his mother to meet his basic needs; specifically, he does not notice the need to eat, drink, or urinate, which have resulted in a few fainting spells and many rushes to the closest restroom. Manny's speech regarding weather and natural disasters is impressive, but this level of vocal communication does not generalize to other topics. Much of his speech is scripted narrative from his favorite videos of natural disasters or weather reports. Manny's special education teacher, Mr. Basu, wants to foster Manny's interests in meteorology and help him socially connect with friends, yet his high-interest area is resulting in some social challenges and Manny's ability to learn new information. Manny will often close his eyes and make loud vocalizations imitating thunder crashes or volcano eruptions in the middle of class when the teacher or other students are speaking. Currently, Manny is not allowed to eat lunch in the cafeteria because he acted like a tornado three days in a row——swiping tables and throwing lunch trays in all directions. For Manny to access social opportunities with peers and increase his learning to hopefully obtain a weather-related job after graduation, Mr. Basu must figure out how to effectively decrease this challenging behavior interfering with Manny's goals.

Overview of Function

Generally, students engage in behaviors because they are effective in producing better circumstances (i.e., access to or avoidance of particular activities, objects, people, sensory experiences). By determining how a student benefits from emitting a challenging behavior, we can identify and

Table 10.1 Four Main Functions of Behavior with Examples

Function	Overview	Hypothesized Example
Sensory	Engaging in a behavior automatically produces a pleasant sensory feeling or automatically avoids an unpleasant sensory sensation.	*Manny might make loud volcano noises because he enjoys the way the noises sound.*
Escape	Engaging in a behavior to get out of or avoid an unpleasant or nonpreferred situation.	*Lily might throw her math manipulatives on the floor to get the academic work removed.*
Attention	Engaging in a behavior to access attention from other people (e.g., teachers, peers, and caregivers).	*Manny might act like a tornado in the cafeteria to make his peers laugh.*
Tangible	Engaging in a behavior to gain access to a preferred item (e.g., toy), activity (e.g., game), or place (e.g., playground).	*Lily might hit her teacher to get "calm down time" in the sensory room with her water table.*

teach an acceptable replacement behavior that produces the same desired outcome. Generally, the purpose a behavior serves for an individual can be categorized by four types of behavioral functions including (a) sensory, (b) escape, (c) attention, or (d) tangible. Behavioral function can be isolated (e.g., a target behavior is maintained by bus driver's attention) or multiply maintained (e.g., a target behavior is maintained by teacher attention and escape from math). More recent evidence suggests that some challenging behavior is likely a result of a synthesized function (e.g., a target behavior is maintained by the escape from independent work to access a classmate's attention; Hanley et al., 2014). See Table 10.1 for the description and example of each isolated behavioral function.

Application of the FBA Process

Conducting an FBA is a collaborative process that allows everyone on the individualized education program (IEP) team to identify and define target behaviors of concern and determine factors related to the persistent occurrence of a student's challenging behavior, including conditions that evoke or serve to trigger behavior and consequences that may inadvertently reward the behavior. Using high-leverage practices described in previous chapters (i.e., Chapters 1 & 3), teachers can collaborate with other members of the IEP team, including the student's family, to conduct an FBA which yields valuable information to allow the student with ESN to better access the curriculum and contribute to a safe and respectful learning environment. FBA results also reveal information that informs goal selection, instructional design, and curriculum modifications that may improve student outcomes. The FBA process can be broken down into six steps overviewed in Figure 10.1. The early steps start broad, are simple to implement, and are relatively subjective in nature. As the team moves further through the process, information gathered about the challenging behavior is more objective pointing to behavioral function(s); however, each proceeding step requires increased expertise to conduct.

Screen: Recognizing the Need for an FBA

Adhering to IDEA (2004), an FBA is required if a student with a disability has been suspended from school due to a challenging behavior for 10 or more days in a school year. Another legal obligation warranting a school district to conduct an FBA is if a change in placement is recommended due to challenging behavior. Additionally, IDEA mandates that an FBA should be considered when

Steps to Conduct a Functional Behavior Assessment

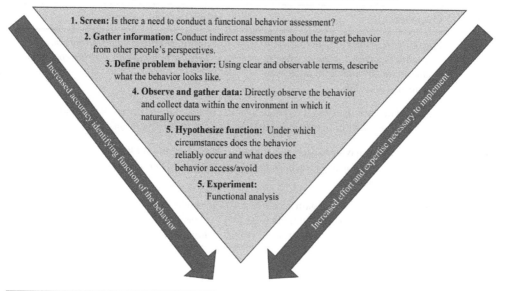

1. Screen: Is there a need to conduct a functional behavior assessment?

2. Gather information: Conduct indirect assessments about the target behavior from other people's perspectives.

3. Define problem behavior: Using clear and observable terms, describe what the behavior looks like.

4. Observe and gather data: Directly observe the behavior and collect data within the environment in which it naturally occurs

5. Hypothesize function: Under which circumstances does the behavior reliably occur and what does the behavior access/avoid

5. Experiment: Functional analysis

Increased accuracy identifying function of the behavior

Increased effort and expertise necessary to implement

Figure 10.1 Process Approach to Conducting a Functional Behavior Assessment

the general classroom behavior management strategies are proving ineffective and the behavior is interfering with the learning environment for the student or for their classmates.

Once the teacher has identified that a student's behavior is adversely affecting their achievement, they need to develop a general description of the behavior and its impact. The description should include specific actions the student emits, events or classroom situations that tend to increase the likelihood of the behavior occurring, consequences that typically follow the behavior, and experiences the student misses as a result of emitting the behavior. Next, the teacher can reach out to the team to ask if anyone else is observing similar behaviors and academic or social impacts during their instructional times with the student.

Gather Information: Indirect Assessments

Having consulted with other team members and determining that a student's behavior is having a negative impact, the teacher can select from a variety of indirect assessment tools to gather more information about the target behavior. Indirect assessments do not require direct observation of the behavior of interest; instead, they rely on another person's account or documentation of the behavior. When using these tools, the teacher looks for clues about physiological and environmental factors that may be causing or contributing to the occurrence of the behavior. Just as Ms. Morelli did with Lily's orthotics, it is important to rule out physiological causes for behavior before moving forward with the FBA process.

Indirect assessments come in the form of records reviews, checklists, rating scales, and open-ended questionnaires. A review of the student's educational file may reveal a previous FBA, or the present levels section in the IEP may describe patterns of behavior in the past. Rating scales and checklists, such as the Questions About Behavior Functions (QABF; Matson et al., 2012 and the Functional Assessment Screening Tool (FAST; Iwata et al., 2013), can be distributed to everyone who is observing the challenging behavior, including other teachers, related service providers, paraeducators, and parents. Open-ended questionnaires and interviews produce more robust information through detailed descriptions of the behavior, events that usually occur immediately before and after the behavior, the preferences of the student, and the interviewee's perception of why the behavior occurs. Examples of open-ended questionnaires include Open-ended Functional Assessment Interview (Hanley, 2009) and the Functional Assessment Interview (O'Neill et al., 1997), both of which are free to download and are in the Resources section.

Defining the Target Behavior of Concern

Creating a clear definition of the challenging behavior helps everyone on the team to understand exactly what the behavior looks like. Much like an IEP goal, behavioral definitions should be objective and measurable. A clear operational definition describes exactly what the student says or does with their body when the behavior is occurring and avoids the use of words that indicate emotions or internal states that are not objectively measurable. The definition should be so clear and concise so that someone who has never seen the student before could read the definition and recognize the behavior when it occurs.

For example, a clear operational definition would not focus on concepts such as angry or frustrated, because two people could interpret those differently. Instead, educators focus on observable behaviors such as grimacing, clenching fists, banging hands on the table, dropping head back and moaning, or other specific actions associated with the student's behavior. Strong definitions include examples and nonexamples of the behavior of interest. This is important because behaviors such as aggression and task refusal can manifest differently in different students. This level of detail and precision allows for accurate and reliable measurement of the behavior of concern.

Lily's challenging behavior is aggression, defined as any instance or attempt to hit or push her teacher and anytime she throws, rips, or swipes task materials. Nonexamples include using fingers to tap a teacher's arm, shoulder, back, etc. to gain attention, or throwing materials designed for throwing during play (e.g., tossing a ball).

Manny's challenging behavior is contextually inappropriate weather reenactment, defined as any instance in which Manny engages in vocal speech sounds that mimic the sounds of natural disasters (e.g., thunder clashes and high wind noises) or physically acts out a natural disaster (e.g., tornados and earthquakes) during a time when he is not authorized to do so. Authorized times for Manny to engage in these behaviors will be addressed in the intervention examples.

Observe and Gather Data: Direct Assessments

Direct assessments of behavior involve observing the challenging behavior as it occurs in real time and collecting objective data on the variables influencing the behavior. This part of the FBA process results in the most accurate information about the target behavior and the events that surround it. An observer records instances of a target behavior and the events that immediately precede and follow it. They also collect data on other environmental conditions (i.e., setting events) that may potentially contribute to the occurrence of the target behavior including the number of students and adults in the classroom, the date and time of the observation, the ongoing activity, and the person(s) interacting with the student. Ultimately, the teacher will use the data collected from direct assessments to hypothesize the function of the behavior by looking at the most frequent antecedent and consequent events, as well as common setting events. Direct assessments include a variety of direct observation forms, such as collecting structured or narrative ABC data, scatterplot data, and baseline counts of the behavior. Direct assessment data should be collected across all the settings in which the behavior occurs, whenever possible. These data can be collected by anyone who is familiar with the student if provided an opportunity to discuss the behavioral definitions and data collection system with the person who developed them. Figure 10.2 shows an example of structured ABC data collected surrounding Lily's challenging behavior and a summary of these data leading to a hypothesis of function(s).

Setting	Location:	Antecedent (What happened *before*)	Consequence (What happened *after*)	Notes
Date: *Feb. 17* Time: *8:30 am* People Present: ☐ Ms. Morelli ☑ Paraeducator ☐ SLP ☐ Other _____	☑ Classroom ☐ Hallway ☐ Cafeteria ☐ Other	☑ Given work or instruction (E) ☐ Preferred item taken away (T) ☐ Teacher attention diverted (A) ☐ Alone and doing nothing (S) ☐ Other _____	☑ Provided verbal reprimand/redirection ("no", "nice hands") (A) ☑ Work/instruction removed (E) ☐ Prompted to keep working/Ignore (S) ☐ Removed from location/activity (E) ☑ Provided a different activity or item (T) ☐ Other _____	*Math work-counting with manipulatives* *Given 5 mins with water tub at desk*
Date: *Feb. 19* Time: *10:00 am* People Present: ☑ Ms. Morelli ☐ Paraeducator ☐ SLP ☐ Other _____	☐ Classroom ☑ Hallway ☐ Cafeteria ☐ Other	☑ Given work or instruction (E) ☑ Preferred item taken away (T) ☐ Teacher attention diverted (A) ☐ Alone and doing nothing (S) ☐ Other _____	☐ Provided verbal reprimand or redirection ("no", "nice hands") (A) ☐ Work/instruction removed (E) ☐ Prompted to keep working (S) ☐ Removed from location/activity (E) ☑ Provided a different activity or item (T) ☐ Other _____	*Transition from sensory room to small-group reading* *Given 5 mins with water tub at desk*

(Collect data for 2-3 weeks)

People Count	Location Count	Common Antecedent Count	Common Consequence Count	
_20_ Ms. Morelli _10_ Paraeducator _3_ SLP _0_ Other	_18_ Classroom _5_ Hallway _0_ Cafeteria _2_ Other	(S) _0_ Sensory (E) _23_ Escape (A) _5_ Attention (T) _10_ Tangible	(S) _2_ Sensory (E) _21_ Escape (A) _7_ Attention (T) _22_ Tangible	

Figure 10.2 Example of Structured ABC Data for Lily's Aggressive Behavior at School

Hypothesize Function(s) of Behavior

Having completed the direct assessment, the teacher must analyze the data to hypothesize the function of the challenging behavior. Referring to the data collected through direct and indirect assessments, the teacher counts the number of occurrences of each type of antecedent and consequent event. The types of events are connected to the four functions of behavior: sensory (automatic), escape, attention, and tangible. Structured ABC data forms allow the user to easily count the number of occurrences of specific antecedent and consequent events. The most frequently counted consequence events typically point to the hypothesized function of the behavior.

For example, the ABC data above show common consequences for Lily's aggressive behaviors at school, which include instructional tasks and materials being removed and Lily being provided a different item or activity (likely water-based play). The data also show that common antecedents include the presentation of work or instructions and/or the removal of preferred items. This suggests that Lily's aggressive behavior is maintained by escape from work demands and access to tangibles (e.g., water play).

Test Hypothesis to Determine Function(s)

If you create a function-based BSP and it is not successful in reducing or eliminating challenging behaviors, then you may need to recruit additional support within your school system to help you complete the last step of the FBA process. This support is often overseen by a Board Certified Behavior Analyst (BCBA) in the form of development, supervision, and training to conduct a functional analysis of the challenging behavior. Broadly, a functional analysis involves altering variables in the environment to evaluate the conditions under which the behavior does and does not occur. That is, they create test conditions by withholding the potential reinforcer (e.g., attention, tangible item, and escape) to see if the student engages in the behavior to access that reinforcer. If the student does engage in the behavior, the BCBA reinforces the behavior by allowing the student to access or avoid the item or event that the student desires. These test conditions are compared to a control condition, in which the environment is set up with free access to reinforcers with the anticipation of observing little to no challenging behavior. There are substantial ethical considerations that one must consider before using functional analysis procedures, including adequate training of the implementer, the safety of the student and others in the classroom, trauma history, and the general well-being of the student.

Two variations of functional analysis are more suited to use in the classroom due to their efficiency: a trial-based functional analysis (Bloom et al., 2013) and the interview-informed synthesized contingency analysis (Hanley et al., 2014). The trial-based functional analysis includes dispersing specific test and control trials throughout the student's school day during naturally occurring times of the day. For example, a single test and control trial to assess if peer attention is maintaining Manny's weather reenactment behavior could be conducted in the cafeteria once a day. The BCBA alternates between test and control conditions of all hypothesized functions to determine which test condition(s) provoke the behavior and which reinforcers cause it to stop. The interview-informed synthesized contingency analysis allows the BCBA to test more an individualized and synthesized (i.e., combined) function in a quick four-to-five session assessment by providing (control) and restricting (test) access to multiple reinforcers at one time. This assessment can be done in as little as 10–20 minutes. The BCBA creates a single test condition that synthesizes two or more hypothesized functions identified by indirect assessment. For example, during Lily's test condition, Ms. Morelli would present work demands and remove access to any water play activities. If Lily aggressed during this time, Ms. Morelli would remove all work demands and allow Lily to play at the water table for about 30 seconds. This process repeats for 5 minutes to give BCBA the opportunity to observe if synthesized environmental variables (i.e., work demands and restricted access to tangibles) can effectively turn the behavior on and off.

Components of a Strong Behavior Support Plan

Based on the results of the FBA process, a BSP is developed to reduce challenging behaviors and improve appropriate behaviors. The BSP explains strategies adults can use to alter the classroom environment to prevent and consistently respond to the challenging behavior. Mindful consideration of the practicality of the BSP and the ability of teachers, paraeducators, and related service providers to follow procedures with fidelity is crucial for the plan's effectiveness. Initially, the BSP makes it easier for the student to access their reinforcers by using the student's baseline data to guide adults' delivery of reinforcers. Implementers of the plan must monitor progress, evaluate effectiveness, and use data to inform BSP updates when necessary. Using behavioral function to guide intervention, a comprehensive BSP incorporates both antecedent interventions, to prevent challenging behavior from occurring, and consequent-based interventions to replace challenging behavior with a safer adaptive behavior. It is critical to select interventions that are individualized and necessary for your student. As more interventions are added to the BSP, teacher and stakeholder implementation becomes more complicated and, likely, unreliable.

Antecedent-based Interventions

Antecedent-based interventions are preventative strategies that are implemented before the challenging behavior occurs; thus, making the behavior less likely to occur by providing the student with small amounts of the reinforcer in advance and lessening the likelihood that challenging behavior will occur to access it. For example, if Manny engages in loud weather vocalization during class to make his peers laugh and ask questions, a teacher can implement a noncontingent reinforcement strategy consisting of providing Manny with scheduled attention breaks at the beginning, middle, and end of each class period (e.g., partner games, praise for weather knowledge, and ask him a question about the weather). With attention from the teacher or peers readily available, Manny's desire for attention is satisfied and he no longer needs to engage in the challenging behavior to obtain it.

Antecedent strategies can target various aspects of the environment (e.g., increasing predictability in routines, increasing the frequency of providing praise, providing opportunities for choice making, presenting an academic task that the student will be successful with before presenting a difficult task, and reviewing social skills for specific situations prior to encountering those situations). Table 10.2 outlines four example antecedent interventions and how they can be implemented to align with a student's FBA results. Although antecedent-based strategies can be implemented as a stand-alone intervention, they do not teach appropriate alternatives to the problem behavior. Thus, their effectiveness is enhanced when combined with consequent-based interventions and implemented as part of a treatment package.

Consequent-based Interventions

Consequent-based interventions are strategies designed to make the problem behavior irrelevant to the student by changing the consequences that follow it. The FBA process determines the function of the behavior, showing us what the student is trying to access or avoid. This information is used to select consequent-based strategies that, when applied consistently, ensure that adults avoid responding to a problem behavior in a manner that reinforces it. Many of these strategies also involve teaching the student pro-social replacement behavior(s) (HLP 8 & 9) that will more efficiently allow the student to access or avoid the specific situation. Problem behaviors provide students with a way to get what they want; if they have a more efficient way to do so, they will no longer need to engage in the problem behavior. For example, teaching a student how to request a break or ask for help provides the student with a functional alternative way to obtain reinforcement (e.g., escape from difficult academic demands) without engaging in the problem behavior. Unless there is a serious threat to safety, reinforcement-only interventions should be implemented prior to considering interventions involving punishment or extinction. Negative outcomes of punishment- and extinction-based procedures include (a) the likelihood of an initial increase in the problem behavior (due to its history of reinforcement), (b) the likelihood of unwanted side effects (e.g., emergence of other problem behaviors such as aggression), and (c) a lack of educational value (i.e., these procedures only teach what not to do rather than what the student should do). Table 10.3 includes definitions and example applications of some consequent-based reinforcement strategies and extinction.

Data Monitoring & Analysis

As with all objective and scientific processes, data tell the story of how things started, how it's currently going, and what needs to be done next. Relying on anecdotal accounts of the behavior from memory is unreliable and misleading. Throughout the FBA process and into BSP implementation, teachers should continuously monitor and document occurrences of the target behavior through systematic data collection. When designing a data collection system, it is important to think about the best way to capture the severity of the behavior within segments of the school day, as opposed to trying to collect behavioral data all day. A complicated data entry system often results in confusion and abandonment; a simple and feasible data collection system will communicate progress when collected often. The following steps align with HLP6 and briefly summarize how to collect, monitor, and graph data, as a prerequisite to evaluating the effectiveness of the BSP and making data-based decisions about what to do next.

1. Using the definition described in Step 3 above, identify times of the school day during which the target behavior is the most problematic. This information is often identified during the indirect assessments described in Step 2 of the FBA process.
   - *Based on Manny's indirect assessments, it is reported that he often engages in weather reenactments during small and whole-group activities. Mr. Basu decides to collect data for the first 10 minutes of morning whole group and the first 10 minutes of math and reading small groups, for a total of 30 minutes of data collection three times a week. Figure 10.3 shows an example of Mr. Basu's data sheet.*

Table 10.2 Antecedent-based Interventions Aligned with Function-based Examples

Intervention	Definition	Function-based Application			
		Sensory	Escape	Attention	Tangible
Noncontingent Reinforcement (NCR)	A reinforcer is provided either continuously or at predetermined times regardless of student behavior.	Manny is provided scheduled access to similar sensory stimulation (e.g., audio of weather noises and videos of earthquakes).	Lily is provided scheduled breaks from academic work demands.	Manny is provided scheduled access to peer attention from a preferred person (specifically peers that enjoy talking about the weather with him).	Lily is provided access to the water table at scheduled times throughout her day.
Choices	The teacher provides multiple options and allows the student to select one of the options or select the order in which all options are completed.	Manny is provided with options of weather noises to listen to with headphones while working independently or is provided a choice between videos to watch of past natural disasters.	Lily chooses the order of work tasks to complete before earning a break.	Manny is provided the choice of which teacher or peer he wants to talk to about the weather during his scheduled times.	Lily is (a) provided with her choice of water-based toys to earn for completing work and/or (b) provided with her choice of item to have with her while working (e.g., water tube and water bead stress ball).
Priming	Exposing a student to information (via discussion, story, video, etc.) about an upcoming activity, event, or situation to prepare the student for what to expect.	Manny is informed about when there will be time to reenact weather events uninterrupted and is informed that the behavior will be interrupted during certain times (e.g., math time).	Lily is informed about how to request a break in an upcoming situation. Ms. Morelli could model the expected behavior by showing Lily a video of a peer raising her hand and handing a break card to an adult to request a break.	Manny is informed about what attention will be like in an upcoming situation. Manny is told that his reenactment behavior will be ignored and interrupted during academic times, and he will receive attention from his classmates during scheduled daily weather reports.	Lily is informed about what she must do before getting an item. Ms. Morelli could read a short story about how Lily needs to complete a math worksheet and then gets to play with a water-based toy (e.g., a water bead stress ball).

(Continued)

Table 10.2 Antecedent-based Interventions Aligned with Function-based Examples *(Continued)*

Intervention	Definition	Function-based Application			
		Sensory	**Escape**	**Attention**	**Tangible**
Visuals	Using materials as reminders or prompts instead of needing an adult to verbally direct the student. Examples include symbol reminders (e.g., symbols on desk to remind student to work quietly and raise his hand), first/then boards (i.e., visual depiction of what has to be completed to earn something), visual schedules, written/ picture prompts for directions, labels, videos, timers, etc.	*Two visuals are alternated on Manny's desk during math class to indicate whether it is an appropriate time to engage in weather reenactment (i.e., "Tornado Time") or remind to act calm with no noises and indicates that weather reenactment will be interrupted during that time (i.e., "Clear Skies").*	*A visual is used to inform Lily how to request a break in different situations. For example, during work time, Lily is shown a video model on her iPad displaying a peer appropriately requesting a break by raising their hand and using picture exchange.*	*A visual schedule is used to inform Manny when he can receive attention for his weather knowledge and reenactment skills. For example, Manny's visual schedule depicts what work must be completed before it is time for him to deliver the current or a past weather report to his class/school.*	*A visual is used to inform Lily when she will have access to her preferred items. For example, Lily has a first/then board that indicates she must complete her math work and then will get to play at the water table.*

Table 10.3 Consequent-based Interventions Aligned with Function-based Examples

Intervention	Definition	Function-based Application			
		Sensory	Escape	Attention	Tangible
Differential Reinforcement of Other Behavior (DRO)	A reinforcer is provided after a set amount of time in which the problem behavior does not occur. Reinforcers are not provided when the problem behavior occurs.	Manny is given an opportunity to watch a weather video or engage in weather reenactment after 30 minutes without any weather reenactment.	Lily is given a break from work demands following 2 minutes without any aggressive behaviors. Escape is not provided when she does aggress.	Mr. Basu provides individualized (e.g., weather related), high-quality, uninterrupted attention to Manny following 10 minutes in which weather reenactment does not occur.	Lily is given access to a water toy after every 5 minutes during which aggression does not occur. The toy is not provided when she aggresses.
Functional Communication Training (FCT)	A communicative response (e.g., verbal language, picture cards, and gestures) is taught to the student as a means of obtaining reinforcers without engaging in the problem behavior.	Manny is given an opportunity to watch a weather video or engage in weather reenactment following raising his hand and asking. Unauthorized weather reenactment is interrupted/blocked from occurring.	Lily is given a break from work demands after she hands Ms. Morelli a picture card to request it. Escape is not provided when aggression occurs.	Mr. Basu provides weather-related, high-quality, uninterrupted attention to Manny following an occurrence of Manny raising his hand and requesting to talk about weather.	Lily is given access to the water table or a water-based toy following an occurrence of an appropriate alternative behavior (e.g., handing the teacher a picture card to request it). Water play is not provided when aggression occurs.

(Continued)

Table 10.3 Consequent-based Interventions Aligned with Function-based Examples *(Continued)*

Intervention	Definition	Function-based Application			
		Sensory	Escape	Attention	Tangible
Differential Reinforcement of Low Rates of Behavior (DRL)	A reinforcer is provided when (a) the rate of a behavior is at or below a predetermined amount or (b) a predetermined amount of time passes between occurrences of the behavior. The predetermined rate is gradually reduced, or amount of time between the occurrences is gradually increased based on student performance.	*Manny is given an opportunity to engage in safe weather reenactment if the behavior occurs two or fewer times in a 30-minute work session.*	*Lily is given a break from work demands if 10 minutes pass between occurrences of aggression.*	*Mr. Basu provides individualized (e.g., weather related), high-quality, uninterrupted attention to Manny if 20 minutes pass between occurrences of the behavior.*	*Lily is given access to water play if she aggresses two or fewer times in a 15-minute time frame or if 10 minutes pass between occurrences of aggression.*
Extinction	Previous reinforcers are no longer provided when the problem behavior occurs.	*An adult blocks Manny from engaging in weather reenactment so that the sensation gained by engaging in the behavior is not felt/heard.*	*Escape from work demands is not provided when Lily aggresses.*	*Attention is not provided when Manny engages in weather reenactment.*	*Access to the water table and water toys is not provided when Lily engages in aggression.*

Partial-Interval Recording		
Directions: Place a (+) if at any point in a single interval the student engages in the target behavior. Place a (–) if the student does not engage in the target behavior at all during a single interval.		
Student: *Manny*	Week of: *March 07*	Interval Length: 1 *minute*
Target Behavior: *Contextually inappropriate weather reenactment (see operational definition)*		

Date:	March 07			March 08			March 11		
Minute	AM Whole-Grp	Math Small-Grp	Read Small-Grp	AM Whole-Grp	Math Small-Grp	Read Small-Grp	AM Whole-Grp	Math Small-Grp	Read Small-Grp
1	–	–	–	–	+	–	–	–	+
2	–	–	+	–	+	+	–	+	+
3	+	+	+	+	–	+	–	+	+
4	+	+	–	–	+	–	+	+	–
5	+	–	–	–	+	–	–	+	–
6	–	–	–	–	+	+	+	+	+
7	+	+	+	–	–	–	+	–	+
8	+	+	+	+	–	+	+	–	+
9	–	+	+	+	+	–	–	+	+
10	–	+	+	–	+	–	–	+	–
Total (+)	16			14			18		
	Total (+) ÷ 30 × 100			Total (+) ÷ 30 × 100			Total (+) ÷ 30 × 100		
Percentage	53%			47%			60%		

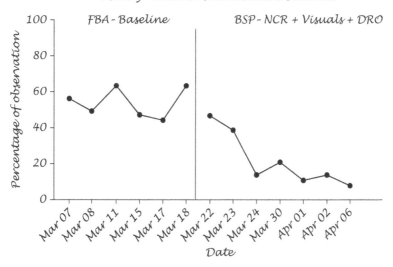

Manny- Weather Reenactment Behavior

Figure 10.3 Data Monitoring and Analysis of Manny's Challenging Behavior at School

2. Collect data within your defined observation time as often as possible, ideally a minimum of three times a week. It is important to stick to a schedule for data collection to avoid bias, such as choosing only to take data on particularly challenging days. Summarize the data from a single observation into a total count, rate, or percentage based on the dimension of behavior being captured.

3. Data should be aggregated into a graph to allow for concise and ongoing evaluation. A visual representation of how much problem behavior is occurring communicates to the IEP team that a BSP is needed and later informs how well the plan is improving the targeted behavior (see Figure 10.3 for an example graph of Manny's behavior before and after implementation of his BSP).

Once a function-based intervention with a combination of antecedent- and consequence-based components is in place, continue to collect data a minimum of three times each week. This formative assessment of problem behavior guides the education team on what to do next. Based on decades of research from Browder et al. (1986), the guidelines outlined in Figure 10.4 can be used to analyze data collected, make a data-based decision, implement the recommended change, and then reevaluate by visually analyzing the data again.

Next Steps Toward Better Practice

1. Challenging behavior in the classroom can be very taxing and frustrating for all involved. Remember to mentally step back from the immediate situation and analyze the environments in which the behavior is and is not occurring.
2. Go through the FBA steps one at a time until you have the data needed to formulate a hypothesis about the function of the problem behavior. Remember to include various key stakeholders (e.g., caregivers, teachers, peers, and related service providers) to provide input and accounts of the behavior in various contexts.
3. When implementing the BSP, give it time. Challenging behavior did not appear overnight, nor will it disappear overnight. Be prepared for and proud of small successes; this means you're on the right track.
4. Don't stop implementing the BSP when problem behavior seems to have disappeared; this can result in resurgence and potentially more harmful topographies. Keep it in place and fade systematically.

If Your Graph Indicates...   Then You Need To...

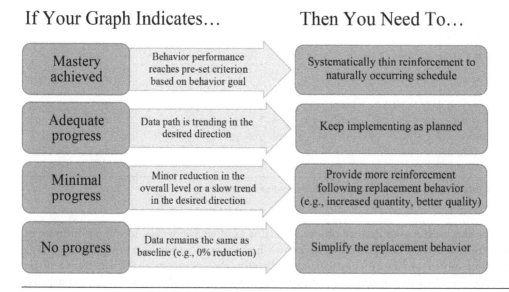

If Your Graph Indicates...		Then You Need To...
Mastery achieved	Behavior performance reaches pre-set criterion based on behavior goal	Systematically thin reinforcement to naturally occurring schedule
Adequate progress	Data path is trending in the desired direction	Keep implementing as planned
Minimal progress	Minor reduction in the overall level or a slow trend in the desired direction	Provide more reinforcement following replacement behavior (e.g., increased quantity, better quality)
No progress	Data remains the same as baseline (e.g., 0% reduction)	Simplify the replacement behavior

Figure 10.4 Recommendations for Making Data-based Decisions

The Big Five

1. All behavior has a function; it serves a purpose for the student. It's our job to figure out what our students with ESN are trying to tell us when they engage in challenging behaviors. This discovery process is referred to as an FBA.
2. Without knowing the function of a behavior, educators and interventionists default to trial and error technologies, most of which are punishment based. This often results in more damage to the learning environment and does not teach the student what they should do instead.
3. The FBA process is comprehensive, investigative, holistic, and scientific. The process is organic, meaning no two students will need the exact same combination of indirect and direct assessments to determine function.
4. A good BSP will not only decrease the behavior of concern when implemented correctly, it will also teach your student an appropriate way to get what they need.
5. To effectively communicate the severity of the problem behavior before the BSP and the extent of behavior change once a BSP is put in place, objective and quantitative data must be collected throughout the FBA and BSP process.

Resources

- Dr. Greg Hanley—Practical Functional Assessment: Understanding Problem Behavior Prior to its Treatment (https://practicalfunctionalassessment.com/)
- Vanderbilt's IRIS Center—Functional Behavioral Assessment: Identifying the Reasons for Problem Behavior and Developing a Behavior Plan (https://iris.peabody.vanderbilt.edu/module/fba/)
- The Association for Positive Behavior Support (https://www.apbs.org/)
- Texas Statewide Leadership for Autism Training (https://www.txautism.net/)
- Connect Ability Canada: Behaviour (https://connectability.ca/2014/06/14/behaviour/)

References

Bloom, S. E., Lambert, J. M., Dayton, E., & Samaha, A. L. (2013). Teacher-conducted trial-based functional analyses as the basis for intervention. *Journal of Applied Behavior Analysis*, 46(1), 208–218. https://doi.org/10.1002/jaba.21

Browder, D. M., Liberty, K., Heller, M., & D'Huyvetters, K. K. (1986). Self-management by teachers: Improving instructional decision making. *Professional School Psychology*, 1(3), 165–175. https://doi.org/10.1037/h0090506

Hanley, G. P. (2009). *Open-Ended Functional Assessment Interview*. https://www.abainternational.org/media/46721/hanleyfainterview.pdf

Hanley, G. P., Jin, C. S., Vanselow, N. R., & Hanratty, L. A. (2014). Producing meaningful improvements in problem behavior of children with autism via synthesized analyses and treatments. *Journal of Applied Behavior Analysis*, 47(1), 16–36. https://doi.org/10.1002/jaba.106

Individuals with Disabilities Education Act, 20 U.S.C. § 1400 (2004).

Iwata, B. A., DeLeon, I. G., & Roscoe, E. M. (2013). Reliability and validity of the functional analysis screening tool. *Journal of Applied Behavior Analysis*, 46(1), 271–284. https://doi.org/10.1002/jaba.31

Matson, J. L., Tureck, K., & Rieske, R. (2012). The questions about behavioral function (QABF): Current status as a method of functional assessment. *Research in Developmental Disabilities*, 33(2), 630–634. https://doi.org/10.1016/j.ridd.2011.11.006

O'Neill, R. E., Horner, R. H., Albin, R. W., Sprague, J. R., Storey, K., & Newton, J. S. (1997). *Functional assessment for problem behavior: A practical handbook* (2nd ed.). Brooks/Cole Publishing Company.

11
Identify and Prioritize Long- and Short-term Learning Goals

Students with Extensive Support Needs
Andrea Ruppar, Sarah Bubash, and Jennifer Kurth

Teachers prioritize what is most important for students to learn by providing meaningful access to and success in the general education and other contextually relevant curricula. Teachers use grade-level standards, assessment data and learning progressions, students' prior knowledge, and IEP goals and benchmarks to make decisions about what is most crucial to emphasize and develop long- and short-term goals accordingly. They understand essential curriculum components, identify essential prerequisites and foundations, and assess student performance in relation to these components.

Supporting Students with Extensive Support Needs

Planning and prioritizing short- and long-term goals for students with ESN requires careful collaboration among teachers, the student, their family, and related service providers. Effective and ethical planning centers the student in the process, and short- and long-term goals are identified using a thorough assessment of the student's desired post-school outcomes, interests, and strengths. To maintain equitable opportunities and experiences in school, curriculum content should be based on age-appropriate grade-level standards. Additionally, team members should teach any skills that might be necessary for the student to fully participate in everyday life. These skills might include social skills, communication skills, self-determination skills, behavioral skills, mobility skills, and adaptive skills such as self-care. Because curriculum content is designed to teach students skills necessary for participating in current and future inclusive environments, students should be taught within the inclusive settings that naturally occasion the use of those skills.

As Billingsley et al. (1996) explained, educational decisions about students with ESN should increase *membership* in a variety of groups, increase *relationships* with peers, and increase *skills* necessary to maintain membership and build relationships. Broadly speaking, short- and long-term goals should prioritize high-impact skills that are generalizable across many different settings and situations and are particularly useful in everyday contexts where individuals with and without disabilities live, work, and play. Because educators plan based on students' current *and future* environments, the short- and long-term goals should be aligned with the overall goal of increasing membership and participation in inclusive communities beyond school.

DOI: 10.4324/9781003175735-12

While access to general education content and teaching meaningful skills in general education settings is the current state of the art for students with ESN, this was not always the case. Students with ESN rarely attended school prior to PL 94-142 in 1975. At the time, students' curriculum content was based on assumptions about their developmental or "mental age." (Browder et al., 2003). This resulted in students spending extensive amounts of time practicing age-inappropriate skills that had little utility in everyday contexts. Students graduated with few skills that would be useful for their lives as adults living in the community. Seeing this as problematic, Brown et al. (1979) described a new approach to curriculum development which came to be known as a *functional curriculum*. In a functional approach, students learned skills that were judged to be useful in their current and future environments, preparing them for lives as adults who lived and worked in typical communities. The functional approach retained dominance as the most widely applied and studied framework in curriculum for students with ESN for several decades (Shurr & Bouck, 2013.).

As Brown et al. (1979) pushed the field to consider inclusive adult workplaces and communities when identifying curriculum for students with ESN, a movement began to promote inclusion in schools as well. Placement of students with ESN in general education classes, rather than in segregated special education classes, raised new questions about how curriculum content should be determined. At first, social skills were emphasized in general education classes, and little attention was given to providing students with access to the content of the classes (Dymond & Orelove, 2001). However, as the No Child Left Behind Act of 2001 and the Individuals with Disabilities Education Act (2004) required all students to be provided access to the general curriculum, questions arose about how this requirement might apply to students with ESN.

Since that time, there have been disagreements about the extent to which educators should "balance" general curriculum content with other skills students might need to learn (Ayres et al., 2011; Courtade et al., 2012; Dymond & Orelove, 2001; Hunt et al., 2012; Timberlake, 2014). It also became evident that students should learn self-determination, to make and express decisions and maintain control over their lives (Shogren et al., 2015). Although some may disagree, most current thinking suggests that curriculum for students with ESN should be grounded in age-appropriate academic and non-academic skills which are contextually relevant and personally meaningful and promote full participation and self-determination in inclusive environments.

Chapter Objectives

Upon reading this chapter, you should be able to do the following:

1. Identify meaningful, high-priority, and generalizable learning goals for students with ESN.
2. Use a person-centered approach to choosing learning goals, including students and families in the process.
3. Engage in cross-disciplinary teaming to develop goals that can be addressed in a variety of environments.
4. Conduct an ecological inventory to identify contextually relevant learning goals.
5. Identify goals aligned with grade-level standards that are personally meaningful for students.

Identify and Prioritize Long- and Short-term Learning Goals

The options for curriculum content are seemingly endless for students with ESN, and it can be difficult for teams to know where to start when selecting curriculum content. Goals need to be meaningful, high priority, and generalizable. Person-centered approaches can help teams narrow the field of possible goals in order to choose the most personally relevant content to teach across a variety of environments. Any given goal should be addressed in more than one inclusive context; if there is no use for a goal in more than one inclusive context, it is not likely to be generalized or maintained—and therefore lacks meaning for the student. Trans-disciplinary teams use ecological assessments to collectively identify common goals. Goals should be grade aligned and should address self-determination, including self-management, self-advocacy, choice and communication, decision-making, and problem-solving.

Identify Meaningful, High-priority, and Generalizable Learning Goals for Students with Extensive Support Needs

Meaningful Goals

Goals that are meaningful make sense from the student's point of view. If it is not clear why a student might need to learn a skill, it is likely that the goal is not meaningful for the student. Teachers should be careful to choose skills based on the students' current and future school, home, community, and/or employment contexts, depending on the student's age. Skills that can be used in these contexts, and advance membership and relationships in these contexts, should be prioritized over isolated skills that are only useful in the context of a special education classroom or therapy office.

Taking the student's point of view also requires teachers to consider the student's personal motivation for learning the skill (e.g., calling friends by name might be reinforcing for a student who is very social). In this way, what is meaningful for one student might not be meaningful for another student. The ultimate function of using the skill should ultimately be reinforcing for the student, and additional reinforcers should no longer be necessary for the student to perform the skill in everyday contexts (Horner et al., 1985).

High-priority Goals

High-priority goals target the most important skills necessary for the student to participate in everyday, age-appropriate activities. Some of the highest priority skills for students with ESN relate to communication, including teaching communicative replacements for challenging behavior. Communication also encompasses literacy, which includes reading, writing, listening, and speaking (Copeland & Keefe, 2018). Skills necessary for participation in age-appropriate general education contexts should also be prioritized, including academic goals focusing on math, social studies, and science; and non-academic goals such as personal management, mobility, social skills, or assistive technology use.

Generalizable Goals

Generalizable goals target skills that are useful in more than one context. Context is especially important to consider when determining if a skill is generalizable. Typically, a skill that is useful in only one context, such as completing a math worksheet, is less generalizable than application of math skills in everyday problem-solving contexts. Selecting a clear generalization strategy (Stokes & Baer, 1977) is helpful to ensure that the skills are useful and reinforcing in a variety of natural contexts.

Use a Person-centered Approach to Choosing Learning Goals, Including Students and Families in the Process

Person-centered approaches address individual needs first, rather than the systems in which they operate. There are a variety of person-centered approaches, such as MAPS, PATH, etc. (O'Brien & O'Brien, 2002). All have the following features in common:

1. The person is at the center: Person-centered planning is rooted in the principles of rights, independence, and choice. It requires careful listening to the person and results in informed set of choices about how the person wants to live and what supports best suit the individual.

2. Family members and friends are full partners: Person-centered planning puts people in context of their family and communities. The contributions that friends and families can make are recognized and valued and give a forum for creatively negotiating conflicts about what is safe, possible, or desirable to improve a person's life.

3. Person-centered planning reflects a person's capacity, what is important to a person (now and for the future), and specifies the support required for the person to participate in and make a valued contribution to their community. Services are delivered in the context of the life a person chooses.

One research-based person-centered planning tool is designed specifically for students with ESN in schools. *Choosing Outcomes and Accommodations for Children (COACH;* Giangreco et al., 2011) guides educational teams through a set of steps for prioritizing a small set of trans-disciplinary goals and planning for instruction. The process begins with an extensive family interview, which guides teachers and families through a process of discussing valued life outcomes and aligning those outcomes to specific academic and non-academic priorities. A trans-disciplinary team then convenes to develop these priorities into shared, measurable IEP goals. A creative problem-solving approach guides conversation and ensures students' instructional and access needs are identified and addressed across team members.

Engage in Trans-disciplinary Teaming to Develop Goals That Can Be Addressed in a Variety of Environments

Trans-disciplinary Teaming

Students with complex access and support needs require a team of professionals who collaborate to plan instruction and assessment. No one person will have in-depth knowledge of all affected areas; however, team members can provide complementary expertise and collectively engage in instruction and planning. Trans-disciplinary goals ensure that multiple team members participate in the planning and implementation of a small set of goals that are useful for the student in many different settings. A trans-disciplinary approach differs from a multi-disciplinary or cross-disciplinary approach because it emphasizes a shared vision and a collection of shared goals across all service providers. This is especially important for teams supporting students with ESN because they require multiple opportunities to practice skills across a variety of environments and with a variety of people to achieve generalization (see Chapter 20, this text). Without trans-disciplinary teaming, a team risks isolated, discipline-specific goals, pullout approaches rather than inclusive services, diminished coordination and communication, and confusion for families (Giangreco et al., 2011).

Writing Team-based Goals

Team-based goals are shared goals across team members. Instead of separate goals related to academics, speech–language pathology, occupational therapy, physical therapy, and other specific disciplines, team goals are a shared set of goals that are addressed by multiple team members. For example, a goal for choice making using picture symbols could be addressed by the following team members in the following ways:

1. The speech–language pathologist ensures the student has the necessary picture symbols available and integrates choice making into her work with the student.
2. The special education teacher identifies opportunities to teach choice making across the school day and at home.
3. The occupational therapist teaches the student to reach for and manipulate the symbol cards.
4. The physical therapist incorporates choice making into mobility activities.

With all team members understanding and addressing a small number of high-priority skills, a student with ESN will acquire and generalize skills more rapidly and reliably.

Example of Trans-disciplinary Teaming

Caroline is a seven year old with multiple disabilities who is transitioning from kindergarten to first grade. She was a full participant in her kindergarten class, and her academic and communication skills advanced rapidly during that year. Most significantly, she learned to use a single-head switch to select a choice using partner-assisted scanning. Reliable use of the head switch has opened opportunities for Caroline to respond to factual questions, identify words and letters, and to learn to use auditory scanning to communicate using a high-tech communication device. Her parents are thrilled with her progress and want to make sure her first-grade year continues in a positive direction.

Ms. Soukup, Caroline's special education teacher, has developed a positive relationship with Caroline's family over the past year, communicating frequently with them about her progress and ongoing support needs. Caroline's next IEP will coincide with her three-year reevaluation. To ensure appropriate supports are provided, and to identify the most useful assessments that will guide long-term planning, Ms. Soukup and the team decide to use *COACH* (Giangreco et al., 2011) to develop a shared vision for Caroline's education. Ms. Soukup invites Caroline's parents to participate in the family interview. First, they discuss valued life outcomes related to home, self-determination, relationships, health and safety, and participation in meaningful activities. Then, they review Caroline's present level of performance in a variety of academic and non-academic areas and identify a small set of high-priority learning outcomes that can be written as trans-disciplinary goals in the IEP. Additionally, these high-priority learning outcomes will guide the team to conduct relevant assessments for Caroline's three-year reevaluation. Supports and additional academic and non-academic learning outcomes are also identified. At Caroline's IEP meeting, team members discussed strategies for collaboration and instruction to collectively support Caroline's progress toward all her IEP goals. At the end of the process, Caroline's mother commented that it was the first time they had ever been asked for their input rather than being presented with a set of professional recommendations to approve.

Conduct an Ecological Inventory to Identify Contextually Relevant Learning Goals

Create Contextually Relevant Learning Goals

Contextually relevant learning goals ensure that students spend adequate time learning skills that are immediately useful in everyday contexts. For students in preschool through 12th grade, age-appropriate general education activities provide natural contexts for students to learn and apply skills. In addition to academic goals that might be important in the context of a variety of general education activities, students should also learn other skills that are relevant to age-appropriate activities across environments. In this way, curriculum content and contexts align and ensure that the student is involved in, and makes progress in, the general education curriculum (Ryndak et al., 2013).

Using an Ecological Inventory

Ecological inventories are a well-researched strategy to identify contextually relevant skills in any environment (Brown et al., 1979; Downing et al., 2015). Conducting an ecological inventory is a relatively straightforward process, requiring no special materials and minimal training. First, the team identifies an overall *domain*, or aspect, of a child's life. Examples of domains include the community, a job, at home, or educational. Within each domain, the team identifies environments. For example, in the educational domain, environments might include the school, bus, after school care, and swimming lessons. Within each environment, there are sub-environments. In a school, some sub-environments might include the child's first-grade classroom, the hallway, the gym, etc.

Within each sub-environment, the student engages in a variety of activities. For example, in the hallway, the student might need to ambulate, identify their locker, put on and take off a coat and boots, keep things stored in a locker, and socialize with peers. From these activities, the team identifies the highest priority skills to ensure the student maintains and increases the membership and relationships within everyday inclusive contexts. For each skill, the team creates a task analysis and identifies the steps in the skill that require additional instruction, as well as steps in which the student would benefit from an accommodation or modification to make the step accessible. A teacher, paraprofessional, or related service provider then uses systematic instruction strategies (see Chapter 16) to teach the student any needed skills within the context of the activity itself.

Example of Ecological Inventory

Andres is a seventh grade student who qualifies for special education under the label of intellectual disability. He attends a large middle school where he participates in theater and enjoys his elective family and consumer science class. He is a full participant in general education English, math, and science classes, where he addresses academic skills. In addition, Andres's family owns a popular restaurant and Andres has begun to help with his family's business. Socially, Andres has recently "come out of his shell" and is taking a more active role in developing peer relationships.

The team identified the following domains in Andres's life:

- Educational
- Social
- Employment
- Home
- Faith

Within the employment domain, the team identified the following environments:

- School store
- The family restaurant

Within the school store environment, the team identified the following sub-environments:

- Storage area
- Cash register

Within the family restaurant, the team identified the following sub-environments:

- Dining room
- Outdoor areas
- Kitchen
- Cash register
- Storage

Across these sub-environments, the team identified the following common activities:

- Keeping a neat and clean work environment
- Using a cash register
- Interacting with customers

Because these skills are useful in multiple environments, the team decided to teach these skills to Andres in the school store. In addition, a team member periodically visited the restaurant to provide support and instruction to Andres there. This had the added benefit of allowing team members to develop strong relationships with Andres' family and observe and identify additional skills that Andres might benefit from learning in school—as well as learning about the supports he uses to access activities outside of school.

Identify Goals Aligned with Grade-level Standards That Are Personally Meaningful for Students

Standards-aligned Objectives

State standards were created to ensure that all students are prepared to function as adults within society and continue their education at the college level (Courtade et al., 2012). The long- and short-term goals of students with disabilities must align with state grade-level content standards for the grade level in which the student is currently enrolled. When planning instruction for students with ESN participating in the alternate assessment, goals and objectives should align to the state's alternate academic achievement standards (see Office of Special Education Programs, 2015) Aligning a student's individual goals with the grade-level standards will ensure that the student is being given access and instruction in the general education curriculum. Courtade et al. (2012) also assert that when state standards are paired with "supplemental instruction in high-priority life skill needs" (p. 8), students will increase their independence in daily living tasks while also expanding the employment opportunities available to them. For example, students who are given instruction in translating data into simple graphs (line, pie, bar, or picture), and how to interpret those graphs, will be able to use that skill in their own life, such as managing expenses, or in a variety of jobs, such as preparing graphs of monthly sales, business expenses, or customer feedback.

Teaching Self-determination

Self-determination is defined as the skills and attitudes a person employs to set goals, make decisions, and solve problems within their life (Shogren et al., 2015). Self-determined students work with educators to select goals that are personally meaningful to the student and align with the student's long- and short-term goals. This connects to the point made earlier in the chapter that goals should be meaningful to the student from their point of view and align with the students' current and future school, home, community, and/or employment contexts. Self-determined students also create plans and solve problems as they work toward meeting the goals they set. As we cannot anticipate what the future job market will look like, it is important that students have the general academic competencies the state standards identify. These academic skills connected to larger and broader life goals will provide students with the knowledge they need to set goals that allow for a greater quality of life, whether this is a job with opportunities for upward mobility, leisure activities, or advocacy work. Educators help create self-determined citizens by ensuring that students with ESN are taught and given opportunities to practice self-determination skills throughout their education. Although not an exhaustive list, some skills that lead to self-determined behavior are the following.

Self-management

Self-management refers to all the skills that an individual utilizes to influence their own behavior (Browder & Shapiro, 1985). Sometimes, these skills are called self-control, and they are important skills to teach because it empowers students to independently monitor and change their own behavior (Browder & Shapiro, 1985). Self-management can involve concepts such as recognizing and regulating emotions (e.g., asking for a break when becoming overwhelmed), monitoring one's own progression through a schedule, planning for task completion (e.g., creating a list of responsibilities needed to be completed), or setting one's own reinforcement schedule. Because self-management is an abstract concept, educators should choose strategies that offer concrete ways of understanding methods to self-regulate.

Goal Setting

Self-determined students have the skills to set and obtain long- and short-term goals. This means that students not only develop the goals themselves, but also create and implement a plan to accomplish the goals set (Shogren et al., 2019). A short-term goal refers to objectives that require a short period of time to complete and are relatively uncomplicated. An example of a short-term goal would be to complete all daily chores before meeting up with friends later that evening. A long-term goal is one that requires a significant amount of time to achieve and usually involves multiple short-term goals that build on one another to be attained. For example, a student might decide that they want to become a chef and own a restaurant. They will first need to graduate high school, then attend and graduate culinary school, work in the kitchen of a restaurant, and obtain funding to open a business.

One way to teach goal setting is through the Self-Determined Learning Model of Instruction (SDLMI; Shogren et al., 2019). This model of instruction provides teachers with a framework to successfully teach students the skills necessary to set and achieve goals through three distinct phases. During the first phase, the teacher supports the student to select a goal to achieve. In the second phase, the teacher supports the student to develop an action plan to attain the goal. In the third and final phase, the teacher supports the student in evaluating their progress toward meeting the goal. The student determines if they have met the goal, or if they should create a new plan or revise their goal. The SDLMI model is used multiple times with a student to give them an optimal number of opportunities to practice the skills in each phase.

Decision-making

The ability to make decisions for oneself is often the skill most thought of when thinking about self-determination. Decision-making is more than making choices and requires students to understand the best and most effective choice going forward because they understand the consequences of that choice. Decision-making involves evaluating the choices available and making a choice based on that evaluation. Teachers often forget to explicitly instruct on how to evaluate choices in the decision-making process. For example, teaching students how to create a pro/con list and to evaluate the options based on that list is a concrete way to teach decision-making.

Problem-solving

Self-determined individuals are problem solvers. This means that they can evaluate a situation, identify obstacles, and identify strategies to navigate obstacles. Many decisions we all make involve some degree of emotional and/or physical risk. Perske (1972) states that to deny people with disabilities the opportunity to make choices that involve emotional or physical risk because they need to be protected diminishes their human dignity. All individuals deserve the freedom and right to make their own decisions. By denying individuals this freedom, it takes away a fundamental human right and relegates them to second-class citizenship. Also, successful problem solvers learn from their failures and correct their strategies based on these failures. Explicitly teaching the steps a person undertakes when problem-solving is one method of teaching this skill. Agran et al. (2002)

taught students with intellectual disability or autism to problem solve by teaching students the sequence of steps in problem solving by having them ask themselves and answer the following questions in sequence: (1) "What is the problem?" and (2) "What can I do about it?" The student was then taught to implement the proposed solution. Once the plan was implemented, the student was then taught to ask, "Did that fix the problem?"

Self-advocacy

Self-advocacy means taking a leadership role in your own life and in the life of your community. Teachers must teach students to advocate for their rights, needs, and desires. This skill is especially important because, as adults, people with disabilities must advocate for the services they need. Students need to understand the supports they need to be successful, as well as where, when, and how to advocate for those supports.

Choices and Communication

Self-determined individuals make choices and communicate those choices to those around them. The importance of an effective and reliable mode of communication cannot be emphasized enough. It is impossible for students to become self-determined if they are unable to communicate with those around them. An effective form of communication could include speech as well as aided and unaided augmentative and alternative communication (AAC). Once a communication system has been established, students should be taught to make choices. The choices made by students should be respected, responded to, and honored whenever possible.

Example of Self-determination

Deondre, a tenth grader with autism, will have his first IEP that formally addresses his transition into adulthood this year. When Deondre was in elementary and middle school, his teachers began work on his self-determination skills by ensuring that Deondre had many choices during the day to practice his choice-making and communication skills. These choices included his preferred reinforcers and the order in which to complete work tasks. Deondre does not communicate verbally and has minimal control of his arms. With this in mind, the elementary school team developed a system for Deondre to communicate by opening his eyes wide to signal yes and closing them tight to signal no.

Self-determination instruction has helped Deondre maintain choice and control in his life. For example, Deondre often is awake at night and comes to school tired. The team has used systematic instruction to teach him to ask for breaks when he is too tired to work and concentrate. In addition, Deondre has begun to recognize when he is starting to get anxious and overwhelmed, cueing himself to ask for a break in class and other situations. His teachers have taught him to self-manage by independently requesting a break during classes and other overwhelming situations by using a switch. Once he has calmed himself down, he is learning to quietly reenter the classroom and request any work that he missed from the teacher or a peer.

Next Steps Toward Better Practice

1. Remember, the process of determining long- and short-term goals must be completed in collaboration with parents and the student.
2. Using a model such as COACH (Giangreco et al., 2011) can help teams develop high priority, individualized, and cross-disciplinary goals.

3. Try completing an ecological inventory for one setting, such as the general education class-room. Start with the beginning of the day and identify the steps a student needs to complete. Then identify students' support needs and potential learning goals within individual activities.

4. An easy way to get started with self-determination instruction is to give students opportunities to make meaningful choices many times per day.

The Big Five

1. Goals for students with ESN are completely individualized. There is no "list" of skills because the goals arise from students' own lives.

2. All goals should be age appropriate and not based on perceived "developmental levels."

3. Teaching in age-appropriate contexts (e.g., general education classes) supports the selection of skills that are contextually relevant to the general education context.

4. Choose skills with a high likelihood of generalization. Try not to teach a skill that will only be useful in one environment.

5. Teach students self-determination skills.

Resources

- Self-determination at University of Kansas: https://selfdetermination.ku.edu/
- Dynamic Learning Maps Professional Development Modules: https://www.dlmpd.com/all-modules-in-alphabetical-order/
- National Center and State Collaborative Curriculum Resources: https://wiki.ncscpartners.org/index.php/Curriculum_Resources
- *Choosing Outcomes and Accommodations for Children* https://products.brookespublishing.com/Choosing-Outcomes-and-Accommodations-for-Children-COACH-P463.aspx
- Person-centered Planning Resources: https://www.personcenteredplanning.org/

References

Agran, M., Blanchard, C., Wehmeyer, M., & Hughes, C. (2002). Increasing the problem-solving skills of students with developmental disabilities participating in general education. *Remedial and Special Education, 23*(5), 279–288. https://doi.org/10.1177/07419325020230050301

Ayres, K. M., Lowrey, K. A., Douglas, K. H., & Sievers, C. (2011). I can identify Saturn but I can't brush my teeth: What happens when the curricular focus for students with severe disabilities shifts. *Education and Training in Autism and Developmental Disabilities, 46*(1), 11–21. https://www.jstor.org/stable/23880027

Browder, D. M., & Shapiro, E. S. (1985). Application of self-management to individuals with severe handicaps: A review. *Journal of the Association for Persons With Severe Handicaps, 10*(4), 200–208. https://doi.org/10.1177/154079698501000403

Browder, D., Spooner, F., Ahlgrim-Delzell, L., Flowers, C., Algozzine, B., & Karvonen, M. (2003). A content analysis of the curricular philosophies reflected in states' alternate assessment performance indicators. *Research and Practice for Persons With Severe Disabilities, 28*(4), 165–181. https://doi.org/10.2511/rpsd.28.4.165

Brown, L., Branston, M. B., Hamre-Nietupski, S., Pumpian, I., Certo, N., & Gruenewald, L. (1979). A strategy for developing chronological age-appropriate and functional curricular content for severely handicapped adolescents and young adults. *The Journal of Special Education, 13*(1), 81–91. https://doi.org/10.1177/002246697901300113

Copeland, S. R., & Keefe, L. (2018). *Effective literacy instruction for learners with complex support needs* (2nd ed.). Brookes.

Courtade, G., Spooner, F., Browder, D., & Jimenez, B. (2012). Seven reasons to promote standards-based instruction for students with severe disabilities: A reply to Ayres, Lowrey, Douglas, & Sievers (2011). *Education and Training in Autism and Development Disabilities, 47*(1), 3–13. https://www.jstor.org/stable/23880557

Downing, J. E., Hanreddy, A., & Peckham-Hardin, K. D. (2015). *Teaching communication skills to students with severe disabilities* (3rd ed.). Brookes Publishing.

Dymond, S. K., & Orelove, F. P. (2001). What constitutes effective curricula for students with severe disabilities? *Exceptionality, 9*(3), 109–122. https://doi.org/10.1207/S15327035EX0903_2

Giangreco, M. F., Cloninger, C. J., & Iverson, V. S. (2011). *Choosing outcomes and accommodations for children: A guide to educational planning for students with disabilities* (3rd ed.). Paul H. Brookes.

Horner, R. H., Williams, J. A., & Knobbe, C. A. (1985). The effect of "opportunity to perform" on the maintenance of skills learned by high school students with severe handicaps. *Journal of the Association for Persons With Severe Handicaps, 10*(3), 172–175. https://doi.org/10.1177/154079698501000308

Hunt, P., McDonnell, J., & Crockett, M. A. (2012). Reconciling an ecological curricular framework focusing on quality of life outcomes with the development and instruction of standards-based academic goals. *Research and Practice for Persons With Severe Disabilities, 37*(3), 139–152. https://doi.org/10.2511/027494812804153471

Individuals with Disabilities Education Act, 20 U.S.C. § 1400 (2004).

No Child Left Behind Act of 2001, Pub. L. No. 107-110, § 101, Stat. 1425 (2002).

O'Brien, C., & O'Brien, J. (2002). The origins of person-centered planning: A community of practice perspective. In S. Holburn, & P. Vietze (Eds.), *Person-centered planning: Research, practice, and future directions* (pp. 3–27). Paul Brookes.

Office of Special Education Programs, November 16, 2015. OSEP dear colleague letter on free and appropriate public education. https://sites.ed.gov/idea/idea-files/osep-dear-colleague-letter-on-free-and-appropriate-public-education-fape/

Perske, R. (1972). The dignity of risk and the MR. *Mental Retardation, 10*(1), 24. https://www.proquest.com/scholarly-journals/dignity-risk-mr/docview/1293657528/se-2?accountid=14605

Ryndak, D., Jackson, L. B., & White, J. M. (2013). Involvement and progress in the general curriculum for students with extensive support needs: K–12 inclusive-education research and implications for the future. *Inclusion, 1*(1), 28–49. https://doi.org/10.1352/2326-6988-1.1.028

Shogren, K. A., Raley, S. K., Burke, K. M., & Wehmeyer, M. L. (2019). *The self-determined learning model of instruction Teacher's guide*. Kansas University Center on Developmental Disabilities.

Shogren, K. A., Wehmeyer, M. L., Plamer, S. B., Forber-Pratt, A. J., Little, T. J., & Lopez, S. (2015). Causal agency theory: Reconceptualizing a functional model of self-determination. *Education and Training in Autism and Development Disabilities, 50*(3), 251–263. http://www.jstor.org/stable/24827508

Shurr, J., & Bouck, E. (2013). Research on curriculum for students with moderate and severe intellectual disability: A systematic review. *Education and Training in Autism and Developmental Disabilities, 48*(1), 76–87. https://www.jstor.org/stable/23879888

Stokes, T. F., & Baer, D. M. (1977). An implicit technology of generalization. *Journal of Applied Behavior Analysis, 10*(2), 349–367. https://doi.org/10.1901/jaba.1977.10-349

Timberlake, M. T. (2014). Weighing costs and benefits: Teacher interpretation and implementation of access to the general education curriculum. *Research and Practice for Persons With Severe Disabilities, 39*(2), 83–99. https://doi.org/10.1177/1540796914544547

12
Systematically Design Instruction toward a Specific Learning Goal
Melinda Jones Ault and Ginevra Courtade

Teachers help students to develop important concepts and skills that provide the foundation for more complex learning. Teachers sequence lessons that build on each other and make connections explicit, in both planning and delivery. They activate students' prior knowledge and show how each lesson "fits" with previous ones. Planning involves careful consideration of learning goals, what is involved in reaching the goals, and allocating time accordingly. Ongoing changes (e.g., pacing and examples) occur throughout the sequence based on student performance.

Supporting Students with Extensive Support Needs

Over the course of their school career, students must learn a host of skills and concepts to meet academic standards and navigate the complex requirements of daily life. Given the limited amount of time students are in school and the large amount of content to be acquired, teachers must systematically design instruction so that their students' learning goals are clearly defined, planned, and sequenced. This ensures that students learn efficiently and can build upon their prior learning to acquire the required content during the time they have in school.

Teachers must provide additional support for students with extensive support needs (ESN) when designing instruction. These students often make gains in smaller increments and at a slower rate than their peers without disabilities and require more intensive, explicit, and systematic support to maximize learning outcomes. This support often requires the repeated presentation of complex concepts using concrete representations prior to more abstract representations (e.g., presenting a physical model of a planet before describing its characteristics). Further, teachers must thoughtfully plan for the use of procedures to facilitate generalization and maintenance to ensure their students can apply both academic and adaptive skills to new contexts. Finally, teachers must find ways to deliver instruction on a vast range of skills (e.g., academic, social communication, and self-determination) within inclusive environments. When designing instruction for students with ESN, teachers should (a) write clear learning goals, so that progress can be clearly assessed, (b) prioritize learning goals during the school career to prepare students for post-school goals, (c) sequence instruction to create logical pathways of learning that build upon prior knowledge to increase understanding and comprehension, and (d) help students make connections and relationships

DOI: 10.4324/9781003175735-13

across skills they are learning to maximize maintenance and generalization (Konrad et al., 2019; McLeskey et al., 2017).

Chapter Objectives

Upon reading this chapter, you should be able to do the following:

1. Write clear learning goals for students with ESN.
2. Describe ways to prioritize learning objectives over a student's school career.
3. Use strategies for sequencing instruction to increase students' understanding and comprehension.
4. Assist students to make connections and relationships across the skills they learn.

Write Clear Learning Goals

Systematically designing instruction begins with teachers writing clear learning goals. When a teacher has selected a learning goal for a student, it must be written so that it can be interpreted by all members of a student's educational team. When written clearly, there is no question when the student has mastered the goal and under what conditions the goal will be demonstrated (Bateman & Herr, 2010). Annual goals are those that the team identifies that the student will accomplish in a school year; however, for individuals with ESN, these annual goals should be broken into short-term objectives or benchmarks (Goran et al., 2020). The goal should include measurable and meaningful performance criteria and should be "challenging" and "appropriately ambitious" to result in meaningful progress (Endrew, 2017, p. 1000). There are a number of models for teachers to use to write goals/objectives (Konrad et al., 2019; Hedin & DeSpain, 2018; Winegarden, 2005). The model presented here uses the CNBC mnemonic to simplify the writing process to include the following components: (a) "C"—the conditions that will be present when the student is expected to demonstrate the skill, (b) "N"—the name of the student for whom the goal is written, (c) "B"—the observable behavior the student will demonstrate, and (d) "C"—the criterion the student will be expected to perform the behavior to indicate mastery. Individualized education program (IEP) goals should include all components of a goal written in one to three sentences. Table 12.1 shows the components of a learning goal using the mnemonic "CNBC."

Condition Statement

Teachers often begin writing a learning goal by detailing the stimulus conditions under which the skill will be performed by the student. The condition statement can be preceded by the word "given" so the educational team knows what conditions should be present when the student is assessed on the learning goal. Students with ESN may have unique circumstances in which conditions will need to be added to the goal and individualized for the student. Conditions may include, but are not limited to, the setting in which the goal will be performed, the specific materials the student will use, the individuals with whom the student will interact, any cues or directives that will be given, the assistive technology the student uses, and the augmentative/alternative communication device of the student.

Observable and Measurable Behavior

Teachers should then write the behavior that the student can actually demonstrate. The behavior must be able to be observed (i.e., seen, heard, tasted, smelled, felt) by the teacher so that it can be accurately measured by anyone on the educational team to determine progress and mastery.

Table 12.1 Examples of Components of Learning Goals

Condition Statement	Name of Learner	Behavior	Criterion
After listening to a passage read aloud from his adapted textbook and given a series of four to five pictures showing characters and actions from the passage.	Joe	Will place the pictures in order from left to right showing the correct sequence of events that occurred in the story.	With no errors for 3 consecutive days.
Given a calculator, a word problem read aloud to her, and a choice of two graphic organizers (one showing a task analysis for addition and one for subtraction).	Janelle	Will select the correct graphic organizer needed to solve the problem, correctly fill in the steps on the organizer, and write the answer to the problem.	For three out of three problems on 3 consecutive days.
Given his augmentative and alternative communication (AAC) device and when asked what music he wants to hear when involved in free time with peers.	Savir	Will navigate his AAC device to indicate his choice of song.	For 2 of 3 consecutive days.
Given a collection of five shapes presented one at a time including circle, pentagon, octagon, square, and triangle (with multiple exemplars presented throughout the day).	Oscar	Will correctly state the shape name.	With 100% accuracy for 3 consecutive days.
Given a shoe with a Velcro fastener placed off of his foot and the task direction to "Put your shoe on".	Bernard	Will place the shoe on his foot and fasten the Velcro within 30 seconds.	For five out of five opportunities across at least 3 days.
When given access to a device with text-messaging capabilities and told to message a friend to invite them to an upcoming event.	Sasha	Will open the text message icon, select her friend's name, type a message about the event that includes the invitation, the location, and the time of the event.	For three out of three opportunities.

Establish Criterion

Teachers then define the criterion or the level at which the student will be expected to perform the behavior *and* the length of time or the evaluation schedule for which they must perform the behavior at this level. The criterion must be in a dimension that can be used to accurately measure the targeted behavior, and the measurement system should match the objective. Teachers also should identify a mastery level that is useful. That is, the criterion should be set at a level that is meaningful for the student in the context of the environment in which they will be using the skill. For example, it may be an appropriate, acceptable, and useful criterion for students to greet individuals in their environment for only 75% of the opportunities during their day. However, a more stringent criterion would be appropriate and useful when teaching a student to correctly follow directions on a job site (e.g., 95% of the opportunities) or to read with fluency to support comprehension, for that skill to be useful, appropriate, and meaningful. In addition to setting the level of mastery, teachers must determine the length of time their students should demonstrate a level of responding in order to have confidence the goal has been mastered. A teacher may not be sure that students have met a goal if it is demonstrated at the criterion level only one time; however, if students demonstrate the skill consistently over a number of evaluation opportunities, the teacher can have more confidence that the goal has been mastered, and so, the number of times a student should demonstrate the skill to meet a goal should be specified. Examples of criterion statements including the level of performance and duration follow: "100% accuracy for three consecutive days," "walks independently for at least 20 feet twice per day for 3 consecutive days," "correctly purchases an item in the store using a debit card for three out of three purchases," or "writes the correct answer to four out of five problems for 3 consecutive days."

A characteristic of some students with ESN is variability in responding. Therefore, for these students, the teacher may need to adjust the criterion to reflect this variability. For example, the criterion component could be written as "independently completes all steps of the task analysis on at least three out of five occasions occurring within the same week" or "achieves at least 80% accuracy for two consecutive days a week across 2 consecutive weeks."

In addition to writing goals that address the acquisition of skills, teachers of students with ESN should consider addressing all phases of learning in the learning goal (i.e., fluency, maintenance, generalization). This will help ensure that instruction is targeted not only at acquisition, but that teachers program for generalization and maintenance.

An additional consideration is that although specificity is important in writing learning goals, writing the conditions and the behavior statements more "loosely" also will drive instruction in a way that can facilitate generalization. Consider the following examples of learning goals that will assist in driving instruction and include components across all phases of learning.

- When it is time for lunch with all needed materials available (condition statement written loosely to facilitate generalization) in the classroom kitchen or at home (across generalization settings), Ripley will independently complete all steps of a task analysis to make a sandwich within 5 min (fluency criterion) for three out of three consecutive lunch periods (acquisition criterion) and will maintain preparing a sandwich for at least 1 year without additional instruction (maintenance criterion). Task analysis includes (a) obtain needed materials and place on preparation surface, (b) remove two pieces of bread from packaging, (c) place main ingredient on one slice of bread, (d) add desired condiment to other slice of bread, (e) place second piece of bread on top of first, (f) cut sandwich in half, and (g) replace all materials.
- When involved in an activity described below (condition statement written loosely with multiple options of activities for generalization) and given choices between two objects (both of which have a graphic symbol + word attached to them), Kendall will select an item by looking at, reaching toward, or touching the desired object (behavior written loosely with options for responding) within 5 s of being given a choice, (fluency criterion) across three activities and 3 days (acquisition criterion). The behavior will maintain for at least 3 months without additional instruction. Example activities include meals (choice between two foods), free time (choice between two toys), math (choice between two manipulatives), and classroom (choice between two friends to sit beside).

Prioritize Learning Goals

Teachers, families/caregivers, and students must prioritize learning goals so students can achieve post-school success. In doing so, teachers should consider the primary concerns of the family/caregiver and student, determine the general education curriculum standards identified for the student's grade level, and identify relevant life skills that incorporate an application of those skills with academic skills.

First, families/caregivers and students may prioritize learning goals as they consider valued life outcomes. Giangreco et al. (2011) published their assessment instrument, *Choosing Outcomes and Accommodations for Children*, to plan educational objectives for individuals with ESN. As a part of the assessment process, the interdisciplinary team is asked to consider the learning objectives and how they relate to individualized valued life outcomes of safety and security, a place to live, meaningful relationships, control and choice, and meaningful activities. During the assessment process, parents also are asked to identify and rank the most important learning goals for the upcoming school year. This prioritization puts the focus on the individualized needs and preferences of the student as learning objectives are identified. Similarly, Hunt et al. (2012) proposed a framework for considering learning objectives by tying them to quality-of-life outcomes in home, friendships, community participation, work, and lifelong learning linked to academic subject area domains.

Second, learning objectives should be developed that provide access to the general education curriculum. With the student's individual needs and preferences identified, the team can consider ways for the student to access grade-level academic content that will be both meaningful for a student and align to state standards. It may be helpful for general education teachers who are part of the interdisciplinary team to discuss the highlights or big ideas of the curriculum for the student's grade level and for the team to have the standards available for review (Courtade & Browder, 2016). Further, many states have developed extensions or alternate assessment targets of priority grade-level standards for students taking alternate assessments. The standards identified for extensions or targets are based on instructional significance and become the foundation for alternate assessments (e.g., Kentucky Department of Education, 2022). As these extensions/targets have been prioritized by the state, they may also be used to guide the development of learning goals. In selecting learning goals, the team should consider each academic content area and focus on priorities for academic learning and skills to access the broader curriculum (Courtade & Browder, 2016). For example, in looking over fourth-grade standards, the team may develop a reading comprehension objective that is aligned to grade level, but also allows for progress in other content areas such as science and social studies.

Third, the educational team should consider the intersection of access and academic standards and the development of meaningful life skills. As mentioned in Chapter 4, ecological assessments and inventories (observation of typical routines and skills by individuals without a disability and compared to a specific student, Browder et al., 2020) can be used to identify those skills needed in current and future environments. Several researchers have focused on embedding life skills instruction within academic content instruction. For example, Chapman et al. (2019) taught students to solve algebraic linear equations in the context of real-life scenarios and then assessed generalization to job tasks performed in the school setting. Karl et al. (2013) taught students to read and define academic content, to compute percentages, and to identify applications of force in physics within meaningful life activities of cooking and grocery shopping. Teachers should design instruction so that individuals learn academic content and meaningful life skills within an ecological inventory framework.

In addition, teachers assist their students in making connections between the academic instruction they receive and its application to their daily routines, as well as when teaching adaptive skills, teachers help students draw connections to academic instruction. *For example, Mr. Jackson has taught a lesson on physics concepts of motion, velocity, acceleration, and force in the classroom setting. When the class goes to the grocery story during a community-based instruction trip, Mr. Jackson embeds and assesses the physics concepts while his students push their carts in the store. Similarly, Mr. Jackson is teaching his student with ESN, Dwayne, a vocational task of raking leaves, placing them in bags, and putting them on the curb for pickup. Dwayne has expressed preferences for jobs that he can do outside. This skill will result in income opportunities for Dwayne in future years, especially in the fall season. Mr. Jackson embeds an academic science lesson on photosynthesis and chlorophyll within the adaptive skill lesson of raking leaves.*

Sequence Instruction to Increase Understanding and Comprehension

Once learning goals have been prioritized, teachers of students with ESN use a variety of techniques to order their instruction so that the learning sequence is logical (makes sense), builds upon students' prior knowledge, and is planned to facilitate student comprehension. Teachers ensure that learning tasks are presented in a simple-to-complex sequence, that they scaffold instruction by providing assistance that facilitates comprehension, that they build student's background information prior to teaching content, and that they maintain their student's learning objectives over time.

Simple to Complex

When teaching new content, the learning sequence should move from simple to complex discriminations. Teachers design instruction so that it begins with those discriminations the student can learn efficiently and moves to those that are more difficult. This will ensure that student errors during instruction are minimized which will reduce future errors as well as keep students motivated as they remain in contact with the reinforcer as instruction progresses. For example, the teacher may begin by sequencing instructional examples that are more easily differentiated and move to responses that purposefully include responses that have shared characteristics, thus making the discriminations more difficult (Grow & Leblanc, 2013; McDonnell et al., 2014). Proper sequencing helps students build upon their prior learning and to understand more complex content as their learning gradually builds over time. When teaching grade-aligned content, teachers of students with ESN must determine if their students have mastered the prerequisite skills needed to ensure mastery of grade-level content. However, these prerequisites can still be linked to and taught within the context of the students' appropriate grade-level standard. For example, while teaching a chemistry lesson, a teacher may work with a student on the skill of identifying "same" and "different" in the context of understanding which solution caused a chemical reaction.

Prompting

Prompting of students is a strategy to increase comprehension because prompts increase the likelihood the student will respond correctly to the task at hand. Both response and stimulus prompts are delivered during instruction as needed to assist the student in responding. Response prompts (e.g., verbal, gestural, model, and physical prompts) are delivered by the teacher after the antecedent stimulus is delivered and before a student responds if assistance is needed. Stimulus prompts are those that modify the antecedent stimulus before it is presented to the student to assist the student in responding correctly. Stimulus prompting includes stimulus shaping, stimulus fading, and superimposition. While teachers initially will deliver prompts that result in correct responding while keeping errors low, they also must plan for the fading of any prompts over time so that students transfer their responding from the prompt used to the stimulus alone. Refer to Chapter 15 for a comprehensive discussion of prompting strategies and how they are systematically faded.

Build Background Information

Prior to teaching new content, teachers should consider what referent and background information students have to support their understanding and learning of that content. For more abstract concepts, students with ESN may not have any referent for the information. It could be they have not had any related experiences with the concepts to be taught and their receptive language level may not allow for understanding of the terms used to illustrate new concepts. Therefore, new content may need to be made more concrete to facilitate understanding. Strategies teachers can use to assist in this include using an anticipatory set prior to reading a new story or passage (e.g., showing and exploring concrete objects the story is about or complete an activity that relates to the content of the story), using photos and videos to illustrate new concepts to develop background information, participating in events or activities that introduce the concepts, simplifying the complexity of the language used in describing the content, using audio sounds to demonstrate or exemplify information that will be presented in the content, teaching and reviewing key vocabulary used in the lesson, and using stories that are personally relevant to the students as the context for teaching the content. Additional strategies for adapting content, which also can support background information and comprehension, are found in Chapter 13.

Consider the scenario of Ms. Espinosa, who is working to increase comprehension and develop background knowledge of her students for upcoming content in her history class. *Ms. Espinosa, a teacher of a secondary inclusive history class, is preparing lessons about World War II. She designs several activities to assist with developing background knowledge and impacting comprehension. First, she takes her entire class, which also includes Keisha, a young woman with ESN who is an augmentative and alternative communication (AAC) device user, to the World War II museum in their local community. While there, the class watches movies about battles in World War II, sees newspaper clippings, views uniforms and other items used during the time, and views news reports. The peer supporting Keisha models the use of vocabulary words, identified by the educational team prior to the visit, on Keisha's AAC device while talking to her about what they are seeing at the museum. Once instruction begins on the World War II unit, Ms. Espinosa provides direct instruction on vocabulary words, ensures that Keisha has textbook information adapted for complexity, and ensures that picture supports and photographs are used to support the information presented to the class. She also adapts the assessments used during class to ensure that Keisha has the vocabulary she needs on her AAC device to respond to questions presented in class, and ensures Keisha's participation in her group's assignment to write and perform a skit on the role of Rosie the Riveter in the war effort.*

Now that Keisha has experiences with the World War II content, future teachers will know that she has learned some background knowledge and referents associated with this historical event and can refer to these events when teaching related historical content.

Maintaining Learning Goals

Teachers also should set schedules to review content and ensure that their students are maintaining the skills and knowledge they have acquired. Once students have mastered the content and skills in the acquisition stage of learning, teachers should check the maintenance of the information as students move to the next scheduled content to be presented. Teachers can insert review trials of previously learned content into new learning sequences to assist in maintenance. The teacher also can schedule regular maintenance checks on previously learned content to ensure responding remains high. If the data indicate the learning has not maintained, then teachers should reteach the content by providing booster sessions as needed until criterion level responding is achieved. Strategies for maintaining skills over time include teaching skills that are immediately useful and frequently demanded. The use of these skills on a regular basis facilitates their maintenance. Other maintenance strategies include thinning the schedule of reinforcement from continuous reinforcement schedules used during acquisition to intermittent schedules of reinforcement that will facilitate maintenance. The goal is for teachers to achieve a schedule of reinforcement used in generalization environments and use reinforcers found in those environments, such as the inclusive classrooms in which students are enrolled.

Assist Students in Organizing New Knowledge and Making Connections with Content

As students with ESN gain new skills and acquire new content, they need assistance to organize their new knowledge and to make connections between previously learned and new content. This involves assisting them in understanding the relationships between the concepts they are learning and how the content relates to their own lives. This involves representing the content/organization/connections concretely in ways that are meaningful to the student and providing opportunities for higher-order thinking.

Graphic Organizers

One way that teachers can assist students in understanding the relationships between prior knowledge and new content as well as between new concepts is to make the connections more concrete by representing them using visual/graphic displays and graphic organizer templates that show and outline connections between content. These templates can assist teachers and students in organizing thoughts, simplifying content, and in making the relationships between concepts more concrete by providing a visual representation of a complex skill or information. Graphic organizers can be used for a variety of purposes including outlining a writing project; showing hierarchical relationships; showing similarities and differences across concepts; and organizing new learning by outlining what students know, what they want to know, and what they learned.

Visual displays and graphic organizers have been incorporated into procedures when teaching students with ESN a variety of academic skills including algebraic equations (Chapman et al., 2019), arithmetic operations (Root et al., 2018), the language arts concept of compare and contrast (Dieruf et al., 2020), and science concepts (Jimenez et al., 2009). Students can be provided with the relevant graphic organizers and also can be taught to discriminate between problem types and select the correct graphic organizer to use to solve problems (Browder et al., 2018; Root et al., 2018). See Chapter 13 for more information about graphic organizers.

Meaningful Stories and Application

Teachers who couch their instruction within meaningful stories for students can assist in making connections. For example, when teachers use a story that is meaningful to the learner to teach content, it connects the learning to the student's life, makes it applicable, brings in their own culture, and perhaps even increases motivation since the nature of the story could be reinforcing. For example, consider the scenario of Ms. Jones who is teaching the concept of greater than and less than to Miguel, who loves to play baseball.

Ms. Jones is teaching a lesson of more than and less than to Miguel's class. She begins the lesson by telling the class she is going to read a story with a problem that they need to help her solve. All students in the class have a copy of the story adapted to their individualized needs. Miguel's story has a photo of a baseball game and pictures above the key words in the story. Students follow along as Ms. Jones reads: Miguel is playing baseball today! His team is named the Bears. He is playing with another team named the Legends. During the game, each team hits the ball and scores some runs. Miguel even scored a home run. When the game is over, the scoreboard showed that the Bears had seven runs and the Legends had five runs. Which team had more runs than the other team? Which team was the winner?

Ms. Jones can use this story as context for teaching a lesson on greater than/less than; it is personally relevant to Miguel; he is motivated and engaged by the content; and he can apply it to his daily life.

Organize Content to Deepen Learning

Teachers may inadvertently limit the depth of learning of their students with ESN. Bloom's taxonomy indicates that teachers can engage their students by having them answer questions and engage in activities on a continuum of cognitive complexity, in which some line of questioning leads to higher-order thinking prompts than others. Teachers of students with ESN tend to ask their students to complete more *remembering* and *understanding* type questions in which students recall information or compare and classify facts and ideas. To deepen understanding and develop higher-order thinking, teachers should intentionally plan and incorporate questions and activities into their lessons that use other levels/cognitive process dimensions of Bloom's taxonomy and require more complex thinking (Wood et al., 2014). For example, when planning comprehension questions related to a short story, a teacher could develop both *remembering* (e.g., What is the name of the author?) and *evaluating* questions (e.g., Why did the author write this? [to persuade, entertain, and inform]) to challenge the student. Then, teachers ensure that students with ESN also are provided the opportunity to respond to these types of questions and that the materials needed to participate in higher-order thinking activities or answer higher-order questions have been modified as needed to allow for their participation (e.g., response options presented with pictures/graphic symbols and response boards planned prior to the lesson on students' AAC devices).

Systematically Assess Student Progress

Teachers who systematically design learning goals must continuously assess the effectiveness of their planning efforts and instructional goals. To do this, teachers continuously monitor their students' progress on the acquisition, fluency, maintenance, and generalization of the knowledge and skills they teach. Teachers also continuously monitor students' ability to use their prior learning to make connections to new learning. Based on the results of this formative assessment, teachers should then make instructional decisions as to whether they need to modify their instruction or continue it as planned. Chapter 6 addresses making data-based instructional decisions.

Next Steps Toward Better Practice

As teachers systematically design their lessons, there are a collection of actionable steps that they can take to ensure they are planning lessons that make connections for their students, build background knowledge, and embed higher-order thinking opportunities. The checklist in Figure 12.1 can be used by teachers to self-assess their lesson plans.

The Big Five

Five takeaways for teachers from HLP 12 include the following:

1. Write learning goals clearly so that all members of current and future interdisciplinary teams can accurately interpret and monitor progress.
2. Use the preferences of families and students, the expertise of general educators, and the results of ecological assessments to prioritize learning objectives over the course of a student's school life.
3. Embed applications of adaptive skills within the context of academic skill instruction.
4. Plan teaching sequences that move from simple to complex, that include development of background information, and that deliver effective prompting to help students develop understanding.
5. Assist students to form connections across content using visual displays (e.g., graphic organizers) and meaningful stories related to the content.

☐	Do I have differential learning outcomes for each student in my lesson?
☐	Have I created assessments to measure outcomes for all students? Are they differentiated to assess progress for all students?
☐	Have I connected with other professionals to collaborate on methods needed to enhance student learning? (SLP, OT, PT, paraprofessional)?
☐	Do I know students' background information related to the content to be taught? Have I planned activities to develop background information if needed?
☐	How will I set up my lesson to support active, engaging instruction (e.g., review classroom expectations, preview lesson objectives in student friendly language, make connections to prior knowledge, use meaningful and culturally relevant stories, and connect learning to real-life outcomes.)?
☐	Did I plan opportunities for all students to communicate during the lesson and ensured they have a communication system to do so?
☐	Do I have frequent opportunities for all students to respond?
☐	Have I planned systematic instruction to support learning of the instructional content (e.g., prompting procedures, error correction procedures, and reinforcement schedules.)?
☐	Do I have instructive feedback planned to deliver to help students elaborate on their responses?
☐	Have I planned for higher-order questions/differentiated tasks to challenge students?
☐	Have I planned for opportunities for students to self-assess their learning progress?
☐	How will I close my lesson (e.g., review of lesson objectives, review of main ideas of the lesson, tie the content back to real-life activities or how the skills are relevant to the student)?

Figure 12.1 Action Steps for Teachers to Evaluate Lessons when Designing Instruction

Resources

- *Choosing Outcomes and Accommodations for Children* https://products.brookespublishing.com/Choosing-Outcomes-and-Accommodations-for-Children-COACH-P463.aspx
- MAST Modules—Students with Significant Disabilities https://mast.ecu.edu/ (see Students with Significant Intellectual Disabilities—Instructional alignment, Adapting books, Story-based lessons, Math instruction)
- Apps and technology tools to assist students in viewing, creating, and collaborating using graphic organizers https://sites.google.com/view/freeudltechtoolkit/graphic-organizers
- TIES Center TIP #14: Academic Standards for Students with Significant Cognitive Disabilities in Inclusive Classrooms: Same Content Standards, Alternate Achievement Standards https://tiescenter.org/resource/tip-14-academic-standards-for-students-with-significant-cognitive-disabilities-in-inclusive-classrooms-same-content-standards-alternate-achievement-standards

References

Bateman, B. D., & Herr, C. M. (2010). *Writing measurable IEP goals and objectives.* Attainment Company.

Browder, D. M., Spooner, F., Courtade, G. C., & Mims, P. J. (2020). Building communication competence. In D. Browder, F. Spooner, & G. Courtade (Eds.), *Teaching students with moderate and severe disabilities* (2nd ed.) (pp. 41–61). The Guilford Press.

Browder, D. J., Spooner, F., Lo, Y., Saunders, A. F., Root, J. R., Davis, L. L., & Brosh, C. R. (2018). Teaching students with moderate intellectual disability to solve word problems. *The Journal of Special Education*, 51(44), 222–235. https://doi.org/10.1177/0022466917721236

Chapman, S. M., Ault, M. J., Spriggs, A. D., Bottge, B., & Shepley, S. L. (2019). Teaching an algebraic equation to high school students with moderate to severe intellectual disability. *Education and Training in Autism and Developmental Disabilities*, 54(2), 161–174. https://www.jstor.org/stable/26663974

Courtade, G., & Browder, D. (2016). *Aligning IEPs to state standards for students with moderate to severe disabilities*. Attainment Company, Inc.

Dieruf, K. B., Ault, M. J., & Spriggs, A. D. (2020). Teaching students with moderate and severe intellectual disability to compare characters in adapted text. *The Journal of Special Education*, 54(2), 80–89. https://doi.org/10.1177/0022466919869978

Endrew, F. v. Douglas County School District Re-1, 137 S. Ct. 988 (2017).

Giangreco, M. F., Cloninger, C. J., & Iverson, V. S. (2011). *Choosing outcomes & accommodations for children: A guide to educational planning for students with disabilities* (3rd ed.). Brookes.

Goran, L., Monaco, E. A. H., Yell, M. L., Shriner, J., & Bateman, D. (2020). Pursuing academic and functional advancement: Goals, services, and measuring progress. *TEACHING Exceptional Children*, 52(5), 333–343. https://doi.org/10.1177/0040059920919924

Grow, L., & Leblanc, L. (2013). Teaching receptive language skills: Recommendations for instructors. *Behavior Analysis in Practice*, 6(1), 56–75. https://doi.org/10.1007/BF03391791

Hedin, L., & DeSpain, S. (2018). SMART or not? Writing specific, measurable IEP goals. *TEACHING Exceptional Children*, 51(3), 100–110. https://doi.org/10.1177/

Hunt, P., McDonnell, J., & Crockett, M. A. (2012). Reconciling an ecological curricular framework focusing on quality of life outcomes with the development and instruction of standards-based academic goals. *Research and Practice for Persons With Severe Disabilities*, 37(3), 139–152. https://doi.org/10.2511/027494812804153471

Jimenez, B. A., Browder, D. M., & Courtade, G. R. (2009). An exploratory study of self-directed science concept learning by students with moderate intellectual disabilities. *Research and Practice for Persons With Severe Disabilities*, 34(2), 33–46. https://doi.org/10.2511/rpsd.34.2.33

Karl, J., Collins, B. C., Hager, K. D., & Ault, M. J. (2013). Teaching core content embedded in a functional activity to students with moderate intellectual disability using a simultaneous prompting procedure. *Education and Training in Autism and Developmental Disabilities*, 48(3), 363–378. https://www.jstor.org/stable/23880993

Kentucky Department of Education. (2022), August 30). *Kentucky Academic Standards - Alternate KSA*. https://education.ky.gov/AA/Assessments/summassmt/Pages/Kentucky-Academic-Standards---Alternate-KSA.aspx

Konrad, M., Hessler, T., Alber-Morgan, S. R., Davenport, C. A., & Helton, M. R. (2019). Systematically design instruction toward a specific learning goal. In J. McLeskey, L. Maheady, B. Billingsley, M. T. Brownell, & T. J. Lewis (Eds.), *High leverage practices for inclusive classrooms* (pp. 157–169). Routledge.

McDonnell, J., Jameson, J. M., Riesen, T., & Polychronis, S. (2014). Embedded instruction in inclusive settings. In D. Browder, & F. Spooner (Eds.), *More language arts, math, and science for students with severe disabilities* (pp. 15–36). Brookes.

McLeskey, J., Barringer, M.-D., Billngsley, B., Brownell, M., Jackson, D., Kennedy, M., Lewis, T., Maheady, L., Rodriguez, J., Scheeler, M. C., Winn, J., & Ziegler, D. (2017). *High-leverage practices in special education*. Council for Exceptional Children & CEEDAR Center. https://ceedar.education.ufl.edu/wp-content/uploads/2017/07/CEC-HLP-Web.pdf

Root, J. R., Henning, B., & Boccumini, E. (2018). Teaching students with autism and intellectual disability to solve algebraic word problems. *Education and Training in Autism and Developmental Disabilities*, 53(3), 325–338. https://www.jstor.org/stable/26563472

Winegarden, B. J. (2005). Writing instructional objectives. https://training.nwcg.gov/pre-courses/m410/Writing_Instructional-Objectives.pdf

Wood, L., Browder, D. M., & Mraz, M. (2014). Passage comprehension and read-alouds. In D. Browder, & F. Spooner (Eds.), *More language arts, math, and science for students with severe disabilities* (pp. 63–84). Brookes.

13
Adapt Curriculum Tasks and Materials for Specific Learning Goals

Pamela J. Mims, Addie McConomy, Jennifer Cook, and Jenny Root

Teachers assess individual student needs and adapt curriculum materials and tasks so that students can meet instructional goals. Teachers select materials and tasks based on student needs; use relevant technology; and make modifications by highlighting relevant information, changing task directions, and decreasing amounts of material. Teachers make strategic decisions on content coverage (i.e., essential curriculum elements), meaningfulness of tasks to meet stated goals, and criteria for student success.

Supporting Students with Extensive Support Needs

High-leverage practice (HLP) 13, Adapt Curriculum Tasks and Materials for Specific Learning Goals, is critical for providing necessary access to general education curriculum for students with ESN. Once educators assess the needs of students, they can adapt tasks and materials to support students in successfully meeting their specific learning goals. This is especially important for students with ESN as their unique needs can create barriers that teachers and paraeducators must adequately address. Removing barriers and providing accessibility using relevant technology, modifications to highlight important information, and reducing and changing requirements for the range and depth of content to be covered can help students with ESN be successful (McLeskey, 2017). Implementing these strategies can lead to increased quality of life for students with ESN.

Chapter Objectives

Upon reading this chapter, you should be able to do the following:

1. Identify strategies for adapting curriculum tasks and materials for specific learning goals for students with ESN.
2. Identify procedures for adapting curriculum tasks and materials for specific learning goals for students with ESN.
3. Identify content enhancements and determine when they can be used in addition to or in place of adaptations to support access to curriculum tasks and materials for specific learning goals for students with ESN.

DOI: 10.4324/9781003175735-14

4. Share examples for adapting curriculum tasks and materials for specific learning goals for students with ESN.

Adaptations

While adaptations are often necessary for students with ESN to access materials and instruction, proactively using the Universal Design for Learning (UDL) framework reduces barriers and improves instructional access for all students. The UDL framework has three guiding principles: engagement, representation, and action and expression. Each of these principles are shaped by guidelines that teachers can use for implementation (Nelson, 2014). When teachers use UDL, they strive to change their classroom learning environment so that all students can be challenged and engaged in meaningful learning (CAST, 2018). UDL can provide guidance for teachers making adaptations to instruction and assessment. The following sections provide specific guidance for teachers on how to adapt tasks to make the general curriculum accessible for students with ESN by focusing on relevant information, changing the task, adjusting the amount of content, and adjusting the depth of content. These strategies also fall under best practice for implementing UDL. For more information, visit the CAST UDL website (web address found below in Resources section).

Focus on Relevant Information

Teachers should begin the process of adapting curriculum tasks and materials by using a team approach. When planning for instruction and adapting curriculum tasks and materials for students with ESN, a collaborative team is critical. Collaborative teams are shown to be beneficial in determining what individual supports may be useful for students with ESN (Browder et al., 2008; Hunt et al., 2004). Teachers need an accurate understanding of a student's learning profile, including prior knowledge and skill gaps, in order to prioritize content. To individualize the content that is prioritized and to provide authentic challenge to individual students, teachers should consider the student's strengths, preferences, abilities, and needs. These data can be collected from IEP team members (including parent/caregivers), observations, and formal assessments, but frequent direct formative assessments should be prioritized (Browder et al., 2020).

Teachers can support students with ESN by adapting text to emphasize relevant information and minimize irrelevant information as appropriate. Targeted information should build on prior knowledge and be necessary for mastering the content. Emphasis should be placed on novel vocabulary, main ideas, and common misconceptions. Emphasis can be made visually by using bolded text, icons, and/or pictures to support understanding of key vocabulary or main ideas. Teachers also should teach students to use the emphasized content by modeling. For example, the teacher may draw attention to a vocabulary word that includes an icon and ask students if they have used that word in the past, what it means to them, and if they can use the word in a statement. Common misconceptions can be addressed by using model/lead/test and providing examples and non-examples (e.g., My turn (teacher says): "Precipitation is liquid that falls from the sky." Together (teacher and student say): "Precipitation is liquid that falls from the sky." Your turn (student says): "Precipitation is liquid that falls from the sky." Teacher: "Now let's look at examples and non-examples." (Shows T-chart). "This is precipitation" (points to an example and repeats). "This is not precipitation" (points to non-examples and repeats). Reducing the information presented on an individual page can also help students with ESN focus on relevant information. Teachers can present only one question or piece of information at a time by using a sheet of cardboard to cover additional content, folding a paper to obscure all concepts but one, or printing content in a way that limits the amount of information displayed at one time.

Changing Tasks

Academic tasks often result in a product (e.g., completed worksheet, diagram, and illustration with caption) representing the student's learning. One initial step in supporting students with ESN is providing directions for completing products in a simplified and accessible format. Directions for completing similar products should be consistent to reduce the cognitive load required for following directions. For example, students may use a binder to submit all their math products. The directions may include circling the final answer. Students will circle their final answer on every math product in the binder, regardless of the format (worksheet, diagram, etc.).

Some students will need more support, and teachers may determine that the best way to make content accessible for students with ESN is to change the task or learning product. Changing the task may require teaching individual (discrete) skills in repetition until they are mastered and can be added to a series (chained) of tasks. When teachers make changes to a learning product for a student with ESN, the teacher should consider the student's learning profile and preferred method of communication. Some products may be presented and responded to orally; a teacher can scribe responses or the student can use speech-to-text software to develop a permanent product. Other options may include using durable response cards (e.g., card stock) or physical manipulatives to indicate responses (e.g., small plastic animal models in place of names of animals printed on worksheet).

Additionally, students with ESN will benefit from academic questioning that is tailored to their preferred response modes or the mode that allows them to independently show what they know. Some students may prefer open-ended questions that allow them to answer with their own words. Other students may need the support offered by multiple-choice response options. Response choices also can be prioritized and emphasized as needed for individual students. Differentiating the response option is an accessible way for teachers to accommodate individual needs. Figure 13.1 provides an example of differentiating the response option.

The concrete, representational, abstract (CRA) instructional framework is an example of changing the task to support all students in mathematics. The use of the CRA instructional framework can support all learners and offers teachers an opportunity to make adaptions to the task. To use this framework with students with ESN in math content, the teacher prepares manipulatives that

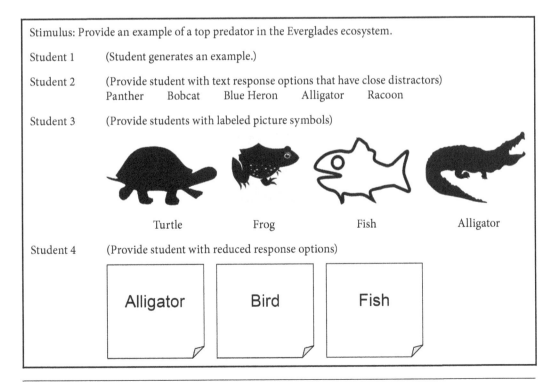

Stimulus: Provide an example of a top predator in the Everglades ecosystem.

Student 1   (Student generates an example.)

Student 2   (Provide student with text response options that have close distractors)
                 Panther   Bobcat   Blue Heron   Alligator   Racoon

Student 3   (Provide students with labeled picture symbols)

                 Turtle   Frog   Fish   Alligator

Student 4   (Provide student with reduced response options)

                 Alligator   Bird   Fish

Figure 13.1 Examples of Ways Students Can Show What They Know

have a one-to-one correspondence to the mathematical problem (i.e., $5 + 2 = 7$ requires seven individually movable items). Once the student has mastered this skill, the teacher can support the learner with representational items, for example, a printed number line. Finally, the problem is presented with no additional support. CRA is an evidence-based instructional framework for providing math instruction to students with learning disabilities (Bouck et al., 2018), which is also effective for students with ESN (e.g., Root et al., 2020; Stroizer et al., 2015).

Adjusting Amount of Content

Teachers must make instructional decisions regarding the amount of content students will master during an instructional session, unit, and within long-range goals. This planning should be supported by assessment data. Once a teacher has prioritized the content that will be taught, they will need to determine the amount of content to provide during each lesson. It can be beneficial to develop a task analysis for content mastery and remove barrier steps that require prerequisite skills, or plan to teach those prerequisite skills in isolation. Once a task analysis is developed, a chaining strategy will need to be chosen. Forward chaining teaches skills in order and prioritizes completing steps, not the whole task, with a focus on mastery of early steps (either individual or in "chunks") before moving on to subsequent steps (Browder et al., 2020). For example, a student may be taught to type their username into a computer log in before being taught to type their password. In total task chaining, the entire task is completed during each instructional session, with explicit instruction on each of the steps that the student has not yet mastered (Browder et al., 2020). In this case, the student would be taught to type their username, password, and click "log in" to complete all steps of the "Log into the computer" task analysis.

Another strategy that can differentiate the amount of content students are responsible for completing is the cloze strategy (Figure 13.2). Blank spaces/lines are inserted for key content, requiring students to fill in the blanks with vocabulary words. This can be a highly individualized strategy to promote engagement while adjusting the depth of the content for each student. When teachers use this strategy, they should begin by (1) removing key content for the students that need the most support, (2) copying the text, (3) removing more content for students who are ready to master more content, and (4) repeating the process until the required number of levels of materials have been prepared. Examples of this process are shown in Figure 13.2 using a paragraph from ReadWorks (2013).

The instructional unit shared above is an adaptation of the CRA that is supported by evidence in math instruction (Bouck et al., 2018). Teachers can provide concrete examples using real objects (e.g., bowl of water), representational examples (e.g., pictures or icons of water), and abstract examples (word only) to support students at a variety of symbolic communication levels throughout each of the stages of learning.

Adjusting Depth of Content

Teachers can provide material adaptation by adjusting depth of content. One commonly used example to adjusting depth of content is using leveled text. Many curricula and websites provide text with similar meanings but leveled to accommodate decoding and vocabulary concerns. An example from the website ReadWorks (2013) is provided in Figure 13.3.

Content Enhancements

Content enhancement is an instructional method that uses evidence-based teaching strategies to help students organize and present content in a manner that demonstrates they can show what they know (Strategic Instruction Model, http://sim.kucrl.org/). Content enhancements can be used in addition to or separate from adaptations. Below, we describe a few content enhancements and,

Key (no words omitted)

The Everglades is a kind of region called a subtropical wetland. This means the area has pretty warm temperatures all year round and that the land is full of water. Water flows from a nearby lake into the Everglades wetlands. The Everglades is sometimes called the "River of Grass" because it is basically a very wide and shallow river.

Students who need more support

The _____ is a kind of region called a subtropical wetland.

This means the area has pretty _____ temperatures all year round and that the land is full of _____.

Water flows from a nearby lake into the Everglades wetlands.

The Everglades is sometimes called the "River of Grass" because it is basically a very wide and shallow _____.

Everglades	Warm	Water	River

*Picture symbols used for students who are beginning with or moving forward with symbols; R in the CRA

Students who need the most support

*Objects for students who need more concrete representation; C in the CRA

Other students may benefit from the key terms but not visual support.

Students who need less support

The _____ is a kind of region called a subtropical _____.

This means the area has pretty _____ temperatures all year round and that the land is full of _____.

Water flows from a nearby _____ into the Everglades wetlands. The Everglades is sometimes called the "River of _____" because it is basically a very wide and shallow _____.

Figure 13.2 Example of Differentiating with a Cloze Strategy

Most content	The Florida Everglades teems with life. Situated at the southern end of the state, between Lake Okeechobee and the Gulf Coast, the Everglades is the largest wilderness east of the Mississippi River. Migratory and wading birds tiptoe through marshy grasslands. Orchids and ferns dot the hardwood forests. Alligators lounge in the shallows and on muddy riverbanks. Mangrove leaves rustle in the wind as the brackish water laps at their roots.
	The Florida Everglades is full of life. It is located at the southern end of the state. The Everglades is a large and wild natural region. For example, many kinds of birds live in the wet and grassy areas. Lots of plants and flowers grow in the forests. Alligators sit in the water and on muddy riverbanks.
Least content	The Florida Everglades is a large natural area at the south end of Florida. It is full of life. Many kinds of birds live in the wet and grassy areas of the Everglades. Different plants live in the forests. Alligators sit in the water and along the muddy sides of rivers.

Figure 13.3 Leveled Text

for each, highlight the benefits, which include ways for the student to access, interact, understand, and retain content; guidelines for use; and suggested examples for application. We highlight three content enhancements that are evidence-based practices (EBPs) for students with ESN: visual supports, adapted text and story-based lessons, and graphic organizers.

Visual Supports

Visual supports are a commonly used communication and teaching support that help students with ESN gain access to information and/or allow increased understanding of a task, message, or expectation. Objects, photographs, and pictures are all examples of common visual supports. The intention of visual supports is to increase independence in learning tasks by improving engagement (Johnston et al., 2004) and decreasing reliance on teachers for prompting and support. One of the biggest benefits for students with ESN who use visual supports is the provision of multiple means of action and expression; the visuals remove barriers allowing students to "show what they know." In Figure 13.1, the use of the visual response options allows students to not only interact with the content, but can provide a reliable way for students to demonstrate understanding of the content. Finally, visual supports can be used to promote generalization and maintenance of skills (e.g., Learning about birds and the visual support for bird in the context of a lesson can generalize and maintain for applicability when using a map to find the birds at a zoo.).

Adapted Text and Story-based Lessons

Researchers have emphasized the importance and impact of adapting text for students with ESN, which can be done through systematic reductions and additions (Lee, 2010). To increase accessibility while maintaining attention to the key ideas, original texts can be adapted through simplification (or reducing the Lexile level) and reducing the amount of text that appears on each page. Additions that can support comprehension include pictures above key vocabulary words, repeated story lines that reinforce the main idea, and definitions and explanations of key vocabulary within the text. In addition to adapting text, creating a systematic approach to progressing through the text can create a predictable routine for teachers and students. One evidence-based approach to increase literacy skills is the use of story-based lessons (SBL; shared story, read aloud; Hudson & Test, 2011). Numerous studies have been conducted that indicate the use of adapted texts and a story-based approach have increased access and comprehension of all academic content areas (Hudson & Test, 2011). Opportunities to ask comprehension questions developed across different levels of Bloom's Taxonomy with a set of response options allow for students to show what they know. Writing activities that occur after a SBL can provide opportunities for students with ESN to demonstrate understanding of concepts learned in the text. Finally, adapted text and SBL can promote retention of concepts and content through repeated readings and the repeated exposure to the systematic process of a SBL (Hudson & Test, 2011).

Following the guidelines for implementing SBL (Jimenez et al., 2007), teachers can promote early literacy skills and overall engagement of students with ESN. For example, a repeated storyline embedded at the bottom of each page of an adapted text allows for a student to demonstrate emergent literacy skills by text pointing to each word in the sentence. Or, when a teacher is reading the text aloud and comes across a targeted vocabulary word, they could stop and ask the student to identify the targeted word on the page.

Adapted texts and SBL provide students with ESN access to content of their same grade-level peers without disabilities, allowing for natural opportunities to not only target grade-aligned standards, but also avenues for addressing personally relevant and age-appropriate content topics (e.g., themes of bullying, sexuality, and friendship). These texts could otherwise be a barrier for students with ESN. Given the text complexity and length of grade-appropriate texts as students age, teachers must continue to consider ways for their students with ESN to access complex texts vs. providing age-/grade-inappropriate texts that may be less complex. For example, instead of providing an eighth-grade student with ESN access to an early elementary picture book, a teacher could provide an adapted version of an eighth-grade novel and use a SBL format to encourage engagement.

Graphic Organizers

Graphic organizers are visual displays used to organize information in a clear, concise, and concrete manner and to effectively facilitate teaching and student learning across age, grade, and skill level (Dye, 2000; Ellis & Howard, 2007). Teachers can use graphic organizers to enhance universally designed lesson content by providing teachers and students alternative means of representation, expression, and engagement while accessing new information (Barton-Arwood & Little, 2013; Knight et al., 2013). Graphic organizers can help students with ESN comprehend and retain information by encouraging active participation and by linking new learning to prior learning (Browder & Spooner, 2011). In recent literature, the use of graphic organizers has been shown to effectively support learning and improve academic outcomes for students with ESN in mathematics (e.g., Cox & Root, 2020), science (e.g., Knight et al., 2013), language arts (e.g., Mims et al., 2012), and social studies (e.g., Schenning et al., 2013). Because graphic organizers are commonly used in K-12 classrooms, they can be easy to find or create online or can be created with common classroom materials (e.g., paper and pencil, computer, tablet, white board, etc.). Students can access graphic organizers either digitally via technology (e.g., presented on a computer or tablet) or hard copy, both of which can be adapted to match the unique instructional and communication profiles of students with ESN. Additionally, graphic organizers can be used with picture symbols, photos, or objects for all students to show understanding and/or organize information in a way that is meaningful to them.

The graphic organizers described below can be adapted to match students' communication and sensory and learning needs. While the general format of each graphic organizer will remain consistent across learners and content, how students interact with (i.e., use/read, input information) the graphic organizer can be adapted to meet individual support needs. For example, for students who are at the presymbolic level of communication (i.e., building awareness of symbols), the teacher, paraeducators, or peer can use objects to represent key vocabulary and to encourage student responding. For students at a concrete symbolic level (i.e., beginning to use symbols), key vocabulary may be presented with objects to promote interest and interaction with content during instruction and provide an array of labeled objects and pictures for students to choose from to demonstrate understanding of key concepts in the graphic organizer.

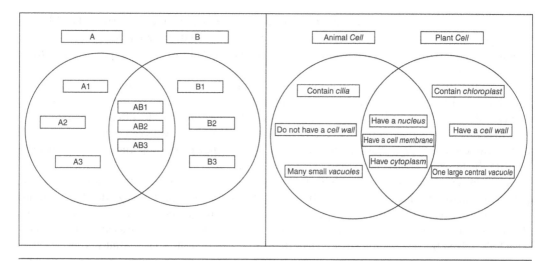

Figure 13.4 Example of a Digital Venn Diagram Before and After Student Input

Note. The figure on the left is an example of a blank Venn diagram template with prepopulated text boxes for speech-to-text input from student. The figure on the right is an example of a Venn diagram comparing animal cells and plant cells that has been completed by a student using speech to text. Key vocabulary words have been *italicized.*

Finally, for students who are at an abstract symbolic level (i.e., uses words and symbols and may demonstrate early reading skills) of communication, teachers can present content in the graphic organizer with words and/or words paired with pictures to promote understanding. Students at this level may write words or choose from a word bank to demonstrate understanding. Finally, universal assistive technologies (e.g., speech to text and text to speech) can be used to make digital graphic organizers accessible to students who are non-emerging or emerging readers and writers and/or students with visual impairments (Cannella-Malone et al., 2015). Figure 13.4 is an example of a Venn diagram template that can be used with speech-to-text in common productivity apps (e.g., PowerPoint, Microsoft Word, and Google).

Graphic organizers are most effective when teachers use explicit instruction with modeling, guided practice, and feedback to teach students how to populate and use the graphic organizer prior to expectations of independent use. By following consistent rules and routines when introducing and using graphic organizers, teachers can help students move from learning how to use a graphic organizer to using a graphic organizer to learn. For this reason, teachers should consider creating a standard set of graphic organizers such as T-Charts; What do you **Know**, What do you **Want** to Know, What did you **Learn** Charts (KWL); and Venn diagrams that can be used across content areas (Baxendell, 2003) to allow students to practice, retain, and generalize their use to learn new concepts across academic areas (Figures 13.4 and 13.5).

The following are tips for using graphic organizers with students with ESN:

- Choose key concepts and vocabulary necessary for understanding the content.
- Create clear and coherent graphic organizers that are free of distracting or extraneous content.
- The complexity of the graphic organizer should match the student's symbolic level of communication, experience, and background knowledge.
- Match the space for information to be input by students to their level of communication (e.g., use of objects, pictures, handwriting, and speech to text).
- Consider using digital graphic organizers (e.g., tablet and computer) with accessibility features when needed.

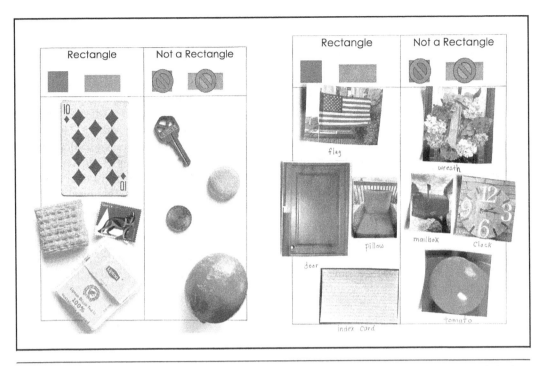

Figure 13.5 Example and Non-example Instruction and Example of Differentiated T-Charts at Presymbolic and Concrete Symbolic Levels

Note. The figure on the left is a T-Chart constructed with objects student brought from home. The figure on the right is the same T-Chart constructed with pictures of items which were labeled by a peer.

Next Steps Toward Better Practice

There are many components within HLP 13: Adapt Curriculum Tasks and Materials for Specific Learning Goals. For teachers of students with ESN, this HLP may be most critical to supporting access to the general curriculum, as we know that students are able to master grade-aligned content when provided with these adaptations and evidence-based instructional practices (Browder et al., 2020). We conclude this chapter with actionable steps teachers can take to begin or improve their use of HLP 13.

Step 1: Choose One Strategy to Do Well and Build from There

Since HLP 13 applies to the entire curriculum, it would be overwhelming (and probably not feasible) to immediately implement all the strategies we described in this chapter. Instead, we suggest teachers select one strategy or content area on which to focus. For example, a focus on supporting students in literacy learning goals could be facilitated by adapting one text and planning corresponding story-based lessons. Using content enhancements such as graphic organizers and manipulatives, perhaps within the CRA framework, would be a practical place to begin if the focus was on a mathematics learning goal. Alternatively, if teachers feel that the most pressing learning goal for their students relates to engagement and communication, perhaps a focus on content enhancements allowing students to "show what they know" such as response cards and visual supports should be prioritized. Once teachers can implement the new strategy well, a second strategy can be initiated while the first is maintained.

Step 2: Collect Usable Data and Use the Data You Collect!

Teachers should be making decisions about learning goal priorities (e.g., Step 1) based on student data. If that is not a frequent or common practice already, it is never too late to start! Simply collecting data is not beneficial to anyone if it is not usable data. Usable data are valid (measure what you intend to measure) and reliable (collected consistently). For students with ESN, it may be helpful to know about the setting or contextual variables around when data were collected—such as the instructional format (e.g., one on one, small group, and whole group), setting (e.g., general education classroom and special education classroom), instructor (e.g., general education teacher, special education teacher, paraeducator, student teacher, and peer), and time of day (e.g., morning and afternoon). These components can help to understand patterns in student data as well as whether students are generalizing skills or applying them to different settings. Having efficient and comprehensive data collection systems is not sufficient—they must be used! Student data should be reviewed regularly (e.g., every one to two weeks) to guide instructional decision-making. Students who are not on track to meet learning goals may need further changes made to increase support, whereas others who have met learning goals are ready for increased challenge (for more information, see HLP 6: use student assessment data, analyze instructional practices, and make necessary adjustments that improve student outcomes).

Step 3: Explicitly Teach Students How to Use Supports

Simply providing students with content enhancements (e.g., task analyses, graphic organizers, manipulatives, and response options) is not sufficient. Students must be taught how to use these appropriately. For example, explicit instruction on how to use graphic organizers and manipulatives to model the mathematical expression *3 x 2* and find the solution would include the following: (a) teacher modeling using their own graphic organizer and manipulatives to make three groups of two, (b) guided practice to give students a chance to practice modeling the problem on their own graphic organizers with immediate error correction with feedback from the teacher, and (c) independent practice modeling the problem (this is when the teacher could take data). When students with ESN are using unfamiliar or novel supports and learning a new or cognitively demanding skill, we recommend separating teaching how to use the supports (e.g., modeling the equation) from the actual skill (e.g., solving the equation) to reduce cognitive load.

Step 4: Use Resources from General Education

Remember the mantra "no more different than necessary" (Browder et al., 2017). Collaboration between general and special education teachers can help to make sure that enhancements and adaptations for learners with ESN are based on the general curriculum of their typically developing peers.

Step 5: Develop Varied Response Methods to Use Across Content Areas

Communication is often one of the primary barriers to progress in academic learning goals for students with ESN. As a result, a critical action step for implementing HLP 13 is developing varied response modes that students can consistently use across content areas. As described above, these may be low tech (e.g., response cards and visual supports) or high tech (e.g., AAC overlays and assistive technology). Regardless of what is chosen, students will not develop independent and successful use of these response modes unless they are consistently available, consistently expected to be used, and consistently reinforced.

The Big Five

In this chapter, we shared information regarding best practice in adapting curriculum tasks and materials for students with ESN. Additionally, we provided several examples of evidence-based practices specific to teaching grade-level academic skills that exemplify this HLP for student with ESN. In summary, there are five big takeaways to consider when adapting curriculum tasks and materials for this population.

1. Consider student strengths, preferences, abilities, and needs while prioritizing goals with a focus on personally relevant content.
2. Collaborative teaming, data collection, and data-based decision-making are critical in planning for how students with ESN can access content and materials.
3. Consider how to make the task accessible for the student so they may independently show what they know.
4. Content enhancements can be a low-effort, high-reward instruction method that integrates evidence-based teaching strategies (e.g., visual supports, manipulatives, adapted text, and graphic organizers) to help students with ESN organize content and share knowledge of grade-aligned academic content.
5. Adaptations and modifications do not have to be difficult to implement. Often, there are subtle changes that can be made, additions to current materials or tasks, or technology added that can make a vast difference in the success of students with ESN.

Resources

Autism Focused Intervention Resources & Modules
https://afirm.fpg.unc.edu/afirm-modules
Assistive Technology Internet Modules
https://atinternetmodules.org/
TIES Center website
https://tiescenter.org/
Project STAIR (Supporting Teaching of Algebra: Individual Readiness)
https://blog.smu.edu/projectstair/category/educator-resources/tailored-professional-development/
    best-practices-for-math-teachers/
MAST Modules
https://mast.ecu.edu/
CAST
https://www.cast.org/our-work/accessibility-inclusive-technology
and
https://www.cast.org/impact/universal-design-for-learning-udl
HLP 13
https://highleveragepractices.org/hlp-13-make-adaptations
Balancing Fidelity and Adaptation: A Guide for Evidence-based Program Implementation
https://pttcnetwork.org/sites/default/files/2021-12/Cooper%20et%20al.%20%282019%29%20
    Balancing%20Fidelity%20%26%20Adaptation.pdf

References

Barton-Arwood, S. M., & Little, A. (2013). Using graphic organizers to access the general curriculum at the secondary level. *Intervention in School and Clinic, 49*(1), 6–13. https://doi.org/10.1177/1053451213480025

Baxendell, B. W. (2003). Consistent, coherent, creative: The 3 c's of graphic organizers. *TEACHING Exceptional Children, 35*(3), 46–53. https://doi.org/10.1177/004005990303500307

Bouck, E. C., Satsangi, R., & Park, J. (2018). The Concrete–Representational–Abstract approach for students with learning disabilities: An evidence-based practice synthesis. *Remedial and Special Education, 39*(4), 211–228. https://doi.org/10.1177/0741932517721712

Browder, D. M., Mims, P. J., Spooner, F., Ahlgrim-Delzell, L., & Lee, A. (2008). Teaching elementary students with multiple disabilities to participate in shared stories. *Research & Practice for Persons With Severe Disabilities, 33*(1-2), 3–12. https://doi.org/10.2511/rpsd.33.1-2.3

Browder, D. M., & Spooner, F. (2011). *Teaching students with moderate and severe disabilities* (1st ed.). The Guilford Press.

Browder, D. M., Spooner, F., Courtade, G. R., & Pennington, R. (2020). Monitoring and enhancing student progress: Getting the most out of data. In D. M. Browder, F. Spooner, & G. Courtade (Ed.), *Teaching students with moderate and severe disabilities* (2nd ed. pp. 191–208). The Guilford Press.

Browder, D. M., Spooner, F., Lo, Y. Y., Saunders, A. F., Root, J. R., Ley Davis, L., & Brosh, C. (2017). *Project solutions implementation manual*. The University of North Carolina at Charlotte. https://access.charlotte.edu/sites/access.charlotte.edu/files/media/solutions/TheSolutionsProject_Manual%20For%20Dissemination.pdf

Cannella-Malone, H. I., Konrad, M., & Pennington, R. C. (2015). ACCESS! Teaching writing skills to students with intellectual disability. *TEACHING Exceptional Children, 47*(5), 272–280. https://doi.org/10.1177/0040059915580032

CAST (2018). Universal Design for Learning Guidelines version 2.2. Retrieved from http://udlguidelines.cast.org

Cox, S. K., & Root, J. R. (2020). Modified schema-based instruction to develop flexible mathematics problem-solving strategies for students with autism spectrum disorder. *Remedial and Special Education, 41*(3), 139–151. https://doi.org/10.1177%2F1540796920949448

Dye, G. A. (2000). Graphic organizers to the rescue! Helping students link—and remember—Information. *TEACHING Exceptional Children, 32*(3), 72–76. https://doi.org/10.1177/004005990003200311

Ellis, E., & Howard, P. (2007). Graphic organizers. *Current Practice Alerts, 1*(13), 1–4.

Hudson, M. E., & Test, D. W. (2011). Evaluating the evidence base of shared story reading to promote literacy for students with extensive support needs. *Research and Practice for Person With Severe Disabilities, 36*(1-2). https://doi.org/10.2511/rpsd.36.1-2.34

Hunt, P., Soto, G., Maier, J., Liboiron, N., & Bae, S. (2004). Collaborative teaming to support preschoolers with severe disabilities who are placed in general education programs. *Topics in Early Childhood Special Education, 24*(3), 132–142. https://doi.org/10.1177/02711214040240030101

Jimenez, B., Browder, D. M., & Trela, K. (2007). Training teachers to follow a task analysis to engage middle school students with moderate and severe developmental disabilities in grade-appropriate literature. *Focus on Autism and Other Developmental Disabilities, 22*(4), 206–219. https://doi.org/10.1177/10883576070220040301

Johnston, S. S., Reichle, J., & Evans, J. (2004). Supporting augmentative and alternative communication use by beginning communicators with severe disabilities. *American Journal of Speech Language Pathology, 12*, 20–30. https://doi.org/10.1044/1058-0360(2004/004)

Knight, V., McKissick, B. R., & Saunders, A. (2013). A review of technology-based interventions to teach academic skills to students with autism spectrum disorder. *Journal of Autism and Developmental Disorders, 43*(11), 2628–2648. https://doi.org/10.1007/s10803-013-1814-y

Lee, A., (2010). Students with significant cognitive disabilities: Adapting books. Modules Addressing Special Education and Teacher Education (MAST). Available at https://mast.ecu.edu/Students%20with%20Significant%20Intellectual%20Disabilities/Adapting%20Books/index.html

McLeskey, J., Barringer, M-D., Billingsley, B., Brownell, M., Jackson, D., Kennedy, M., Lewis, T., Maheady, L., Rodriguez, J., Scheeler, M. C., Winn, J., & Ziegler, D. (2017, January). *High-leverage practices in special education*. Council for Exceptional Children & CEEDAR Center. https://ceedar.education.ufl.edu/wp-content/uploads/2017/07/CEC-HLP-Web.pdf

Mims, P. J., Lee, A., Browder, D. M., Zakas, T., & Flynn, S. (2012). The effects of a treatment package to facilitate English/language arts learning for middle school students with moderate to severe disabilities. *Education and Training in Autism and Developmental Disabilities, 47*(4), 414–425. https://www.jstor.org/stable/23879635

Nelson, L. L. (2014). *Design and deliver: Planning and teaching using universal design for learning*. Brookes Publishing.

ReadWorks. (2013). Pythons invade the Florida Everglades. https://www.readworks.org/article/Pythons-Invade-the-Florida-Everglades/70e9c396-91f6-46b8-9fb0-27ab30ad57f1#!articleTab:content/

Root, J. R., Cox, S. K., Gilley, D., & Wade, T. (2020). Using a virtual-representational-abstract integrated framework to teach multiplicative problem solving to middle school students with developmental disabilities. *Journal of Autism and Developmental Disorders, 51*(7), 2284–2296. https://doi.org/10.1007/s10803-020-04674-2

Schenning, H., Knight, V., & Spooner, F. (2013). Effects of structured inquiry and graphic organizers on social studies comprehension by students with autism spectrum disorders. *Research in Autism Spectrum Disorders, 7*(4), 526–540. https://doi.org/10.1016/j.rasd.2012.12.007

Stroizer, S., Hinton, V., Flores, M., & Terry, L. (2015). An investigation of the effects of CRA instruction and students with autism spectrum disorder. *Education and Training in Autism and Developmental Disabilities, 50*(2), 223–236. https://www.jstor.org/stable/24827537

14

Teach Cognitive and Metacognitive Strategies to Support Learning and Independence

Joanna Ryan and Jessica Bowman

Teachers explicitly teach cognitive and metacognitive processing strategies to support memory, attention, and self-regulation of learning. Learning involves not only understanding content but also using cognitive processes to solve problems, regulate attention, organize thoughts and materials, and monitor one's own thinking. Self-regulation and metacognitive strategy instruction are integrated into lessons on academic content through modeling and explicit instruction. Students learn to monitor and evaluate their performance in relation to explicit goals and make necessary adjustments to improve learning.

Supporting Students with Extensive Support Needs

Federal education laws require schools to provide all students, including students with extensive support needs (ESN), with instruction that promotes progress in the general grade-level curriculum. Special education research shows that students with ESN can gain knowledge and skills aligned with the general curriculum when provided with instruction that effectively supports their learning (McDonnell et al., 2020). As educational planning teams develop individualized programs for students, they must consider students' access to all aspects of their grade-level general curriculum, including academic content, settings, and instructional frameworks. Plans that conceptualize students' curriculum access within each of these areas may help to ensure that students receive meaningful and enriched educational experiences in a way that aligns with education laws.

As students learn from the general curriculum, they also need to learn to use strategies that promote the independent and generalized use of academic skills. When educational teams can use instructional methods that link academic instruction to functional outcomes, students' learning of knowledge and skills aligned with the general curriculum becomes more socially significant (Hunt et al., 2012). That is, when students can meaningfully use the skills they learn in "real-life" situations outside of the immediate instructional environment, grade-level curriculum content learning becomes more valuable to students' short- and long-term life outcomes. Cognitive and metacognitive strategy instruction can help teachers promote students' generalized use of the skills they learn during classroom instruction. These practices have been described in high-leverage practice (HLP) resources for students with mild and moderate disabilities (Kennedy et al., 2020) and have received some attention in resources describing educational practices for students with ESN. As with any

DOI: 10.4324/9781003175735-15

performance skill, teachers can clearly define and systematically teach these processes for students with ESN.

Chapter Objectives

Upon reading this chapter, you should be able to do the following:

1. Define the term *cognitive strategies* and provide everyday examples of cognitive strategies used by students with ESN.
2. Define the term *metacognition* and describe the steps students complete when using metacognitive strategies.
3. Describe the importance of cognitive and metacognitive strategies for helping students to generalize skills and increase independence.
4. Describe ways to teach cognitive strategies and metacognition for students with ESN.
5. Describe the importance of fading instructor support when teaching students to use cognitive and metacognitive strategies.

What Are Cognitive Strategies? What Is Metacognition?

Education resources that describe best practices for students with mild and moderate disabilities highlight the importance of goal-setting and reflective processes to independent and generalized learning (Graham et al., 2016). This idea can also be applied to instruction and learning for students with ESN, and these practices have been taught using frameworks such as the self-determined learning model of instruction (SDLMI; Kansas University Center on Developmental Disabilities, n.d.), structured inquiry-based instruction (Ryan et al., 2019), and modified schema-based instruction (MSBI; Cox & Root, 2020). As these ways of teaching are used, it is important to provide instruction using strategies that have been shown to be effective for students with ESN. This chapter addresses two ideas described in education literature, *cognitive strategies* and *metacognition*, and presents a conceptualization of them in terms of evidenced and HLPs for students with ESN.

Educational researchers and practitioners use the term *cognitive strategies* to describe the skills that students learn to help them to solve problems or take action during academic tasks and daily living situations. Cognitive strategies involve using processes, physical tools, and ways of thinking to support task completion and action-taking within specific situations (The IRIS Center, 2015). One way to think of cognitive strategies is as a type of prompt that does not need another person. Cognitive strategies are self-management strategies used to complete tasks and take action. These strategies can be used to support many activities and areas of academic and daily life, help make complex or vague processes systematic and concrete, and make these processes easier to teach and learn. Students can use strategies for solving math problems, planning the next steps to complete functional tasks, demonstrating comprehension of written passages, organizing materials and the time it takes to complete tasks, self-managing behaviors needed to successfully complete tasks, and remembering information required to complete activities. Chelly, a student with ESN, uses cognitive strategies to complete academic activities in a ninth-grade general education English-language arts classroom. Each day, the class completes a timed written reflection. Chelly completes her reflection using a graphic organizer that includes areas labeled "who," "where," and "what." The organizer is a cognitive strategy that helps her remember the type of information she needs to write and helps her put the information into an order she can use to develop sentences. She also has difficulty remembering how to correctly spell common words during reflection writing and often asks peers or instructors for help. A paraprofessional worked with her to develop an acronym for the word "said." When she needs to write the word "said," she thinks, "Sam and I danced," to remember the order of the letters. Table 14.1 shows examples of cognitive strategies for approaching a variety of academic and functional situations.

Table 14.1 Task Dimensions and Cognitive Strategies

Dimensions of Successful Task Completion	Examples of Cognitive Strategies to Support Each Dimension
Organizing materials	Checklists for materials needed to complete a task or participate in an activity
	Graphic organizers to arrange materials
	Environmental organizational systems, such as bins, folders, or sorting tubs
Remembering to begin a task or activity	Alarms
	Interval timers
	Calendars
	Graphic organizers for note-taking
	Physical reminders such as sticky notes or environmental arrangement
Remembering steps in a process	Visually presented task steps
	Lists
	Mnemonics
	Tallying the number of times a process was used
	Graphic organizers
Completing a task or activity within a time limit	Visual timers
	Check-in system
Gathering necessary information	Charts
	Graphic organizers
	Highlighting text
Attending to and remaining engaged with a task or activity	Reinforcement systems
	Interval timers
	Check-in, check-out systems

Metacognition involves a person's observation and assessment of the cognitive strategies they select to solve problems and to take action in their day-to-day lives. When people encounter problems or actionable situations, they need to be able to plan, monitor, and assess the strategies they use as they take action or resolve issues. These are typically "covert" skills that others cannot directly observe and include the sequence of thoughts that occur as a person evaluates outcomes and determines needed steps to resolve a problem or take effective action. In educational contexts, metacognition has been used to describe the ways that students "think about learning." This can include planning, monitoring, and assessing ways of gaining and using information during learning activities.

The use of metacognitive strategies can be taught using known effective instructional practices for students with ESN. These skills are necessary to help students independently use cognitive strategies and academic skills beyond the immediate instructional setting. Metacognitive skills instruction involves affecting observable, measurable, "overt" student behaviors through instructional prompting and then fading prompts that require the student's use of overt actions.

Teaching students with ESN to use metacognitive strategies can help promote the independent and generalized use of the cognitive strategies and academic skills they learn in the classroom. Metacognitive strategy instruction provides a general framework that can help move students' cognitive strategies and academic skills from the classroom instructional setting into other areas of their school day, homes, and communities. For example, Maxwell, an 11th-grade student with ESN, uses the math skills he was taught in the classroom to determine the number of bills he needs to put into his wallet each morning before he leaves the house. During math groups at school, he has learned several cognitive strategies for approaching real-world problems involving grouping and addition in the classroom, including using manipulatives, using the calculator on his phone, and drawing a graphic organizer to determine sums of money. Before he heads to school, Maxwell looks at the list of activities he will participate in for the day on his phone calendar. He looks at which activities will need money (lunch, snack from the school store, and basketball game after school) and then draws and uses a graphic organizer to help him determine how many bills he will need to put in his wallet. He thinks about the amount of money in his wallet and decides that it seems like it is about the right amount based on the amount that he has taken on similarly scheduled days. He determines that the graphic organizer helped him select the correct amount of money. Maxwell's consideration of the "correctness" of the amount of money he put in his wallet and his decision that the graphic organizer was helpful involved his use of metacognitive skills. The following sections describe how teachers can plan and implement cognitive and metacognitive strategy instruction in instructional and generalized settings.

Teaching Cognitive Strategies

Due to the various tasks and situations that cognitive strategies can support, there is not one specific process for their selection, development, and instruction. Although strategies may widely vary across students and situations, some steps are common when selecting and developing cognitive strategies for students with ESN.

Identify Student Support Needs Related to the Task or Activity

Different students need different types of supports to complete tasks and activities. For example, one student may need strategies for remembering the sequence of task steps to select and use a resource for answering a question during social studies class, while another student can recall the task steps but needs supporting strategies to remain engaged for the duration of the lesson. To identify the type of support a student needs, teachers should think about the dimensions of the task or activity that require prompting or assistance from another person. Table 14.1 shows examples of task or activity dimensions that may need consideration when developing cognitive strategies to support task or activity completion, including gathering necessary information, organizing materials, and remembering steps in a process, among other dimensions. As cognitive strategies are identified, it is important to collect baseline data to help with gathering information about how well the strategy works over time.

Incorporate the Student's Strengths and Preferences

After identifying the dimensions of the task or activity that need support or prompts from another person, it is important to develop cognitive strategies that leverage what the student already knows how to do. Incorporating student interests and preferences can help make cognitive strategies engaging and meaningful for students. For example, a student who consistently forgets to bring their lunchbox to the cafeteria and has a strong technology strength and interest in a personal device might use the alarm or reminder features on the device to plan a signal to get the lunchbox.

List the Steps Involved in the Strategy

If the cognitive strategy will require the student to use a series of steps, writing out each of the steps that the student will use can help with instructional planning. Chapter 16 describes task analysis, the process used to determine each of the steps a person uses when a skill is performed. Olivia's special education teacher uses a task analysis during a morning check-in routine each day to teach Olivia to program her phone with several reminder alarms. These alarms cause Olivia's phone to vibrate and show a picture of the activity she needs to complete during certain times of the day. For example, she sets alarms to remind her to take her supplies to the art classroom and take her ID card to the cafeteria. There are multiple steps involved in setting each alarm on her phone, including (1) determining the best time to set the alarm, (2) locating the alarm app on the phone, and (3) editing and saving the alarm time and picture within the app. Olivia can find the alarm app on her phone, but needs help to choose alarm times and program the alarms. The steps she cannot complete independently need instruction so she can complete them by herself.

Determine a Plan for Teaching Each Step

Teaching students with ESN to independently use each step in a cognitive strategy uses the same types of instructional procedures that are used to teach other meaningful academic and functional skills. There are many evidenced and high-leverage instructional practices that can be used to provide instruction, including systematic prompting (Chapter 15), reinforcement (Chapter 8), and self-monitoring strategies. Before teaching a student to use a cognitive strategy, it is important to have a clear and well-considered plan for teaching each step that uses instructional procedures known to work for students with ESN. As Olivia's teacher considers ways to teach her to complete the step of choosing the best times to program reminder alarms on her phone app, she thinks about how Olivia has learned other skills. Her teacher knows that Olivia quickly learns new skills when provided with visual supports and response prompting using time delay. Olivia's teacher prepares a daily visual schedule with text, pictures, and times of important daily activities. She plans to use a progressive time delay procedure to teach Olivia to select several times to program into her alarm app.

Embed the Use of Strategies into Other Situations

Planning opportunities for a student to use a cognitive strategy outside of the immediate instructional situation and during a variety of academic and non-academic situations can help to promote the student's generalized and independent use of the strategy. Determining these additional opportunities may involve reviewing the student's daily schedule of activities to determine and plan learning trials in more natural situations. For example, Ana's second-grade teacher uses a graphic organizer and counting blocks to teach her to use 1:1 correspondence during math instruction in the general education classroom. The teacher also provides Ana with an opportunity to use the skill during lunch lineup. During lunch lineup, Ana is responsible for handing lunch tickets to classmates as they line up to walk to the cafeteria. She gives one ticket to each classmate who indicates they will be getting a cafeteria lunch, counting each ticket with support from her peers.

Fade Instructor Support

A significant purpose of cognitive strategy instruction is to promote students' completion of tasks and activities without prompting from other people. From the start, it is important to have a plan to fade instructional prompting and supports given by a teacher or other person as the student uses the cognitive strategy. Using evidenced instructional procedures to fade support, including systematic prompting procedures, can promote student independence on a more efficient timeline. Andy is a sixth-grade student with ESN who is learning to use a graphic organizer and word bank to write out his ideas during an English-language arts lesson. At first, his teacher used modeling and verbal prompts every time Andy used the organizer and word bank. Andy has recently started becoming more proficient with these cognitive strategies, and his teacher has been systematically fading the model and verbal prompt during instruction. Andy's teacher plans to completely fade the model and verbal prompt to allow Andy to independently write or place words into parts of the graphic organizer.

Fade or Adapt Use of the Strategy

If a cognitive strategy is intrusive or stigmatizing, it is important to fade or adapt the student's use of the strategy so that the student can perform the skill in a more natural or age-appropriate way. For example, it is more stigmatizing for a high-school student to use counting bears and a graphic organizer to solve math problems in a general education classroom than using virtual manipulatives on a phone app or tablet.

More About Metacognitive Strategies

Researchers have shown that students with ESN can learn to complete complex academic tasks and cognitive strategies when teachers use evidence-based instruction. However, when students are not also taught processes that help them use these skills outside of instructional situations, they may only be able to use them under specific circumstances. For example, Daniel can proficiently multiply and divide single-digit numbers on paper when working in a small group. He does not use these skills in any functional way outside the instructional setting. With instruction, he could use this skill in more natural situations, such as planning a number of pages to read each day to complete a reading assignment. Metacognitive strategy instruction can help students use academic skills and cognitive strategies in various academic and functional situations. The steps in metacognition include *planning*, *monitoring*, and *assessing* the use of skills and strategies related to task completion, problem-solving, or activity participation (Kennedy et al., 2020). When students can *plan*, they can identify a goal or problem and then choose a cognitive strategy to approach it. When they can *monitor* the strategy they selected to address a problem or goal, they can initiate the use of the cognitive strategy and then determine if it helps to move toward meeting the goal or resolving the problem (and identify when they are "stuck"). When students can *assess* the effectiveness of their plan, they can determine when the strategy is completed and determine if it resulted in a meaningful solution or result.

Strategies to plan, monitor, and assess learning and performance can be taught along with most academic and functional curriculum lessons for K-12 students. Table 14.2 shows how students can plan, monitor, and assess learning and performance during an academic and a functional skills lesson.

Teaching Metacognitive Strategies

Teaching students to ask questions about the processes supporting their learning and then act based on responses to these questions is a common way to teach metacognitive strategies. Figures 14.1 and 14.2 show examples of worksheets that teachers might use to guide students to ask and answer questions as they learn.

Teachers can use explicit instruction (see Chapter 16) to teach students to ask and respond to metacognitive questions during many types of curricular content lessons, including lessons to teach academic, functional, vocational, communication, leisure, and social or emotional skills.

Table 14.2 Examples of Metacognitive Strategy Use

		Mathematics Lesson	**Solving a Functional Problem**
Planning	Setting a goal or identifying a problem Choosing a cognitive strategy to use	What am I trying to find out? How will I solve this problem?	What is the problem? What can I do to work on the problem?
Monitoring	Using the chosen cognitive strategy Determining if the strategy allows progress toward the goal or resolution	Use a graphic organizer and manipulatives to guide thinking. Am I getting closer to finding an answer or am I stuck?	Use the strategy. Am I getting closer to solving the problem or am I stuck?
Assessing	Determining when the strategy is completed Determining if the goal was met or the problem was resolved Determining if a new cognitive strategy needs to be tried	Did I find an answer? Does the answer make sense? If it does not make sense, what else can I try?	Did I finish using the strategy? Did I solve the problem? If I did not solve the problem, what else can I try?

During instruction, students learn to ask and respond to questions about the planning, monitoring, and assessment of the use of cognitive strategies that surround and support their learning. Students may attend, respond, and react to these questions with the support of peers or educational staff, and questions may be presented and responded to verbally, visually, or using objects. For example, when Alejandro is asked how he plans to gather information about an assigned historical event, his teacher offers him a choice between doing his research on a computer (represented by a mouse) or a book (represented by his library card). Teachers need to consider students' individual instructional support needs when planning metacognitive strategy instruction. Students who use alternative and augmentative communication (AAC) systems need to access their systems during instruction so they can use relevant vocabulary. Scaffolded supports and other HLPs for providing instruction for students with ESN can help to promote effective and efficient metacognitive skills instruction. It is important to plan for fading instructional prompts and cues to promote independent use of these skills.

In addition to providing explicit instruction during instructional times, it is important to plan opportunities for students to generalize the use of metacognitive strategies during other academic and non-academic situations throughout the school day. The following sections describe the use of explicit instruction to teach the use of metacognitive skills using questioning and visual supports. Figure 14.1 shows an example of questions teachers may use to guide metaccognition in a math lesson. A description of a math lesson taught by Mr. McDonnell shows how a teacher might provide this instruction.

Mr. McDonnell is a third-grade general education teacher. His class is working on adding and subtracting multi-digit whole numbers and checking the reasonableness of their solutions. Mr. McDonnell has worked with Ms. Jackson, the special education teacher, to teach and reinforce several cognitive strategies to the entire class, including Eleanor, a student with ESN. Eleanor has learned various cognitive strategies to use during math activities, such as graphic organizers, manipulatives, and strategies for checking her answers for correctness.

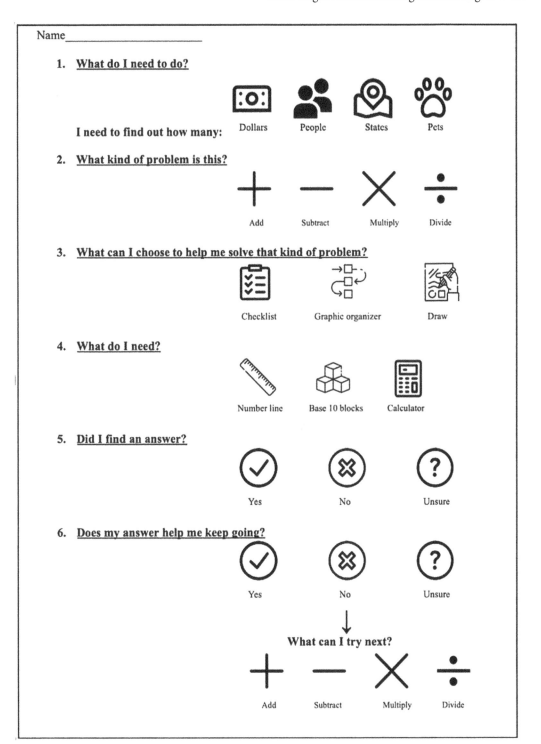

Figure 14.1 Questions to Guide Metacognition during a Math Lesson

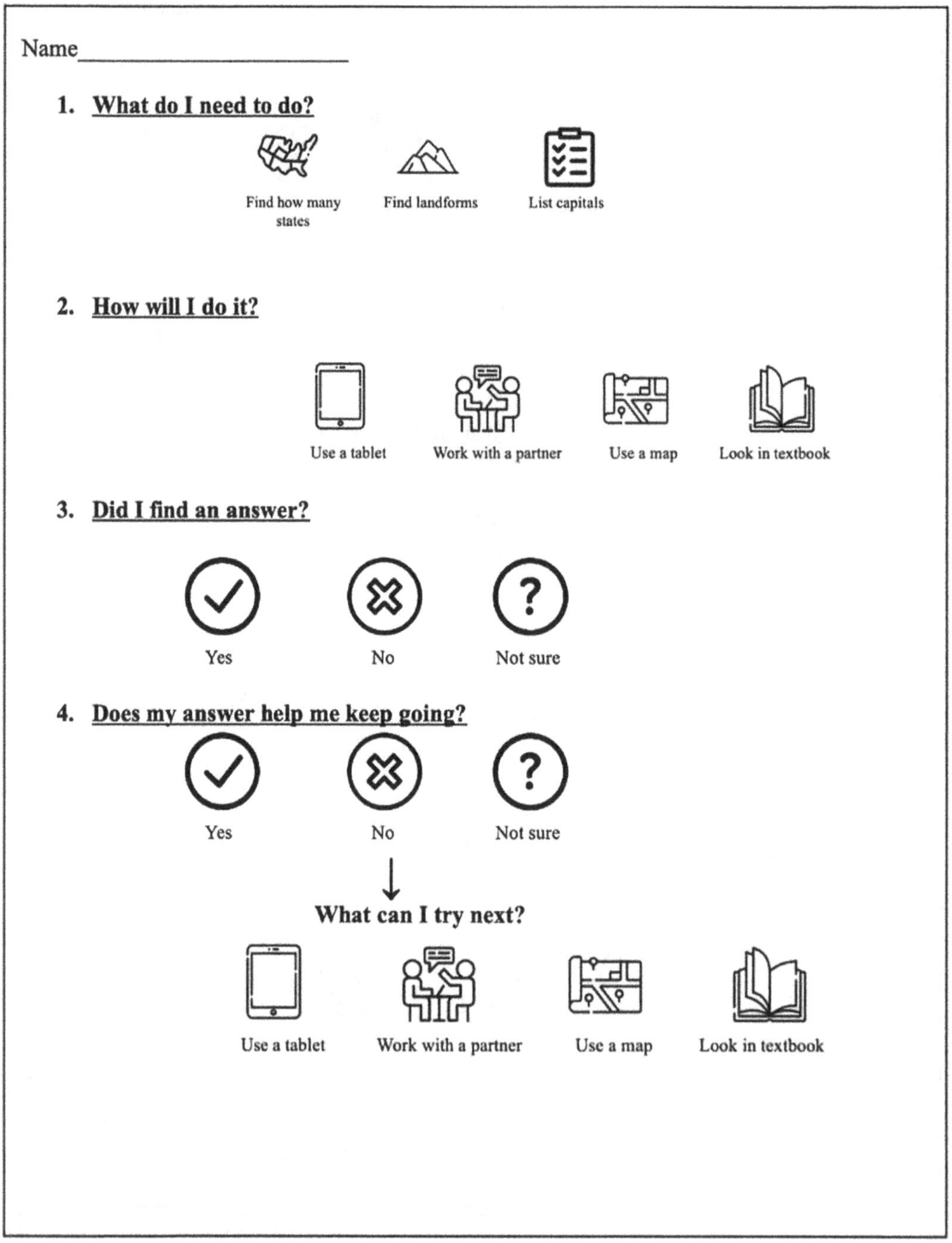

Name_____

1. **What do I need to do?**

Find how many states   Find landforms   List capitals

2. **How will I do it?**

Use a tablet   Work with a partner   Use a map   Look in textbook

3. **Did I find an answer?**

Yes   No   Not sure

4. **Does my answer help me keep going?**

Yes   No   Not sure

↓

What can I try next?

Use a tablet   Work with a partner   Use a map   Look in textbook

Figure 14.2 Questions to Guide Metacognition during a Social Studies Lesson

Teach Students to Plan

The first step in teaching students with ESN to use metacognitive strategies is to explicitly teach students to identify a goal or problem and also to teach them to choose a cognitive strategy for approaching the goal or problem.

Teach Students to Identify a Goal or Problem

When students plan to complete a task, solve a problem, or participate in an activity (including learning), they must first determine the goal to reach or the problem they are trying to solve. This will help the student choose a cognitive strategy to help move toward a goal or resolution. Teachers can support this step by teaching content in a meaningful way and directing students to ask questions and take action in response to these questions. For example, when a lesson requires students to use a map to identify the landforms in a state, a teacher may provide relevant content for the task (such as displaying the landforms a traveler might see on a road trip) and then ask, "What do you need to do? Do you need to find the landforms, list the capitals, or count the number of states?" Figure 14.2 shows questions a teacher may use to guide metacognition during a social studies lesson.

Teach Students to Select a Cognitive Strategy

After students have identified a goal or problem, they identify a cognitive strategy to use to work toward the goal or resolution. The strategy they select may require materials, which also need to be identified. Questions that students may answer to choose a cognitive strategy include "How can I find an answer?" and "What do I need to get started?" A student with ESN may select between many cognitive strategies to complete a writing activity, including using a graphic organizer, acronyms, sentence stems, or word banks. Teachers can develop cognitive strategy maps to help students select a cognitive strategy appropriate for a task or problem. Figure 14.3 shows an example of a cognitive strategy map for reading.

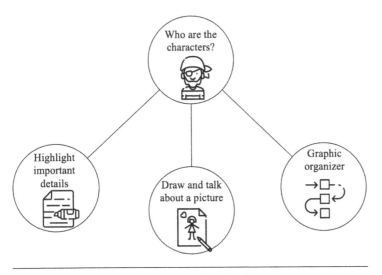

Figure 14.3 Cognitive Strategy Map for Reading Comprehension

As small group math instruction continues in Mr. McDonnell's classroom, Eleanor's group talks through a word problem and how they might solve the problem. The problem reads, "A book has 320 pages. Leron has already read 118 pages. How many pages does he have left to read?" All students have their own meta-cognitive strategy worksheet to help them think through the problem using the Plan, Monitor, and Assess framework. Figure 14.4 shows these *worksheets.*

Mr. McDonnell prompts the group to think about what they are trying to find out and gives them a moment to underline parts of the word problem that might help them figure it out. While they are writing, he hands Eleanor her metacognitive strategy sheet (see Figure 14.4) *and reads her choices aloud to her quietly, "Eleanor, what are we trying to find out?"*

"Reading."

"Yes, Leron is reading in this problem. What are we trying to find out? Are we trying to find how many books he has read, how many pages he has left to read, or how many pictures are in his book?"

Eleanor points to the icon, indicating that she is trying to find out how many pages he has left to read. Mr. McDonnell gives her a thumbs up, and Eleanor marks it with her pencil. Once the group has discussed what they are trying to find out, Mr. McDonnell reminds them that they need to plan to address the task or problem. He says, "Draw or circle the operation you think we might use to solve this problem, and a tool you might use to solve it."

He turns to another student in the group to assist them in re-reading the word problem. While he does that, another student leans over to Eleanor and prompts her to choose an operation and a strategy or tool on her sheet. Eleanor indicates that she will add and use base 10 blocks with a graphic organizer. When each person has written their operation, Mr. McDonnell tells them to hold them up and explain their selection.

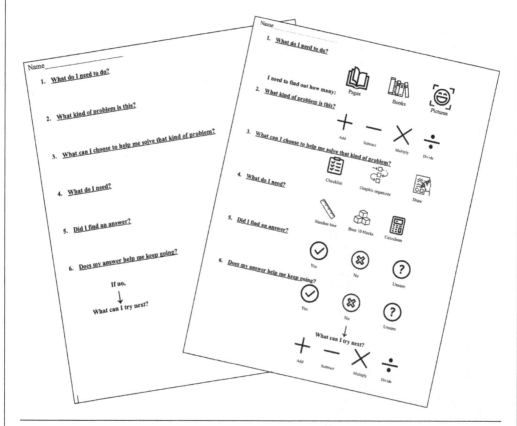

Figure 14.4 Mr. McDonnell's Worksheets

Teach Students to Monitor

Once students have identified a goal and determined a plan, they will need to implement the cognitive strategy they selected and monitor the way they use it.

Teach Students to Use the Selected Cognitive Strategy

Students will need to know when and how to start using the selected cognitive strategy. To ensure that students can independently initiate use of the strategy, teachers can have a well-developed plan to fade instructor support during cognitive strategy instruction. They can also plan a variety of opportunities for students to practice, initiating use of the strategy throughout the school day.

Teach Students to Monitor Progress Toward the Goal

Students will also need to be able to determine if the cognitive strategy they selected does or does not help them to get closer to their goal or the problem resolution. Questions that students may answer and act upon in this area include "Am I getting closer to finding an answer?" or "Do I know what to do next?" Teachers can support students as they monitor their progress using these questions, including checklists or systematic prompting and fading (McConomy et al., 2021).

The math lesson continues in Mr. McDonnell's classroom. After providing reinforcing and corrective feedback to Eleanor and others in the group about their plans to solve the word problem, Mr. McDonnell tells students to find a solution to the problem and to monitor their work as they progress. Since Eleanor's prioritized learning goals involve being able to add and subtract multi-digit whole numbers to the nearest ten or hundred, she solves the equation "300-100 = __." Mr. McDonnell reminds students to look back at how they planned to solve the problem. Eleanor points to her selection of adding and using base 10 blocks in the graphic organizer and takes these manipulatives out of her desk to solve the problem. She starts by counting out three hundreds flats into the first section of the graphic organizer and then stops working. Her tablemate asks if she knows what to do next, and Eleanor shakes her head "no."

Her tablemate says, "You counted three hundreds, now you take one away!" Eleanor takes one hundreds flat away, leaving her with two hundreds flats.

Mr. McDonnell turns his attention to Eleanor and says, "Count by hundreds with me to find out how many pages—100 pages, 200 pages."

Eleanor looks back at her worksheet and repeats to herself, "200 pages."

Mr. McDonnell is excited to see Eleanor independently counting by hundreds, as he has purposefully included opportunities for students to use skip counting to estimate the sums of numbers throughout the day (e.g., whenever multi-digit numbers come up naturally in the school day, such as estimating how many days left of school or how many more minutes before lunch starts).

Teach Students to Assess

When students finish a task or activity, they need to assess the completeness and accuracy of the outcomes of their actions.

Teach Students to Identify When the Strategy Is Complete

Students will first need to identify when they have finished using a cognitive strategy when assessing their work. Questions that students may answer and act upon to determine if they have finished their planned approach include "Is there anything else I need to do?" or "Did I complete my plan?" Teachers might use self-monitoring checklists or task analyses to teach students to identify when they have completed a strategy.

Teach Students to Evaluate Outcomes

Finally, students will need to determine if they met their goal or resolved a problem. Questions that students can ask and answer may include "Did I do what I was trying to do?" or "Does this answer make sense?" Returning to the original goal identified in the planning phase could help students determine whether they have completed the task and whether their solution makes sense and addresses the original goal.

Mr. McDonnell concludes his math lesson. Once each student has found a solution to the word problem, Mr. McDonnell asks students to consider if their answer makes sense. If it makes sense, they share their reasoning with the group. First, he asks Eleanor to share her estimate, "Eleanor, about how many pages did you estimate Lebron still had left to read?"

Eleanor holds up the two hundreds flats and says, "200 pages." Mr. McDonnell announces to the group, "Eleanor calculated an estimate for us by rounding the numbers; thank you, Eleanor! Does that answer what you were trying to find out?"

Eleanor nods her head to say, "Yes."

Mr. McDonnell asks another student to share their reasoning. The student says, "I got about 200; I used friendly numbers to subtract 120 from 320 and got 200, and then added 2 back in and got 202. He still had 202 pages left in his book to read."

Plan Generalization Opportunities

Combining curricular instruction with metacognitive strategy instruction can help promote the use of skills beyond the immediate instructional setting into other academic and non-academic areas of a student's life. Students need to practice using the skills and strategies outside of the isolated instructional setting for this to occur. Teachers can plan specific opportunities for students to use metacognitive strategies in more meaningful, naturalistic ways to address problems or tasks that they may encounter within a variety of environments. To ensure that these plans are enacted, teachers may need to include information about generalization opportunities in instructional plans and may need to contrive practice situations throughout the school day.

Plan to Fade Instructor Support

All students, including students with ESN, will need teacher support as they learn to use metacognitive strategies. Explicit, highly prompted instruction is valuable for teaching new skills for students with ESN, but a plan for fading teacher support is essential for promoting independent and generalized use of metacognitive skills. To fade intensive instructional supports, teachers may begin to use more wait time or to use less intrusive prompting strategies. Using less intrusive prompting strategies may include moving from direct verbal prompts (such as "Now you set your timer to 2 minutes!") to indirect verbal prompts (such as "What do you need to do next?"). Teachers could also transition from teacher-provided prompts to less intrusive or more naturalistic prompts such as peer prompts, self-monitoring checklists, or technology-aided prompting systems.

Next Steps toward Better Practice

Beginning to teach cognitive and metacognitive strategies along with academic and functional skills can seem complicated. It is okay to start small with one student during one lesson and then grow from there! Follow these steps to get started:

1. When providing academic and functional skills instruction during one lesson with one student, become aware of teacher prompting and think about how to teach one or more cognitive strategies to replace the teacher prompt.

2. Teach multiple cognitive strategies to replace the teacher prompt and fade teacher prompting.
3. Plan opportunities for the student to use the cognitive strategies during and outside of planned instructional times.
4. Use explicit instruction to teach metacognitive strategies during planned instructional times and plan to fade instructor support.
5. Plan opportunities for the student to practice using the metacognitive strategies throughout the school day, during academic and non-academic situations.

The Big Five

This chapter presented several ideas about cognitive strategies and metacognition, including descriptive information about these HLPs and some procedures for teaching them. There are several big ideas to take from all of this information, including the following: (1) Teaching cognitive and metacognitive strategies can help students to use skills in a generalized and independent way, (2) there are ways to teach academic content aligned with the general curriculum that can also promote functional skills learning, (3) cognitive and metacognitive skills can be taught using the same high-leverage and evidenced instructional procedures that are used to teach other meaningful skills for students with ESN, (4) it is important to explicitly teach these strategies during planned instructional times, and (5) it is also important to plan opportunities for students to use these strategies outside of the isolated instructional setting, in other academic and non-academic situations throughout and beyond the school day.

Resources

To learn more about cognitive strategies and metacognition, investigate these resources:

Clausen, A., Reyes, E. N., Wakeman, S., & Collins, B. (2020). High-Leverage Practices (TIPS Series: Tip #9). Minneapolis, MN: University of Minnesota, TIES Center. https://publications.ici.umn.edu/ties/foundations-of-inclusion-tips/special-education-high-leverage-practices-for-instruction-in-inclusive-settings

Kennedy, M. J., Cook, L., & Morano, S. (2020). HLP 14: Use Cognitive and Metacognitive Strategies. https://highleveragepractices.org/hlp-14-use-cognitive-and-metacognitive-strategies

PROGRESS Center (2021). Cognitive and metacognitive strategies: What do teachers need to know?. American Institutes for Research. https://promotingprogress.org/sites/default/files/2021-08/Cog-MetaCog-Strategies-508.pdf

References

Cox, S. K., & Root, J. R. (2020). Modified schema-based instruction to develop flexible mathematics problem-solving strategies for students with autism spectrum disorder. *Remedial and Special Education*, 41(3), 139–151. https://doi.org/10.1177/0741932518792660

Graham, S., Bruch, J., Fitzgerald, J., Friedrich, L., Furgeson, J., Greene, K., Kim, J., Lyskawa, J., Olson, C. B., & Smither Wulsin, C. (2016). Teaching secondary students to write effectively (NCEE 2017-4002). Washington, DC: National Center for Education Evaluation and Regional Assistance (NCEE), Institute of Education Sciences, U.S. Department of Education. Retrieved from the NCEE website: http://whatworks.ed.gov.

Hunt, P., McDonnell, J., & Crockett, M. A. (2012). Reconciling an ecological curricular framework focusing on quality of life outcomes with the development and instruction of standards-based academic goals. *Research and Practice for Persons With Severe Disabilities*, 37(3), 139–152. https://doi.org/10.2511/027494812804153516

Kansas University Center on Developmental Disabilities. (n.d.). *Self-determination*. Retrieved October 15, 2021, from https://selfdetermination.ku.edu/

Kennedy, M. J., Cook, L., & Morano, S. (2020). HLP 14: Use cognitive and metacognitive strategies. https://highleveragepractices.org/hlp-14-use-cognitive-and-metacognitive-strategies

McConomy, M. A., Root, J., & Wade, T. (2021). Using task analysis to support inclusion and assessment in the classroom. *TEACHING Exceptional Children*. Advance online publication. https://doi.org/10.1177/00400599211025565

McDonnell, J., Jameson, J. M., Bowman, J. A., Coleman, O., Ryan, J., Eichelberger, C., & Conradi, L. (2020). Assessing generalization in single-case research studies teaching core academic content to students with intellectual and developmental disabilities. *Focus on Autism and Other Developmental Disabilities, 35*(3), 143–152. https://doi.org/10.1177/1088357620902500

Ryan, J., Jameson, J. M., Coleman, O. F., Eichelberger, C., Bowman, J. A., Conradi, L. A., Johnston, S. S., & McDonnell, J. (2019). Inclusive social studies content instruction for students with significant intellectual disability using structured inquiry-based instruction. *Education and Training in Autism and Developmental Disabilities, 54*(4), 420–436. http://www.daddcec.com/etadd.html

The IRIS Center. (2015). *Intensive intervention (part 1): Using data-based individualization to intensify instruction*. Retrieved October 15, 2021, from https://iris.peabody.vanderbilt.edu/module/dbi1/

15
Provide Scaffolded Supports

Response and Stimulus Prompts
Timothy Riesen, Shamby Polychronis, and Sarah Ivy

Scaffolded supports provide temporary assistance to students so they can successfully complete tasks that they cannot yet do independently and with a high rate of success. Teachers select powerful visual, verbal, and written supports; carefully calibrate them to students' performance and understanding in relation to learning tasks; use them flexibly; evaluate their effectiveness; and gradually remove them once they are no longer needed. Some supports are planned prior to lessons, and some are provided responsively during instruction.

Supporting Students with Extensive Support Needs

Individualized instruction designed to promote the acquisition, generalization, and maintenance of academic, functional, and community skills is the foundation of special education and related services. Targeted instruction should involve teaching elementary- and secondary-age students academic and functional skills to engage in inclusive educational and community settings. This chapter focuses on the use of scaffolded supports. Scaffolded supports are used to provide students with individualized assistance and support to successfully acquire and maintain a variety of emerging academic, functional, and community skills. The scaffolded supports are systematically faded as the student masters the target skill across multiple environments. This chapter describes how teachers can use prompting strategies to promote near-errorless learning and the maintenance and generalization of skills across educational and community environments. The chapter also will provide examples of implementing response-prompting instructional programs for an elementary and secondary student.

Chapter Objectives

Upon reading this chapter, you should be able to do the following:

1. Describe the principles of response prompting.
2. Describe the principles of stimulus prompting.
3. Select an appropriate prompting strategy for teaching students specific academic and functional skills.

DOI: 10.4324/9781003175735-16

4. Identify the essential components of prompting strategies.
5. Develop instructional programs for elementary- and secondary-age students, including a data collection method to monitor student progress toward independence.

Student Vignettes

Maria. *Maria is an eight year old with extensive support needs (ESN) in the third grade attending her local neighborhood school in an inclusive classroom. She speaks English in school and primarily Spanish at home, typically combining three to four words at a time in conversation. She can name all the letters of the alphabet and recognize her name in print. She inconsistently makes the correct sounds for some letters in English but does not blend sounds when decoding. For about a month, the special education teacher has been using a tier-2 reading curriculum in a small group with Maria and two other students. Based on performance data, the special educator has determined that Maria needs a more structured, systematic approach to develop sight word recognition.*

Eddy. *Eddy is a 17-year-old student with ESN. Eddy participates in work-based learning as outlined in his transition plan. Eddy expressed interest in working at a pizza restaurant during his transition planning meetings. His teacher developed a community-based, work-based learning opportunity at a local pizzeria and arranged for Eddy to spend approximately 3 hours per week learning several novel tasks related to working in a pizzeria including making pizzas, assembling pizza delivery boxes, and stocking the pizza preparation stations.*

Principles of Response Prompting

Response prompting is an errorless learning strategy designed to assist students in acquiring academic (Jameson et al., 2008; Polychronis et al., 2004), functional (Ivy & Hatton, 2014), or community-based (Riesen & Jameson, 2018) skills across carefully designed instructional trials. Errorless learning combines positive reinforcement with a prompt or cue that reduces a student's chance of making incorrect responses. Response prompts are teacher behaviors or cues systematically presented to a student to increase the student's likelihood of responding correctly. Prompts are faded until the student can independently perform the skill under natural conditions (Collins et al., 2001). Teachers can use a single prompt or combine prompts during instructional trials. Prompts are typically categorized using a hierarchy representing the least intrusive prompts to the most intrusive prompts. They may include indirect verbal prompts, direct verbal prompts, gestures, model prompts, and physical prompts.

1. *Indirect verbal prompt:* An indirect verbal prompt is an indirect verbal statement that cues a student about an expected response. For example, "What do you need to do now?" or "What is next?"
2. *Direct verbal prompt:* A direct verbal prompt explicitly cues the student about the expected response. For example, "This word is map, say map." or "Place the pepperoni on the pizza."
3. *Gestural prompt:* Non-verbal teacher prompts or gestures that draw attention to the stimulus material, such as pointing to the word map or the pepperoni.
4. *Model prompt:* The teacher demonstrates how to perform the expected response.
5. *Physical prompt:* A teacher may use a full physical prompt such as hand-over-hand prompting to guide the student to a correct response. A teacher may use a partial physical prompt, such as touching a hand or an elbow. For example, the teacher might tap the student on the elbow to cue them to pick up pepperoni.

Teachers should prepare for response-prompting programs by identifying the student's learning objective and conducting a baseline probe of the student's performance on the objective. The baseline probe is an essential step. It helps the teacher identify how much of the target skill the student can complete independently and the level of assistance or the type of prompt the student needs if they cannot complete it independently. The baseline probe also is used to identify the *controlling prompt* and *non-controlling prompts*. The delivery of the controlling and non-controlling prompts is contingent on the response-prompting strategy being implemented. The controlling prompt is a prompt that reliably ensures that a student responds correctly when asked to complete discrete or chained skills or tasks (Wolery et al., 1992). For example, the controlling prompt for a student who is learning geography words may be a direct verbal prompt—"This word is map, say map." When this prompt is delivered, the student consistently says "map." A non-controlling prompt also increases the probability of a correct student response, but the prompt does not always elicit a correct response from the student. For example, if the controlling prompt is a verbal prompt, and the teacher delivers an indirect verbal prompt "What is this?" and the student responds correctly by saying the word "map," the teacher would reinforce the student and move to the next word. If the student does not respond or incorrectly responds, a teacher implementing a system of least prompts (SLP) program would deliver the next intrusive prompt up to the controlling prompt.

Response prompting requires teachers to incorporate several important elements into their instructional programs. Teachers begin each instructional trial by delivering a cue designed to ensure that the student focuses on the targeted skill or task. For example, a teacher might say, "Are you ready to learn?" or "Are you ready to work?" and wait for the student to verbally or non-verbally acknowledge the teacher. Once the student acknowledges the teacher and attends to the task, the teacher presents the instructional cue designed to elicit the student's response. An example of an instructional cue may include the teacher saying, "It's time to read the geography words." or "It's time to assemble a pizza box." Once the instructional cue is provided, the teacher begins instruction by inserting a prompt between the instructional stimulus (e.g., directive or material that evokes a response) and the student's response. The response interval, the time the teacher waits before a prompt, and the type of prompt a teacher uses are contingent on the response-prompting strategy. For example, if a teacher uses the SLP, the teacher would wait a predetermined interval before delivering the first non-controlling prompt. If the student did not respond, the teacher would provide each non-controlling prompt up to the controlling prompt. The teacher should also implement appropriate error correction and reinforcement procedures. Finally, the teacher should collect data on student responses and graph the data to adjust the instruction based on data patterns.

The primary goal of response prompting is to fade prompts and transfer control from the teacher's prompt to the naturally occurring target instructional stimulus (Wolery et al., 1992). The student's correct behavior should change or transfer over time so that the student recognizes and responds to naturally occurring cues. At that point, the student will be able to independently complete the target behavior or skill without prompting from the teacher.

Educators can use several response-prompting procedures to teach the acquisition of academic, functional, and community skills, including graduated guidance, the SLP, most-to-least prompting, constant and progressive time delay, and simultaneous prompting (SP; Collins et al., 2018). Table 15.1 provides information about the critical features of each prompting strategy.

Graduated Guidance

Graduated guidance is a prompting procedure designed to teach skills requiring some level of assistance. A graduated guidance instructional program requires the teacher to make decisions about the intensity of the physical prompt in the moment to support a student in completing an action or task without errors. Compared to other response-prompting strategies, graduated guidance is more fluid and responsive to student behavior in real time because the teacher varies the level of physical support moment to moment as needed. Physical support can vary in terms of intensity, location, or both. Intensity refers to the intrusiveness of the physical support, with full hand-over-hand assistance being the most intrusive, whereas a slight and brief touch is the least intrusive. Location refers to where the physical support is provided on the body, for example, the hand, wrist, forearm, elbow, or shoulder.

Table 15.1 Prompting Features

Prompting Strategy	Considerations	Steps for Implementation
Graduated Guidance	• Useful for discrete or chained tasks and behaviors that require physical assistance. • Most effective with cooperative learners (avoid use with those resistant to physical contact). • Can adjust physical guidance within sessions. • Begin with the least intrusive prompt level with demonstrated success.	• Give instructional cue. • If student does not respond or begins to respond with an error, immediately use the physical prompt needed to ensure a correct response. • Provide verbal reinforcement for all prompted and unprompted correct responses. • Shadow student response during acquisition. • Continue instruction until the student performs the task independently and error-free.
System of Least Prompts	• Useful for building skill acquisition and fluency for chained responses. • Use at least three levels of prompts. • Provides students with an opportunity to be independent before providing increasing levels of support.	• Give instructional cue. • Use the predetermined response interval before prompting. • Provide verbal reinforcement for prompted and unprompted correct responses. • Provide the next intrusive prompt in the hierarchy with the appropriate response interval for incorrect or no responses. Continue to prompt up to the controlling prompt. • Continue instruction until the student meets established independent performance criteria.
Most to Least	• Useful for new skill acquisition of discrete or chained responses. • Most effective when the student can demonstrate the prerequisite skill(s) for the task. • Reduces errors by providing high levels of support before fading to less-intrusive prompts.	• Give instructional cue. • Begin instructional trials with the controlling prompt. • Provide verbal reinforcement for prompted and unprompted correct responses. • Fade prompts from most to least assistance according to established criteria. • For incorrect or no responses, provide the previous prompt level. • Periodically conduct test probes using the least intrusive prompting levels. • Continue instruction until the student meets established independent performance criteria.

(Continued)

Table 15.1 Prompting Features (*Continued*)

Prompting Strategy	Considerations	Steps for Implementation
Time Delay	• Provides a delay that gives students an opportunity to be independent before providing the controlling prompt. • Works well with verbal prompts. • Useful for skill acquisition and building fluency. • Controlling prompt delivered after a preset interval that remains constant. • Controlling prompt is delivered after a preset interval that increases progressively.	• Give instructional cue. • To ensure the student knows how to respond, use 0-second delay with the controlling prompt for the first several instructional trials. • Following the 0-s condition, insert a predetermined time delay (*constant or progressive*). • Provide verbal reinforcement for prompted correct responses. • For incorrect or no responses, repeat the prompt. • Continue instruction until the student meets established independent performance criteria.
Simultaneous Prompting	• Useful for new skill acquisition, particularly discrete skills. • Designed to minimize errors by providing a controlling prompt delivered after a 0–second delay interval.	• Give instructional cue and immediately provide the controlling prompt. • Provide verbal reinforcement for correct responses. • Periodically, conduct probe. During the probe session, give the task direction, wait for the predetermined response interval for the student to respond, and record student response. No prompts or error correction is provided during the probe session. • Continue instruction until student meets established independent performance criteria.
Stimulus Prompting	• Useful for new skill acquisition, particularly discrete and motor skills. • Involves the manipulation of the configuration of the target stimulus across learning trials. • Highly effective and efficient for teaching skills that have not successfully developed through other methods.	• Give an instructional cue and present the target stimulus and the prompt simultaneously. • Conduct instructional trials by transferring stimulus control to the natural cure by gradually decreasing the exaggerated manipulations of the target stimulus across trials. • Provide the next intrusive prompt in the hierarchy with the appropriate response interval for incorrect or no responses. Continue to prompt up to the controlling prompt. • Continue instruction until student meets establish independent performance criteria.

Adapted from Collins et al. (2018). Response prompting as an ABA-based instructional approach for teaching students with disabilities. *Teaching Exceptional Children, 50*(6), 343–355.

When implementing graduated guidance, the teacher begins instruction with the physical support required for the student to perform a task accurately and then fades support, in terms of intensity and/or location, as quickly as possible. Within a given opportunity, the teacher may increase and decrease support as needed as certain parts of the task may be more or less difficult or even dangerous for the student to complete. As the student begins to perform all or part of the task independently, the teacher "shadows" the student by remaining close to them with hands in a ready position to increase support as needed to prevent errors. Additionally, the teacher might provide verbal descriptions for each task step. Providing such descriptions may support a student to respond appropriately to verbal prompts in the future.

System of Least Prompts

The SLP requires a teacher to systematically use a hierarchy of prompts sequenced from the least to the most level of assistance. There are several important considerations to developing a SLP program. First, when implementing SLP, teachers need to identify a minimum of three levels of prompts in the hierarchy that will be used during instruction (Wolery et al., 1992). The first level is the opportunity to respond to the natural cue. The second and subsequent levels are prompts arranged from the least intrusive to the most intrusive concluding with the controlling prompt. Second, the teacher needs to determine the length of the response interval (the time before a prompt is delivered). Decisions about the appropriate response interval are based on student characteristics and are typically between 3 and 5 seconds. Third, the teacher should determine the most efficient strategy to reinforce correct responses and select the appropriate feedback for incorrect responses. Finally, the teacher should systematically collect data on student performance to implement and adjust the program based on data patterns (Wolery et al., 1992).

Applied example.
After observing Eddy at the pizzeria, the teacher develops instructional programs for each vocational task. The following example illustrates how the teacher used the SLP to teach Eddy how to assemble pizza boxes. The teacher decided that a diagram of the pizza box that included labels for each of the required folds would help during the instructional process (see Figure 15.1). The teacher uses letters to label each of the required folds for pizza box assembly, which helps the teacher develop a task analysis for pizza box assembly; the diagram is also used as a visual aid during instruction.

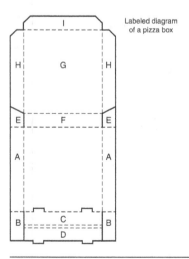

Labeled diagram of a pizza box

Figure 15.1 A Figure of a Pizza Box with All the Parts/Folds Labeled

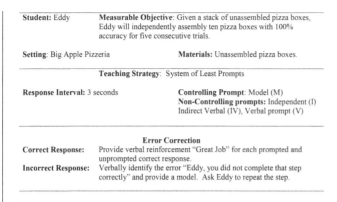

Student: Eddy	**Measurable Objective**: Given a stack of unassembled pizza boxes, Eddy will independently assembly ten pizza boxes with 100% accuracy for five consecutive trials.
Setting: Big Apple Pizzeria	**Materials:** Unassembled pizza boxes.
	Teaching Strategy: System of Least Prompts
Response Interval: 3 seconds	**Controlling Prompt**: Model (M) **Non-Controlling prompts:** Independent (I) Indirect Verbal (IV), Verbal prompt (V)

Error Correction

Correct Response:	Provide verbal reinforcement "Great Job" for each prompted and unprompted correct response.
Incorrect Response:	Verbally identify the error "Eddy, you did not complete that step correctly" and provide a model. Ask Eddy to repeat the step.

Figure 15.2 A Sample Instructional Script for the Task of Pizza Box Assembly

Once the diagram was complete, the teacher develops a ten-step task analysis for pizza box assembly. The teacher conducts a baseline on Eddy assembling pizza boxes. During baseline, the teacher assesses Eddy's ability to assemble the pizza box without any prompting. During instruction, the teacher delivers prompts sequenced from the least intrusive to the most intrusive prompt until Eddy correctly performs each step on the task analysis. The teacher notes the controlling prompt, in this case, is a model. The teacher develops an instructional script that outlines how to implement the instructional program with fidelity (Figure 15.2). The script includes the measurable objective, setting, and materials. The teacher also includes information about the controlling and non-controlling prompts. The teacher also outlines the response interval (the time the teacher waits before delivering a prompt on the hierarchy) and error correction procedures.

To begin instruction, the teacher obtains the student's attention by asking, "Are you ready to work?" and then delivers the instructional cue, "Eddy, it is time to assemble pizza boxes." Eddy does not respond within the 3-second response interval. The teacher increases the amount of assistance and moves up the prompt hierarchy until Eddy responds. The teacher documents the type of prompt that elicited correct responses on the instructional data sheet (Figure 15.3). During the initial phase of instruction, the teacher praises Eddy after each step on the task analysis. The teacher summarizes the percentage of correct unprompted responses for baseline and instructional trials and continues instruction until Eddy independently assembles pizza boxes for three consecutive trials.

Student: Eddy
Measurable Objective: Given a stack of unassembled pizza boxes, Eddy will independently assembly 10 pizza boxes with 100% accuracy for three consecutive trials.
Setting: Big Apple Pizzeria
Materials: Unassembled pizza boxes.

Steps	Baseline 1	2	3	Instruction 4	5	6	7	8	9	10
1. Place unassembled box on the assembly table with the print side down	V	IV	IV	V	I	I	I	I	I	I
2. Fold the "A" flaps up towards the ceiling	M	M	M	M	V	IV	IV	I	I	I
3. Fold "B" flaps in towards the center of the box	M	M	M	M	M	IV	IV	I	I	I
4. Fold "C" flap toward the ceiling.	M	M	M	V	M	V	IV	IV	I	I
5. Bend "D" flap over "B" flaps until tab locks into place	M	M	V	V	IV	IV	I	I	I	I
6. Fold "E" flaps in towards the center of the box	M	M	V	M	V	IV	IV	IV	I	I
7. Fold "H" flaps toward the ceiling	M	V	M	V	V	IV	I	I	I	I
8. Fold "I" flap toward the center of the box	M	M	V	V	V	IV	IV	IV	I	I
9. Fold "G" section over assembled section to form a box	M	M	M	M	M	V	IV	I	IV	I
10. Insert tabs to complete the pizza box assembly	V	V	V	I	I	I	I	I	I	I
Percent of unprompted Correct Responses	0	0	0	10	20	20	40	70	90	100

Summary Data

%	%	%	%	%	%	%	%	%	%
100	100	100	100	100	100	100	100	100	100
90	90	90	90	90	90	90	90	90	90
80	80	80	80	80	80	80	80	80	80
70	70	70	70	70	70	70	70	70	70
60	60	60	60	60	60	60	60	60	60
50	50	50	50	50	50	50	50	50	50
40	40	40	40	40	40	40	40	40	40
30	30	30	30	30	30	30	30	30	30
20	20	20	20	20	20	20	20	20	20
10	10	10	10	10	10	10	10	10	10
0	0	0	0	0	0	0	0	0	0

Figure 15.3 A Sample Self-graphing Data Collection Sheet for Assembling Pizza Boxes

Most-to-Least Prompts

The most-to-least strategy also requires at least three levels of prompting and requires that instruction begins by providing the most amount of assistance (i.e., controlling prompt) during the beginning phases of instruction. The prompting is systematically faded across instructional sessions until the student can perform the task independently. To fade the prompts across sessions, the teacher determines the criterion for decreasing the level of assistance. For example, a teacher may establish a criterion of two consecutive successful trials at a verbal prompt. Once the student successfully performed the target behavior for two trials, the teacher fades to an indirect verbal and so on until the student independently performs the task across multiple sessions. The most-to-least procedure also requires periodic probe sessions at the least intrusive prompting level. The probe sessions allow the teacher to periodically determine if the student correctly responds with less assistance. If the teacher determines the student correctly responds at a less intrusive prompt, specific adjustments are made to the established criteria outlined in the instructional program.

Time Delay

Time delay uses a single controlling prompt, delivered at a pre-specified delay interval following an instructional cue. The instructional cue is a task direction or environmental stimulus that cues the student to perform a behavior. There are two phases of instruction when using time delay—a 0-second (0 s) phase and a time-delay phase. There are two types of time delay: constant time delay (CTD) and progressive time delay (PTD).

Regardless of the type of time-delay procedure used, instruction begins with the 0-s delay phase during which an instructional cue is provided (e.g., "What word is this?") followed immediately by the controlling prompt (e.g., "School"). The purpose of the 0-s delay coupled with the controlling prompt is to ensure that the student reliably and correctly responds to the instructional stimulus. One can think of this as the teaching phase of instruction. After the student has demonstrated prompted correct behavior several times in 0-s delay trials, the teacher switches to the time-delay phase of instruction (e.g., 5 s for the student to read "school"). In the time-delay phase, the teacher provides the instructional cue and then waits for the pre-specified time-delay interval giving the student an opportunity to respond independently. If the student does not respond within the delay, the teacher provides the controlling prompt followed by more time for the student to respond. If the student responds incorrectly, the teacher needs to implement an error correction procedure. For example, if the student was supposed to read the sight word "school" and says "church," the teacher would say, "that word is school, say school."

In CTD, the time-delay interval is always the same for each trial and should be selected based on the student's processing speed required to do the behavior (e.g., 5 s). In PTD, the time delay is first a very brief interval (e.g., 0.5 s) and is increased by small intervals with subsequent opportunities (e.g., increase to 1 s, 1.5 s, 2 s, etc.). The controlling prompt never changes in CTD or PTD unless adjustments are necessary due to student errors.

Applied example.
Maria's teacher decides to use constant time delay because of its usefulness for building fluency. She surveys Maria's family, friends, the general education teacher, and her related service providers about meaningful and motivating words for Maria to learn. She also interviews Maria directly about her preferences for particular people, activities, and places. Based on the survey results, the teacher identifies 15 high-interest words to begin instruction and decides she will teach them in sets of five at a time. She creates word cards using 3 x 5 index cards and includes several copies of each word for instruction. She also helps Maria decorate a box to collect word cards that she has learned and bring them home to read with her family. The teacher identifies places and contexts where Maria will encounter the words she is learning and plans to create opportunities to read the words she is learning in those natural contexts to promote generalization.

Now that the teacher has materials prepared, she makes the final decisions to prepare for instruction and writes out a script (Figure 15.4). Based on Maria's typical response time, the teacher decides that 5 s will

Student: Maria

Measurable Objective: Given a set of 5 words with 3-5 opportunities to read each word for a total of 15-25 instructional trials, Maria will independently read aloud the words correctly with 100% accuracy for two consecutive sessions.

Setting: Small group   **Materials:** Word cards

Teaching Strategy: Constant Time Delay

Instructional Cue: "what word is this?" or "read this word"
Time Delay: 5 seconds

Controlling Prompt: Verbal Model (sound out each letter while pointing to it, then read the word aloud)

Error Correction

Correct Responses: Provide verbal reinforcement "Great Job, that word is ____!" for each prompted and unprompted correct response.

Prompted Error: Verbally identify the error "No, that word says _____" and move on to the next word.

Unprompted Error: Verbally identify the error and remind student to wait, "No, that word says _____, remember to wait if you are not sure," and move on to the next word.

No Response: Remind the student to read the word after your prompt "remember to read the word after me" and move on to the next word.

Figure 15.4 A Sample Instructional Script for Teaching Sight Work Recognition

give Maria enough time to read the word out loud if she knows it. To support generalization, she will vary her instructional cue with statements like "What word is this?" or "Read this word." Maria imitates verbal language, so the teacher decides that a verbal prompt will be effective as a controlling prompt. To support decoding (without directly teaching it), she chooses to include a model of her sounding out the word as she points to each letter in the controlling prompt immediately before the verbal prompt. Once Maria reaches mastery criterion with a word, a copy of the word card will go in her box to take home and practice, and the teacher will create opportunities to read that word in more natural contexts. The teacher identifies mastery as when Maria reads a word correctly 100% of the time over two consecutive instructional sessions.

The teacher creates a data collection form to record Maria's responses for each opportunity to read a word (Figure 15.5). The possible responses include Maria correctly responding before the controlling prompt (i.e., independent), correctly responding after the controlling prompt (i.e., prompted correct), incorrectly responding before or after the controlling prompt (i.e., error), or making no response after the controlling prompt. The teacher decides that she will respond to errors without excitement. She will matter-of-factly tell Maria she made an error and provide the correct answer (i.e., "No, that word is _____"). If Maria makes an error before the controlling prompt, she'll remind Maria to wait, "Wait, if you are unsure."

Student: Maria

Measurable Objective: Given a set of 5 words with 3-5 opportunities to read each word for a total of 15-25 instructional trials, Maria will independently read aloud the words correctly with 100% accuracy for 2 consecutive sessions.

Setting: Small group
Materials: Word cards – Set 1

I – unprompted correct, **P** – prompted correct, **E** – prompted/unprompted error, **NR** – no response

Steps		Session								
	0s delay			5s delay						
	1	2	3	4	5	6	7	8	9	10
1. Manuel	NR	P	P	E	E	P	P	E	I	I
2. Ms. Roder	P	P	P	P	P	P	P	P	I	I
3. Manuel	P	P	P	P	P	P	P	P	I	I
4. Storybots	P	P	P	P	P	P	P	I	I	I
5. Bracelets	P	P	P	P	P	I	I	I	I	I
6. Storybots	P	P	P	P	P	I	I	I	I	I
7. Restroom	P	P	P	P	P	I	I	I	I	I
8. Ms. Roder	P	P	P	P	P	P	P	E	I	I
9. Restroom	P	NR	P	P	P	P	I	I	I	I
10. Bracelets	NR	P	P	P	I	I	I	I	I	I
11. Manuel	P	P	P	P	P	P	P	P	I	I
12. Storybots	P	P	P	P	P	I	I	I	I	I
13. Restroom	P	P	P	P	P	P	I	I	I	I
14. Ms. Roder	P	P	P	P	P	P	I	I	I	I
15. Bracelets	P	P	P	P	I	I	I	I	I	I
16. Bracelets	P	P	P	I	I	I	I	I	I	E
17. Storybots	P	P	P	P	P	P	I	I	I	I
18. Ms. Roder	P	P	P	P	P	P	P	P	I	I
19. Manuel	P	P	P	P	P	P	I	I	I	I
20. Restroom	P	P	P	P	I	I	I	I	I	I
Percent of Unprompted Correct Responses	0	0	0	5	20	40	65	70	100	95

Summary Data

%	%	%	%	%	%	%	%	%	%
100	100	100	100	100	100	100	100	100	100
90	90	90	90	90	90	90	90	90	90
80	80	80	80	80	80	80	80	80	80
70	70	70	70	70	70	70	70	70	70
60	60	60	60	60	60	60	60	60	60
50	50	50	50	50	50	50	50	50	50
40	40	40	40	40	40	40	40	40	40
30	30	30	30	30	30	30	30	30	30
20	20	20	20	20	20	20	20	20	20
10	10	10	10	10	10	10	10	10	10
0	0	0	0	0	0	0	0	0	0

Figure 15.5 A Sample Self-graphing Data Collection Sheet for Sight Word Recognition

Simultaneous Prompting

SP is an errorless learning technique in which the controlling prompt is always delivered immediately following the presentation of the instructional stimulus. Student data are collected during separate probe or test trials, conducted prior to SP trials, during which a teacher presents the instructional stimulus and provides an opportunity for the student to respond independently. This procedure is particularly useful for teaching new discrete or chained tasks. It can also help students avoid practicing incorrect responses that may occur when using a time-delay procedure. Some teachers have found this prompting procedure highly effective because they do not have to differentially respond to correct and incorrect responses (Morse & Schuster, 2004).

Principles of Stimulus Prompts

Stimulus prompts involve the manipulation of instructional stimuli across learning trials and involve the techniques of stimulus fading and stimulus shaping (Cengher et al., 2018). These techniques can be time- and labor-intensive, and so, they are often overlooked in favor of other methods. However, stimulus prompting is highly effective for students who have had difficulty gaining skills through other response-prompting methods.

Stimulus shaping requires the teacher to systematically alter the shape or form of the target instructional stimulus so the student begins to recognize defined features of the target material. For example, a teacher implementing a shaping program to teach reading sight words could initially introduce an image of the intended word. As the student demonstrates success, the teacher would gradually transform the image into the written word. For example, an instructor teaching a student the word "apple" might partially transform the apple into the letter "a" followed by the letters "pple." Gradually, the teacher continues to transform the image until only the word is presented.

Stimulus fading requires the teacher to alter or introduce a new element to the target stimulus. The additional element is systematically faded over time. For example, a teacher implementing a fading program to teach color names initially presents students with flashcards that have the color names written in color-coordinated ink. The ink color gradually fades to black as the student demonstrates success across successive trials. Another example is teaching a discrimination task for a student to learn their name. In this example, the teacher presents the student with three options, including the student's larger and bolded name. Over time, the teacher fades their name back to a matching intensity and size as the other options. This process encourages the student to pay attention to the relevant features (e.g., beginning letters in the word) rather than the irrelevant ones (e.g., font color and size).

Next Steps toward Better Practice

There are several steps that teachers can follow to begin or improve their use of prompting strategies. Each of the steps, outlined below, align with the principles of high-leverage practices:

1. *Identify a goal for a particular student.* Similar to the present level of performance statement on an IEP, consider the gap between what the student should be able to do or wants to be able to do and what they are currently able to do.
2. *Analyze struggles.* Teachers should analyze areas where a student struggles in academic and functional skills and consider the following: (a) Does the student have the background knowledge needed to be successful or is this a new skill for them? (b) Is the student making simple mistakes because they may need to go back and practice previously mastered skills? Is the student noticing and attending to the natural or instructional cue? and (c) Does the student need to work on accomplishing the task independently? Additional considerations may include

specific student characteristics such as aversion to physical guidance, dependency on verbal prompts, and access to appropriate behavioral and communication supports.

3. *Select an appropriate prompting strategy.* Considering the struggles identified in the previous step, use the information in Table 15.1 to select a prompting strategy that will work well for both the skill being taught and the unique needs of the student.

4. *Design an instructional script.* This document should detail the measurable objectives, steps of the selected prompting strategy, and student-specific error correction and reinforcement strategies.

5. *Practice with other professionals.* Teachers should implement new programs with colleagues to practice the strategy, get feedback, and increase fidelity. This will also help reduce unnecessary plateaus and student frustration.

6. *Train team members.* Once an instructional program has been developed and the prompting and assessment protocols are well defined, teachers should train team members to implement the program with fidelity. Training to fidelity will help increase the number of instructors who can work with the student and free up time for the teacher to attend to other responsibilities.

The Big Five

Developing scaffolded instructional supports, such as response and stimulus prompts, is an important component of teaching students with extensive support needs to be independent in academic and community environments. Teachers who support students in a variety of inclusive education and community environments should use targeted instructional strategies to support students in acquiring, generalizing, and maintaining skills needed for independence. There are several big five takeaways to ensure that the scaffolded supports align with high-leverage instructional practices. Teachers should

1. Understand the instructional parameters and the application of a broad array of prompting strategies.

2. Understand how to collect baseline probes to identify (a) level of performance, (b) level of assistance or the type of prompt, and the (c) controlling and non-controlling prompts.

3. Understand how to deliver appropriate reinforcement and error correction procedures.

4. Understand how to fade the use of prompts.

5. Understand the utility of each prompting strategy for individual students and the type of skills that the student is learning. The type of prompting strategy the teacher selects should be based on how the student learns best and the type of discrete or chained skill being taught.

Resources

https://transitionta.org/effectivepractices
https://iris.peabody.vanderbilt.edu/resources/high-leverage-practices/
https://ccrs.osepideasthatwork.org/teachers-academic/evidence-based-practices-instruction
https://www.understood.org/en/school-learning/for-educators/universal-design-for-learning/what-is-explicit-instruction
https://autismpdc.fpg.unc.edu/evidence-based-practices
https://ebip.vkcsites.org/

References

Cengher, M., Budd, A., Farrell, N., & Fienup, D. M. (2018). A review of prompt-fading procedures: Implications for effective and efficient skill acquisition. *Journal of Developmental and Physical Disabilities*, 30(2), 155–173. https://doi.org/10.1007/s10882-017-9575-8

Collins, B. C., Branson, T. A., Hall, M., & Rankin, S. W. (2001). Teaching secondary students with moderate disabilities in an inclusive academic classroom setting. *Journal of Development and Physical Disabilities, 13*(1), 41–59. https://doi.org/10.1023/A:1026557316417

Collins, B. C., Lo, Y.-Y., Park, G., & Haughney, K. (2018). Response prompting as an ABA-based instructional approach for teaching students with disabilities. *Teaching Exceptional Children, 50*(6), 343–355. https://doi.org/10.1177/0040059918774920

Ivy, S. E., & Hatton, D. D. (2014). Teaching skill acquisition to individuals with blindness: A systematic review of response prompting procedures. *International Review of Research in Developmental Disabilities: Current Issues in the Education of Students With Visual Impairments, 46*, 55–100. https://doi.org/10.1016/B978-0-12-420039-5.00005-8

Jameson, M., McDonnell, J., Polychronis, S., & Riesen, T. (2008). Embedded, constant time delay instruction by peers without disabilities in general education classrooms. *Intellectual and Developmental Disabilities, 46*(5), 346–363. https://doi.org/10.1352/2008.46:346-363

Morse, T. E., & Schuster, J. W. (2004). Simultaneous prompting: A review of the literature. *Education and Training in Developmental Disabilities, 39*(2), 153–168. https://www.jstor.org/stable/23880063

Polychronis, S. C., McDonnell, J., Johnson, J. W., Riesen, T., & Jameson, M. (2004). A comparison of two trial distribution schedules in embedded instruction. *Focus on Autism and Other Developmental Disabilities, 19*(3), 140–151. https://doi.org/10.1177/10883576040190030201

Riesen, T., & Jameson, J. M. (2018). A comparison of prompting procedures to teach work tasks to transition-aged students with disabilities. *Education and Training in Autism and Developmental Disabilities, 53*(1), 100–110. https://www.jstor.org/stable/26420430

Wolery, M., Ault, M. J., & Doyle, P. (1992). *Teaching students with moderate to severe disabilities: Use of response prompting strategies.* Longman.

16
Provide Intensive Instruction and Use Explicit Instruction

Belva C. Collins

HLP 16: Teachers make content, skills, and concepts explicit by showing and telling students what to do or think while solving problems, enacting strategies, completing tasks, and classifying concepts. Teachers use explicit instruction when students are learning new material and complex concepts and skills. They strategically choose examples and non-examples and language to facilitate student understanding, anticipate common misconceptions, highlight essential content, and remove distracting information. They model and scaffold steps or processes needed to understand content and concepts, apply skills, and complete tasks successfully and independently.

HLP 20: Teachers match the intensity of instruction to the intensity of the student's learning and behavioral challenges. Intensive instruction involves working with students with similar needs on a small number of high priority, clearly defined skills or concepts critical to academic success. Teachers group students based on common learning needs; clearly define learning goals; and use systematic, explicit, and well-paced instruction. They frequently monitor students' progress and adjust their instruction accordingly. Within intensive instruction, students have many opportunities to respond and receive immediate feedback with teachers and peers to practice what they are learning.

Supporting Students with Extensive Support Needs

Students who have extensive support needs (ESN) can include those with significant intellectual ability, dual sensory impairment, challenges in motor ability, complex healthcare needs, or any combination of these. Most educators will agree that the context for teaching students with ESN should be the most inclusive environments possible and should include instruction on the same content that students would receive if they did not have a disability. To do this, instructors must consider how instruction will take place using evidence-based practices (i.e., those that have been found to be effective through a rigorous research process) and must critically analyze how content can be taught in a way that is meaningful and relevant in the student's life. Most evidence-based practices for students with ESN had their genesis in research conducted on teaching functional life skills, such as cooking (e.g., Graves et al., 2005), laundry (Taylor et al., 2002), self-care (Norman

DOI: 10.4324/9781003175735-17

et al., 2001), or recreational tasks (e.g., Seward et al., 2014) in segregated settings. An emerging database, however, has demonstrated that these practices can be applied in inclusive classrooms where core content is taught (e.g., Collins et al., 2007; Heinrich et al., 2016; Tekin-Iftar et al., 2017) without sacrificing the need for specially designed instruction that is both explicit and intensive, two of the high leverage practices (HLPs; McLeskey et al., 2017). Systematic instruction consists of explicit and intensive practices that are evidence-based and can be applied across instructional settings and curricular content.

The basis for systematic instruction is applied behavior analysis (ABA; Pennington, 2019), a field that is often misunderstood by those who are not familiar with the research (Collins et al., 2018). A chief misconception is that ABA requires instructors to teach repeated trials in isolation disregarding where skills will be needed. In contrast, ABA is a flexible practice that allows instructors to individualize instruction as they teach skills in applied settings. This requires instructors to be skilled in analyzing how learners acquire content and how they will need to apply it in their daily lives. Once this is accomplished, instructors teach in a systematic fashion that is explicit and intensive. *Explicit instruction* (HLP 16) is intentional and direct, while *intensive instruction* (HLP 20) requires instructors to teach at a dosage strong enough for a learner to reach criterion in a timely fashion. When using systematic instruction, there are no assumptions that a student with ESN will develop concepts through exposure or hands-on exploration or will automatically be able to apply what has been taught. Instead, data drive instructional practices as the student meets objectives for acquisition, fluency, maintenance, and generalization.

To facilitate desired outcomes, systematic instruction should be nearly errorless, which means that students receive sufficient support and feedback to experience success and thus, have access to reinforcement (e.g., positive feedback). This chapter provides general guidelines for instructors on how to conduct explicit and intensive instruction for students with ESN, while Chapter 15 goes into greater detail on the specific systematic evidence-based procedures to accomplish this through scaffolding (HLP 15). Throughout this chapter, the term "instructor" will be used since the person delivering explicit and intensive instruction may be the special education teacher, a paraprofessional, a peer tutor, or someone else on the student's interdisciplinary team (e.g., general education teacher, parent, related service personnel).

Chapter Objectives

Upon reading this chapter, you should be able to do the following:

1. Distinguish between explicit and intensive instruction.
2. Provide a rationale for using explicit and intensive instruction in teaching students with ESN.
3. Provide examples of explicit and intensive instruction as the foundation for systematic instruction.

Explicit Instruction (HLP 16)

The fundamental component for explicit instruction is the instructional trial, which is the basic component of the instructional session.

The Instructional Trial

All instructional trials, regardless of context, have three parts: (a) the antecedent (A) or target stimulus (TS), (b) the behavior (B) or response (R), and (c) the consequence (C). Before an instructor can present an instructional trial, however, it is imperative that the instructor has the student's attention by presenting an attentional cue (AC). Collins (2022) used the following formula to demonstrate this sequence:

$$(AC)A \rightarrow B \rightarrow C$$

or

$$(AC)TS \rightarrow R \rightarrow C$$

Note that terms across these formulas will be used interchangeably throughout this chapter.

Attentional Cue and Response

To ensure attention is secured, the instructor must provide an AC and then wait for an attentional response before proceeding with instruction. The AC can be general or specific. When using a *general AC*, the instructor may address the entire class or the individual (e.g., "Eyes on me!"). In most cases, this will be sufficient to draw the attention of students to the instructor and will result in a *general attentional response* (e.g., students look at instructor or materials). If not, the instructor can provide a *specific AC* that requires an action focused on the relevant aspects of the stimulus to be performed by the entire class (e.g., "Put your finger on the word and trace its letters.") or by the individual (e.g., "Zoe, name the letters in the word."). This would be followed by a *specific attentional response* by the class (e.g., all students trace the letters in a word with their fingers) or by the individual (e.g., Zoe states the letters in the word). The instructor may find it effective to provide a general AC for the entire class and a specific AC only for those who need it.

Target Stimulus

Once attention is secured, the next step is to make clear to the student what the instructor expects the learner to accomplish. This is known as the antecedent or target stimulus, and it signals that a behavior or response should occur to demonstrate the expected outcome of instruction and access reinforcement. The goal of instruction is that students apply what has been learned in natural contexts. For example, a student who has been taught to read and define vocabulary should be able to read and understand it in natural settings, as when reading and using measurement terms (e.g., half cup, one tablespoon, two pints) while cooking even if the items have been adapted (e.g., red line at the half cup mark on a full cup, picture recipe card showing one tablespoon or two pints), or a student who has been taught to calculate percentages should be able to do this when required in natural settings, such as calculating a tip in a restaurant or tax on a purchase in a store by checking off steps of a task analysis while using a calculator. In these cases, the natural target stimulus would be the printed words in a recipe or stated price on a receipt or price tag. During instruction, however, it is necessary to explicitly state what the instructor is asking the student to do by providing a clear task direction when teaching vocabulary (e.g., "What word?", "What does this word mean?", "Touch the picture that shows what this word means") or teaching the calculation of percentage (e.g., "Use your checklist and calculator to find 20% of this amount."). When instruction reflects the real world as task directions are paired with natural stimuli, students should ultimately be able to apply the learning they have acquired where and when it is needed, whether or not a task direction is presented. Note that, when students have difficulty with hearing or comprehending directions, the instructor might use alternate options, such as pictures, manual signs, written words, or a combination of these, to convey what is expected.

Behavior or Response

In providing explicit instruction, the expected behavior should be both measurable and observable. While an instructor may want a student to "appreciate," "understand," or "realize" what is being taught, it is impossible to know if a student can do this unless these terms are stated using clear behavioral descriptions. A student's *appreciation* might be measured by requiring them to make a statement of affirmation. For example, a student in an art class might be required to *list* elements of painting by a specific artist (e.g., "Van Gogh's paintings have bright colors and swirling motions."). A student's *understanding* of something might be measured by requiring them to *demonstrate* competency (e.g., use a ruler and a formula to calculate area and perimeter of a box). A student's realization of something might be measured by requiring them to *state* the outcome of a science experiment (e.g., state that water became a solid when it froze at a specific temperature and became a gas when it boiled at a specific temperature). "List," "demonstrate," and "state" would be behavioral terms that describe explicit actions that can be observed and measured to determine that learning has taken place. Note that, when students have challenges in communication, options to replace verbal responses might be using an augmentative communication device, forming manual signs, or pointing to pictures or words.

Consequence

The consequence following the response in the instructional trial influences whether or not a student will perform a desired behavior or correct response in the future. When a student makes a desired response, it is important to reinforce the response, and positive verbal feedback may be a reinforcer for some students. This can be general (e.g., "Good job!" "Nice work!") or specific (e.g., "Yes, red and yellow combine to make orange.", "Right! 2 plus 2 equals 4."). During initial learning, it is important to provide this feedback consistently and frequently. Once a student reaches the criterion (and not before), positive feedback can be faded (e.g., every other trial, at the end of an instructional session) and become less descriptive. This reflects the real world where reinforcement may be delivered less frequently and will facilitate maintenance of the behavior over time. What is most important is that the positive consequence for correct responses should be individualized since what is reinforcing to one student may not be reinforcing to another. For example, praise may be sufficient feedback for some students while others may be more reinforced by a pat on the back, a high five, a gold star, a sticker, or participation in an activity. When tangible individualized reinforcers are necessary, it is always good practice to pair them with praise and positive statements.

Just as it is important to provide appropriate consequences for correct responses, it also is important to provide corrective feedback for incorrect responses. This allows the student to both recognize an error and have a model for the correct response. For example, the instructor may state the correct pronunciation or spelling of a vocabulary word (e.g., "You forgot the 'U.' Square is spelled S-Q-U-A-R-E.") as the instructor writes, states, or points to letters or demonstrate how a math problem should have been solved (e.g., "Stop. You need to add here instead of subtract like this…") as the instructor models with a second calculator.

Types of Systematic Instruction

Model-Lead-Test

The lesson plan shown in Table 16.1 demonstrates the use of the AC, presentation of the target stimulus, response, and consequence within a *model-lead-test* procedure (the most basic form of systematic explicit instruction). In this instructional format, the instructor first *models* the behavior or response that the student is expected to perform (e.g., demonstrates how to work a long division problem using a calculator). The instructor then *leads* the student in performing the behavior

Table 16.1 Lesson Plan Demonstrating Key Components of Instruction in a Core Content Biology Lesson

Unit	Biology: One-Celled Organisms
Lesson 1	Identifying One-Celled Organism.
Materials	Microscope, pond water containing one-celled organisms, microscope slides, eye dropper, pictures of various one-celled organisms, animals, and concrete objects.
Objective	After looking at a magnified drop of pond water on a slide, Zeke will independently and correctly touch a corresponding picture of a one-celled organism by selecting from an array of pictures showing one-celled organisms and other distractors (e.g., animal, concrete object) across three trials.
Prerequisite Instruction	Teacher shows the class examples of one-celled organisms in a PowerPoint presentation or a book. The teacher then models how to prepare a slide and use the microscope before placing students in pairs for hands on activity. Zeke's peer assists him in placing drop of pond water on slide, putting it under microscope, and focusing microscope.
Model-Lead-Test Procedure	*Model:* Instructor (teacher or peer) looks in microscope, selects a picture of an organism, and says, "Look. This is what I saw when I looked in the microscope. This is a one-celled organism." *Lead:* Instructor says, "Now, you try it," then guides Zeke in looking in microscope and selecting picture of the corresponding organism. Zeke repeats this until he is making the correct response. *Test:* Instructor provides the opportunity for Zeke to independently perform task, as follows:
Attentional Cue and Response	General Cue: "Zeke, are you ready to show me what you have learned?" General Response: Zeke sits up straight and nods his head.
Task Direction (Target Stimulus)	Instructor says, "Zeke, point to a picture of a one-celled organism that looks like what you saw in the microscope." Zeke may look back and forth as many times as needed before making a selection.
Response (Behavior)	From an array of five pictures (i.e., three single-cell organisms and two distractors), Zeke points to a picture of a one-celled organism.
Consequence	Correct response: "Great job! You selected a picture of an amoeba (paramecium, euglena). That is a one-celled organism." Incorrect response: "No, that is not a one-celled organism. That is a dog (ball). You should have seen a one-celled organism that looked like one of these (show correct choices). Let's look in the microscope and try again." Instructor repeats test sequence for three trials.
Data Collection	Peer assists Zeke in gluing selected pictures of one-celled organisms to a worksheet and writing their names beneath the pictures to create a permanent product for assessment. The number of correct pictures on the worksheet is later entered on the daily graph. This lesson repeats until Zeke meets the objective criterion.
Lesson Extension	Once Zeke can identify single-cell organisms, subsequent lessons will focus on identifying similarities and differences across organisms. Real-life connections will be made in discussing sources of water, as well as pure and contaminated water for drinking (e.g., "One-celled organisms live in pond water that may make you sick if you drink it. You should drink water from the tap or a bottle."). Note that trials on other instructional targets can be embedded in the lesson, such as math, fine motor, and communication skills.

(e.g., provides guided practice by assisting the student in working long division problems by giving explicit directions and feedback). Finally, the instructor *tests* to determine if the student can independently perform the desired behavior (e.g., gives learner a sheet of long division problems to complete independently). This three-step process is repeated continually until the student meets the preset performance criteria on the test (e.g., 100% correct responses on 10 long division problems). While the model-lead-test strategy is a common practice, it can lead to frustration on the part of a student with ESN who needs more explicit support for learning to occur. This support can be provided through two types of systematic instructional strategies that involve scaffolding by providing specific individualized prompts that increase the likelihood of a correct response and can be faded when no longer needed: stimulus and response prompting.

Stimulus Prompting

Stimulus prompting involves adding a prompt (P) or directly manipulating the target stimulus, prior to the task direction that can be faded over time. Collins (2022) has conceptualized stimulus prompting like this:

$$(P)TS \rightarrow R \rightarrow C$$

As an example, the instructor may print color words in the corresponding color (e.g., word red printed in red font) and then fade the color of the print to black over time, or the instructor may provide the corresponding number of dots next to a numeral and fade the dots over time. An additional example of stimulus prompting includes presenting an array of response choices and then indicating the correct response by placing it in closer proximity to the learner prior to giving the task direction.

Response Prompting

Response prompting involves adding a prompt following the task direction or target stimulus but prior to the student's response. Collins (2022) has conceptualized response prompting like this:

$$TS \rightarrow (P)R \rightarrow C$$

As with stimulus prompting, the prompt is faded when no longer needed. Chapter 15 lists and describes the various response prompting procedures (i.e., graduated guidance, most-to-least prompting, simultaneous prompting, system of least prompts, time delay) when the HLP of *scaffolding* is presented. For the purposes of this chapter, it is enough to mention that stimulus and response prompting are two types of systematic instruction that are preferable to the model-lead-test procedure because they are likely to result in fewer errors and result in more efficient learning for individuals with ESN. For additional information on explicit instruction using response prompting procedures, consult Browder et al. (2020), Ault and Shepley (2019), Collins (2022), and Wolery et al. (1992), as listed in the reference section of this chapter.

Intensive Instruction

Because students with ESN most likely will require multiple trials of instruction across multiple sessions to reach a preset criterion, it is necessary to prioritize what will be taught by clearly defining both the behavior that is being addressed and the criterion for mastery of that behavior. Most curricula in general education are comprised of instructional units on a specific topic in which a large amount of content is presented. Individualized education programs (IEPs) for students with ESN, however, hone in on specific objectives that interdisciplinary team members (e.g., instructors, paraprofessionals, parents, related service personnel, students with disabilities) have identified as being crucial for mastery if acquired skills are to be useful and applied in a student's life. An instructional unit may have a predetermined number of lessons designed to teach specific content before the instructor moves to the next unit whether or not students have mastered the unit content. Figuring out how to provide enough instruction for a student to master specific skills within the unit content requires intensive instruction that may involve supplemental instruction or extend across instructional units. For example, a student being taught numeral identification and basic counting can continue to work on those skills across math units on operations (e.g., addition, subtraction, multiplication, and division), fractions, measurement, and money. A student who is being taught letter identification and basic phonics can continue to work on those skills across subjects where vocabulary is presented, as can a student who is being taught to form letters of the alphabet or construct basic sentences and paragraphs. Intensity refers to the dosage (e.g., number and frequency of trials and opportunities to respond) of explicit instruction necessary to master skills over time.

Potential Instructional Formats

There is not a single format for delivering intensive instruction. Instead, the instructor must take into consideration what is being taught and how it should be presented. Some skills are best taught on an *individual* basis. This includes academic skills such as writing personal information, or daily living skills such as dressing for gym class. In both cases, the skill may require a personalized model and hand-over-hand guidance. It may be advantageous to teach other skills in a *small group* format where students have the opportunity to observe and learn from each other whether all group members are being taught the same content or each is being taught different content. This also includes academic skills such as participating in a hands-on science experiment, or daily living skills such as preparing a meal in a consumer science class. Finally, there are times when instructors will present content in a *large group* format (e.g., lecture, demonstration). In this case, the instructor can concentrate on *embedding* instructional trials for the learner with ESN within the lesson. For younger students, this might occur by inserting trials of numeral or letter recognition during play with blocks containing letters and numerals or during read-aloud time in the book center. For older students, this might occur by inserting trials of numeral or letter recognition while discussing a book in a literature class or inserting trials on personal management or safety in a health class unit. It is clear that the more trials of explicit and intensive instruction on specific objectives can be inserted across activities or units of study, the more likely it is that students with ESN will master the content.

Potential Instructors

Whichever format is used to provide instruction (and it is recommended that all formats be considered when planning the daily instructional schedule), the professional literature has shown that who delivers instruction can vary as long as the person conducting instruction has received adequate training to be proficient in the delivery of explicit instruction. In addition to special education teachers, there is evidence that effective instructors can include general education teachers (e.g., Tekin-Iftar et al., 2017), paraprofessionals and peers (e.g., Britton et al., 2017; Heinrich et al., 2016), related service providers (e.g., Roark et al., 2002), and family members or caregivers (e.g., Mobayed et al., 2000). The more individuals trained to deliver explicit instruction, the greater the intensity of instruction will be since it can be delivered across settings (e.g., academic classes, extracurricular activities, and homework assignments) throughout the day.

For explicit instruction to be effective, it is important that instructional strategies be delivered with a high degree of *reliability* (i.e., accuracy). This means that, if the special education teacher is not the person delivering instruction, alternate instructors must be trained to a high degree of proficiency. Most coaching on instructional strategies involves several training components that can include providing written materials, modeling what is expected in person or by sharing video, role-playing, observing the person in training in person or through video, providing feedback in real time either in person or through electronic audio, and answering questions. Whatever method for coaching is used, it should continue until competency is demonstrated.

Key Elements of Explicit and Intensive Instruction

So far, this chapter has described the basic components of a trial of explicit instruction and the format and instructor options for increasing the intensity of that instruction. This final section describes the key elements involved in conducting explicit and intensive instruction by presenting the decisions that an instructor must make when teaching a student with ESN.

Discrete Skills and Chained Tasks

Each basic behavior or response that is being taught to a student with ESN can be classified as a *discrete* skill. A discrete skill consists of a single one-step behavior that can be observed and measured. For most students, this is easy to determine. A student can write a letter of the alphabet or a numeral. A student can make a "yes" or "no" response to a question or provide a simple answer in a single statement. A student can perform a mathematical operation to produce an answer, such as adding two numbers or using a calculator. For some students with ESN, however, even these basic skills must be divided into smaller components. A student with ESN may need to be taught to make multiple strokes to form a single letter of the alphabet or a numeral; perform several steps to activate an augmentative communication device to respond to a question; or individually count dots, tics on a number line, or fingers to add two numbers or multiple steps to operate a calculator. In this case, a discrete skill for one student may be a chained task for another.

A *chained task* is made up of a sequence of discrete skills linked together to form a more complex behavior. To perform a skill, the student will need to complete each step of the chain. It is possible that the student may already have mastered some steps of the chain but still need help on others. For example, a student may know how to enter numbers into a calculator but need to be taught how to enter the function keys (e.g., +, −, =). Progress on learning a chained task is sometimes measured by whether a student increases the number of performed steps over time and whether or not the learner can perform the entire chained task. In addition, progress on learning is sometimes determined by whether a student needs less assistance over time and whether or not the skill can be performed independently. If some steps are too difficult for a student with ESN, adaptations can be made (e.g., premeasured ingredients for a student who cannot measure but can complete the other steps of assembling a snack).

Teaching a chained task requires a *task analysis*. This means that all steps must be listed with the recognition that sometimes steps of a chained task must be performed in a *specific order* to get the desired outcome or sometimes steps can sometimes be performed in a *functional order* (i.e., out of sequence) if the outcome is still the same. In addition, the instructor may choose to teach one step of the chain at a time beginning with the first step and proceeding forward (i.e., *forward chaining*) or beginning with the last step and proceeding backward (i.e., *backward chaining*). The most common way to teach a chained task, however, is to teach the *total task* (i.e., all steps at the same time), giving the student the opportunity to perform mastered steps independently and receive instruction on the remaining steps. If necessary, chained tasks also can be taught through *chunking* long chains into short, more manageable groups of steps, such as teaching a snack time routine by breaking the chain into the steps for making a drink, making peanut butter and crackers, serving the snack, and cleaning up.

Whether the instructor is using explicit instruction to teach a discrete skill or a chained task, the intensity of instruction must be considered. This requires determining how many trials of instruction will occur throughout the day and how those trials will be provided. It is important to remember that the more opportunities a learner has to respond per instructional session and throughout the day (i.e., the more intense the instruction), the more efficient instruction is likely to be. In other words, learners likely will acquire new content in a shorter period of time (e.g., fewer days or weeks). There are several options for delivering instruction: (a) massed trials, (b) spaced trials, and (c) distributed trials.

Massed Trial Instruction

Massed trials are presented in a sequence with no other types of instruction between trials and can be conceptualized (where X = one trial) as illustrated in the following manner (Collins, 2022): XXXXX. An instructor may choose to present a series of flashcards in succession or a set of several word problems to solve. The more trials per instructional session, the more intense the instruction and the greater the likelihood that learning will take place in a shorter period of time.

Spaced Trial Instruction

Spaced trials are presented in a manner to allow the student to stop and think between instructional trials and can be conceptualized in the following manner (Collins, 2022): X X X X X. This works well in a small group lesson in which the instructor conducts a trial (or several massed trials) with a student per turn, conducts instructional trials with other members of the group, and then conducts another trial (or several massed trials) with the student. This can be exemplified by a small group lesson focused on reading where each student takes a turn to read a word, a sentence, or several sentences. Spaced trials facilitate social skills by teaching turn-taking skills and can allow *observational learning* to occur as students watch each other receive instruction.

Distributed Trial Instruction

Distributed trials are another way to increase the intensity of learning. Distributed trials are presented in a manner that is natural, with instructional trials occurring throughout the day, often across settings and instructors, and can be conceptualized in the following manner where X = instruction on a specific skill and Y = instruction on another skill (Collins, 2022): X Y X Y X Y. Distributed trials have the advantage of learning taking place where it is needed instead of in isolation. For example, an instructor might conduct an instructional trial on name-writing in each class where the student with ESN must identify personal work, when checking into a special event, and when keeping score in a game.

Distributed trials are also a way of *embedding* instruction into a large group lesson. This is especially appropriate in inclusive general education settings where instructors are more likely to use large group formats for instruction. For example, an instructor who is teaching a novel can embed a trial of numeral identification when pointing to page numbers or the table of contents, color identification when discussing the book's cover or pictures, and vocabulary when selecting highlighted words for the student to identify and define as the lesson proceeds. This type of instruction can be repeated with various texts across classes, thus combining explicit and intensive instruction in a natural manner.

Phases of Learning

There are four phases of learning that should be considered in planning explicit and intensive instruction: (a) acquisition, (b) fluency, (c) maintenance, and (d) generalization. Students may be at different phases, depending on the skill being taught. The phase of learning being addressed will influence the design of instruction.

Acquisition

Acquisition is initial learning. During this phase, students are provided frequent opportunities to practice skills that are continuously reinforced.

Fluency

Fluency is how well a student performs a skill. An acquired skill needs to be fluent enough to be useful in real life. For example, a student with ESN must be able to respond to requests for personal information (e.g., orally, in writing, using augmentative device) within a specified interval of time following a request. The student also must be able to enter a PIN when using a debit card with an electronic device (e.g., ATM, computer, check-out of store) before the system closes down. Fluency can be facilitated during acquisition by requiring a response to be made within a specified amount of time (e.g., 3 seconds) during an instructional trial.

Maintenance

Maintenance refers to the performance of a skill after instruction has ended. Instructors should never make the assumption that a student with ESN will retain a skill just because the criterion was met a specific point in time. Skills should be revisited and reassessed periodically to determine if they are being retained; if not, remedial instruction may be necessary. Maintenance can be facilitated by requiring multiple sessions of mastery performance across days to determine when criterion has been met (i.e., overlearning) and by fading reinforcement (e.g., praise) during instructional trials once a learner has met the criterion to better reflect the real world where reinforcement may not be readily available.

Generalization

Perhaps the most important phase of learning is *generalization* because, if a skill is not generalized, it is useless in the real world. Generalization is the ability of a student to perform skill under conditions that are different than during instruction. This may be the ability to perform a skill with different materials (e.g., write name on assignment, type name on a computer, enter name in blocks on a form), in response to different people (e.g., the instructor, a community member, an employer), and across different settings (e.g., classroom, gym, home). Generalization can be facilitated by varying instructional materials, varying instructors, or teaching across settings. Another strategy is to teach with materials that reflect those that will be found in the real world (e.g., pictures of real survival signs instead of picture drawn in black and white, real money instead of play money, fasteners on real clothing instead of fasteners on dolls). Once criterion is reached, the instructor should assess whether the student can perform a skill under novel, untrained conditions not used during instruction. If not, it will be necessary to continue instruction with the novel conditions.

Data Collection

Explicit and intensive instruction requires that instructional data be recorded on a frequent basis, with daily data on sessions of trials being optimal. Data also should be graphed as soon as possible after they are collected. This is because it is crucial to make instructional decisions based on data. The teacher should consistently analyze student data to determine if (a) progress is occurring as expected, (b) if inadequate progress is occurring, (c) if no progress has been made, and (d) if variable performance is occurring (i.e., sometimes showing the expected performance and sometimes not). While any trained instructor can be taught to reliably record and graph data, the special education teacher will most likely be responsible for making data-based decisions on whether to continue instruction as is or make adaptations, although feedback may be solicited from members of the interdisciplinary team.

Next Steps toward Better Practice

When implementing explicit and intensive instruction with students with ESN, teachers should consider the following guidelines:

1. Before implementing explicit instruction with a student with ESN, practice until accurate and fluent with the instructional procedure and elicit feedback (e.g., self-assessment when watching a video, peer-feedback when receiving advice from an observer).
2. Once fluent in using explicit instruction, share strategies with others in the student's environment (e.g., paraprofessionals, peer tutors, parents, related service providers) to facilitate generalization across people and settings.
3. When coaching others in the use of explicit instruction, model the strategy, and then consider providing direct feedback both during instruction (e.g., face-to-face comments, comments via bug-in-the-ear technology) and following instruction (e.g., verbal discussion, written feedback).
4. Collect and graph data from instructional trials or sessions to be used in determining the *effectiveness* (i.e., if the student makes progress or meets criterion) and *efficiency* (i.e., how many sessions or how much time it takes the student to meet criterion) of instruction and make changes, as indicated (e.g., change instructional procedures, change instructional materials, increase the intensity of instruction by adding additional trials).

The Big Five

When planning explicit and intensive instruction for students with ESN, consider the following take-aways from this chapter:

1. Two key components of systematic instruction are the use of explicit (i.e., direct) and intensive (i.e., frequent) instructional trials.
2. Systematic instructional trials are comprised of an AC, an antecedent (i.e., target stimulus), a behavior (i.e., response), and a consequence (e.g., feedback).
3. Systematic instruction is flexible in that it can be applied across content and easily embedded in ongoing units of instruction.
4. Systematic instruction should be individualized for each student with ESN, taking into consideration the student's age, ability, and needs for support.
5. Systematic instruction requires data-based decision-making to determine what works and does not work with each student.

Resource

- The Iris Center website (https://iris.peabody.vanderbilt.edu/)—search for explicit and intensive instruction.

References

Ault, M. J., & Shepley, C. N. (2019). Stimulus control and prompting strategies. In R. Pennington (Ed.), *Applied behavior analysis for everyone* (pp. 108–122). AAPC Publishing.

Britton, N. S., Collins, B. C., Ault, M. J., & Bausch, M. E. (2017). Using a constant time delay procedure to teach support personnel to use a simultaneous prompting procedure. *Focus on Autism and Other Developmental Disabilities, 32*(2), 102–113. https://doi.org/10.1177/1088357615587505

Browder, D. M., Spooner, F., Courtade, G. R., & Contributers (2020). *Teaching students with moderate and severe disabilities* (2nd ed.). Guilford Press.

Collins, B. C. (2022). *Systematic instruction for students with moderate and severe disabilities* (2nd ed.). Brookes Publishing.

Collins, B. C., Evans, A., Galloway, C. G., Karl, A., & Miller, A. (2007). A comparison of the acquisition and maintenance of teaching functional and core content in special and general education settings. *Focus on Autism and Other Developmental Disabilities, 22*(4), 220–233. https://doi.org/10.1177/10883576070220040401

Collins, B. C., Lo, Y., Park, G., & Haughney, K. (2018). Response prompting as an ABA-based instructional approach to teaching students with disabilities. *TEACHING Exceptional Children, 50*(6), 343–355. https://doi.org/10.1177/0040059918774920

Graves, T. B., Collins, B. C., Schuster, J. W., & Kleinert, H. (2005). Using video prompting to teach cooking skills to secondary students with moderate disabilities. *Education and Training in Developmental Disabilities, 40*(1), 34–46.

Heinrich, S., Collins, B. C., Knight, V., & Spriggs, A. D. (2016). Embedded simultaneous prompting procedure to teach STEM content to high school students with moderate disabilities in an inclusive setting. *Education and Training in Autism and Developmental Disabilities, 51*(1), 41–54. https://www.jstor.org/stable/26420363

McLeskey, J., Barringer, M.-D., Billingsley, B., Brownell, M., Jackson, D., Kennedy, M., Lewis, T., Maheady, L., Rodriguez, J., Scheeler, M. C., Winn, J., & Ziegler, D. (2017, January). High-leverage practices in special education. Council for Exceptional Children & CEEDAR Center. http://ceedar.education.ufl.edu/wp-content/uploads/2017/07/CEC-HLP-Web.pdf

Mobayed, K. L., Collins, B. C., Strangis, D., Schuster, J. W., & Hemmeter, M. L. (2000). Teaching parents to employ mand-model procedures to teach their children requesting. *Journal of Early Intervention, 23*(3), 165–179 https://doi.org/10.1177/10538151000230030601

Norman, J. M., Collins, B. C., & Schuster, J. W. (2001). Using video prompting and modeling to teach self-help skills to elementary students with mental disabilities in a small group. *Journal of Special Education Technology, 16*(3), 5–18. https://doi.org/10.1177/016264340101600301

Pennington, R. C. (2019). *Applied behavior analysis for everyone.* AAPC Publishing.

Roark, T. J., Collins, B. C., Hemmeter, M. L., & Kleinert, H. (2002). Including manual signing as non-targeted information when teaching receptive identification of packaged food items. *Journal of Behavioral Education. 11*(1), 19–38. https://doi.org/10.1023/A:1014381220940

Seward, J., Schuster, J. W., Ault, M. J., Collins, B. C., & Hall, M. (2014). Comparing simultaneous prompting and constant time delay to teach leisure skills to students with moderate intellectual disabilities. *Education and Training in Autism and Developmental Disabilities, 49*(3), 381–395. https://www.jstor.org/stable/23881258

Taylor, P., Collins, B. C., Schuster, J. W., & Kleinert, H. (2002). Teaching laundry skills to high school students with disabilities: Generalization of targeted skills and nontargeted information.

Education and Training in Mental Retardation and Developmental Disabilities, 37(2), 172–183. https://www.jstor.org/stable/23879828

Tekin-Iftar, E., Collins, B. C., Spooner, F., & Olcay-Gul, S. (2017). Teaching teachers to use systematic instruction to teach core content to students with ASD. *Teacher Education and Special Education, 42*(3), 225–245. https://doi.org/10.1177/0888406417703751

Wolery, M., Ault, M. J., & Doyle, P. M. (1992). *Teaching students with moderate to severe disabilities: Use of response prompting strategies.* Longman.

17
Use Flexible Grouping
J. Matt Jameson and Susan S. Johnston

Teachers assign students to homogeneous and heterogeneous groups based on explicit learning goals, monitor peer interactions, and provide positive and corrective feedback to support productive learning. Teachers use small learning groups to accommodate learning differences, promote in-depth academic-related interactions, and teach students to work collaboratively. They choose tasks that require collaboration, issue directives that promote productive and autonomous group interactions, and embed strategies that maximize learning opportunities and equalize participation. Teachers promote simultaneous interactions, use procedures to hold students accountable for collective and individual learning, and monitor and sustain group performance through proximity and positive feedback.

Supporting Students with Extensive Support Needs

Previous chapters have established the importance of inclusion and the benefits of inclusive classrooms while emphasizing the need for teacher-controlled systematic instruction for students with ESN. Placement in inclusive settings influences the range of **instructional arrangements** (i.e., grouping arrangements) that students with ESN experience. Instructional arrangements, in turn, affect the learning and communication/social opportunities in the environment. While inclusive settings have more opportunity for whole and small group activity (McDonnell et al., 2000), instruction in general education classrooms has historically been characterized by whole-class instruction and homogenous student groups (e.g., same age and ability) that are often permanent and assigned based on teacher assessment of individual student learning (Kennedy & Fisher, 2001). In this instructional arrangement, students are asked to listen to the teacher, follow directions, take notes, and answer questions as they are asked (Downing, 2010). Unfortunately, students with ESN may have communication, visual, or auditory skills that impact their participation in these large group instructional arrangements (Carter et al., 2008). Using intentional flexible (i.e., heterogeneous) small group arrangements allows students to be grouped based on individual interests, communication/social skills, and varying performance levels (Brown et al., 2020; Collins, 2012). This chapter will describe HLP 17, using intentional and flexible student grouping as an instructional arrangement for students with ESN to increase the opportunities for learning and to practice communication/social skills.

DOI: 10.4324/9781003175735-18

A misconception about teaching students with ESN is that systematic instruction on core academic content and IEP goals must be provided in a one-on-one instructional format with massed discrete trials in a separate setting. While systematic instruction requires some form of direct instruction, these opportunities do not need to be one-on-one with a teacher, massed, or done in a special education setting. Students with ESN have acquired skills taught with systematic instructional procedures in small group formats (e.g., simultaneous prompting, progressive time delay, constant time delay, the system of least prompts). In addition, research has shown that students with ESN in inclusive settings are more engaged while working in small groups than in the traditional large group instructional arrangement (Steinbrenner & Watson, 2015) and that their engagement is highest when working in small groups with general education peers without disabilities (Logan et al., 1997). Communicative and social interactions occurred more often within small group instructional formats and when students were not receiving direct support from a paraprofessional or special educator (Carter et al., 2008). In addition to the social and learning benefits, small groups also provide the opportunity for observational learning and cooperative learning.

Research has shown students with ESN learn by watching others in small group instructional arrangements (e.g., Mechling et al., 2007). This can result in an increase in instructional efficiency through observational learning. Observational learning occurs when students acquire content by observing other students' instructional opportunities and acquiring non-targeted information (Collins, 2012). If students in the group are taught the same tasks, including the same non-targeted information, observational learning can increase the potential for more rapid learning. If students in the group are taught different lessons, including different non-targeted information, observational learning increases the potential for a more significant amount of learning to take place (Fickel et al., 1998). In addition to observational learning, small heterogeneous learning groups provide the opportunity for cooperative learning experiences. Cooperative learning in mixed ability group arrangements has numerous benefits for teachers and students with ESN (and their peers) in inclusive settings (Hunt et al., 1994). These benefits include (a) more efficient use of teacher and student time, (b) increased opportunities for observational learning, imitating a teacher or classmate's model of a correct response, and acquisition of incidental information, (c) increased social interaction among peers and opportunities to practice communication/social skills, and (d) increased opportunities to prepare and practice for inclusive environments where group arrangements are commonly used (Brown et al., 2020; Collins, 2012). This chapter will provide professionals with a framework for using instructional HLPs described in the previous chapters (e.g., systematic instruction) in intentional small group learning arrangements for students with ESN that maximize learning and communication/social opportunities.

Chapter Objectives

Upon reading this chapter, you should be able to do the following:

1. Describe the rationale and purpose behind small mixed ability groups for students with ESN.
2. Be able to make intentional choices for student grouping arrangements in inclusive settings.
3. Be able to utilize peers to provide instructional supports for students with ESN.
4. Be able to support peers and create support networks for students with ESN.

Application of the Practice: Make Intentional Instructional Decisions When Using Small Groups

Used in conjunction with systematic instruction (e.g., instructional cue, stimulus presentation, response prompting, objective and measurable behavior, error correction, and differential reinforcement), small heterogeneous learning groups provide students and teachers with an efficient and effective instructional arrangement for inclusive settings. Students can be assigned to groups by teacher selection, student selection, or random selection. Teachers are encouraged to use all three selection methods of grouping depending on the content being taught and activities planned, but this chapter will focus on teacher-selected small heterogeneous groups as an intentional instructional intervention to maximize opportunities for observational and cooperative learning and communication/social interactions.

Flexible Grouping to Support Instruction and Learning

When designing instructional groups, teachers should consider (a) designing and using instructional tasks and stimuli to maximize the instructional opportunities for observational learning, (b) having clear expectations for student responses (i.e., individual responses, group responses, or cooperative learning), and (c) integrating opportunities for cooperative and peer-supported learning.

Instructional Tasks and Stimuli

When instructing students in a group, teachers have four options to choose from in terms of task and stimuli selection. Groups should maximize the opportunities for instruction on targeted skills (i.e., skills identified in IEP goals) and observational learning. Students can be taught (a) the same task using the same stimuli, (b) different tasks using the same stimuli, (c) the same task using different stimuli, or (d) different tasks using different stimuli (Collins, 2012).

The Same Task and the Same Stimuli for All Members of the Group

The teacher will teach the same targeted skill with the same stimuli for all small group members in this arrangement. The targeted skill(s) and instructional materials are the same for all students. *For example, Mr. Rainey teaches four students in his inclusive kindergarten to discriminate community safety signs identified and prioritized through ecological assessment. The stimuli include 15 community safety sign photos. The targeted skill for all four students, both those with and those without disabilities, is to expressively (i.e., verbally) identify the same 15 community safety signs. Mr. Rainey sequentially provides a new stimulus presentation and opportunity to respond to each group member arranged around a round table. The individual student responses will depend on which stimulus they are presented with, and Mr. Rainey records data for each instructional trial for his one student with ESN in the small group.*

The Same Task and Different Stimuli for Each Member of the Group

Another option for small group instruction is to teach the same task but use different stimuli. The targeted skill is the same, but the instructional materials are different. *In this example, Mr. Rainey teaches six students in his inclusive kindergarten to expressively (i.e., verbally) identify photos of community signs. One of the students has intellectual disability and a visual impairment and uses tactile stimuli. All six students are taught the same targeted skill (i.e., expressive identification of community safety signs). Each was assigned different stimuli (i.e., five different community signs were introduced to each student, and one student used tactile signs). After two weeks of instruction using this group every other day, Mr. Rainey observed that all the students were verbally identifying signs that the other students were working on. This is an example of the students learning non-targeted content.*

Different Tasks for Each Member of the Group Using the Same Stimuli

In this instructional arrangement, each small group member has a different targeted learning objective that can be taught using the same stimuli for each group member. *For example, using a stimulus set of 15 safety signs, Mr. Rainey teaches four students in his inclusive kindergarten skills targeting their individual learning needs. One student is discriminating colors on the signs, two are working on identifying the shapes of the signs, and another is working on discriminating letters on the signs. All students work on individualized content with the same stimulus set of 15 safety signs. After two weeks of instruction using this group one time per day, Mr. Rainey observed that the student discriminating colors began to use shapes when describing the signs. This is an example of a student learning non-targeted content.*

Different Tasks and Stimuli for All Members of the Instructional Group

In this instructional arrangement, each small group member is working on a different learning objective taught using individualized stimuli for each group member. Teaching each student a different task using different stimuli may require additional preparation on the part of the teacher. Still, it may require less instructional time while promoting observational learning as students are exposed to both non-targeted goals and instructional stimuli. *For example, Mr. Rainey teaches a literacy lesson to four students in his inclusive kindergarten at a square table with the students sitting across from each other. One student who has ESN is deafblind and is working with a tactile board to learn prepositions (e.g., on, under, next to). One student has ESN and limited verbal speech and is working on the behavioral objective of sitting in her chair and increasing pre-reading skills (e.g., correctly holding a book, turning pages). One peer without disabilities is working on identifying initial and terminal consonant sounds in consonant-vowel-consonant (CVC) words in grade-level books, and another is independently reading. All students are working on individualized content and using different stimuli. After 20 minutes of instruction, Mr. Rainey notices that the student working on pre-reading skills has started to imitate the identification of the consonant sounds she has seen her classmate working on. She has begun to learn a non-targeted skill without systematic instruction.*

In summary, the efficiency of instruction for both students and teachers increases when students acquire discrete or chained non-targeted content through observational learning. This happens when students acquire this non-targeted information as it is inserted as instructive feedback during the delivery of instructional trials (e.g., inserted in the task cue, prompt, or consequence). Including non-targeted information in a small group format has the added advantage of allowing students to acquire additional information inserted in their targeted instruction and non-targeted information inserted in the targeted instruction of others in the group (Ledford et al., 2008). Teachers in inclusive settings need to intentionally design educational arrangements and processes that allow students with ESN to meaningfully and successfully participate in the academic and social activities of the general education classroom.

Table 17.1 shows a two-column table with text describing strategies and examples for embedding non-targeted information into instructional trials.

Vignette: Zeke

Zeke is a fifteen-year-old with Down syndrome, Other Health Impairments (OHI), and ESN who attends his neighborhood high school. Zeke is fully included in all his high school classes and gets support through co-teaching, paraprofessional, and peer supports arranged by his IEP team. Zeke has basic academic and functional skills and strong communication and social skills. Still, he needs support engaging in the general education content and staying engaged in the activities and routines in the general education classrooms. Zeke's IEP team is interested in supporting the development of his general education content knowledge and communication/social skills through the intentional design and use of flexible grouping arrangements in his general education classes. Zeke's special education teacher and general education 10th-grade Earth Science Teacher have spent time collaborating to design a learning environment where Zeke spends the majority of each science class in heterogeneous small learning groups with peers without disabilities. Zeke works on a balance of IEP goals and general education content that have been intentionally designed to maximize his opportunities for learning and social engagement.

Table 17.1 Embedding Non-targeted Information into Instructional Trials. A Two-column Table with Text Describing Strategies and Examples

Strategy	Example
Add non-targeted information to the prompt	Roark et al. (2002) taught students with ESN to identify foods (targeted skill) while including manual signs for the words in the prompt as non-targeted information. Four secondary students identified packaged food using a constant time delay procedure. The non-targeted content was the manual sign of the item. The students with ESN learned to discriminate the packaged food items. In addition, they were all able to learn some of the manual signs presented as non-target content.
Add non-targeted information to the stimulus	Daugherty et al. (2001) included non-target content in the antecedent event, teaching counting (targeted skill), and colors (non-targeted content). The instructor would present the items on the table and say, "Count the red blocks." The student was given the color in the task direction simultaneously without distracting the students from the task or adding instruction time to the lesson. All students met their targeted objectives in counting and learned the non-targeted content related to color.
Add non-targeted information to the consequence	Taylor et al. (2002) taught four high school students with moderate to severe disabilities to do laundry using task analysis (targeted skill) and to recognize laundry sight words (non-targeted content). During instruction on the task analysis, the teacher would say the word, show it on a flashcard, and then point out the word on the washing machine or in the natural environment while teaching the task analyzed skill of doing a load of laundry. All students learned non-targeted content.

Student Responses

Teachers have two ways to organize student responses in small group instructional arrangements: individual or group responses (Collins, 2012).

Individual Student Responses

In an intrasequential group arrangement, each student receives one-on-one instruction in the small group arrangement (Collins et al., 1991). The teacher can sequentially or randomly present instructional trials to each student giving individual cues, stimulus presentation, response prompt, and error correction or differential reinforcement to each student individually and all students observe the instruction of the other group members. *For example, Zeke's science teacher, Miss Kowalski, begins some instructional sessions each week with small groups where she has identified students who need targeted support. The groups change frequently but generally include Zeke and four peers from the general education class. Miss Kowalski provides 15 minutes of instruction where she addresses Zeke's IEP goals of measuring different states of matter (i.e., measuring a volume of liquid or mass of a solid) and different instructional targets she identifies for his general education peers through weekly assessments using an intrasequential model. Miss Kowalski usually provides a specific instructional cue, expects a specified response, and provides instructional feedback to each student, one at a time. Sometimes she will rotate sequentially through the students in the group; sometimes, she will randomly choose which student is provided an opportunity to respond. Students are usually working on different skills using different stimuli.*

In an intersequential model, each learner in the group works together to complete a task by completing individual steps. In this arrangement, each student has a targeted learning objective that can be addressed as they complete one step in a group activity. *For example, Miss Kowalski has small lab groups several times a week. She frequently changes the group compositions but generally has four peers without disabilities, a student with a specific learning disability, and Zeke grouped for the lab activities. Today the lab requires students to select a container and estimate the volume of liquid that will exactly fill the container when frozen. Zeke picks the container for the group, one student without a disability estimates the volume of water they should add. Zeke measures and adds the water (i.e., his IEP goal). Another student without disabilities records the hypothesis, procedures, and outcomes in a shared lab book. The student with a specific learning disability completes an iPad-based graphic organizer that guides the process using a Problem-Hypothesis-Test-Results-Reflect format, and the final student reports the results to the rest of the class. Each student has a different task and uses both the same and different stimuli to complete a single task.*

Group Responses

Group responses could simply be simultaneous choral responses to a single stimulus. While this does increase the instructional efficiency (e.g., four students responding to a single stimulus takes less time than each student getting an individual instructional opportunity), this arrangement does not provide the same opportunities for observational learning, instructional feedback, and social interaction that the individual response models offer. In contrast, small cooperative groups maximize these opportunities and may be the ideal instructional arrangement for students with ESN in inclusive settings. At a minimum, there is evidence that cooperative learning is an effective instructional arrangement for students with ESN (Jimenez et al., 2012). Cooperative learning groups are defined as 2–10 mixed ability students working together to accomplish a specified learning task (Brown et al., 2020; Collins, 2012). Brown et al. (2020) describe several keys to designing cooperative learning groups for students with ESN. They suggest teachers ensure that: (a) students are heterogeneously assigned to groups for instruction, (b) instructional activities are designed to encourage groups to work together, (c) students are taught processes for organizing assigned academic tasks within the group, (d) students are taught social and communication skills necessary to support each other and resolve differences to complete assignments, and (e) students are assessed individually to monitor progress and make data-based decisions. *For example, Miss Kowalski uses cooperative learning groups throughout each weekly Earth Science lesson. She changes group compositions each week as the activities and learning objectives change. This week the group has been studying changing states of matter. The group met at the start of the lesson and worked together using an inquiry-based approach to establish what they knew about states of matter, what they wanted to know, and what they expected to learn. Miss Kowalski structures this process so each student has the opportunity to interact in the group in this inquiry process. Students all have rotating roles (e.g., scribe, lab manager, scientist, research assistant) in the group, which has clearly defined expectations in the initial inquiry-based explorations. She also collects data and provides prompts for Zeke's IEP goal of increasing skills in group interactions through eye contact, attending to relevant stimuli, and waiting for his turn. This week there were also multiple naturally occurring opportunities to collect data on Zeke measuring the volume of liquids (an IEP goal).*

Peer Supports for Learning

In addition to the benefits of cooperative and observational learning, small group instructional formats also provide opportunities for increasing instructional efficiency through the use of peer supports. Peers can implement curricular, instructional, or ecological adaptations and provide assistance and feedback in completing assigned tasks. Research on the use of peers to deliver instructional programs to students with significant cognitive disabilities extends back more than four decades (e.g., Jenkins & Jenkins, 1981), and peer support strategies are an established evidence-based practice for students with ESN. Most importantly, research has shown that students with ESN and their peer supports benefit from the arrangements (Carter et al., 2009). Peer support arrangements vary widely in the intended focus and intensity. Teachers may utilize a single peer to deliver highly structured systematic instruction or assign several students informally to provide social supports. Whatever arrangement is used, the peer support strategies must be designed to maximize all students' learning and social opportunities in the small group arrangement.

Teachers should consider the following when using peers in small group instructional arrangements (Brown et al., 2020). First, teachers need to identify students with ESN and peers without disabilities who may benefit from peer support arrangements. It is essential to consider the academic and social characteristics of all students and the student's preferences. Students with ESN should have a say about who they want to work with, and peers should express interest and willingness to be a support. Second, students should be oriented to their roles and responsibilities as peer supports. This can include more informal orientation and information about the strategies to support students with ESN in academic and social activities to more structured training to provide systematic instruction embedded in the classroom activities (Brock et al., 2016). It is important that all students know their roles and responsibilities and are provided support and training by teachers and paraprofessionals to facilitate the interactions and instruction. Third, teachers must provide ongoing monitoring of the peer support arrangement to ensure that the students benefit socially and academically. This can include informal observations of the interactions and academic activities or more formal monitoring of progress on targeted skills and the fidelity of peers' use of systematic instruction. It is important to remember that when a peer without a disability fills the role of teacher, that peer's interactions with the student with ESN may be less likely to be reciprocal and directed toward communication or socializing. Teachers may want to both assign more than one peer to support students with ESN (Carter & Kennedy, 2006) but also provide frequent opportunities for the student with ESN to work with and meet new students in the class. *Zeke works in a variety of small group instructional arrangements in Miss Kowalski's 10th-grade Earth Science class. Miss Kowalski has designed several peer support strategies to help Zeke in these groups. She often has two students without disabilities that she has trained to deliver embedded instructional trials into the naturally occurring opportunities in the small groups. These students were taught how to identify times to provide instruction, deliver an instructional cue, use constant time delay response prompting strategies, provide error correction and differential reinforcement, and collect instructional data. She will often have these students deliver supplemental instructional opportunities on targeted IEP goals in small group arrangements. Miss Kowalski monitors the fidelity with which the peers use the instructional procedures, evaluates the data they collect to make instructional decisions, and meets with them weekly to talk about their instruction with Zeke. She also uses a small group of peers (i.e., peer support network) she has identified to provide social support for Zeke in science class and school and community activities. They also receive an orientation and ongoing support to provide Zeke with communication and social opportunities as appropriate. She mixes these peer supports in heterogeneous small group activities whenever she can.*

Teachers must remember that instructional context, or grouping arrangements, influence the academic and communication/social opportunities for students with ESN. Heterogeneous small group arrangements should be intentionally designed to maximize instructional efficiency through the use of observational, cooperative, and peer-supported learning and social opportunities. In addition, these arrangements provide opportunities for peer-to-peer supports which are increasingly recognized as a viable strategy to avoid the adverse effects of one-on-one paraprofessional supports in academic and social interactions between students with ESN and their peers without disabilities and benefit all students in the inclusive classroom (Carter et al., 2015).

Figure 17.1 shows a text box discussing the use of the Good Behavior Game as a group contingency behavior management intervention.

Supporting Student Behavior in Small Groups

There are three types of group contingencies, (a) independent, (b) dependent, and (c) interdependent, used to support on-task behavior. Research suggests that all group contingencies are effective, as evidenced by studies that show an increase in on-task behaviors and a decrease in disruptive behaviors (Wahl et al., 2016). Researchers have suggested using the Good Behavior Game (GBG), a strategy with a strong effect in reducing disruptive and off-task behaviors of all students, including students with ESN. The Good Behavior Game (GBG) is a Tier I group contingency classroom management intervention used to promote appropriate behaviors in students (Conradi et al., 2021). Students are assigned to teams, given points as the teams exhibit appropriate behaviors, and then the team that accumulates the highest number of points is rewarded. While implementing the game, teachers commonly recognize appropriate behaviors, teach prosocial skills and classroom expectations, give feedback about inappropriate behavior and verbal praise, and reward students while reinforcing their appropriate behaviors (Flower et al., 2014). Not only has the GBG proved to be a practical Tier I strategy for teachers to use, but students with ESN have benefitted and show increased rates of engagement and fewer interfering behaviors (Conradi et al., 2021).

Figure 17.1 Supporting Student Behavior in Small Groups. A Text Box Discussing the Use of the Good Behavior Game as a Group Contingency Behavior Management Intervention

Flexible Grouping to Support Communication Skills and Social Interactions

As described, in addition to academic skills, flexible grouping can support communication skills and social interactions. Research suggests that many students with ESN continue to be served in non-inclusive settings (e.g., Kleinert et al., 2015; Thurlow et al., 2020). This may be due, in part, to the complex communication needs frequently experienced by students with ESN (Robinson & Soto, 2021). However, the complex communication needs of students with ESN can often be supported through augmentative and alternative communication (AAC) in the context of flexible groupings in inclusive settings (Beukelman & Light, 2020; Robinson & Soto, 2021). In addition to developing communication skills, incorporating intervention strategies into flexible groupings may support social relationships with peers, thereby decreasing the feelings of isolation and loneliness that have been reported by AAC users (Cooper et al., 2009; Therrien, 2019).

Vignette: Anna
Anna is a four-year-old child with cerebral palsy and ESN who enjoys dress-up and pretend play activities in her inclusive preschool classroom. Although Anna uses a limited number of vocalizations when interacting with others, her vocalizations are not usually understood by communication partners. Anna is learning to communicate expressively by pointing to pictures on her speech-generating device (SGD). Anna seems to enjoy playing alongside her peers. However, her teachers have noted that she rarely interacts with them during the preschool day. Anna's teachers are interested in supporting the development of Anna's communication skills and social relationships in the context of flexible grouping.

When utilizing flexible grouping to support the communication and social skill development of students with ESN, teachers must pay particular attention to (a) designing strategies based on individual student needs, (b) providing clear expectations and multiple opportunities to respond, and (c) using flexible grouping in concert with other HLPs and EBPs.

Identify Individual Student Needs

Depending upon the communication skills of the student with ESN, individual student needs might involve increasing the use of a variety of pragmatic functions, developing skills related to conversational functions, and/or increasing the complexity of communication skills (Johnston & Blue, 2019). Using a variety of pragmatic functions involves communicating for a range of purposes, such as commenting, requesting, and rejecting. The development of conversational functions includes the ability to take turns, repair communication breakdowns, and initiate/maintain/terminate interactions. Increasing the complexity of communication skills includes learning new vocabulary and combining known vocabulary to more clearly articulate thoughts and ideas.

> *Assessment and observation reveal that Anna currently uses her SGD during interactions with adults but does not use it to interact with peers. The team is interested in teaching Anna to comment and request when interacting with peers, and they identify two target behaviors for instruction. The first target behavior is for Anna to request a turn with desired objects/activities by selecting a button on her SGD that says, "Can I have a turn?" The second target behavior is for Anna to comment by selecting a button on her SGD that says, "This is fun!"*

Clear Expectations and Multiple Opportunities to Learn/Practice Communication Skills

After identifying student communication needs, teachers should establish clear expectations for the group activity and ensure multiple opportunities to practice the identified communication skills. Expectations will vary based upon the activity and group members. However, expectations regarding communication might include having only one student speak at a time and ensuring that all students are given a chance to speak. In addition to establishing clear expectations, teachers must also ensure that students have multiple opportunities to engage in the target behavior. Because flexible grouping requires collaboration and interaction among group members, opportunities to support communication skill development will occur naturally. For example, in the context of a first-grade cooperative learning math activity where students are using fractions to prepare and bake cupcakes, there will be multiple opportunities to give, receive, and exchange ideas and information.

> *The team notes that Anna and a small group of peers frequently congregate in the dramatic play area, where a variety of dress-up and pretend play items are located. The expectations of activities in the dramatic play area include collaboration (i.e., working together to create a pretend meal) and interaction (i.e., taking turns feeding and dressing a doll) which makes it well suited to teach Anna to request turns and comment. The team notes that there are several naturally occurring opportunities for Anna to engage in the target behaviors during this activity. For example, Anna frequently looks expectantly toward peers when they are playing with toys that she enjoys (creating natural opportunities for Anna to use her SGD to say, "Can I have a turn?"). Further, she vocalizes with delight when peers include her in interactions (creating natural opportunities for Anna to use her SGD to say, "This is fun?").*

Use Flexible Grouping in Concert with Other HLPs and EBP

As with all HLP's, flexible grouping is not a standalone practice. When supporting communication and social interactions, teachers should use other HLPs and evidence-based practices in conjunction with flexible grouping. Included among the practices that may be particularly well-suited for supporting communication skill development in the context of flexible grouping are aided language modeling and communication partner instruction. Aided language modeling involves communication partners using the student with ESN's AAC system in interactions (Allen et al., 2017;

Romski & Sevcik, 1996; Sennott et al., 2016). For example, when participating in a science experiment, a peer might (a) point to the chemical reaction occurring in a test tube, (b) say, "Look, it's starting to bubble!," and (c) press "LOOK" and "BUBBLE" on the student with ESN's speech-generating device. Communication partner instruction involves teaching adults and peers to use strategies to support the communication of the student with ESN. Communication partner instruction might include teaching adults and peers to create communication opportunities, use expectant delay, prompt communication, and recognize/respond to communicative behaviors (e.g., Biggs et al., 2018; Johnston et al., 2003)

> *Anna's teachers incorporate several HLPs into the play activity, including the use of scaffolding, explicit instruction, and assistive technology. Further, Anna's teacher provides training and support to communication partners. Specifically, peers and other adults in the classroom are provided with information about Anna's communication skills and target behaviors and how to model communication using Anna's SGD.*

Flexible Grouping that Extends Beyond the Classroom

In addition to supporting academic and communication skill development, flexible grouping can extend beyond the classroom. Peer network interventions include the use of flexible grouping and have been used to increase social interactions and support the development of social relationships for students with ESN (e.g., Biggs et al., 2018; Carter et al., 2013; Hochman et al., 2015). Peer network interventions are implemented in non-academic contexts, are organized and facilitated by school staff, including three to six peers who support a student with ESN, and are focused on developing new friendships and building social skills. Peer networking interventions include creating opportunities for the group to interact during social activities and teaching peers strategies for serving as an effective communication partner to the student with ESN (Biggs et al., 2018).

Next Steps toward Better Practice

This section will describe some actionable guidelines that practitioners can use to improve their use of small heterogeneous group learning arrangements to support students with ESN:

1. Classroom instructional arrangements should maximize the time students spend in small teacher-designed mixed-ability groups that increase opportunities for learning and communication/social interactions with peers.
2. The size and composition of the small groups should be flexible and should vary according to the content of instruction and student characteristics and relationships. Try new groups frequently to see what works.
3. Small group arrangements should be organized to provide students with the support they need to succeed. Often this may mean that students with ESN may need smaller group sizes to maximize the amount of time they can spend with the teacher.
4. Rotate materials and concepts taught, use multiple examples of each concept, and use individualized stimulus materials for each student to optimize observational learning opportunities in small groups.
5. Try using fast-paced and randomly sequenced instructional trials to keep students engaged in the small group activities.
6. Regularly monitor small groups to ensure students are focused on targeted stimuli, providing or observing targeted responses, and are engaged with the learning of all group members.

7. When identifying effective peer supports in small groups for students with ESN, consider the preference of the student with ESN, age-appropriate, the interest of the peer, the school attendance of the peer, shared interests, existing social networks, and the peer's communication/social skills.
8. Provide orientation and on-going support to facilitate meaningful social interactions.

The Big Five

This chapter presented a structure for teachers to use while designing instructional arrangements that maximize the opportunities for learning and communication/social opportunities for students with ESN. There are several big ideas to take from this information. You should know:

1. Inclusion leads to more opportunities for heterogeneous small group learning, which benefits all.
2. The considerations for intentional student grouping choices and cooperative learning groups.
3. The process for using peers to serve as instructional supports.
4. The process for using peers to serve as social and communication supports.
5. The process for developing peer support networks.

Resources

- HLP #17: Use Flexible Grouping https://highleveragepractices.org/hlp-17-use-flexible-grouping. This video provides an overview of the background and rationale for HLP #17: Flexible Grouping.
- The University of Minnesota, National Center on Educational Outcomes/TIES Center https://publications.ici.umn.edu/ties/communicative-competence-tips/how-peers-can-support-aac-use-by-students-with-significant-communication-needs. This website provides information regarding how peers can support students who use AAC within and outside of classroom activities.
- Kentucky Peer Support Network https://www.kypeersupport.org/. This website provides information and resources related to peer support arrangements and peer networks.
- https://www.youtube.com/playlist?list=PLCkBP2csbOsvoTdGk4JczRYDwseRNIe49. This series of five videos includes supporting relationships between students with and without disabilities, specifically focusing on students with ESN.
- Waisman Center, Natural Supports Project http://www2.waisman.wisc.edu/cedd/naturalsupports/sharedactivities.php. This website includes information and resources on creating natural supports for students with ESN through shared activities, valued roles, and genuine relationships.

References

Allen, A. A., Schlosser, R. W., Brock, K. L., & Shane, H. C. (2017). The effectiveness of aided augmented input techniques for persons with developmental disabilities: A systematic review. *Augmentative and Alternative Communication*, 33(3), 149–159. https://doi.org/10.1080/0743461 8.2017.1338752

Beukelman, D., & Light, J. (2020). *Augmentative and alternative communication: Supporting children and adults with complex communication needs* (5th ed.). Paul H. Brookes.

Biggs, E. E., Carter, E. W., Bumble, J. L., Barnes, K., & Mazur, E. (2018). Enhancing peer network interventions for students with complex communication needs. *Exceptional Children*, 85(1), 66–85. https://doi.org/10.1177/0014402918792899

Brock, M. E., Biggs, E. E., Carter, E. W., Cattey, G. N., & Raley, K. S. (2016). Implementation and generalization of peer support arrangements for students with severe disabilities in inclusive classrooms. *The Journal of Special Education*, 49, 221–232.

Brown, F., McDonnell, J., & Snell, M. E. (2020). *Instruction of students with severe disabilities* (9th ed.). Pearson.

Carter, E. W., Asmus, J., Moss, C. K., Cooney, M., Weir, K., & Fesperman, E. (2013). Peer network strategies to foster social connection among adolescents with and without severe disabilities. *Teaching Exceptional Children, 46*(4), 51–59. https://doi.org/10.1177/004005991304600206

Carter, E. W., Cushing, L. S., & Kennedy, C. H. (2009). *Peer Support strategies for improving all students' social lives and learning.* Paul H. Brookes.

Carter, E. W., & Kennedy, C. H. (2006). Promoting access to the general curriculum using peer support strategies. *Research and Practice for Persons with Severe Disabilities, 31*(4), 284–292.

Carter, E. W., Moss, C. K., Asmus, J., Fesperman, E., Cooney, M., Brock, M. E., & Vincent, L. B. (2015). Promoting inclusion, social connections, and learning through peer support arrangements. *Teaching Exceptional Children, 48*(1), 9–18.

Carter, E. W., Sisco, L. G., Brown, L., Brickham, D., & Al-Khabbaz, Z. A. (2008). Peer interactions and academic engagement of youth with developmental disabilities in inclusive middle and high school classrooms. *American Journal on Mental Retardation, 113*(6), 479–494. https://doi.org/10.1352/2008.113:479-494

Collins, B. C. (2012). *Systematic instruction for students with moderate and severe disabilities.* Paul H. Brookes Publishing Company.

Collins, B. C., Gast, D. L., Ault, M. J., & Wolery, M. (1991). Small group instruction: Guidelines for teachers of students with moderate to severe handicaps. *Education and Training in Mental Retardation, 26*(1), 18–32. https://www.jstor.org/stable/23878629

Conradi, L. A., Ryan, J., Fudge, O., Jameson, J. M., Fischer, A. J., Farrell, M., & McDonnell, J. (2021). Effects of the good behavior game on students with severe disabilities. *Education and Training in Autism and Developmental Disabilities, 56*(4), 454–465.

Cooper, L., Balandin, S., & Trembath, D. (2009). The loneliness experiences of young adults with cerebral palsy who use alternative and augmentative communication. *Augmentative and Alternative Communication, 25*(3), 154–164. https://doi.org/10.1080/07434610903036785

Daugherty, S., Grisham-Brown, J., & Hemmeter, M. L. (2001). The effects of embedded skill instruction on the acquisition of target and nontarget skills in preschoolers with developmental delays. *Topics in Early Childhood Special Education, 21*(4), 213–221.

Downing, J. (2010). *Academic instruction for students with moderate and severe intellectual disabilities in inclusive classrooms.* Corwin.

Fickel, K. M., Schuster, J. W., & Collins, B. C. (1998). Teaching different tasks using different stimuli in a small heterogeneous group. *Journal of Behavioral Education, 8*(2), 219–244. https://doi.org/10.1023/A:1022887624824

Flower, A., McKenna, J. W., Bunuan, R. L., Muething, C. S., & Vega, R. Jr (2014). Effects of the good behavior game on challenging behaviors in school settings. *Review of Educational Research, 84*(4), 546–571.

Hochman, J. M., Carter, E. W., Bottmea-Beutal, K., Harvey, M. N., & Gustafson, J. R. (2015). Efficacy of peer networks to increase social connections among high school students with and without autism. *Exceptional Children, 82*(1), 96–116. https://doi.org/10.1177/0014402915585482

Hunt, P., Staub, D., Alwell, M., & Goetz, L. (1994). Achievement by all students within the context of cooperative learning groups. *Journal of the Association for Persons with Severe Handicaps, 19*(4), 290–301. https://doi.org/10.1177/154079699401900405

Jenkins, J. R., & Jenkins, L. M. (1981). *Cross age and peer tutoring: Help for children with learning problems. What research and experience say to the teacher of exceptional children.* The Council for Exceptional Children.

Jimenez, B. A., Browder, D. M., Spooner, F., & Dibiase, W. (2012). Inclusive inquiry science using peer-mediated embedded instruction for students with moderate intellectual disability. *Exceptional Children, 78*(3), 301–317. https://doi.org/10.1177/001440291207800303

Johnston, S., & Blue, C. W. (2019). Teaching communication skills. In F. Brown, M. Snell, & J. McDonnell (Eds.), *Instruction of students with severe disabilities* (9th ed.). Pearson.

Johnston, S., McDonnell, A., Nelson, C., & Magnavito, A. (2003). Teaching functional communication skills using augmentative and alternative communication in inclusive settings. *Journal of Early Intervention, 25*(4), 263–280. https://doi.org/10.1177/105381510302500403

Kennedy, C. H., & Fisher, D. (2001). *Inclusive middle schools*. Paul H. Brookes.

Kleinert, H., Towles-Reeves, E., Quenemoen, R., Thurlow, M., Fluegge, L., Weseman, L., & Kerbel, A. (2015). Where students with the most significant disabilities are taught: Implications for general curriculum access. *Exceptional Children, 81*(3), 312–329. https://doi.org/10.1177/0014402914563697

Ledford, J. R., Gast, D. L., Luscre, D., & Ayres, K. M. (2008). Observational and incidental learning by children with autism during small group instruction. *Journal of Autism and Developmental Disorders, 38*(1), 86–102. https://doi.org/10.1007/s10803-007-0363-7

Logan, K. R., Bakeman, R., & Keefe, E. B. (1997). Effects of instructional variables on engaged behavior of students with disabilities in general education classrooms. *Exceptional Children, 63*(4), 481–497. https://doi.org/10.1177/001440299706300404

McDonnell, J. M., Thorson, N., & McQuivey, C. (2000). Comparison of the instructional contexts of students with severe disabilities and their peers in general education classes. *Research and Practice for Persons With Severe Disabilities, 25*(1), 54–58. https://doi.org/10.2511/rpsd.25.1.54

Mechling, L. C., Gast, D. L., & Krupa, K. (2007). Impact of SMART board technology: An investigation of sight word Reading and observational learning. *Journal of Autism and Developmental Disorders, 37*(10), 1869–1882. https://doi.org/10.1007/s10803-007-0361-9

Roark, T. J., Collins, B. C., Hemmeter, M. L., & Kleinert, H. (2002). Including manual signing as nontargeted information when using a constant time delay procedure to teach receptive identification of packaged food items. *Journal of Behavioral Education, 11*(1), 19–38. https://doi.org/10.1023/A:1014381220940

Robinson, N. B., & Soto, G. (2021). AAC in schools: Mastering the art and science of inclusion. In B. Ogletree (Ed.), *Augmentative and alternative communication: Challenges and solutions* (pp. 81–116). Plural Publishing.

Romski, M. A., & Sevcik, R. A. (1996). *Breaking the speech barrier: Language development through augmented means*. Brookes Publishing.

Sennott, S. C., Light, J. C., & McNaughton, D. (2016). AAC modeling intervention research review. *Research and Practice for Persons With Severe Disabilities, 41*(2), 101–115. https://doi.org/10.1177/1540796916638822

Steinbrenner, J. R. D., & Watson, L. R. (2015). Student engagement in the classroom: The impact of classroom, teacher, and student factors. *Journal of Autism and Developmental Disorders, 45*(8), 2392–2410. https://doi.org/10.1007/s10803-015-2406-9

Taylor, P., Collins, B., Schuster, J. W., & Kleinert, H. (2002). Teaching laundry skills to high school students with disabilities: Generalization of targeted skills and nontargeted information. *Education and Training in Mental Retardation and Developmental Disabilities, 37*(1), 172–183. https://www.jstor.org/stable/23879828

Therrien, M. (2019). Perspectives and experiences of adults who use AAC on making and keeping friends. *Augmentative and Alternative Communication, 35*(3), 205–216. https://doi.org/10.1080/07434618.2019.1599065

Thurlow, M. L., Ghere, G., Lazarus, S. S., & Liu, K. K. (2020). *MTSS for all: Including students with the most significant cognitive disabilities*. The University of Minnesota, National Center on Educational Outcomes/TIES Center. Retrieved from https://nceo.umn.edu/docs/OnlinePubs/NCEOBriefMTSS.pdf

Wahl, E., Hawkins, R. O., Haydon, T., Marsicano, R., & Morrison, J. Q. (2016). Comparing versions of the good behavior game: Can a positive spin enhance effectiveness? *Behavior Modification, 40*(4), 493–517.

18
Use Strategies to Promote Active Student Engagement

Channon K. Horn

Teachers use a variety of instructional strategies that result in active student responding. Active student engagement is critical to academic success. Teachers must initially build positive student–teacher relationships to foster engagement and motivate reluctant learners. They promote engagement by connecting learning to students' lives (e. g., knowing students' academic and cultural backgrounds) and using a variety of teacher-led (e.g., choral responding and response cards), peer-assisted (e. g., cooperative learning and peer tutoring), student-regulated (e.g., self-management), and technology-supported strategies shown empirically to increase student engagement. They monitor student engagement and provide positive and constructive feedback to sustain performance.

Supporting Students with Extensive Support Needs

Decades of research provides substantial evidence that when students have frequent opportunities to actively engage with content during an instructor-directed lesson, they learn more, exhibit greater rates of on-task behavior, have less challenging behavior, and their instructor has immediate feedback pertaining to the overall effectiveness of the lesson (MacSuga-Gage & Simonsen, 2015). Studies conducted across multiple content areas and preschool, elementary, middle-, and high-school classrooms with students with and without disabilities have repeatedly demonstrated positive academic and behavioral outcomes associated with the use of active student engagement strategies. Whether students are taught in the general education classroom during whole-group instruction, in a resource setting during small-group instruction, or in one-on-one intensive instructional arrangements, one of the biggest predictors of student achievement is having meaningful opportunities to actively engage in a well-designed lesson.

Historically, teachers have taught students with extensive support needs (ESN) primarily in segregated classrooms. Instruction was centered on the academic, social communication, and functional skills of each student and was provided in one-on-one or small-group instructional arrangements. This model provided students with opportunities to actively engage with the material being taught. However, as best practice has shifted to educating students with ESN in inclusive environments, instructors must ensure that students continue to have high numbers of opportunities to meaningfully engage with the same content and within the same instructional groupings as their peers.

DOI: 10.4324/9781003175735-19

Active student engagement is defined as any observable response made to an instructional stimulus (e.g., directive, presentation of material) during an instructional sequence (MacSuga-Gage & Simonsen, 2015). Students with and without ESN may respond in many ways during instruction. Students may actively respond during a lesson through engaging in hands-on activities, constructing or generating permanent products, or responding individually or as a part of a group to a teacher question or cue. Students with ESN may be more likely to respond with varied modalities including using speech, gestures, or written responses; selecting a picture or words on a speech-generating device; touching a word, picture, or object from an array; or directing eye gaze. Despite their form, these responses provide instructors the opportunity to check their students' understanding of content. The planning and provision of opportunities for students to respond is essential to instructional delivery.

Chapter Objectives

Upon reading this chapter, you should be able to do the following:

1. Define active student engagement strategies.
2. Implement active student engagement strategies in the learning trial.
3. Adapt active engagement strategies using no tech/low-tech as well as high-tech assistive technologies.
4. Describe the benefits associated with active engagement strategies.

Active Engagement

Active student engagement is commonly associated with the opportunity to respond or actively engage with the content being presented. Active student engagement is in direct contrast to passive involvement or the "sit and get" method of instruction. Active engagement typically includes activities in which students are engaged in writing, drawing, reading, doing, or talking whereas passive engagement simply results in students listening, watching, or just being present when an activity occurs (Kurth et al., 2015). Another important distinction between active and passive student engagement strategies is the expectation of feedback. Active student engagement strategies typically result in an abundance of feedback, but passive instructional strategies occur without any expectation of feedback from the instructor.

Active student engagement can be as simple as a yes/no response to an instructor-directed question or as complex as a student developing a diagram to demonstrate understanding of a scientific process. Students with ESN acquiring daily living skills might be actively engaged by performing the first step in a task analysis for tooth brushing or activating their switch on an adapted blender to assist in the preparation of pureed food for lunch. The modality in which the student responds or the type of task in which they are responding varies depending on the needs of the student, how they reliably respond to information, and the task being presented. Instructors must carefully plan for active engagement in all classroom activities including those in 1:1, small-group, whole-group, or cooperative learning group instructional arrangements. Consider the scenario of Ms. Conley who is ensuring the active participation of all third-grade students in her class. *Ms. Conley, a third-grade general education instructor, developed cooperative learning groups in order for students to demonstrate their knowledge as it relates to communities during a social studies lesson. Each group was assigned two categories to compare and contrast. Ms. Conley was mindful of constructing groups and assigning specific roles to each individual so that everyone could actively respond. When assigning Cali, a student with ESN who communicated through receptive identification when provided a field of three, she was mindful of each students' strengths and areas of need. Cali's group was assigned the task of developing a Venn diagram using visual images to compare and contrast rural versus urban communities. Cali was asked to glue the items under the appropriate heading after the group had discussed each image. Cali communicated her response by receptively agreeing or disagreeing to comments made by her peers. "I think a picture of a field should go under the heading of rural, do you agree Cali?" At which time, she responded with either a gesture or by receptively selecting yes or no on her communication board. She then glued the picture under the rural heading.* As you can see from this scenario, Ms. Conley was intentional in developing a lesson in which all students, including Cali, would have the opportunity to actively engage in the task.

Student Benefits

The positive student outcomes associated with active engagement include increased skill acquisition (Brophy & Good, 1986; McLeskey et al., 2019), enhanced rates of on-task behavior (Haydon et al., 2013), diminished instances of off-task behavior (Sutherland et al., 2003), increased opportunities for students to receive performance feedback, and increased opportunities for instructors to provide feedback on student performance. Although these positive outcomes are well documented for students with ESN (e.g., Berrong et al., 2007; Bolt et al., 2019; Bondy & Tincani, 2018), the literature indicates that the vast majority of these students' instructional day is spent passively engaged in the curriculum. Pennington and Courtade (2015) found that students with ESN spent on average 42% of the school day passively engaged in instruction, approximately 13% of the time engaged in off-task behaviors, and an additional 6% of the time engaged in extended periods of time with no clear expectation. Bitterman et al. (2013) found that students with ESN spent a mere 39% of the school day being actively engaged in the acquisition of curriculum content compared to their peers without disabilities who spent an average of 59.4% of the school day actively engaged in academically relevant content.

Although these data may be startling, the implications are clear. All students, with and without disabilities, need and benefit from frequent, meaningful, opportunities to actively engage with the curriculum. The universal design for learning (UDL) framework provides a set of principles that should be used during the development of all curricula for all individuals. The outcome of UDL should generate equal opportunities for all students to access, engage with, and demonstrate their knowledge of material taught including students with ESN. One of the three guiding principles of the UDL framework is *multiple means of action and expression*. This principle is of particular importance when educating individuals with ESN and when considering active responding. All learners must be provided "alternative modalities for expression, both to level the playing field among learners and to allow the learner to appropriately (or easily) express knowledge, ideas, and concepts in the learning environment" (CAST, 2018, Options for Communication & Expression section). However, this will not occur without instructors adequately planning and preparing lessons for the diverse learners they will teach to ensure active engagement opportunities for all. When all students in the class are actively engaged, off-task behavior decreases, on-task behavior increases, and academic achievement is enhanced (Horn et al., 2021; McLeskey et al., 2019).

Instructor Benefits

Although the positive student outcomes associated with active student engagement are well documented, the benefits for instructors also are invaluable. Frequently, instructors wait until the end of instruction to assess students' learning (i.e., summative assessment) instead of acquiring information about student progress throughout the instructional period using formative assessment. Instructors may read an entire chapter before asking questions pertaining to the vocabulary or the characters being introduced. The implementation of active engagement strategies during instruction allows instructors to check for understanding along the way. Acquiring real-time performance data on individual students allows instructors to make immediate changes to their instructional sequences. The instructor can determine if information should be retaught or if the lesson can progress as originally designed. Data are imperative to making an accurate decision, and active engagement strategies provide a way to collect data in real time in an effort to make an accurate determination about the teaching and learning that is occurring during instruction.

Instructor Planning and Implementation

Careful planning and implementation will facilitate the effective use of active engagement strategies. Table 18.1 shows planning considerations the instructor should make to ensure students are actively engaged in their lessons. The following example depicts how those considerations would be used in the classroom setting during a whole-class lesson in which the instructor planned for active engagement using choral responding. *While reading Charlotte's Web (White & Williams, 1952) aloud to her class, Ms. Mathias established a goal of teaching new vocabulary words to her students. Ms. Mathias had previously selected the vocabulary words to be taught. Once the vocabulary words had been determined, she intentionally considered the needs of her learners. Most students in the class could respond by writing; however, one of her students, Drew, communicated by pointing to objects. After carefully considering the goal of the lesson and the needs of her learners, Ms. Mathias designed a plan of action for whole-class active engagement. She knew most students would do well writing their answers using a whiteboard, and for Drew, she knew she needed to gather objects for him to use when responding. Her vocabulary was preselected and objects were chosen to convey the meaning of the words presented. As the story was read aloud and Wilbur was introduced as the runt of the litter, Ms. Mathias displayed an object depicting a runt (i.e., a plastic figure of a pig that was small and thin) and explained that "runt means the smallest of the litter." She also showed a non-example of a plump plastic pig while saying, "This is not the runt. He is bigger than the smallest one in the litter." Later, when Ms. Mathias implemented active student engagement strategies as part of her formative assessment plan, she said, "Class show me what does the word runt mean?" Instead of only allowing one student to verbally respond, she planned for all students to show their response by*

Table 18.1 Planning and Implementation Considerations for Active Engagement

Planning	Implementation
• What kind of instructional format will be used in the lesson? (1:1, small group, pairing of students, whole group, or cooperative learning groups) • How will they be asked to engage (e.g., completing an activity, responding chorally, or using a student response system)? • When will the opportunities to respond be presented during the lesson? • How will the opportunities be individualized for all learners in the lesson? • Who is needed to assist learners with ESN and in what way? • What materials are needed to ensure all learners are able to comprehend and respond? (e.g., visual supports provided, response cards prepared, or all students have whiteboards) • Do students need to be taught how to respond? • How will data be collected?	• Ensure pairing of peer or facilitation by paraprofessional for students with ESN to provide supports for responding to active engagement opportunities. • Provide directions for active responding in ways that are effective for all learners in the group. • Provide adequate response time for all learners. • Provide a clear signal for students to show their response if using choral responding. • Reinforce correct responding. • Provide corrective feedback for incorrect responding. • Gather and analyze data in terms of who is responding and accuracy of responses. • Reteach content to students who respond incorrectly.

writing on individual whiteboards or by selecting which of the two objects they think best showed a runt (for Drew). Once Ms. Mathias provided the cue, "Class show me," all students responded in their chosen modality. The students using whiteboards wrote the meaning of the word and held it up for the teacher to see. Drew selected the "runt" when presented with the two pig figures of varying sizes and held it up for the teacher to see. Upon scanning the students and their responses, Ms. Mathias had immediate information on who was comprehending the vocabulary being introduced in the book. If the majority of students responded correctly, she used behavior-specific praise, "Excellent job, runt means the smallest, and Wilbur was the smallest pig born." If the majority of students responded incorrectly, then Ms. Mathias would know she needs to do additional teaching on the vocabulary being taught as the lesson progresses.

Purposes of Active Engagement Strategies

The scenarios in this chapter show how instructors use active engagement strategies when planning instruction in the classroom. The instructor should expect that using these strategies will provide opportunities for instructors to assess student learning, to increase on-task behavior, and to increase the opportunities for students to respond. The remaining sections will highlight the purposes of using active engagement.

Assess Student Learning

The purpose of promoting active student engagement is multifaceted. However, the primary purpose should be to ensure students are acquiring the information being taught. Facilitating active engagement in the classroom allows the instructor to determine if the instruction is effective or if additional teaching or a modification to one's teaching practices is required. For example, an instructor may ask students in whole-group instruction to "Solve for x," while displaying the problem $x + 6 = 10$ to the class. If the majority of the class responded with 16 (by writing their response on a whiteboard), the instructor would know that this content should be retaught and offer additional opportunities for the students to perform the skill. For one student with ESN, the instructor planned for a peer to assist in setting up the equation $10 - 6$. If the student with ESN made an error in selecting the correct operation key, the teacher would know that more discrimination training is required.

Increase On-Task Behavior

The secondary purpose of consistent, meaningful opportunities to actively engage in the lesson is to increase students' rate of on-task behavior. The research evidence supports that high rates of active student engagement result in increased rates of on-task behavior, which frequently aids in the acquisition of the material being taught (Horn et al., 2021). When students are on task, instructors can disseminate information in a more efficient and effective manner instead of pausing throughout the lesson to redirect off-task behavior which delays the pace of instruction. Maintaining a brisk pace of instruction assists students in remaining on task. Students who are actively engaged in a lesson have fewer opportunities to create and or engage in off-task behavior. Hence, instructors who have been intentional in ensuring that all students have the opportunity to engage in the content spend more time teaching and less time correcting challenging behavior. Efficient delivery of instruction occurs when lessons are well planned, materials are readily available, and opportunities to respond are intentionally embedded throughout the lesson. The more efficiently instruction can be delivered, the more likely all learners are to attend to the content being taught rather than extraneous distractors that naturally occur in the educational environment.

Provide Increased Opportunities to Respond

Prior to considering active student engagement strategies, it is important to have a basic understanding of the learning trial. The learning trial consists of a three-term contingency, frequently illustrated in the form of an antecedent–behavior–consequence. The learning trial sets the occasion for students to actively engage in the lesson and demonstrate their knowledge of the information being taught. *Consider a scenario in which Mr. Choo presents a question to a whole or small group of learners: "What was the 15th state admitted to the union in 1792?" This question is the antecedent. This is followed by the opportunity for the students to produce a response, or demonstrate the behavior, of answering the question. After the response, Mr. Choo provides a consequence in the form of confirming and praising the response (e.g., "Great, Kentucky is the 15th state admitted to the union.") or providing corrective feedback if the response was incorrect (e.g., "Remember, Kentucky was the 15th state admitted to the union.").* When considering the learning trial presented in inclusive settings, instructors should give special consideration to students with ESN and may need to make modifications for those learners.

It is during the behavior or response component of the learning trial in which active engagement strategies are implemented. Responses for each learner in the class should be individualized. For example, in response to the question "What is the Bluegrass state?" a student may emit a verbal response (i.e., "Kentucky"), touch Kentucky on a provided map, or select Kentucky from a field of three presented via an eye gaze board. Instructors should carefully consider the design of the opportunities to respond they provide. First, they should ensure all students in the class have a way to respond during instruction (e.g., speech, gestures, context appropriate pictures, and speech-generating device). Second, they should plan opportunities to respond such that they occur throughout the entire lesson. Third, they should ensure that an adequate response time is provided for all learners, including those with physical disabilities, to generate their response. Fourth, they should consider whether peer supports can be used to assist the student with ESN in responding. Finally, they must consider a feasible and consistent method for collecting data on student responses

Active Group Response Techniques

When instructors move from individual opportunities to respond in one modality to whole-class response strategies that occur in a variety of modalities, they can assess all students' performance. Strategies that promote opportunities for all students to respond simultaneously (i.e., choral responding and response cards) to an instructor-directed question or stimulus are more efficient and have been associated with increased rates of on-task behavior (Haydon et al., 2013) and academic success (McLeskey et al., 2019).

Choral Responding

Choral responding is an effective, whole-class response strategy that can be used with students of all ages across all content areas. Students respond in unison following the presentation of an instructional stimulus or task direction (e.g., "What word?" "Mix two drops of red dye and two drops of blue dye." and "Figure the least common denominator."). It is an effective and cost-effective method to promote active student engagement in all classrooms. Prior to implementing choral responding into the classroom environment, students must be taught the predetermined signal that cues them to respond. In some cases, instructors will pose a question, provide an adequate response interval, and then cue students to respond at the same time. The cue to respond can be a gesture (pointing to the class), an auditory signal (a clap of the hands) or a verbal phrase ("The answer is …" and "Everyone tell me now."). The important feature is that students have been taught to respond to the signal when provided. One of the benefits of choral responding is the autonomy of the student's individual responses. Students who are confident often respond with certainty, while those students who are unsure tend to mumble, wait to respond, or fail to produce a response. The clarity of the response provides the instructor with formative data pertaining to the students' knowledge or lack of knowledge associated with the question asked. For example, if the whole class responds with confidence, the instructor should proceed with the lesson, but if the majority of students lack confidence, evidenced by mumbled responses or delayed responding, the instructor should take a moment to offer clarification.

When using choral responding with students with ESN, instructors should adhere to the recommendation provided above in relation to student response modes, prepared communication supports (e.g., augmentative/alternative communication devices and core and fringe vocabulary), and use of peer supports. When instructors are prepared, they are able to implement opportunities to respond efficiently and effectively and place their students' needs at the center of instructional programming. Instructors can refer to Table 18.1 to ensure their planning is student centered. When choral responding is intentionally used on a consistent basis, it can have a powerful impact on the number of opportunities students are given to respond, the rate of on-task behavior evidenced, and how efficiently the effectiveness of the lesson can be evaluated.

Response Cards

Response cards are another strategy that can be used to promote active engagement with all learners when responding to instructor-directed questioning. Response cards are signs or cards that are simultaneously displayed or completed by all students participating in the lesson to show the instructor their response to a question or direction (Ault & Horn, 2018). Response cards come in a variety of formats and occur along the assistive technology continuum. Low-tech/no-tech student response systems include printed pictures or words, whiteboards, yes/no paddles, as well as students holding thumbs up or down. Figure 18.1 shows examples. The implementation of response cards resembles the same process as choral responding in that students must be taught the signal that cues them to display their response so that all responses are viewed simultaneously. Low-tech response cards are easy to implement, inexpensive to create, and increase student engagement. The implementation of traditional, low-tech response cards provides the opportunity for all students to respond simultaneously during the instructional session, providing the instructor with immediate feedback on all students' performance (Schnorr, et al., 2016). Consider the scenario of Ms. Alsulami who is teaching a lesson on punctuation to her class of second graders. She decides to implement response cards to increase the opportunities to respond for her class. *Each student in Ms. Alsulami's language arts class had a whiteboard and expo marker, and Cooper, a student with ESN, was given premade response cards due to his limited fine motor abilities. The premade response cards were made from cardboard, and each contained one punctuation mark. The instructor gave the direction, "Class I am going to read a sentence, and I want you to show me what type of punctuation mark should be placed at the end of my sentence. Are you ready?" Students were given the opportunity to access their materials, and then, the learning trial was provided. "Class, show me what type of punctuation should go at the end of this sentence, 'Do you have a cat at home'." The sentence was stated twice, and then, Ms. Alsulami said, "Show me!" On her cue, all students displayed their response. The majority of students wrote a question mark on their whiteboard and held it up for the instructor to see, while Cooper touched the premade card with the question mark. The accommodation allowed Cooper to participate in the lesson and demonstrate his understanding of the material being taught.*

High-Tech Student Response Systems

Recently, response cards have evolved into high-tech student response systems which offer greater opportunities for differentiation. Class-wide clicker systems allow students to electronically submit

Figure 18.1 Response Card Examples

their response to instructor questions with the advantage that the data submitted can be collected for immediate or future use. The cost of clicker systems has been negated by other options for choral responding, which are currently offered at low or no cost, such as Plickers (https://get.plickers.com/) or Kahoot (https://kahoot.com/home/mobile-app/). Plickers allows students to display their response to a multiple-choice question via a preprinted QR code that is individually displayed and captured when the instructor scans the whole class with a smart device (Common et al., 2020). Plickers eliminates the need for every student to have a device but offers the same autonomy of whole-class response systems and the benefit of data being captured on individual responses for immediate or future use (Kent, 2019).

The push for one-to-one device programs in many schools offers endless opportunities for use as high-tech response cards (Kaur, 2020). One-to-one device programs strive to provide all students with either a laptop, Chromebook, or tablet device to use throughout the school day. A plethora of applications can be downloaded that allow individuals to draw, locate pictures or symbols, use speech to text, use word prediction, and or work collaboratively with peers in response to an instructor-posed question or stimulus. Once students have had the opportunity to formulate their response, the instructor provides the signal that cues students to display their work for immediate feedback.

The advantage of response cards is the ease with which they can be differentiated to meet the needs of the students and the lesson being taught. Not all individuals need to have the same response card, and not all individuals will have the ability to respond with total independence. For example, if students are asked to use the Padlet app, an interactive bulletin board (https://www.padlet.com) to illustrate the process of evaporation, some students may be able to create the entire evaporation process and some students may be able to add arrows depicting the movement of the water, while other students may simply circle which picture illustrates the process of evaporation from a field of two. Digital response cards have the ability to be differentiated to the lesson and to the student, but it will not occur without planning on the part of the instructor.

Adequate planning and preparation are key features when using active engagement strategies. It is important to begin with the end in mind and ask questions: What are the objectives of the lesson? What are the needs of the students? What strategy will be used to keep all students actively engaged? How can students convey their knowledge in a manner that capitalizes on individual strengths? How will the instructor use the student responses to drive future instruction?

Next Steps toward Better Practice

In order to facilitate active student engagement on a consistent basis, special education instructors, paraprofessionals, and related service providers will need to be intentional about changing their own behavior. Initially, instructors can collect data on the number of opportunities they provide for students to actively engage in the learning process to serve as a baseline against which they can evaluate their efforts to improve their teaching behaviors. Instructors can ask themselves: How many questions are asked to the whole class and to students with ESN? Each opportunity would constitute one tally or one opportunity to actively engage with the content or material being presented. Instructors can then use the answers to these questions as baseline data to which they can compare their future performance when implementing active engagement strategies. Once the data have been gathered, instructors should look at the information critically. If the data indicate that all students have equal opportunities to consistently actively engage throughout the lesson, the instructor can be encouraged that their efforts are successful. If the data show gaps, the instructor can implement strategies to improve. Other class members can assist. For example, instructors can preplan opportunities for student engagement and allow paraprofessionals to cue when the opportunity is near. If the instructor presents content using PowerPoint, for example, create slides with whole class response opportunities built in. If peer supports are available in the classroom, have them track the number of opportunities students have to respond during a selected period of time. Often the realization that the behavior is being monitored will create positive changes. When working alone, instructors can set a timer for preplanned intervals and at the end of each interval provide an opportunity for students to actively engage in the learning process. Regardless of how instructors go about creating active student engagement opportunities, remember to use the information students are providing to drive future instructional sequences and assess if additional practice opportunities are needed or if students are acquiring the content.

Active student engagement strategies have the ability to positively impact student academic and behavioral outcomes. However, the strategies used must be intentionally selected and aligned with the material being taught and the needs of the students being educated. Increasing the number of opportunities students have to respond throughout the lesson increases the occurrence of on-task behavior, leading to positive student outcomes.

The Big Five

1. In order for students to actively engage in the learning process, they must be given consistent opportunities to engage in meaningful learning that is both interesting and motivating.
2. Active engagement strategies provide instructors with immediate opportunities to provide performance feedback to all students, not just the students who willingly engage.
3. Active engagement strategies can be differentiated to meet the individual needs of the students.
4. Active engagement strategies provide instructors with opportunities to make moment-to-moment decisions regarding the teaching and learning process.
5. Active engagement strategies are correlated with positive measurable outcomes on student learning and behavior.

Resources

Several technology resources can be used to increase active responding including the following:

- BoomCards (https://www.boomlearning.com/)—Electronic learning activities that provide instant feedback and allow for progress monitoring.
- Doodle Buddy (https://apps.apple.com/us/app/doodle-buddy-paint-draw-app/id313232441)—Electronic white board that allows students to draw or write individual responses.
- Kahoot (https://kahoot.com/home/mobile-app/)—Game-based, learning platform that captures student data in real time.
- Padlet (https://padlet.com/)—Online bulletin board that allows students to work collaboratively or individual on a task or topic.
- Plickers (https://get.plickers.com/)—Rapid-response online polling app; students respond through an individualized QR code.
- ShowMe (https://www.showme.com/)—Virtual whiteboard that allows students to create and share videos.

References

Ault, M. J., & Horn C. K. (2018). Increasing active engagement: Guidelines for using student response systems. *Journal of Special Education Technology, 33*(3), 207–216. https://doi.org/10.1177/0162643418775745

Berrong, A. K., Schuster, J. W., Morse, T. E., & Collins, B. C. (2007). The effects of response cards on active participation and social behavior of students with moderate and severe disabilities. *Journal of Developmental and Physical Disabilities, 19*(3), 187–199. https://doi.org/10.1007/s10882-007-9047-7

Bitterman, A., Gray, L., & Goldring, R. (2013). *Characteristics of Public and Private Elementary and Secondary Schools in the United States: Results From the 2011–12 Schools and Staffing Survey* (NCES 2013-312). U.S. Department of Education. Washington, DC: National Center for Education Statistics. Retrieved 10/11/2021 from http://nces.ed.gov/pubsearch.

Bolt, T. D., Hansen, B. D., Caldarella, P., Young, K. R., Williams, L., & Wills, H. P. (2019). Varying opportunities to respond to improve behavior of elementary students with developmental disabilities. *International Electronic Journal of Elementary Education, 11*(4), 327–334. https://doi.org/10.26822/iejee.2019450791

Bondy, A. H., & Tincani, M. (2018). Effects of response cards on students with autism spectrum disorder or intellectual disability. *Education and Training in Autism and Developmental Disabilities, 53*(1), 59–72.

Brophy, J., & Good, T. (1986). Instructor behavior and student achievement. In M. C. Wittrock (Ed.), *Third handbook of research on teaching* (pp. 328–375). Macmillan.

CAST (2018). Universal Design for Learning Guidelines version 2.2. Retrieved from http://udlguidelines.cast.org

Common, E. A., Lane, K. L., Cantwell, E. D., Brunsting, N. C., Oakes, W. P., Germer, K. A., & Bross, L. A. (2020). Instructor-delivered strategies to increase students' opportunities to respond: A systematic methodological review. *Behavioral Disorders, 45*(2), 67–84. https://doi.org/10.1177/0198742919828310

Haydon, T., Marsicano, R., & Scott, T. M. (2013). A comparison of choral and individual responding: A review of the literature. *Preventing School Failure, 57*(4), 181–188. https://doi.org/10.1080/1045988x.2012.682184

Horn, C. K., Ackerman, K. B., & Hitch, E. J. (2021). Applying high leverage practices to increase active engagement and on-task behavior of students with intellectual disabilities during literacy activities. *Journal of Special Education Technology*. Advance online publication. https://doi.org/10.1177/01626434211019395

Kaur, D. (2020). Post-positivist approach to factors that influence k-12 instructors' use of iPads and chromebooks. *International Journal of Technology In Education and Science, 4*(1), 26–36.

Kent, D. (2019). Plickers and the pedagogical practicality of fast formative assessment. *Teaching English With Technology, 19*(3), 90–104.

Kurth, J. A., Lyon, K. J., & Shogren, K. A. (2015). Supporting students with severe disabilities in inclusive schools: A descriptive account from schools implementing inclusive practices. *Research and Practice for Persons With Severe Disabilities, 40*(4), 261–274. https://doi.org/10.1177/1540796915594160

MacSuga-Gage, A. S., & Simonsen, B. (2015). Examining the impact of opportunities to respond on student outcomes: A systematic review of the literature. *Education and Treatment of Children, 38*(2), 211–240. https://doi.org/10.1353/etc.2015.0009

McLeskey, J., Maheady, L., Billingsley, B., Brownell, M., & Lewis, T. (Eds.). (2019). High leverage practices for inclusive classrooms. Routledge. https://doi.org/10.4324/9781315176093

Pennington, R. C., & Courtade, G. (2015). An examination of teacher and student behavior in classrooms for students with moderate and severe disability. *Preventing School Failure, 59*(1), 40–47. https://doi.org/10.1080/1045988X.2014.919141

Schnorr, C. I., Freeman-Green, S., & Test, D. W. (2016). Response cards as a strategy for increasing opportunities to respond: An examination of the evidence. *Remedial and Special Education, 37*(1), 41–54. https://doi.org/10.1177/0741932515575614

Sutherland, K. S., Alder, N., & Gunter, P. L. (2003). The effect of varying rates of opportunities to respond to academic requests on the classroom behavior of students with EBD. *Journal of Emotional and Behavioral Disorders, 11*(4), 239–248. https://doi.org/10.1177/10634266030110040501

White, E. B., & Williams, G. (1952). *Charlotte's web.* Harper & Brothers.

19

Use Assistive and Instructional Technologies

Anya S. Evmenova and Roba Hrisseh

Teachers select and implement assistive and instructional technologies to support the needs of students with disabilities. They select and use augmentative and alternative communication (AAC) devices and assistive and instructional technology products to promote student learning and independence. They evaluate new technology options given student needs; make informed instructional decisions grounded in evidence, professional wisdom, and students' individualized education program (IEP) goals; and advocate for administrative support in technology implementation. Teachers use the universal design for learning (UDL) framework to select, design, implement, and evaluate important student outcomes.

Supporting Students with Extensive Support Needs

The long-term goal of education is developing independent, knowledgeable, skilled, and contributing members of society (Ryndak et al., 2012). The reauthorization of the Individuals with Disabilities Education Improvement Act (IDEA, 2004) as well as the Every Student Succeeds Act (ESSA, 2015) increased the expectations for students with extensive support needs (ESN) to access, actively participate, and improve educational outcomes along with their peers without disabilities. Despite the evidence that they can succeed, learn more, and learn at faster rates within inclusive general education settings, students with ESN continue to be taught in restrictive settings (Kurth et al., 2019; Saunders et al., 2019; Spooner et al., 2019). One way to facilitate access to general education curriculum and provide flexible academic activities for students with ESN is to use high-leverage practices (HLPs), specifically, implementing assistive and instructional technologies. This chapter offers descriptions of some of the most effective technologies used by students with ESN. It also provides descriptions on effective technologies for both special and general education teachers to support the needs of this unique population across domains, curriculum areas, and in a variety of educational settings.

Chapter Objectives

Upon reading this chapter, you should be able to do the following:

1. Identify practical examples of research-based assistive, instructional technology (IT), and UDL interventions to support various areas of need for students with ESN across different settings.

DOI: 10.4324/9781003175735-20

2. Apply free or affordable technologies (both low tech and high tech) as well as principles of UDL for students with ESN across domains.
3. Review key components of independent technology use by students with ESN in inclusive environments.

HLP #19——Use Assistive and Instructional Technologies

HLPs are "practices that are used frequently in classrooms and have been shown to improve student outcomes" (McLeskey et al., 2017, p. 7). Furthermore, these practices are supported by research evidence and can be applied across contexts. HLP #19 encourages teachers to select and implement appropriate assistive and instructional technologies as well as the principles of UDL in order to support the needs of students with disabilities. The world of technology is multifaceted and can look very different depending on specific learner characteristics. Teachers need to be aware of where and when to apply this variety of technologies. But first, it is important to differentiate between the technology types and their importance for students with ESN.

Defining Assistive Technologies

The definition of assistive technology (AT) includes two parts: AT devices and AT services. AT device has been originally defined in the Technology-Related Assistance to Individuals with Disabilities Act (Tech Act) of 1988 (P. L. 100-407) as "any item, piece of equipment, or product system whether acquired commercially off the shelf, modified, or customized that is used to increase, maintain, or improve functional capabilities of individuals with disabilities." There is a continuum of AT devices from simple, readily available low-tech devices (e.g., pencil grips and hand-made pointing devices) to more complex and expensive (e.g., communication systems, electronic devices, and software programs). Unfortunately, for students with ESN, the use of AT is often limited to providing access to educational activities rather than improve their learning and social outcomes. For example, students with autism spectrum disorder and intellectual disability may have access to an AAC device, but rarely use it in a meaningful way during the instruction or for conversing with peers (Chung et al., 2012).

The use of AT is mandated by law. Since the 1997 reauthorization of IDEA, educators are required to "consider whether the child requires assistive technology devices and services" (34 C.F.R. § 300.346[2][v]) during each IEP meeting. However, it often equates to the consideration of only an AT device, but not the service. AT services need to be put in place if we strive for that effective implementation of technology. The original definition of an AT service was expanded in the Individuals with Disabilities Education Act (IDEA) of 2004 as "any service that directly assists a child with a disability in the selection, acquisition, or use of an assistive technology device". The AT services include the following:

a. The evaluation of the needs of a child with a disability, including a functional evaluation of the child in their customary environment;
b. Purchasing, leasing, or otherwise providing for the acquisition of assistive technology devices by such child;
c. Selecting, designing, fitting, customizing, adapting, applying, maintaining, repairing, or replacing assistive technology devices;
d. Coordinating and using other therapies, interventions, or services with assistive technology devices, such as those associated with existing education and rehabilitation plans and programs;
e. Training or technical assistance for a child with a disability or, if appropriate, that child's family; and

f. Training or technical assistance for professionals (including individuals providing education or rehabilitation services), employers, or other individuals who provide services to employ or are otherwise substantially involved in the major life functions of that child. (P.L. 108-446 § 1401(2)).

Unfortunately, the lack of focus on AT services may result in overall dissatisfaction, underutilization, and abandonment of an AT device (Ranada & Lidstrom, 2017). Even if mainstream technology is used to provide AT supports to students with ESN in inclusive settings, it needs to be carefully selected, individualized based on the specific abilities and needs of the individual student, and evaluated during implementation.

Instructional Technologies

Mainstream or IT in the classrooms aims to facilitate learning and make it more engaging. The use of technology has recently seen a great growth, with many school districts starting to move to 1:1 technology initiatives, allowing students to have individual devices with Internet access. These initiatives benefit all learners including those with ESN. For example, a group of students with significant disabilities in an elementary school may receive a variety of individual devices without the need to share them. For one student, it is a laptop set up just like the one used by his peers without disabilities; for another one, it is an iPad with a communication application as well as a number of instructional applications to practice literacy and math skills; and for the third student, it is a desktop computer with a touch screen allowing for more device stability.

Overall, the use of IT aims to close the achievement gap between students with and without disabilities (U.S. Department of Education, 2017). Indeed, the same device can be instructional for some students in facilitating their learning, yet can be assistive for others by offering them opportunities not otherwise available. For example, a student with physical disabilities needs an iPad in order to access books and turn pages, while reading books on an iPad may be an alternative and more engaging option for other students.

The transparency of smartphones, tablets, and personal computers with a myriad of built-in accessibility features is certainly exciting. It contributes to the inclusion of individuals with ESN into education and society. It also offers solutions when regular AT equipment is unavailable either due to its cost, user eligibility, IT security settings, or users not wanting to be identified as having a problem. Nowadays, students in inclusive classrooms may use individual devices, allowing those with disabilities easy access to various technology programs without having to look different (Evmenova, 2020). Easy access to communication apps on mainstream tablets has also resulted in the shift to enhanced social communication across environments (Klein, 2017).

Defining Universal Design for Learning

In light of increasing expectations toward active participation of all learners in the general education curriculum, educators constantly search for potential venues to provide quality academic education to their students, including those with ESN. UDL is a scientifically based framework that aims to reshape the curricula development to remove barriers and meet the needs of a wide spectrum of learners (Meyer et al., 2014). Three UDL principles require teachers to provide (1) multiple means of engagement, motivating learners in different ways; (2) multiple means of representations, presenting content in multiple ways; and (3) multiple means of action/expression, allowing students to demonstrate their learning in multiple ways. The Every Student Succeeds Act (ESSA, 2015) encourages educators to design assessments using UDL principles and adopt technology that aligns with UDL. Students with ESN can benefit from UDL-based inclusive instructions full of textual, visual, auditory, multimedia, and technology-based supports. For these students, UDL flexibility may be applied to alternative content (e.g., academic and functional) that is relevant; supports, materials, and services (e.g., technology, prompting, and human support) needed to succeed in a task; and appropriate formative and summative assessments that align with individual goals linked to standards (Ryndak et al., 2012). So, what are some ways to practically implement all this technology in the classrooms?

Assistive Technology Options for Students with ESN

AT for students with ESN often includes using assistive communication technology. Ways to support learners' communication skills are very important for successful participation of students with ESN in various learning environments. Teachers should consider both low-tech and high-tech examples of augmented and alternative communication (AAC).

Low-tech Picture-based Systems to Improve Communication and Social Interactions

A variety of AAC can be used as an alternative to verbal communication. Low-tech AAC includes tools and strategies that do not include batteries or electronics such as printed communication boards, charts, cards, books, etc. The user selects letters, words, and/or symbols on the chart to share their message. That can be done by direct pointing, using different pointers (e.g., head pointer, mouth stick, and light pointer), or eye gaze. The Picture Exchange Communication System (PECS) is an example of a low-tech and affordable communication system that can help learners with ASD and other developmental disorders learn functional communication and increase verbalizations (Bondy & Frost, 2011; Lamb et al., 2018). In addition to relying on pictures or icons, PECS includes a teaching protocol with six phases. They are (1) learning to communicate (exchange single pictures for items or activities); (2) distance and persistence (generalize using single pictures in different places); (3) picture discrimination (choose from two or more pictures); (4) sentence structure (construct simple sentences on a detachable sentence strip); (5) answering questions (use PECS to answer "What do you want?" question); and (6) commenting (comment and answer other questions). Implementation of PECS with fidelity is required in order to achieve improved communication outcomes (Lamb et al., 2018).

Among students with ESN, many do not use speech, signs, or graphic symbols for their communication (Geist et al., 2021). Project CORE from the Center for Literacy and Disability Studies at University of North Carolina at Chapel Hill has created aided AAC materials to support universal core vocabulary for students with significant disabilities who rely on body movements, facial expressions, and vocalizations to communicate. Aided AAC requires external materials to get the message across. The Universal Core vocabulary includes a set of 36 frequently used words and are available to be used by direct pointing or touch, eye gaze selection, and partner-assisted scanning or can be used with speech-generating devices. Based on the research evidence, K-12 students demonstrate positive changes in their communication skills when having access to the Universal Core symbolic communication materials (Geist et al., 2021). Preschoolers with ASD also have shown improvements in communication measured by the Communication Matrix and changes in social interactions (Dorney & Erickson, 2019). These boards are available for free download and printing (http://www.project-core.com).

Speech-generating Devices to Access Educational Tasks

High-tech AAC refers to computerized speech-generating devices. For years, these included dedicated devices that could be obtained from a few specialized companies (e.g., Prentke Romich Company – https://www.prentrom.com and Tobii Dyanvox – https://us.tobiidynavox.com). Today, many AAC applications are available for download and use on *Apple iPads* (https://www.fluentaac.com/bestaacapps). In addition to improving communication and social interactions, AAC devices offer opportunities for students to participate in general education curriculum. For example, a third-grade student with severe disabilities and complex communication needs (CCN) can participate in literacy instruction and contribute to class discussion about a story character's traits. First, the student can use a single-message AAC device with a recorded "that's it" message. During a read-aloud, when the student hears something important about the target character, the student can click on the "that's it" message to cue peers without disabilities that this item is something that should be written down into the graphic organizer. Then, the student uses their high-tech AAC to contribute to brainstorming terms that were used to describe the character. If a term does not exist in the AAC device, peers can help add words to the AAC device (Sheldon & Erickson, 2020).

Similarly, secondary students with CCN can be successful in a public high school using AAC applications on the iPad (e.g., Proloquo2Go, LAMP, and Tobii Dynavox Compass). But some students may need help in effectively using AAC during an instructional activity. For example, instructional assistants may need to model AAC use during reading and talking activity. MODELER (model, encourage, and respond) is one strategy that guides support personnel through modeling how to speak using AAC, providing time delay, and responding to student communication attempts. This strategy has shown to increase communication turns for secondary students with CCN and has also made it easier for untrained educators to support a meaningful educational intervention (Newton & Sennott, 2017). Regardless of the specific AAC program or application, it is imperative to provide access to this AT for students with ESN and support it with AT services such as evaluation, coordination among educators, and training for all involved members.

Instructional Technology Supports for Students with ESN

As was mentioned earlier, technology can be instructional for some learners and assistive for others. But while AT aims to provide alternative access to a task that is not possible otherwise, IT enhances teaching and learning. Here are just a few examples of how technology can enhance consistency in teaching and independence in learning by students with ESN.

Augmented/Virtual Reality to Practice Various Skills

Emerging technologies such as augmented and virtual reality offer experiences that simulate real-world experiences. While augmented reality (AR) is a real world enhanced with a layer of additional content, virtual reality (VR) creates an entire new simulated world. A body of research exists on the effectiveness of VR on skill-specific performance by young adults with ESN (Mak & Zhao, 2020). The specific skills included driving skills addressed via VR driving simulation; interview skills via Virtual Interactive Training Agents (ViTA) and Virtual Reality–Job Interview Training (VR-JIT); pedestrian skills and following road signs via Neuro software; and other daily living skills via VR games. In turn, AR intervention created with a free mobile application with embedded digital content (e.g., *Boardmaker* picture symbols, video models, and audio) was effectively used to teach young children with ESN and CNN how to properly brush their teeth (Cihak et al., 2016). But AR/VR interventions can also support students in learning academic skills such as math. For example, an AR intervention created using HP Reveal supported high-school students including those with ESN to model how to solve math problem (Kellems et al., 2019). While HP Reveal application is no longer available, there are many other free programs that can allow educators creating AR/VR environments for their students (e.g., ARKit and Google Cardboard).

Video Modeling to Improve Social Skills

Video-based instruction is an evidence-based strategy for teaching various skills to learners with ESN (Park et al., 2019). There are different types of video modeling that can be used with

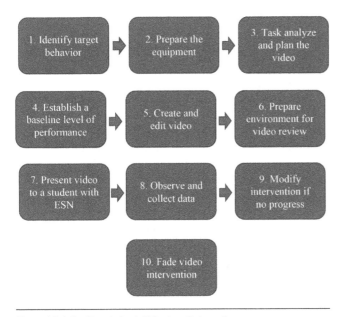

Figure 19.1 Ten Steps to Create Video-based Interventions

this population of students including (a) video modeling—watching a model perform the target task; (b) video prompting—a model completing one individual step of the larger task at a time; (c) video self-modeling—edited video to show a user performing the exemplar behaviors, etc. Video modeling has been used to improve numerous skills for kids and adults with ESN. For example, video modeling has shown to improve social skills for improving employment skills for adults with ID (Park et al., 2020). The improved skills included offering help, appropriately answering feedback, and requesting further clarification when directions were unclear, and were mostly maintained two weeks after the intervention. More importantly, all participants reported to really enjoy the video modeling intervention because it was similar to watching TV.

Video modeling sessions to teach a skill can be very efficient (e.g., delivered quickly and consistently across the users; Park et al., 2020). Furthermore, making videos is no longer a daunting task. The majority of mobile devices and laptops offer such features as video and picture recording. Sophisticated devices even offer different editing options. These features can easily be used for video modeling in the classroom, employment, and daily living (Alsuhaibani et al., 2016). The 10 steps for creating and using video-based interventions are illustrated in Figure 19.1.

Universal Design for Learning and Students with ESN

While UDL does not eliminate the need for more individualized accommodations including AT, it can greatly increase access, participation, and progress in general education instruction for students with ESN. But in addition, UDL also makes learning accessible to all the other learners by removing the barriers. A joint implementation of UDL and AT is often needed to enhance educational experiences for the target population.

Wearable Technology to Support Self-regulation

One of the guidelines under the multiple means of engagement UDL principle is to provide options for self-regulation. Self-regulation is an ability to control one's behaviors while attaining a specific learning or behavioral goal (Zimmerman, 1995). For students with ESN, learning content, mastering skills, and being motivated to use complex self-regulation skills can be particularly challenging. In both K-12 and postsecondary settings, they often rely on a teacher, an assistant, or another adult to manage self-regulated learning and engage in goal setting, self-monitoring, and self-evaluation. But these supports can be more consistently and discreetly delivered using technology. Mainstreamed wearable technology (e.g., smart watches) that is capable of collecting and analyzing data from a user in real time in order to provide feedback has been recently examined as the way to support learners with ESN (Black et al., 2020). This type of technology has been shown to improve academic outcomes, communication skills, social interactions, as well as independent living skills (Benssassi et al., 2018). Many educators recognize the advantages of using wearable technologies for teaching and learning. Some common suggestions include providing prompts, recording and sharing video models (e.g., when a quick video clip demonstrating a simple step is played on a smart watch), offering simulations (e.g., where users can experience an environment), improving social engagement (by providing alerts to remain on task), practicing social interactions and expressions, and providing immediate feedback without distracting other students (Bower & Sturman, 2015). Many of these suggestions can support students with ESN in various environments while completing different tasks.

For example, a WELLI wearable technology application has been shown to support students' participation, learning, and independence in inclusive postsecondary courses (Evmenova et al., 2019). Young adults with intellectual or developmental disability (IDD) were able to engage in general education college-level courses without overreliance on the support personnel. This resulted in increased independence and non-stigmatizing autonomy. These young adults did not look or feel different than their typical peers when wearing a smart watch that delivered the prompts to them. This app was recently further developed to offer prompts about emotional state and suggest strategies for calming down (see Figure 19.2). While it hasn't been tested with typical students, a wearable technology application supporting self-regulation and emotional regulation of users might benefit all learners regardless of their abilities and needs.

UDL Representation during Shared Reading and Literacy Instruction

Literacy instruction has historically been an area of concern for students with ESN, as it often focuses on isolated skills instruction such as basic vocabulary (Coyne et al., 2012). However, the technology implemented within the multiple means of representation UDL principle makes access to more complex and balanced literacy instruction possible. Shared story reading has been shown to be effective for teaching literacy to students with ESN (Alison et al., 2017). Alison and colleagues enhanced shared reading experiences for three elementary students with ASD who were also English language learners by using e-texts with embedded prompting on vocabulary and comprehension. Thus, instead of relying on an adult or peer reader to read aloud, students were able to independently access texts and interact with them in personalized ways. The stories were created using *GoTalk NOW* application and were displayed on an iPad2. For each of the six WH questions, a separate screen was created to include definitions, quizzes, and feedback. Participating students demonstrated improved understanding and ability to answer WH questions while reading grade-aligned texts. Using technology made reading both physically and cognitively accessible for these learners with ESN (Alison et al., 2017).

If there are no resources to purchase an iPad, teachers can create similar interactive UDL talking books using free *PowerPoint* or *Google Slides*. Each page can have a block of text ranging from one word to multiple paragraphs depending on the students' needs supported by images. Both programs allow recording narration for each slide. The narration can be recorded for the whole block of text or for each word separately. Animation features allow built-in supports (e.g., pop-up definition of the word when clicking on the word) as well as interactive activities. Thus, students

Figure 19.2 WELLI Wearable Application for Individuals with IDD

can take a quiz and/or test their comprehension by choosing from an array of options hyperlinked to either a celebration slide (for the right answer) or the corrective feedback slide (for the incorrect answer). Built-in buttons on the page can be set up to allow students unlimited attempts to return to the question screen as many times as needed.

Computer-assisted Instruction to Provide Gradual Levels of Support

Providing gradual levels of support is one of the ways to support multiple means of action/expression UDL principle. Computer-assisted instruction (CAI) offers opportunities to learn and receive feedback (through various games and simulations) while using a computer or another device. Built-in text, graphics, audio, and other interactive features allow for scaffolding. Combined with explicit instruction, engaging and motivating CAI is often used for practicing basic skills in reading and math. In a recent investigation, CAI (both on tablets and on traditional computers without touchscreen) was used for vocabulary instruction for both elementary and secondary students with

ESN (Mize et al., 2018). It was highly effective for this population of students, especially those at the secondary level. The important features of CAI associated with improved outcomes and increased motivation for students with ESN included visual supports (e.g., images, animations, graphics, and dynamic highlighting of text as it's being read aloud), auditory supports (e.g., sounding out the word or sentence, and auditory corrections), and feedback (e.g., basic feedback provided by a computer or specific feedback provided by a teacher).

CAI can provide initial instruction, extra practice, and necessary remediation across different subjects. It is one of the evidence-based practices for learning and practicing math by students with ESN (Saunders et al., 2019; Snyder & Huber, 2019; Spooner et al., 2019). While some of these studies utilized specialized CAI programs (e.g., *IntelliTools Classroom Suite*), others used free tools such as *PowerPoint*, *Google* images and *YouTube* videos, *Quizlet* (www.quizlet.com), etc. With intentional design embedding additional instructional components (e.g., systematic instruction, constant time delay, simultaneous prompting, corrective feedback, and reinforcement), it is possible to create a robust CAI even without the extensive resources. It is also important to note that in all aforementioned research, while the teacher or instructor remained near the user in case of technical difficulties, most studies included pre-intervention training to ensure that students with ESN could operate and navigate the programs independently (Snyder & Huber, 2019).

Effective and Independent Technology Use

Promoting students' learning and independence is the most important premise of any technology use. Independence across various domains and quality of life are important educational goals for students with ESN, the majority of whom score very low on overall independence, have difficulty finding both competitive or supported employment positions, and are not able to choose their own homes or roommates (Ryndak et al., 2012). As has been previously discussed throughout the chapter, technology allows more independence in accessing educational experiences for these students. However, the overall satisfaction and continuous use of technology by students with ESN is dependent on the effective implementation of AT services (Ranada & Lidstrom, 2019). It should start with careful evaluation of the student's needs and ways to address those needs with AT, IT, or UDL. Even readily available, IT programs and apps should be carefully selected based on the desired outcome. For example, a SETT framework can be used to determine the S—student needs (both abilities and needs), E – environment(s) where task occurs, T – top-priority tasks of immediate concern, as well as T – tools (both devices and services; low tech and high tech) that might support the expected outcomes (Zabala, 2005). At this point, teachers may reach out to AT specialists or other technology professionals in order to use appropriate assessments. One critical consideration when choosing an IT or technology to support UDL is its accessibility. When designed without accessibility in mind, technology may become a bigger barrier rather than a solution for users with ESN.

After obtaining and adjusting the technology, collaboration with other educators and related service providers is crucial. Finally, training for a child, professional working with the child, and family members need to take place in order to ensure the implementation of the technology with fidelity. All students, but especially those with ESN, benefit from explicit and strategic instruction and should receive extensive modeling and ample opportunities for practice with any technology (Israel, 2019). An intensive training is even more important if users do not have prior experiences with the given tool. Additional focus should be given to any prerequisite skills required to effectively use the technology (e.g., using a mouse, activating buttons, etc.). Moreover, this is not the end of the journey. Teachers should continuously monitor student progress in the targeted activities and use data to make decisions about any refinements to the technology plan (Evmenova, 2020). This is a highly iterative process.

Next Steps toward Better Practice

Educators can take several steps towards effective, efficient implementation of HLP #19:

1. Understand the differences between technology types and their interactions.
2. Explore free and available low- and high-tech resources.
3. Collaborate with related service providers and other key stakeholders to brainstorm best technology solutions.
4. Integrate technology into instructional and/or other activities across settings.
5. Consider how the student, parents, and all involved educators will be trained on the technology and supported throughout its use.

The Big Five

1. **Technology is the way to ensure access and participation in education.** Using technology with the students with ESN should never be the goal. It can be truly transformational, but the effective implementation depends greatly on the teachers' and other professionals' knowledge and ability to seamlessly integrate technology into various classroom activities. Having easier access to technology items should be just the beginning of the process.
2. **AT consideration should focus on both devices and services.** Educators should never stop at considering the device, whether it is AT, IT, or technology used to support UDL in the classroom. Without AT services in place, the devices are more likely to be abandoned (even if they are a great match to the user's needs) (Ranada & Lidstrom, 2019).
3. **Collaboration between major stakeholders is key for both technology assessment and implementation.** Meeting the needs of students with ESN requires collaboration between educators, families, students, and community (Ryndak et al., 2012). This extends to the technology selection and use. Coordinating with other professionals is an important AT service that should not be overlooked.
4. **Technology does not have to be complex and expensive, but it needs to be implemented with fidelity.** All HLPs grouped under instruction aim to provide explicit, strategic, flexible, evidence-based, and well-designed instruction for students with disabilities. This instruction is expected to be delivered with fidelity (McLeskey et al., 2019). There are many free or inexpensive technology supports designed specifically for students with ESN. But even those have to be implemented with fidelity in order to improve students' learning and engagement.
5. **UDL and mainstream technology may decrease the need for additional accommodations.** Providing instructional materials in multiple formats may broaden their use, even if more customized AT is still necessary. For example, accessible educational materials (AEM—https://aem.cast.org/) offer accessible text and instructional materials in a variety of formats. These materials may require the use of the customized text-to-speech program that reads text out loud for the user that fits individual needs or can be accessed by a freely available text-to-speech program (e.g., Natural Reader—https://www.naturalreaders.com).

Resources

Learn more about AT: Georgia Tech——Tools for Life: https://gatfl.gatech.edu/index.php
Learn more about UDL: CAST——https://www.cast.org/
Learn more about integration of AT and IT: CITIES——https://cites.cast.org/

References

Alison, C., Root, J. R., Browder, D. M., & Wood, L. (2017). Technology-based shared story reading for students with autism who are English-language learners. *Journal of Special Education Technology*, *32*(2), 91–101. https://doi.org/10.1177/0162643417690606

Alsuhaibani, A., Evmenova, A. S., & Graff, H. (2016). Video-based educational interventions for individuals on the autism spectrum: A literature review. *Good Autism Practice, 17*(1), 54–60.

Benssassi, E. M., Gomez, J.-C., Boyd, L. E., Hayes, G. R., & Juan Ye (2018). Wearable assistive technologies for autism: Opportunities and challenges. *IEEE Pervasive Computing, 17*(2), 11–21. https://doi.org/10.1109/MPRV.2018.022511239

Black, M. H., Milbourn, B., Chen, N. T. M., McGarry, S., Wali, F., Ho, A. S. V., Lee, M., Bölte, S., Falkmer, T., & Girdler, S. (2020). The use of wearable technology to measure and support abilities, disabilities and functional skills in autistic youth: A scoping review. *Scandinavian Journal of Child and Adolescent Psychiatry and Psychology, 8*, 48–69. https://doi.org/10.21307/sjcapp-2020-006

Bondy, A., & Frost, L. (2011). *A picture's worth: PECS and other visual communication strategies in autism* (2nd ed.). Woodbine House.

Bower, M., & Sturman, D. (2015). What are the educational affordances of wearable technologies? *Computers and Education, 88*, 343–353. https://doi.org/10.1016/j.compedu.2015.07.013

Chung, Y.-C., Carter, E. W., & Sisco, L. G. (2012). Social interactions of students with disabilities who use augmentative and alternative communication in inclusive classrooms. *American Journal of Intellectual and Developmental Disabilities, 117*(5), 349–367. https://doi.org/10.1352/1944-7558-117.5.349

Cihak, D. F., Moore, R. J., Wright, R. E., McMahon, D. D., Gibbons, M. M., & Smith, C. (2016). Evaluating augmented reality to complete a chain task for elementary students with autism. *Journal of Special Education Technology, 31*(2), 99–108. https://doi.org/10.1177/0162643416651724

Coyne, P., Pisha, B., Dalton, B., Zeph, L. A., & Smith, N. C. (2012). Literacy by design: A universal design for learning approach for students with significant intellectual disabilities. *Remedial and Special Education, 33*(3), 162–172. https://doi.org/10.1177/0741932510381651

Dorney, K. E., & Erickson, K. (2019). Transactions within a classroom-based AAC intervention targeting preschool students with autism spectrum disorders: A mixed-methods investigation. *Exceptionality Education International, 29*(2), 42–58. https://doi.org/10.5206/eei.v29i2.9401

Every Student Succeeds Act of 2015, Pub. L. No. 114-95 § 114 Stat. 1177 (2015).

Evmenova, A. S. (2020). Implementation of assistive technology in inclusive classrooms. In D. Chambers (Ed.), *Assistive technology to support inclusive education* (Volume 14, pp. 177–193). Emerald Publishing Limited.

Evmenova, A. S., Graff, H. J., Motti, V. G., Giwa-Lawal, K., & Zheng, H. (2019). Designing a wearable technology intervention to support young adults with IDD in inclusive postsecondary academic environments. *Journal of Special Education Technology, 34*(2), 92–105. https://doi.org/10.1177/0162643418795833

Geist, L., Erickson, K., Greer, C., & Hatch, P. (2021). Initial evaluation of the project core implementation model. *Assistive Technology Outcomes and Benefits, 15*(1), 29–47. https://www.atia.org/wp-content/uploads/2021/03/V15_Geist_etal.pdf

Individuals with Disabilities Education Act, 20 U.S.C. § 1400 (2004).

Israel, M. (2019). Use assistive and instructional technologies. In J. McLeskey, L. Maheady, B. Billingsley, M. Brownell, & T. Lewis (Eds.), *High-leverage practices for inclusive classrooms* (pp. 264–278). Routledge.

Kellems, R., Cacciatore, G., & Osborne, K. (2019). Using an augmented reality–based teaching strategy to teach mathematics to secondary students with disabilities. *Career Development and Transition for Exceptional Individuals, 42*(4), 253–258. https://doi.org/10.1177/2165143418822800

Klein, C. (2017). Communication and developing relationships for people who use augmentative and alternative communication. *Assistive Technology Outcomes and Benefits, 11*(1), 57–65.

Kurth, J. A., Ruppar, A. L., Toews, S. G., McCabe, K. M., McQuestion, J. A., & Johnston, R. (2019). Considerations in placement decisions for students with extensive support needs: An analysis of LRE statements. *Research and Practice for Persons With Severe Disabilities, 44*(1), 3–19. https://doi.org/10.1177/1540796918825479

Lamb, R., Miller, D., Lamb, R., Akmal, T., & Hsiao, Y.-J. (2018). Examination of the role of training and fidelity of implementation in the use of assistive communications for children with autism spectrum disorder: A meta-analysis of the picture exchange communication system. *British Journal of Special Education, 45*(4), 454–472. https://doi.org/10.1111/1467-8578.12243

Mak, G., & Zhao, L. (2020). A systematic review: The application of virtual reality on the skill-specific performance in people with ASD. *Interactive Learning Environments.* Advance online publication. https://doi.org/10.1080/10494820.2020.1811733

McLeskey, J., Barringer, M.-D., Billingsley, B., Brownell, M., Jackson, D., Kennedy, M., Lewis, T., Maheady, L., Rodriguez, J., Scheeler, M. C., Winn, J., & Ziegler, D. (2017). *High-leverage practices in special education.* Council for Exceptional Children & CEEDAR Center.

Meyer, A., Rose, D. H., & Gordon, D. (2014). *Universal design for learning: Theory and practice.* CAST.

Mize, M. K., Park, Y., & Moore, T. (2018). Computer-assisted vocabulary instruction for students with disabilities: Evidence from an effect size analysis of single-subject experimental design studies. *Journal of Computer Assisted Learning, 34*(6), 641–651. https://doi.org/10.1111/jcal.12272

Newton, C., & Sennott, S. C. (2017). Impact of the MODELER AAC strategy for secondary students with complex communication needs. *The Journal on Technology and Persons With Disabilities, 5,* 252–269. http://hdl.handle.net/10211.3/190216

Park, J., Bouck, E. C., & Duenas, A. (2020). Using video modeling to teach social skills for employment to youth with intellectual disability. *Career Development and Transition for Exceptional Individuals, 43*(1), 40–52. https://doi.org/10.1177/2165143418810671

Park, J., Bouck, E., & Duenas, A. (2019). The effects of video modeling and video prompting interventions on individuals with intellectual disability: A systematic literature review. *Journal of Special Education Technology, 34*(1), 3–16. https://doi.org/10.1177/0162643418780464

Ranada, A. L., & Lidstrom, H. (2019). Satisfaction with assistive technology device in relation to the service delivery process – A systematic review. *Assistive Technology, 31*(2), 82–97. https://doi.org/10.1080/10400435.2017.1367737

Ryndak, D. L., Orlando, A.-M., & Duran, D. (2012). Serving students with extensive support needs in general education contexts in a reconceptualized system of education. In L. C. Burrello, W. Sailor, & J. Kleinhammer-Tramill (Eds.), *Unifying educational systems: Leadership and policy perspectives* (pp. 135–155). Routledge.

Saunders, A. F., Root, J. R., & Jimenez, B. A. (2019). Recommendations for inclusive educational practice in mathematics for students with extensive support needs. *Inclusion, 7*(2), 75–91. https://doi.org/10.1352/2326-6988-7.2.75

Sheldon, E., & Erickson, K. (2020). Emergent literacy instruction for students with significant disabilities in the regular classroom. *Assistive Technology Outcomes and Benefits, 14,* 135–160. https://www.atia.org/wp-content/uploads/2020/06/ATOB-V14-A9-SheldonErickson.pdf

Snyder, S., & Huber, H. (2019). Computer assistive instruction to teach academic content to students with intellectual disability: A review of the literature. *American Journal of Intellectual and Developmental Disabilities, 124*(4), 374–390. https://doi.org/10.1352/1944-7558-124.4.374

Spooner, F., Root, J. R., Saunders, A. F., & Browder, D. (2019). An updated evidence-based practice review on teaching mathematics to students with moderate and severe developmental disabilities. *Remedial and Special Education, 40*(3), 150–165. https://doi.org/10.1177/0741932517751055

U.S. Department of Education (2017). *Reimagining the role of technology in education: 2017 national education technology plan update.* https://tech.ed.gov/files/2017/01/NETP17.pdf

Zabala, J. (2005). Ready, SETT, go! Getting started with the SETT framework. *Closing the Gap Computer Technology in Special Education and Rehabilitation, 23*(6), 1–3.

Zimmerman, B. J. (1995). Self-regulation involves more than metacognition: A social cognitive perspective. *Educational Psychologist, 30*(4), 217–221. https://doi.org/10.1207/s15326985ep3004_8

20
Teach Students with Extensive Support Needs to Maintain and Generalize New Learning across Time and Settings

Sara Snyder and Rachel Cagliani

Effective teachers use specific techniques to teach students to generalize and maintain newly acquired knowledge and skills. Using numerous examples in designing and delivering instruction requires students to apply what they have learned in other settings. Educators promote maintenance by systematically using schedules of reinforcement, providing frequent material reviews, and teaching skills that are reinforced by the natural environment beyond the classroom. Students learn to use new knowledge and skills in places and situations other than the original learning environment and maintain their use in the absence of ongoing instruction.

Supporting Students with Extensive Support Needs

Generalization and maintenance may not occur for some students with extensive support needs (ESN) if instructional approaches do not specifically address these outcomes. This chapter focuses on the importance of generalization and maintenance, strategies to promote generalization and maintenance, and how to plan, implement, and assess students' generalization and maintenance. The strategies included in this chapter can be used to meet the needs of a wide variety of students with ESN, including students with multiple disabilities and sensory impairments.

Chapter Objectives

Upon reading this chapter, you should be able to do the following:

1. Describe teaching strategies that promote generalization.
2. Develop a plan for how to facilitate response and stimulus generalization of skills.
3. Describe how to support maintenance by changing reinforcement schedules.
4. Develop a plan for when and how often to assess skill maintenance.
5. Describe how to make data-based decisions that support maintenance.

Generalization

Generalization is when a student can perform a skill in new ways or contexts beyond the original way it was taught. It is an essential for all types of skills including behavioral (e.g., raise your hand

DOI: 10.4324/9781003175735-21

and wait to be called on to speak), academic (e.g., graph data on a coordinate plane), and daily living skills (e.g., washing hands) as it facilitates independence across contexts. Generalization should be considered a critical outcome of instruction for students with ESN.

Response and Stimulus Generalization

There are two broad categories of generalization. *Stimulus generalization* is when after learning to respond in the presence of one stimulus (e.g., saying "Planet" when presented with a picture of Jupiter) the student responds to other stimuli with similar features (e.g., Mars and Uranus) without being taught to do so (Collins, 2012). Stimuli can be any changes in the environment that affect an individual's behavior (e.g., teacher directions, presentation of instructional materials, change in settings, or communicative partner). Teachers should plan to vary stimuli during instruction so the student learns to respond to all possible variations. For instance, Mr. Wayne is teaching the different forms of precipitation. To promote generalization, Mr. Wayne would show his student multiple photographs depicting precipitation, including rain, sleet, hail, and snow. Within this stimulus set, he has numerous photos of each concept. For example, he has photographs of rain that depict both heavy downpours and light rain. For each picture, Mr. Wayne's student responds correctly with one response describing all the photos: precipitation. Mr. Wayne uses multiple photographs of precipitation, so the student learns there are many examples of precipitation.

Response generalization is when a student uses a new behavior to respond to some stimulus without prior instruction. (Collins, 2012). For example, Ms. Fields is working with Ahmad on representing a quantity with different addends. She teaches Ahmad to represent the number six by arranging two groups of three manipulatives. Ahmad then creates quantities of six by showing three groups of two. Additionally, after training with only unifix cubes he can show groups using a variety of materials, including plastic counters, drawing circles on a whiteboard, or using his fingers. In this example, there is one stimulus ("show me groups that add up to 6"), and Ahmad can demonstrate multiple responses or ways of showing six items.

The ultimate goal is to teach students to use new skills under a range of situations and apply skills in new ways to solve everyday problems. For example, Dennis has been working on greeting people who approach him using his alternative and augmentative communication (AAC) device. His teacher, Ms. Diaz, has taught him to greet a variety of people, including peers, other teachers in the school, his bus driver, and the principal, by activating his AAC device to say hello. She notices that Dennis begins to greet new people as they approach. This is stimulus generalization: multiple stimuli (new people) and one response ("Hello"). Next, Ms. Diaz teaches response generalization by teaching Dennis a variety of informal greetings to use with peers and formal greetings to use with adults.

Strategies to Promote Generalization

Select Meaningful Skills for Instruction

One factor that may improve generalization is selecting meaningful skills for both the student and the student's caregivers by conducting person-centered planning, ecological inventories, and preference assessments. For example, George is a 15-year-old student with multiple disabilities who needs intensive support. His mother has indicated that George does not open his mouth and accept food on a spoon when offered during meal times. She reports that George's nurse and teachers have observed the same issue across settings. George's teacher develops an intervention where George is presented with two food choices, and George is taught to choose a food to eat by looking toward the food he wants. The person assisting him with meals then presents a spoonful of George's food selection. Since George depends on caregivers for assistance during meals, because he eats often, eats a wide variety of foods, and eats at both home and school, this skill of indicating choice by looking toward a preferred food from a choice of two might generalize well to all conditions where the skill is needed. George's mother was interested in this intervention and began to implement the intervention at home, which also promotes generalization as instruction occurs across relevant people, places, and times.

Train Diversely

Teachers can use *multiple exemplar instruction* to enhance stimulus generalization. Multiple exemplar instruction simply means "many examples," or in this case, many stimuli (Collins, 2012). When teaching the geographic landform *island*, Mr. Anderson shows Amelia multiple representations (e.g., photographs, illustrations, and videos) of islands that present stimulus variations (e.g., tropical, desert, large, and small islands). This will facilitate Amelia's understanding that islands vary by color, shape, and size.

Teachers also can vary the exemplars to ensure students attend to the important features of the stimuli rather than the non-relevant features. When teaching the student to identify letters by name, the teacher may present different examples of a letter B, including upper and lowercase. The Bs may be different colors or fonts, printed on the computer and written using various writing utensils. The Bs may be presented in different ways, such as on flashcards, within text, on a whiteboard, or on signs around the school. When identifying B, the form or shape of the letter is the important feature. The font, size, and color of the letter are non-relevant features.

Teachers can use a variety of tactics to select the different stimuli to use in multiple exemplar instruction. For example, Mr. Chin is teaching Ben to read the time on a clock to the half hour (e.g., 9:30). He looks at the different clocks in Ben's environments and observes that Ben has a digital clock on his smartphone, an analog clock in his classroom, and a digital clock in the gym. Mr. Chin speaks to Ben's father, who notes that the family has a digital clock on the oven that the family refers to often. Mr. Chin uses this information to develop exemplars as they appear on the different clocks in Ben's life. Mr. Chin also varies the irrelevant features of the exemplars to assist Ben with focusing on the relevant features during instruction. The exemplars show time as it appears on the oven clock (with green digits) and as it appears on Ben's smartphone (in large white numbers). The exemplars also depict the numbers written in different ways since some clocks show numbers with all straight lines.

Teachers can also facilitate response generalization by teaching multiple exemplars of a response. For example, Mr. Lewis is working with Erika on saying goodbye when ending social interactions. Mr. Lewis teaches a variety of appropriate farewells, such as vocalizing bye, see you later, *adios*, and waving and bumping fists with the communicative partner.

Train Loosely

When teaching procedures are highly teacher controlled, they are always implemented in the same way. This may not support generalization. Another option is to *train loosely* by modifying the instructions that occur just before the student responds (Stokes & Osnes, 1989). For example, when asking the student to touch state capitals on the map of the US, the teacher can vary the instructions or antecedents by saying "Touch Richmond," "Where is Atlanta?" "Show me Columbia," and "Can you find Nashville?" The teacher may conduct this instruction in a variety of locations in the classroom (e.g., work table and desk) and using a variety of U.S. maps that vary in size, shape, or color.

Training loosely also includes varying how reinforcement is provided both in content and schedule. The teacher may use a variety of praise statements, such as "excellent!" and "great work!" and response-specific praise like "Terrific! You found the capital of Georgia!" The teacher can alternate the type of reinforcement across trials. For example, the student may get praise for the first correct response, a high five for the second correct response, and a token for the third correct response.

Program Common Stimuli: Items or People

Teachers of students with ESN must balance teaching several responses to various stimuli while ensuring the student recognizes something in the learning environment that reminds them of how to respond (Stokes & Osnes, 1989). If the student cannot identify any similarities to previous learning opportunities, they may not recall how to respond correctly. Two stimuli that could be held constant across learning contexts are physical stimuli (items) and social stimuli (people).

Teachers may choose to hold some physical stimuli or item constant across learning opportunities to assist the student with knowing how to respond across opportunities (Stokes & Osnes, 1989). The teacher may ensure this item is always present in the learning environment or teach the student how to bring the item to various settings. Teachers should select physical stimuli that are meaningful to the activity and student. Mr. Nguyen is teaching Michelle how to measure various items throughout the school using a tape measure. Mr. Nguyen initially selected this skill after completing person-centered planning, where Michelle expressed interest in building furniture at her family's business. Mr. Nguyen taught Michelle how to open the tape measure, use the hook to place one end of the tape measure on one side of the item she's measuring, and stretch the tape to the other side of the item. Once the tape measure is stretched out, Mr. Nguyen taught Michelle how to identify the number on the opposite side of the item from the hook and to record that number on her paper. Mr. Nguyen wants Michelle to have practice with this across various items and settings, so he brings Michelle around the school to gather measurements of several pieces of furniture. Mr. Nguyen incorporates common salient physical stimuli by presenting Michelle with the same tape measure every time she needs to measure something but trains diversely by incorporating various items to measure. Mr. Nguyen chose to keep the tape measure the same to support Michelle, who has an intellectual disability and vision impairment. The tape measure is adapted to meet Michelle's vision accommodations. By using the same tape measure that Michelle is familiar with across learning contexts, the item may remind Michelle how to respond correctly when asked to measure something. Michelle's teacher can further plan for generalization by teaching Michelle how to self-mediate the physical stimuli or teach her to bring the important physical stimuli with her when relevant and necessary.

In another example, Ms. Hicks is teaching their student Senai how to budget her money for groceries to create her grocery list before her shopping trip at her neighborhood store. Ms. Hicks teaches Senai to use the store's mobile app to make her list and ensure the items she picks add up to be less than her budgeted amount of money. The following day, Ms. Hicks and Senai go to the store to purchase the items. Senai carries the mobile device with the store's application to find the items she planned to purchase located in several different places. The mobile device serves as a self-mediated physical stimulus for planning and purchasing items within a budget.

Students with ESN may also benefit from incorporating familiar people across various teaching environments. In some situations, teachers may be unable to train across environments initially. In these situations, incorporating common salient social stimuli (Stokes & Osnes, 1989), such as a familiar adult or student, may help a student with ESN generalize the behavior to a new environment. For example, Mrs. Tallon taught her student Jordan to use the restroom at school. Now, Jordan no longer wears diapers while at school. Mrs. Tallon is very excited about Jordan's progress and knows if this skill can be generalized to all aspects of Jordan's life beyond the classroom, he will be able to be more involved in his community, and his family will be able to save money. Mrs. Tallon meets with Jordan's family and creates a plan to spend a few days during her post-planning at the end of the school year at Jordan's home to help support his family in generalizing remaining dry and using the restroom to his home environment. In this example, Mrs. Tallon is the salient social stimuli. Teachers should be sure to have a plan to eventually fade the salient social stimuli to prevent students from only being able to respond correctly in the presence of the person.

Use Commonly Occurring Reinforcers Delivered on Typical Schedules

Some students with ESN acquire new skills and demonstrate previously learned skills solely by relying on the reinforcers commonly available in inclusive environments such as teacher praise, high fives, and trips to the prize box. For example, a high-school biology instructor may provide positive reinforcement like praise for a lab well done, high scores for lab completion, etc. However, for some students with ESN, teachers may need to provide reinforcers that do not commonly occur in other environments (e.g., access to preferred items or other activities) for the student to learn the skill. The ultimate goal is to work toward commonly occurring reinforcers to promote the student's access to inclusive settings.

Schedules of reinforcement describe how much of a reinforcer is given and how often. Teachers might initially provide a large amount of a reinforcer very frequently to keep the student with ESN engaged and responding to instruction. Special education teachers need to plan how to transition the learner to reinforcement schedules that are typical in inclusive settings.

Teach Student Behaviors That Promote Access to Reinforcement

Teacher praise is a commonly used reinforcer that ideally should frequently occur in inclusive settings. Teachers may need to teach students with ESN to engage in behaviors that recruit or gain access to praise. For example, teachers may have to teach students to raise their hand and keep it raised until the biology teacher approaches and then teach students how to show the biology teacher their progress within the lab group. Without the skill of recruiting teacher attention, the student cannot access teacher praise. Attention from peers is also a potential reinforcer available in inclusive settings. Still, a student with ESN cannot benefit from peer attention unless the student with ESN knows how to appropriately recruit and maintain the peer's attention. A first step may be to teach students to greet a peer and then ask a social question to start a conversation.

Reinforce Generalized Responses

Teachers should provide reinforcement when the student demonstrates generalized responses to increase the likelihood that they will occur again in the future. For example, Ms. Barnes is teaching Joe (fifth grade) to greet others. Instruction on this skill typically occurs in the special education classroom. One morning, Ms. Barnes and Joe are walking in the hallway together. Joe independently greets Mr. Trost, the school media specialist. After the greeting, Ms. Barnes then provides behavior-specific praise to Joe: "Joe, I just saw you greet Mr. Trost just like we've been working on in class! Awesome!"

Planning, Implementing, and Assessing Generalization

Planning for Instruction That Promotes Generalization

Teachers will need to plan for teaching for skill generalization, rather than hoping the generalized responding will occur independently. This process should begin with a skills assessment. What skill does the student need to learn, and what are the contexts in which the student should demonstrate the skill? Next, the teacher should develop learning objectives that specifically address generalization. By writing objectives that address generalization, the teacher sets a generalization plan in motion that outlines all the contexts in which the student is expected to do the skill. Next, the teacher should brainstorm all the ways the student should generalize the new skill. See the planning table for an example of the planning process (Figure 20.1).

Planning for Generalization

✓ Conduct assessments (e.g., ecological and preference assessments, and person-centered planning)
✓ Write observable & measurable generalization objectives
✓ Brainstorm options for stimulus generalization
  ○ Across people,
  ○ Across activities,
  ○ Across settings,
  ○ Across materials,
  ○ Across times of day
✓ Brainstorm options for response generalization
✓ Target a variety of ways to vary instruction to promote generalization

Example of Generalization Planning

✓ **Student name, grade:** Rick, post-graduate (age 21)
✓ **Results from the assessment:** The assessment indicated Rick would like to use an electronic personal planner
✓ **Objective**: When told event information, Rick will record a variety of events in an electronic personal planner for five events with 100% accuracy.
✓ **Brainstorm options for stimulus generalization:**
  ○ People: Any person who tells the student about an upcoming event (teacher, friend, caregiver, receptionist from the dentist office, and advertising on social media)
  ○ Activities: All types of events, including required events (doctor's appointments, and upcoming quiz in class) and fun events (upcoming get together)
  ○ Settings: In all classes, when checking out at the doctor's office, in conversation with people who communicate upcoming events
  ○ Materials: Use a variety of writing utensils on different pages of the planner
  ○ Times of day: Any time of day when Rick needs to write down an upcoming event
✓ **Brainstorm options for response generalization:**
  ○ Type the event
  ○ Voice to text entry

Figure 20.1 Generalization Planning Tool That Can Be Used to Determine How They Can Teach for Generalization in Multiple Contexts

Implementing Strategies That Promote Generalization

One approach is to teach a skill to mastery in one context before teaching in a new context or teaching additional responses. One issue with this approach is that it may take a long time for the student to demonstrate mastery, thereby delaying instruction in other contexts or on additional relevant responses. Students with multiple disabilities and/or sensory impairments may present with characteristics that further lengthen the time it takes to master a skill.

A more efficient approach may be implementing generalization strategies during initial skill acquisition and writing learning objectives that address generalization from the outset of instruction (see Figure 20.2). This approach may be more efficient because it exposes the student to all plausible conditions. For example, Dr. Jones is teaching Mandy to count dollar bills. His generalization planning includes response generalization, where Mandy practices this skill by buying different items with various combinations of bills. Dr. Jones also plans for stimulus generalization. Mandy's practice opportunities include multiple paraprofessionals, peer tutors, locations (e.g., school spirit store, grocery store, and school coffee shop), and times of the day.

Objectives written for skill generalization

✓ When shown a recipe on a website, in a cookbook, or on a food package, Rebecca will follow the written recipe to cook the meal for up to a five-step recipe, with 100% accuracy across ten different recipes presented in a variety of formats.

✓ When provided with an equation with a missing quantity (for totals up to 20), Josephine will demonstrate solving the equation for the missing value with four different kinds of manipulatives with 90% accuracy for four consecutive instructional sessions

---

Figure 20.2 An Example of Written Learning Objectives That Address Generalization

Assessing Generalization

Teachers should assess stimulus and response generalization by ensuring their data collection materials account for this information. For instance, when recording the student's response, the teacher should also note the stimuli presented before the correct response. Similarly, the teacher should record the student's response following the presentation of a stimulus when multiple responses are being taught. By collecting this information in addition to accuracy, teachers can monitor that correct responding is occurring in response to multiple stimuli and across multiple responses.

Maintenance: Generalization across Time

Not only should students carry their skills to new contexts, but also students should continue to perform the skills long after instruction ends. Maintenance refers to the student continuing to perform the skill at a socially valid level after instruction has been completed (Ledford et al., 2019). Maintenance can be conceptualized as generalization across the dimension of time. The maintenance of a skill is an important outcome of instruction. Without maintenance, instruction every day and every year would be like starting all over again, with students never progressing to more complex skills because the teacher continually has to reteach basic skills.

Maintenance can be a problem for all students, not just students with ESN. For instance, even after several years of foreign language instruction in high school, someone may struggle to recall the most basic words and phrases later in life. Maintenance may be particularly challenging for students with ESN due to characteristics related to disability, such as impaired short- and long-term memory.

Strategies That Promote Maintenance

Select Meaningful Skills for Instruction

The phrase "use it or lose it" brings up an important component of teaching for maintenance. For skills to maintain, they must be meaningful to the student and their life. If students do not have opportunities to apply this skill outside of the instructional context, they will likely "lose" or forget the skill. Therefore, teachers need to ensure sufficient opportunities to respond. In the previous example, Mr. Nguyen taught Michelle to use a tape measure. After learning how to measure various pieces of furniture, Michelle will be able to assist her family in their shop after school, on the weekends, and well beyond her time in Mr. Nguyen's class. Meaningful skills will maintain better than skills that are not meaningful to the student. Teachers of students with ESN can determine whether or not a skill is meaningful to a student by engaging in person-centered planning and ecological assessment to prioritize learning outcomes and design instructional programs.

Thin Reinforcement Schedules

Ensuring maintenance also involves planning to transition to more manageable schedules of reinforcement than required during the acquisition phase (Ledford et al., 2019). Initially, when teaching a student with ESN a new skill, teachers provide a dense schedule of reinforcement. For example, during the acquisition phase of learning, teachers of students with ESN may provide a reinforcer every time the student engages in the correct response. This is known as a continuous reinforcement schedule or a fixed ratio (FR1) schedule of reinforcement. For students to continue engaging in the behaviors after instruction has stopped, teachers of students with ESN must plan to thin the schedule of reinforcement and plan for more commonly available reinforcers to take the place of reinforcers used during initial phases of learning (e.g., teacher praise and token economy). As mentioned in the previous section on generalization, if the goal is for the student to be included in environments with peers without disabilities, planning to transition to the types of reinforcers and reinforcement schedules typical in those settings will be important. Teachers can determine the typically occurring schedule of reinforcement by considering how frequently students without ESN access reinforcement for similar tasks and work toward a similar schedule.

When a student has demonstrated mastery of the skill with the continuous schedule of reinforcement, teachers must gradually thin the schedule of reinforcement, so the student learns to engage in the behavior without accessing reinforcement after every occurrence or only intermittently. Intermittent schedules of reinforcement can ensure the maintenance of a skill over time (Martens et al., 2011). Intermittent schedules of reinforcement involve only providing a reinforcer after either a **fixed** number of occurrences (e.g., every third response = FR3) of the behavior or an average or **variable** number of occurrences (e.g., third, seventh, and ninth response = VR 3). Variable schedules are preferred, as fixed schedules of reinforcement are more predictable to the student and make the behavior less likely to maintain after instruction has stopped. Teachers of students with ESN should move from continuous schedules of reinforcement to fixed schedules of reinforcement. Finally, the student should transition to variable schedules that match the naturally occurring schedules typical in more inclusive environments. Variable schedules are beneficial in the classroom because they decrease the predictability of reinforcement, making the behavior more likely to persist, and they are more manageable to implement for teachers. A commonly used schedule thinning progression is FR1, FR2, and VR3 (Ledford et al., 2019). FR1 means fixed ratio of one, where every correct response produces reinforcement. FR2 indicates a fixed ratio of two, where reinforcement is provided for every two correct responses. VR3 means a variable ratio of three, where reinforcement is provided about every three responses (sometimes two and sometimes four).

The following example illustrates a possible progression of reinforcer delivery. Miss Singh is teaching her student Charlotte to read and follow directions. Miss Singh presents Charlotte with various three- to five-word sentences on clipboards, notecards, or an iPad and tells Charlotte to read the sentence and do what the instructions say. She will move on to the next phase after Charlotte meets the following mastery criterion for initial acquisition: five sessions of 100% correct responding across 20 different directions with at least two teachers and two settings. Notice that this mastery criterion also includes information about skill generalization: 20 different directions, at least two teachers, and two settings. Once Charlotte reaches the mastery criterion, Miss Singh plans to thin the schedule of reinforcement across the following four phases. In Figures 20.3–20.6, the X indicates the trials where a reinforcer will be provided after the student responds correctly. Where an X is not present, the student responded correctly but does not access reinforcement. In other words, the X indicates that every time Charlotte will receive access to a preferred activity contingent on correctly reading the three- to five-word sentence and doing what the sentence says.

Correct Response	1	2	3	4	5	6	7	8	9	10	11	12
	X	X	X	X	X	X	X	X	X	X	X	X

Figure 20.3 This Chart Shows a Fixed Ratio Schedule of Reinforcement for a Student

Correct Response	1	2	3	4	5	6	7	8	9	10	11	12
		X		X		X		X		X		X

Figure 20.4 This Chart Shows a Fixed Ratio 2 Schedule of Reinforcement for a Student

Correct Response	1	2	3	4	5	6	7	8	9	10	11	12
Session 1	X			X				X		X		

Figure 20.5 This Chart Depicts a Variable Ratio 3 Schedule of Reinforcement

Correct Response	1	2	3	4	5	6	7	8	9	10	11	12
												X

Figure 20.6 This Chart Depicts a Natural Schedule of Reinforcement in an Inclusive Setting

Phase 1: Fixed Ratio 1 (FR1)

Miss Singh gives Charlotte the reinforcer (access to a preferred activity) after each time Charlotte vocally reads one sentence and then does what the sentence says to do (See Figure 20.3).

Phase 2: Fixed Ratio 2 (FR2)

Miss Singh gives the reinforcer after every two instances of correct responding. Therefore, Charlotte accesses the reinforcer on the second, fourth, sixth, etc., time she correctly reads a sentence and does what the sentence says to do (See Figure 20.4).

Phase 3: Variable Ratio 3 (VR3)

Miss Singh delivers the reinforcer after an average of every three instances of correct responding. The following table illustrates Phase 3 (See Figure 20.5).

Phase 4: Naturally Occurring Schedules of Reinforcement and Embedded Reinforcers

In this phase, the schedule of reinforcement is thinned or reduced even further (See Figure 20.6). In more inclusive settings, students may be required to engage in a greater number of correct responses before accessing reinforcers. Teachers can also change the way they provide reinforcers. For example, rather than providing the preferred activity contingent on correctly reading sentences, Charlotte's final direction to read states, "take a break." By making the last step "take a break," we rely on negative reinforcement, receiving a break when you complete all of your work, to maintain the behavior.

Once Charlotte has reached the mastery criterion, and the schedule of reinforcement is thinned to the more typical rate indicated in Phase 4, Ms. Singh ensures Charlotte will have regular opportunities to practice this skill in a meaningful way. Before learning this skill, Charlotte received several teacher prompts and directions to navigate her day at school. Miss Singh plans for Charlotte to have more independence across her school day by presenting directions typed on paper or the iPad rather than through vocal teacher directives to incorporate Charlotte's new skill.

Planning and Assessing for Maintenance

When planning to ensure a skill is maintained, the first step is to write a learning objective that reflects maintenance across time. A rigorous mastery criterion indicates how many times the student has to demonstrate the skill at mastery levels to be considered mastered. This may promote overlearning.

Assessing maintenance is not a one-time event, but something the teacher should continue regularly after instruction has ended. One approach would be to choose a particular instructional session during the week to conduct maintenance probes (e.g., every Tuesday at 12:30). The maintenance probe would involve the teacher measuring independent performance without response prompting. An ideal schedule would be to check for skill maintenance as often as it typically occurs but vary the day and time to identify student-level factors impacting maintenance probes.

Before reteaching a skill, teachers should conduct more than one maintenance probe. If the student performs poorly during one maintenance probe, the student has not necessarily lost the skill, but it does indicate a need to probe for maintenance again soon to identify a pattern consistent with skill loss. In this case, the teacher may conduct another maintenance probe the next day rather than wait until the following week. Consider creating additional opportunities in the day for the student to practice the skill in addition to structured maintenance probes. See Figure 20.7 for a maintenance planning tool teachers can use to ensure maintenance.

To evaluate maintenance, Ms. Singh conducts maintenance probes with Charlotte each week to ensure she can still read the sentences and follow the written directions. Charlotte uses this skill frequently throughout the week, but data collection only occurs once a week. Since Miss Singh's schedule is so busy with other students, meetings, etc., she adds a reminder in her phone to record data at one specific time each week. Miss Singh graphs these data to make data-based decisions about whether Charlotte is maintaining the skill, and if not, what kind of additional instruction is needed to relearn the skill. Figure 20.8 demonstrates those data and Miss Singh's decision-making process.

As depicted in Figure 20.8, Miss Singh continued to collect data once Charlotte reached mastery criterion to ensure the skill was maintained beyond initial acquisition. The data points in maintenance are spaced out because Miss Singh only collected data once per week. During the maintenance phase, Ms. Singh recorded one probe where Charlotte could only read 60% of the sentences. Ms. Singh conducted two more probe sessions over the next two days to confirm if Charlotte had not retained the skill. Data confirmed that Charlotte's performance was below the mastery criterion (100% accuracy) across three days. Miss Singh reintroduced instruction to reteach the skill. Once Charlotte met the mastery criterion again, Miss Singh continued to collect maintenance data once per week.

Maintenance Planning

- Write observable and measurable maintenance objectives that support overlearning by including rigorous mastery criteria.
- What can be done to ensure that the skill is meaningful, increasing the likelihood of being maintained?
- How often will the skill be assessed to see if it is maintained once instruction is over?
- Define criteria to resume instruction if the skill is not maintained.
- What kind of teaching will occur if the skill is not maintained?

Maintenance Planning Example

- Learning objective: When shown a picture of a school object, Rocio will vocalize the name of the school object across 20 objects with 90% accuracy on four out of five learning sessions.
- To make the skill meaningful, the teacher will teach Rocio school items that she commonly uses at school. During learning activities, the teacher will ask Rocio to name the item that she is using during the activity. The teacher will also focus on school items she may use in her afterschool program and at home.
- The teacher will assess this skill once a week to ensure Rocio has maintained the skill.
- If Rocio scores less than 60% accuracy on one maintenance probe, the teacher will conduct two additional maintenance probes over the next two school days.
- If all three data points indicate performance below 60%, the teacher will resume instruction until consistent correct responding occurs.

Figure 20.7 Maintenance Planning Tool That Can Be Used to Determine How to Assess for Maintenance after Instruction Has Ended

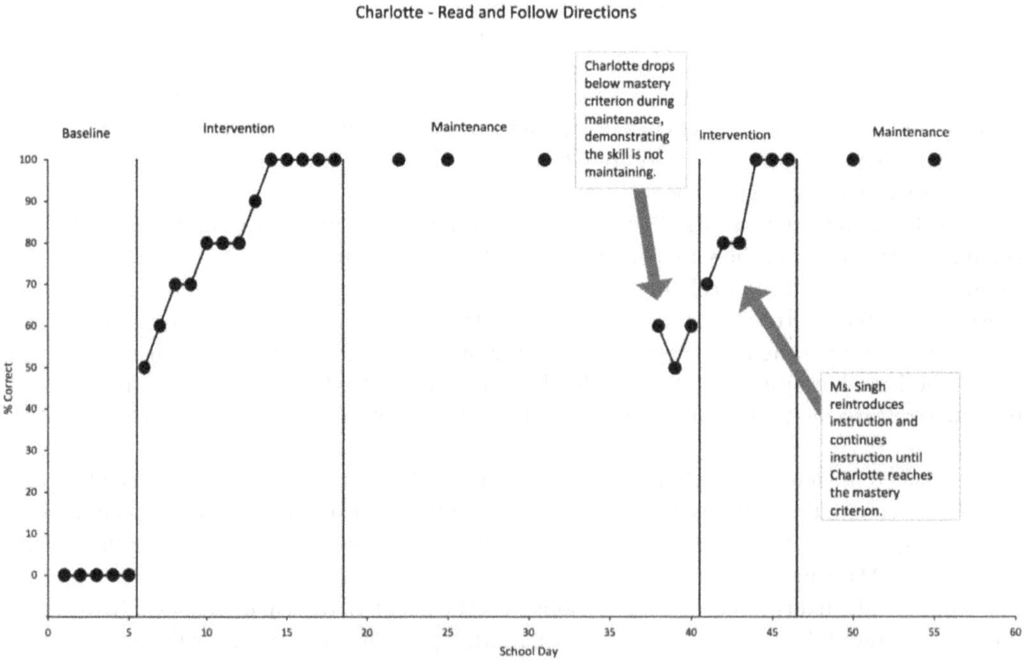

Figure 20.8 A Graph Showing a Student's Performance during Intervention, When Maintenance Probes Were Conducted and When Instruction Was Initiated When There Was a Lack of Maintenance

Checklist for Maintenance

✓ Once a student demonstrates the mastery criterion for initial acquisition, plan to collect data on the behavior once a week for at least three months.

✓ If initial instruction involves a continuous schedule of reinforcement or a schedule of reinforcement not feasible long term, make a plan to thin the schedule of reinforcement. First, begin by only providing the preferred stimuli contingent on correct responding every other instance. Once correct responding maintains, provide the preferred stimuli an average of every three instances of correct responding. From here, plan to gradually increase the required responses to access the preferred stimuli until a more manageable schedule is reached.

✓ Plan to incorporate naturally occurring opportunities for reinforcement or contingencies similar to less-restrictive settings.

✓ Go back to teaching when a student's performance on a skill drops below the mastery criterion for three or more days.

Figure 20.9 This Checklist Outlines What Teachers Should Do to Monitor Skill Maintenance

Continuing to assess skill maintenance can feel daunting. However, as long as the system for defining and measuring behavior is set up from the beginning of instruction, teachers should be able to quickly determine if a skill has been maintained and when to reteach. Figure 20.9 shows a checklist that may help plan for maintenance across students and skills.

Next Steps toward Better Practice

1. Complete the planning for generalization table on page 255.
2. Based on the completed table, decide on ways to vary instruction to promote generalization.
3. Create an action plan by determining who, when, what, and where the plan for generalization will occur.
   a. Who? When? Look at the class schedule and determine the best time based on when this student receives this instruction and staff availability. If additional staff is needed, make a plan to train those staff members. Be sure to explain to staff why teaching across people is necessary.
   b. What? Determine any additional materials that need to be created and plan for an organization to ensure multiple exemplars are presented at the correct time.
   c. Where? If different settings are necessary, work with school administration and teachers to ensure the setting is available at the time and for the desired purpose. Be prepared with a rationale for why additional settings are necessary.
4. If there is no data collection system in place, set one up. Collecting and graphing data will allow for data-based decision-making and to observe change over time. Seeing graphs change can be rewarding and provide evidence that all the hard work in planning for generalization and maintenance was worth the extra effort.
5. Put the plan into action!

The Big Five

1. Use strategies that promote both response and skill generalization.
2. Make a teaching plan for all the ways the skill should be generalized.
   a. Conduct person-centered planning, ecological assessments, and preference assessments.
   b. Consider generalization across activities, times of day, settings, people, and materials.
   c. Consider the various behaviors that could serve the same purpose.

3. Teach skills that are relevant to the student and incorporate reinforcers typically available in the student's environment to ensure generalization and maintenance.
   a. Communicate the plan to all stakeholders.
   b. Consider steps to thinning the schedule to common maintaining contingencies.
4. Make a plan to assess skill maintenance periodically (more than one time) and graph those data to make data-based decisions about whether or not a skill maintains.
5. When a skill does not maintain, go back to teaching.

Resources

- AIM: Naturalistic Interventions Module: https://autisminternetmodules.org/mod_intro.php?mod_id=93
- AIM: Prompting: https://autisminternetmodules.org/mod_intro.php?mod_id=43
- AFIRM Naturalistic Intervention Module Amsbary, J., & AFIRM Team. (2017). *Naturalistic intervention.* Chapel Hill, NC: National Professional Development Center on Autism Spectrum Disorder, FPG Child Development Center, University of North Carolina. Retrieved from http://afirm.fpg.unc.edu/Naturalistic-intervention

References

Collins, B. (2012). *Systematic instruction for students with moderate and severe disabilities.* Brookes Publishing Company.

Ledford, J., Lane, J. D., & Barton, E. E. (2019). *Methods for teaching in early education.* Routledge.

Martens, B. K., Daly, E. J., & Begeny, J. C. (2011). Behavioral approaches to education. In W. W. Fisher, C. C. Piazza, & H. S. Roane (Eds.), *Handbook of applied behavior analysis* (pp. 385–401). The Guilford Press.

Stokes, T. F., & Osnes, P. G. (1989). An operant pursuit of generalization. *Behavior Therapy, 20*(3), 337–355. doi: https://doi.org/10.1016/S0005-7894(89)80054-1.

21

Provide Positive and Corrective Feedback

Margaret G. Werts

> The purpose of feedback is to guide student learning and behavior and increase student motivation, engagement, and independence, leading to improved student learning and behavior. Effective feedback must be strategically delivered and goal directed; feedback is most effective when the learner has a goal and the feedback informs the learner regarding areas needing improvement and ways to improve performance. Feedback may be verbal, nonverbal, or written and should be timely, contingent, genuine, meaningful, age appropriate, and at rates commensurate with task and phase of learning (i.e., acquisition, fluency, maintenance). Teachers should provide ongoing feedback until learners reach their established learning goals.

Supporting Students with Extensive Support Needs

All individuals need feedback to learn to act in ways that are socially, educationally, economically, and personally beneficial. The receipt of feedback lets individuals know how they are doing in relation to the expectations of others or the requirements of specific tasks or activities. Feedback is ubiquitous in all aspects of daily life. Across school, home, and community contexts, individuals benefit from feedback provided by those around them. It helps learners acquire the skills needed to navigate the complex demands of the unique environments they encounter in their lives. Feedback can be overt (e.g., a peer delivers a high five or a teacher provides some verbal error correction) or subtle in nature (e.g., a teacher nods in agreement to the entire class or a student's incorrect response prevents them from completing the next step of a task). Students with extensive support needs (ESN) may have difficulty evaluating the accuracy of their performance from subtle or naturally occurring consequences and thus often need additional support in the form of explicit feedback.

Chapter Objectives

Upon reading this chapter, you should be able to do the following:

1. Define and deliver feedback and praise to students with ESN.
2. Note and measure types and rates of praise and feedback being given in the classroom, home, or community environments.

DOI: 10.4324/9781003175735-22

3. Observe students to determine if reinforcers are effective.
4. Add additional information to teaching trials (non-target information and instructive feedback) to increase teaching efficiency.
5. Assist and teach students to recruit teacher feedback and praise.

What Is Feedback?

Simply, feedback is information about our performance. It can take many forms including spoken, written, gestural performance feedback, or the modeling of correct performance. Further, learners can receive feedback across their senses (e.g., visual, auditory, and kinesthetic). Understanding the ways in which feedback can be delivered and is experienced by students can help educators plan for effective feedback delivery. For example, a teacher might need to plan to deliver feedback differently for some of her students with sensory impairments. They might provide a blind student with verbal or tactile feedback on the correct placement of toothpaste on a toothbrush or a student who is deaf and blind with tactile cues to indicate a peer is within close proximity.

Three Ways Feedback Supports Students

Feedback can help students in three ways (Hattie, 2012; Hattie & Timperley, 2007). First, feedback can let students know whether they have accurately completed a task or performed a skill. It also can help students identify when they have made an error and provide specific information related to the error. This information can help prevent students from making similar errors in the future. *For example, Phillip is working on identifying work materials with his name. The teacher shows Phillip his name on a box of materials and asks, "Whose name is here?" When he answers, "That's my name, Phillip," the teacher praises his reading and lets him know that it did, indeed, say Phillip. If Phillip points to another student's name, the teacher responds, "That says Jose." She then corrects his response and says, "This one says Phillip."*

Second, feedback can provide students with additional information to assist them in responding correctly. If a student is asked to perform a behavior but makes an error or indicates they are unsure of how to respond, the teacher can provide additional feedback to assist them in completing the task. *For example, Mr. Jones is asking Maya, a young adult working in a library, to alphabetize files. She begins by placing all files beginning with "a" in the file box; however, she then hesitates when selecting the next files that begin with "b." Mr. Jones provides feedback that assists Maya in knowing what comes next. He says, "Look at your alphabet chart. After 'a' comes 'b.'" Maya then goes on to select the "b" files to place in the file box.*

Third, feedback can be used to provide additional or extra information to the student beyond just confirming the accuracy of their response. The teacher can extend the content being delivered as part of the feedback for the student responding. *For example, Sylvia is working in center time with her favorite activity of building blocks and learning to build a multiple-block tower. When she builds a four-block tower, Mr. Jackson provides praise, "Great, you built a tower with four blocks!" He then provides additional information on socially interacting with others by saying and modeling, "You can ask Sam to help you with the tower by handing him a block to put on your tower. Like this."*

Across these three uses of feedback, teachers consistently provide praise, encouragement, and information about performance. This dense or continuous schedule of feedback and reinforcement supports students' skill acquisition (Hattie et al., 2016). Only after students can perform skills accurately and consistently should teachers begin to shift to intermittent schedules of feedback.

What Is Praise?

Praise is a verbal statement, gesture, or any action indicating that a teacher, supervisor, parent, or peer approves of the student's behavior or response (Brophy, 1981; Cavanaugh, 2013; Reinke et al., 2008). Praise can also be considered a low-cost effective reinforcement mechanism when it is valued by the student and serves to increase future occurrences of behaviors followed by praise. Praise can be divided into two broad categories: general praise and behavior-specific praise. General praise, observed most often in classrooms (Floress & Beschta, 2018), is any statement or action that communicates that another person is pleased with or approves of a student's behavior. For example, after a student with autism uses a number line to solve a math problem, a teacher might say, "Good work" or "Fantastic." General praise is positive but conveys no specific information about performance or reasons as to why praise was given. Behavior-specific praise describes the particular response or feature of the response for which praise was provided. It goes beyond delivery of approval to include a specific and explicit description of the approved or desired behavior, clearly making connections between students' behavior and approval (Hawkins & Heflin, 2011). For example, the teacher may state, "I like the way you poured water into the cake mix without spilling it" or "You did a good job presenting the plot of the novel" or "You used the right task analysis to solve the math problem" (Briere et al., 2015; Jenkins et al., 2015).

Non-target Extra Information and Instructive Feedback

Feedback can be used to inform as well as extend instruction. Non-target information is extra or additional information that can be added to any part of a learning task or trial. It is not targeted for instruction; students are not required to respond to the information and are not praised if they do. Rather, it is additional information the teacher just exposes the student to or provides (Werts et al., 1995). If it is inserted into the consequence of a trial—that is, with the praise or reinforcer following the target behavior, it is called instructive feedback. Adding planned non-target information is a technique allowing a student to be exposed to and to learn additional information or behaviors in almost the same amount of instructional time needed to teach the initial teaching objective (Albarran & Sandbank, 2019; Werts et al., 1995). For a sequence with non-target information delivered during the consequence of a learning trial, the teacher presents a task or a question related to the target behavior and gives time for the student to respond, either guided or independently. After the student responds, the teacher lets the student know whether their response is correct or provides any needed guidance, and then inserts the planned extra non-target information. Students, from preschoolers to adolescents and adults, with a wide range of abilities and levels of support needs have learned a majority of this extra information when presented during instruction (Werts et al., 1995). Further, presenting non-target information has been demonstrated effective during one-on-one teaching (Ault et al., 2017), small-group instruction (Colozzi et al., 2008; Cromer et al., 1998), and when short questions were embedded in independent seatwork (Caldwell et al., 1996). It also has been implemented effectively by teachers (Collins & Stinson, 1994), therapists (Stewart et al., 1997), paraprofessionals (Ledford et al., 2008; Parrott et al., 2000), and other students (Collins et al., 1995; Tekin-Iftar, 2003). Finally, researchers have shown that it can be effective when embedded within instructional technology (Ault et al., 2017).

Consider the following scenario: *Chris has an IEP goal of naming coins. Additionally, his team has identified a goal of stating monetary values of each coin. His math teacher, Mr. Lam, prepares four envelopes, one for each coin (penny, nickel, dime, and quarter) and puts one coin in each. On the back of the envelope, he writes the monetary value. He has decided that Chris would benefit from questions distributed throughout the instructional day. He chooses the hours between 10 am and noon because Chris is in math class and the cafeteria during that time each day. Mr. Lam lists the order in which he will present coins to Chris varying the order each day, giving Chris three opportunities to respond to each coin, for a total of 12 trials. He will use a constant time-delay procedure, a well-established near-errorless learning technique (Werts et al., 2003). For each opportunity, he approaches Chris, takes the coin out of its envelope, hands it to him, and asks, "What coin is this?" (task direction). Initially, Mr. Lam immediately models the answer, "Dime" (prompt). Chris repeats the response, and Mr. Lam praises him and shows the envelope with ten cents written on it and says, "A dime is 10 cents." (extra information). Once Chris consistently names the coins with the immediate model, Mr. Lam fades the model by inserting a delay interval prior to delivering the model prompt. Chris continues to receive praise and extra information for each coin correctly identified. Chris is not expected to repeat this information, and he does not receive any feedback from Mr. Lam if he does. After Chris is able to name all of the coins to criterion, Mr. Lam tests him on his ability to state the monetary value of each coin. He finds that even though the extra information was not targeted, he has learned the monetary values for three out of the four coins.*

It is important to note that extra information also can be added to other elements of an instructional trial. For example, teachers can add non-targeted information to instructional materials and task directives (Daugherty et al., 2001). For example, when teaching a student to name numbers, the teacher also might provide non-target information on written words. The teacher shows the word "two" and says, "This is the word for this number" and then shows the numeral "2" and asks, "What's this number?" A teacher also can add information to prompts in a series of steps in a task (Fiscus et al., 2002). For example, a student is learning to follow a task analysis to complete a science experiment. Anytime the teacher needs to deliver a prompt (i.e., a verbal direction of the next step of the experiment), they also present a card showing conversions of liquid measurements and states what is on the card (i.e., "8 ounces = 1 cup").

Adding non-target information can increase the efficiency of instruction (Ault et al., 1989; Werts et al., 1995) because more information can be acquired in less instructional time. Extra information can be related or unrelated to the initial instructional target. Related extra information might require a student to respond in the same way but to a different instructional stimulus. For example, a student may be presented with uppercase letters to name, while also presented with non-targeted lowercase letters. It may also be related but require a quite different response. For example, when teaching a middle schooler to read the word "wallet," the teacher might also present the definition "a container for cards and money." Unrelated extra information presents endless opportunities for exposing to students to a range of content items. For example, when a student is calculating the better deal on two brands of beans (target response), the teacher might show a healthy eating diagram and point to healthy protein section, saying "Beans are healthy proteins that you want to eat a lot of." Instructive feedback can be used to provide an application of the academic content to the real world. Multiple research studies have been conducted indicating that instructive feedback can be used to increase the rapidity of learning for future targets after they were directly targeted in later instruction (Holcombe et al., 1993; Wolery et al., 1991). *For example, Tyriq's teacher added vocabulary words that he would need in the next science unit during other lessons. She asked Tyriq to respond to a question (task direction), "Tyriq, what is the sum of these numbers?" and then presented a word card and said, "This says 'Catalyst.'" When the class moves to the next chapter in science class, Tyriq will have a knowledge of the written and spoken word and can then learn, as target information, a definition of catalyst.*

Teaching Students to Recruit Praise and Feedback

Students need feedback, but teachers cannot be everywhere at once. Therefore, students with ESN have been taught to self-assess and to appropriately recruit teacher praise (Craft et al., 1998; Hemmeter et al., 2012). Students also have been taught when to ask for help (Connell et al., 1993; Stokes et al., 1978) notify teachers when they are within a certain distance, and when a task or job is complete. They might be taught to raise a hand or to ask, "How am I doing?" "Look what I have done" or "Look, I'm finished." Researchers have shown that teachers often respond to these requests within 20 s, permitting reinforcement of both academic and recruitment behaviors (Stokes et al., 1978).

Kiika, a first grader with intellectual disability, had difficulty cleaning up when told and getting ready for the next activity during the school day. Because she responded well to positive attention from her teacher, her educational team decided to teach her to use a simple behavior chart. A laminated file folder had photos of her putting materials in a box and standing in line to move to the next activity. Kiika practiced with Pat, her teacher, through rehearsal, repetition, and modeling, placing Velcro checkmarks on the photos following transitions. When she could accurately place the checkmarks with assistance, Pat let her do more of the self-assessment independently. She was taught that it was most effective to ask for teacher attention under several conditions: when she had completed a task, when she had marked the folder, when Pat was within 3 feet, and when Pat was not busy talking with another student. They also taught Kiika to walk up to Pat and show the folder or to announce that she was finished with a task ("I'm done." "Look at this." and "I cleaned up, now."). When she had asked appropriately, Pat praised her for the task and for soliciting attention appropriately. Through intentional teaching of ways to ask for attention and praise, Kiika received more feedback and positive interactions with Pat enabling her to self-monitor and benefit from teacher praise. She was also learning to act independently in the classroom.

Rates of Praise

Unfortunately, levels of feedback in many educational settings are insufficient to facilitate positive student outcomes (Delquadri et al., 1986; Gorton et al., 2021; Scott et al., 2011). Further, as mentioned above, teachers often rely on general rather than behavior-specific praise (Floress & Beschta, 2018). However, we do know that teachers can increase their use of feedback with careful planning and supports (Hawkins & Heflin, 2011; Kalis et al., 2007; Sutherland et al., 2000). This often involves collecting data on current levels of feedback delivery, setting goals for improvement, and monitoring progress. A step-by-step plan for helping teachers observe their reinforcement, analyze, and reflect on their responses, and make positive changes for increasing praise is shown in Table 21.1.

As a reminder, teachers must keep in mind that although praise is a reinforcer for many students, there are some students for whom praise is not a reinforcer and some in which it could actually serve as a punisher (i.e., decrease the future occurrence of behavior if praise was used as a consequence); therefore, reinforcer preference assessments should be conducted for all students prior to their use (Fisher et al., 1992; Lee et al., 2010; Piazza et al., 1996).

Next Steps toward Better Practice

There is much that teachers can do to ensure their effective use of feedback. They can organize their instructional routines to ensure students are successful and have opportunities to receive feedback. This involves planning instructional activities that consider students' current repertoires and arranging routines and activities in ways that increase predictability for students.

1. Include wait time for the student to respond. Occasionally, students need time to move or to speak, due to a delay in motor activity levels or processing time. Preempting a response deprives the student of opportunities to receive reinforcement due to teacher impatience rather than knowledge of answers or actions needed. Errorless learning ensures students have access to correct responses and remain in contact with the reinforcer while prompts are systematically and gradually faded.
2. Foster a positive relationship with each student so that they can receive positive reinforcement and praise. Teachers who have paired themselves with reinforcers act as a reinforcing agent for their students.
3. Provide a ratio that favors praise over corrective statements striving to use a ratio of 4:1 (Walker et al., 2004).
4. Consistently reinforcing desirable behaviors, answers, and actions will lead to more rapid acquisition. In early stages of learning, give reinforcement to all correct responses. As skills develop, thin the reinforcement schedule to an intermittent schedule.

Table 21.1 To Increase Rates of Praise in the Classroom

Action	Process	Data Collection

Observe; reflect	Audio or videotape the classroom during a selected time (e.g., instructional, transitional, or social). Repeat observations during this time over several days.
	Ask a colleague, paraprofessional, or an administrator to observe during selected times.
	Think through class time and what motivators are used with individual students with ESN.
		Frequency—how often
		Type
		  General
		  Behavior specific
		Tone
		  Positive
		  Reprimand
		Who
		  Individual or group
		  Equitable
		Consistency
		Immediacy
		Quality—what is being said

Analyze	Consider the following: Do all students receive reinforcement or praise? Is reinforcement individualized for student preference? Do some students receive more reinforcement or praise than others? Do individuals receive more positive reinforcement than correction? Are statements/reinforcers age and developmentally appropriate? Is praise/reinforcement delivered in proximity to desired behavior? Are student's behaviors changing/improving in response to reinforcement?	Yes/No

Plan; implement the plan	Set teacher goals based on data gathered and analysis.
	Receive training and coaching based on goals.
	Collect data on teacher progress toward goals.
		Frequency—how often
		Type
		  General
		  Behavior specific
		Positive—praise or
		  correction
		Who
		  Individual or group
		  Equitable—do all students receive praise/ reinforcement
		Consistency
		Immediacy
		Quality—what is being said
		Effectiveness

Observe; reflect	Conduct further observation and reflection based on analyses of data and adjust ratios and rates of praise and reinforcement. Receive feedback from coach and adjust plan if needed.	

5. Reinforcement and praise should come as close in time to desired behaviors as possible. With time in between, alternative behaviors or actions can be inadvertently reinforced.

6. Ensure reinforcement is not being provided to unwanted behaviors by giving negative attention to student behaviors. Sometimes a student may want the teacher's attention and act out, call out inappropriately, or engage in aggressive actions to get attention. When adults and peers in the environment react, they are reinforcing inappropriate behaviors. Once reinforced, these become difficult to "unlearn."

7. When praising students, make sure that they understand what is being praised. A student who hears, "Good job," may not know exactly what was good. Teachers can assist by praising and then stating the specific behavior that was done well. Behavior-specific praise helps future performance.

8. All persons in the classroom or teaching environments can be involved in consistently and reliably providing reinforcement and praise to the student. Teachers, paraprofessionals, school personnel, maintenance staff, administrative staff, and others can work cohesively and in concert to strengthen and support desired actions. This will take time to inform all about objectives and goals for each student. In planning meetings or in circulated documents, teachers can inform staff in and out of classrooms what behaviors need to be noticed and how to acknowledge actions in a way that is reinforcing to each individual student.

9. Praise, other reinforcers, and feedback can be used in conjunction with other HLPs to maximize the benefit to the students.

The Big Five

1. Students benefit from praise, reinforcement, and information about performance and expectations.

2. People throughout students' environments can assist in delivering coherent and immediate feedback. Training and collaboration are the keys to having a consistent rate and a feedback-rich environment.

3. Students should be given feedback that is specific to expected tasks desired and to student's needs.

4. Students can be taught to ask for feedback from teachers, peers, family members, and community members.

5. Feedback can be used to teach extra information and to introduce concepts and facts to be taught later leading to more efficient use of instructional time.

Resources

The National Center for Pyramid Model Innovations
(NCPMI) http://challengingbehavior.fmhi.usf.edu

This project, funded by the Office of Special Education Programs, supports capacity of state and local programs to implement early childhood multi-tiered systems of support to improve social, emotional, and behavioral outcomes of young children with, and at risk for, developmental disabilities or delays.

The IRIS Center https://iris.peabody.vanderbilt.edu/

The IRIS Center, funded through the Office of Special Education Programs, US Department of Education, is dedicated to improving education outcomes for all children, especially those with disabilities from birth through age 21, through the use of effective evidence-based practices and interventions. Modules for self-study include case study units, study guides, video examples, and activities.

Center on Positive Behavioral Interventions and Supports (PBIS) https://www.pbis.org/

The Technical Assistance Center on PBIS supports schools, districts, and states to build capacity for implementing a multi-tiered approach to social, emotional, and behavior support. The purpose is to improve the capacity of state and local agencies to enhance school climate and school safety, improving conditions for learning. It provides organizational models, demonstrations, dissemination, and evaluation tools needed to implement the practice across contexts.

Autism Focused Intervention Resources & Modules (AFIRM)
https://afirm.fpg.unc.edu/afirm-modules

AFIRM Modules present step-by-step processes of planning for, using, and monitoring the behavior plans of learners with ASD from birth to 22 years of age. Modules include an introduction to basics of each evidence-based practice, guides to preparing to use practices, steps in implementation, and steps for monitoring.

Division for Early Childhood of the Council for Exceptional Children

Division for Early Childhood. (2014). *DEC recommended practices in early intervention/Early childhood special education 2014.* http://www.dec-sped.org/recommendedpractices

DEC-recommended practices are a set of guidelines that are intended to bridge the gap between research and practice. They offer guidance to persons who work with young children who have or are at risk for developmental delays or disabilities. The list includes practices that shown to result in better or more rapid results for children and families.

References

Albarran, S. A., & Sandbank, M. P. (2019). Teaching non-target information to children with disabilities: An examination of instructive feedback literature. *Journal of Behavioral Education, 28*(1), 107–140. https://doi.org/10.1007/s10864-018-9301-3

Ault, M. J., Baggerman, M., & Horn, C. (2017). Effects of an app incorporating systematic instruction to teach spelling to students with developmental delays. *Journal of Special Education Technology, 32*(3), 123–137. https://doi.org/10.1117/0162643417696931

Ault, M. J., Wolery, M., Doyle, P. M., & Gast, D. L. (1989). Review of comparative studies in instruction of students with moderate and severe handicaps. *Exceptional Children, 55*(4), 346–356. https://doi.org/10.1177/001440298905500410

Briere, D. E., Simonsen, B., Sugai, G., & Myers, D. (2015). Increasing new teachers' specific praise using a within-school consultation intervention. *Journal of Positive Behavioral Interventions, 17*(1), 50–60. https://doi.org/10.1177/1098300713497098

Brophy, J. (1981). Teacher praise: A functional analysis. *Review of Educational Research, 51*(1), 532–532. https://doi.org/10.3102/00346533051001005

Caldwell, N. K., Wolery, M., Werts, M. G., & Caldwell, Y. (1996). Embedding instructive feedback into teacher-student interactions during independent seat work. *Journal of Behavioral Education, 6*(4), 459–480. https://doi.org/10.1007/BF02110517

Cavanaugh, B. (2013). Performance feedback and teachers' use of praise and opportunities to respond: A review of the literature. *Education & Treatment of Children, 36*(1), 111–137. http://www.jstor.org/stable/42900606

Collins, B., Branson, T., & Hall, M. (1995). Teaching generalized reading of cooking product labels to adolescents with mental disabilities through the use of key words taught by peer tutors. *Education and Training in Mental Retardation and Developmental Disabilities, 30*(1), 65–75. http://www.jstor.org/stable/23879140

Collins, B. C., & Stinson, D. M. (1994). Teaching generalized reading of product warning labels to adolescents with mental disabilities through the use of key words. *Exceptionality, 5*(3), 163–181. https://doi.org/10.1207/s15327035ex0503-3

Colozzi, G. A., Ward, L. W., & Crotty, K. E. (2008). Comparison of simultaneous prompting procedure in 1: 1 and small group instruction to teach play skills to preschool students with pervasive developmental disorder and developmental disabilities. *Education and Training in Developmental Disabilities, 43*(2), 226–248. http://www.jstor.org/stable/23879932

Connell, M. C., Carta, J. J., & Baer, D. M. (1993). Programming generalization of in-class transition skills: Teaching preschoolers with developmental delays to self-assess and recruit contingent teacher praise. *Journal of Applied Behavior Analysis, 26*(3), 345–352. https://doi.org/10.1901/jaba.1993.26-345

Craft, M. A., Alber, S. R., & Heward, W. L. (1998). Teaching elementary students with developmental disabilities to recruit teacher attention in a general education classroom: Effects on teacher praise and academic productivity. *Journal of Applied Behavior Analysis, 31*(3), 399–415. https://doi.org/10.1901/jaba.1998.31-399

Cromer, K., Schuster, J. W., Collins, B. C., & Grisham-Brown, J. (1998). Teaching information on medical prescriptions using two instructive feedback schedules. *Journal of Behavioral Education, 8*(1), 37–61. https://doi.org/10.1023/A:1022812723663

Daugherty, S., Grisham-Brown, J., & Hemmeter, M. L. (2001). The effects of embedded skill instruction on the acquisition of target and nontarget skills in preschoolers with developmental delays. *Topics in Early Childhood Special Education, 21*(4), 213–221. https://doi.org/10.1177/027112140102100402

Delquadri, J., Greenwood, C. R., Whorton, D., Carta, J. J., & Hall, R. V. (1986). Classwide peer tutoring. *Exceptional Children, 52*(6), 535–542. https://doi.org/10.1177/001440298605200606

Fiscus, R. S., Schuster, J. W., Morse, T. E., & Collins, B. C. (2002). Teaching elementary students with cognitive disabilities food preparation skills while embedding instructive feedback in the prompt and consequent event. *Education and Training in Mental Retardation and Developmental Disabilities, 37*(1), 55–69. http://www.jstor.org/stable/23879583

Fisher, W., Piazza, C. C., Bowman, L. G., Hagopian, L. P., Owens, J. C., & Slevin, I. (1992). A comparison of two approaches for identifying reinforcers for persons with severe and profound disabilities. *Journal of Applied Behavior Analysis, 25*(2), 491–498. https://doi.org/10.1901/jaba.1992.25-491

Floress, M. T., Beaudoin, M. M., & Bernas, R. S. (2021). Exploring secondary teachers' actual and perceived praise and reprimand use. *Journal of Positive Behavior Interventions, 24*(1), 46–57. https://doi.org/10.1177/10983007211000381

Floress, M. T., & Beschta, S. L. (2018). An analysis of general education teachers use of praise. *Psychology in the Schools, 55*(10), 1188–1204. https://doi.org/10.1002/pits.22187

Gorton, K., Allday, R. A., Lane, J. D., & Ault, M. J. (2021). Effects of brief training plus electronic feedback on increasing quantity and intonation of behavior specific praise among preschool teachers. *Journal of Behavioral Education.* Advance online publication. https://doi-org.proxy006.nclive.org/10.1007/s10864-020-09427-w

Hattie, J. (2012). *Visual learning for teachers: Maximizing impact on learning.* Routledge.

Hattie, J., Fisher, D., & Frey, N. (2016). Do they hear you? *Educational Leadership, 73*(7), 16–21.

Hattie, J., & Timperley, H. (2007). The power of feedback. *Review of Educational Research, 77*(1), 81–112. https://doi.org/10.3102/003465430298487

Hawkins, S. M., & Heflin, L. J. (2011). Increasing secondary teachers' behavior-specific praise using a video self-modeling and visual performance feedback intervention. *Journal of Positive Behavior Interventions, 13*(2), 97–108. https://doi.org/10.1177/1098300709358110

Hemmeter, M. L., Ostrosky, M. M., & Corso, R. M. (2012). Preventing and addressing challenging behavior: Common questions and practical strategies. *Young Exceptional Children*, 15(2), 32–46. https://doi.org/10.1177/1096250611427350

Holcombe, A., Wolery, M., Werts, M. G., & Hrenkevich, P. (1993). Effects of instructive feedback on future learning. *Journal of Behavioral Education*, 3(3), 259–285. https://doi.org/10.1007/BF00961555

Jenkins, L. N., Floress, M. T., & Reinke, W. (2015). Rate and types of teacher praise: A review and future directions. *Psychology in the Schools*, 52(5), 463–476. https://doi.org/10.1102/pits.21835

Kalis, T. M., Vannest, K. J., & Parker, R. (2007). Praise counts: Using self-monitoring to increase effective teaching practices. *Preventing School Failure: Alternative Education for Children and Youth*, 51(3), 20–27. https://doi.org/10.3200/PSFL.51.3.20-27

Ledford, J. R., Gast, D. L., Luscre, D., & Ayres, K. M. (2008). Observational and incidental learning by children with autism during small group instruction. *Journal of Autism and Developmental Disorders*, 38(1), 86–103. http//:doi.org/10.1007/s10803-007-0363-7

Lee, M. S. H., Yu, C. T., Martin, T. L., & Martin, G. L. (2010). On the relation between reinforcer efficacy and preference. *Journal of Applied Behavior Analysis*, 43(1), 95–100. https://doi.org/10.1901/jaba.2010.43-95

Parrott, K. A., Schuster, J. W., Collins, B. C., & Gassaway, L. J. (2000). Simultaneous prompting and instructive feedback when teaching chained tasks. *Journal of Behavioral Education*, 10(1), 3–19. https://doi.org/10.1023/A:1016639721684

Piazza, C. C., Fisher, W. W., Hagopian, L. P., Bowman, L. G., & Toole, L. (1996). Using a choice assessment to predict reinforcer effectiveness. *Journal of Applied Behavior Analysis*, 29(1), 1–9. https://doi.org/10.1901/jaba.1996.29-1

Reinke, W. M., Lewis-Palmer, T., & Merrell, K. (2008). The classroom check-up: A class wide teacher consultation model for increasing praise and decreasing disruptive behavior. *School Psychology Review*, 37(3), 315–332. https://doi.org/10.1080/02796015.2008.12087879

Scott, T. M., Altern, P. J., & Hirn, R. G. (2011). An examination of typical classroom context and instruction for students with and without behavioral disorders. *Education and Treatment of Children*, 34(4), 619–641. https://doi.org/10.1353/etc.2011.0039

Stewart, S. R., Gonzalez, L. S., & Page, J. L. (1997). Incidental learning of sight words during articulation training. *Language, Speech, and Hearing Services in Schools*, 28(2), 115–126. https://doi.org/10.1044/0161-1461.2802.115

Stokes, T. F., Fowler, S. A., & Baer, D. M. (1978). Training preschool children to recruit natural communities of reinforcement. *Journal of Applied Behavior Analysis*, 11(2), 285–303. https://doi.org/10.1901/jaba.1978.11-285

Sutherland, K. S., Wehby, J. H., & Copeland, S. R. (2000). Effect of varying rates of behavior-specific praise on the on-task behavior of students with EBD. *Journal of Emotional and Behavioral Disorders*, 8(1), 2–8. https://doi.org/10.1177/106342660000800101

Tekin-Iftar, E. (2003). Effectiveness of peer delivered simultaneous prompting on teaching community signs to students with developmental disabilities. *Education and Training in Developmental Disabilities*, 38(1), 77–94. https://www.jstor.org/stable/23880187

Walker, H. M., Ramsey, E., & Gresham, F. M. (2004). *Antisocial behavior in school: Evidenced-based practices* (2nd ed.). Wadsworth/Thomson Learning.

Werts, M. G., Caldwell, N. K., & Wolery, M. (2003). Instructive feedback: Effects of a presentation variable. *The Journal of Special Education*, 37(2), 124–133. https://doi.org/10.1177/00224669030370020601

Werts, M. G., Wolery, M., Holcombe, A., & Gast, D. L. (1995). Instructive feedback: Review of parameters and effects. *Journal of Behavioral Education*, 5(1), 55–75. https://doi.org/10.1007/BF02110214

Wolery, M., Cybriwsky, C. A., Gast, D. L., & Boyle-Gast, K. (1991). Use of constant time delay and attentional responses with adolescents. *Exceptional Children*, 57(5), 462–474. https://doi.org/10.1177/001440299105700509